YEAR BOOK

JULY 1, 1998–AUGUST 31, 1999

AMERICAN PHILOSOPHICAL SOCIETY

Held at Philadelphia for Promoting Useful Knowledge

AMERICAN PHILOSOPHICAL SOCIETY

Independence Square   Philadelphia   1999

The Year Book constitutes the annual report of the American
Philosophical Society. All rights reserved.

For more information, see our website: www.amphilsoc.org.
General phone number: 215-440-3400
Library Fax number: 215-440-3423
Philosophical Hall Fax number: 215-440-3436

Library of Congress catalog card no.: 39-2934
ISBN: 0-87169-950-8
US ISSN: 0065-9762

CONTENTS

AMERICAN PHILOSOPHICAL SOCIETY 1999–2000

OFFICERS

Patron   The Governor of Pennsylvania

President   Frank H. T. Rhodes

Vice Presidents   Mildred Cohn, 1997–2000
   Victor McKusick, 1999–2002   Mary Patterson McPherson, 1998–2001

Curator, Fine Arts   Henry A. Millon

Curator, Jefferson Garden   William H. Frederick, Jr.

Treasurer   Theodore L. Cross, 1997–2000

Secretaries   Baruch Blumberg, 1999–2002 Helen North, 1999–2002

Executive Officer   Alexander G. Bearn

Librarian   Edward C. Carter II

Councillors

1997–2000		1998–2001	1999–2002
I	Owen Gingerich	Val Fitch	Rudolph Marcus
II	Günter Blobel	Purnell Choppin	Thomas Eisner
III	Harriet Zuckerman	Loren Graham	Bernard Bailyn
IV	Jaroslav Pelikan	Morton White	Martin Ostwald
V	Vincent McKusick	William B. Eagleson, Jr	Theodore Cross

Executive Committee

Arlin Adams	Hanna H. Gray	Frank H. T. Rhodes
Alexander Bearn	Mary Patterson McPherson	Jonathan Rhoads
Britton Chance	Martin Meyerson	Torsten Wiesel
William B. Eagleson, Jr.	Henry Millon	Hatten Yoder
William Frederick, Jr.	Helen North	
Robert F. Goheen	Ludo Rocher	

The President and Executive Officer are members of all committees except the Audit Committee. The first member named in each committee is Chairman.

COMMITTEES

Audit

Martin Meyerson	1998–2001	William T. Golden	1999–2002
Alan S. Blinder	1997–2000		

Finance

William B. Eagleson, Jr.	1999–2002	Mary Patterson McPherson	
Arlin M. Adams	1999–2002		1999–2002
Theodore L. Cross	1999–2002	Martin Meyerson	1999–2002
David P. Eastburn	1999–2002	Jonathan E. Rhoads	1999–2002
Robert F. Goheen	1999–2002	Lewis H. Van Dusen, Jr.	1999–2002
Herman H. Goldstine	1999–2002		

Library

Hatten S. Yoder, Jr.	1997–2000	Ruth Patrick	1999–2002
Edward C. Carter II	ex officio	Jeremy Sabloff	1998–2001
Charles C. Gillispie	1998–2001	Anthony F. C. Wallace	1999–2002
Stanley Katz	1999–2002	Russell F. Weigley	1998–2001
Helen F. North	1998–2001	Theodore J. Ziolkowski	1999–2002

Publications

Alexander G. Bearn		Donald R. Kelley	1999–2002
Glen W. Bowersock	1997–2000	Mabel L. Lang	1997–2000
Ward H. Goodenough	1999–2002	Bruce Metzger	1999–2002
Lionel Gossman	1997–2000	Helen North	1999–2002
Oleg Grabar	1999–2002	Noel M. Swerdlow	1998–2001
Henry M. Hoenigswald	1997–2000		

Meetings

Alexander G. Bearn		Marshall Clagett	1999–2002
Glen W. Bowersock	1997–2000	Ansley J. Coale	1996–1999
George F. Carrier	1996–1999	David P. Eastburn	1997–2000
Britton Chance	1997–2000	E. Allan Farnsworth	1998–2001

Val Fitch	1998–2001	Jerrold Meinwald	1998–2001
Herbert Friedman	1997–2000	Helen North	1998–2001
Stanley N. Katz	1997–2000	Barbara Oberg	1999–2002
Edwin Kilbourne	1999–2002	Gerard Piel	1997–2000
Lawrence Klein	1999–2002	Jonathan E. Rhoads	1997–2000
Mabel L. Lang	1997–2000		

Research

Ludo Rocher	1998–2001	Stanley Katz	1997–2000
Mildred Cohn	1998–2001	Fernando Nottebohm	1999–2002
Robert Dyson	1997–2000	Peter Paret	1999–2002
Herman H. Goldstine	1998–2001	Russell F. Weigley	1998–2001
Ward Goodenough	1998–2001		

Nomination of Officers

Helen North	IV 1999–2002	Lawrence R. Klein	III 1998–2001
Herbert Friedman	I 1999–2002	Glen W. Bowersock	IV 1999–2002
Robert Austrian	II 1999–2002	William T. Golden	V 1999–2002

Advisory on Election of Members

Arlin M. Adams, President   Alexander G. Bearn, Executive Officer

CLASS I		CLASS II	
Chairman		*Chairman*	
Herbert Friedman	1997–2000	Lawrence Bogorad	1998–2001
Class Representative		*Class Representative*	
Owen Gingerich	1999–2002	Maclyn McCarty	1997–2000

CLASS III		CLASS IV	
Chairman		*Chairman*	
Lawrence Klein	1998–2001	Henry A. Millon	1998–2001
Class Representative		*Class Representative*	
Joyce Appleby	1997–2000	Ward Goodenough	1997–2000

CLASS V	
Chairman	
Vincent McKusick	1998–2001
Class Representative	
William T. Golden	1998–2001

Class Committees on Membership

CLASS I: *Mathematical & Physical Sciences*

Herbert Friedman	1997–2000
Val L. Fitch	1997–2000
Andrew M. Gleason	1997–2000
Donald F. Hornig	1997–2000
Saunders Mac Lane	1997–2000
Alvin M. Weinberg	1997–2000

CLASS II: *Biological Sciences*

Lawrence Bogorad	1998–2001
Robert Austrian	1998–2000
Purnell W. Choppin	1997–2000
Thomas Eisner	1997–2000
Peter Grant	1997–2000

CLASS III: *Social Sciences*

Lawrence R. Klein	1998–2001
Gregory C. Chow	1997–2000
Philip D. Curtin	1998–2001
Gordon S. Wood	1999–2002
Harriet Zuckerman	1997–2000

CLASS IV: *Humanities*

Henry A. Millon	1998–2001
Anthony Grafton	1999–2002
Mabel L. Lang	1999–2002
Brunilde Ridgway	1998–2001

CLASS V: *The Arts, Professions, and Public Affairs*

Vincent McKusick	1998–2001
Joel E. Cohen	1997–2000
Sheldon Hackney	1998–2001
Stanley Katz	1998–2001
Mary Patterson McPherson	1998–2001
Frank E. Taplin	1997–2000

Clinical Investigator Fellowship (formerly Daland)

Victor A. McKusick	1997–2000	Maclyn McCarty	1997–2000
Robert Austrian	1997–2000	Jonathan E. Rhoads	1997–2000
John Loeb	1999–2002		

Barzun Prize

Peter Paret	1999–2000	Donald R. Kelley	1997–2000
Bernard Bailyn	1999–2002		

Franklin Medals

Vincent L. McKusick	1999–2002	Harriet Zuckerman	1999–2002
Owen Gingerich	1999–2002		

Jayne Lectures

Britton Chance	1999–2002	Jonathan E. Rhoads	1999–2002

Jefferson Medal

Robert F. Goheen	1997–2000	Mary Patterson McPherson	
Anne d'Harnoncourt	1997–2000		1997–2000
Christian Habicht	1997–2000		

Lashley Award

Eric R. Kandel	1997–2000	Larry R. Squire	1999–2002
Floyd Bloom	1998–2001	Torsten N. Wiesel	1997–2000
Sanford Palay	1998–2001		

Lewis Award

James Barr	1999–2002	I. Bernard Cohen	1999–2002
Glen W. Bowersock	1999–2002	Mabel L. Lang	1997–2000
Alfred D. Chandler	1997–2000		

Magellanic Premium

Charles P. Slichter	1999–2002	Gerry Neugebauer	1997–2000
Herbert Friedman	1997–2000	Vera Rubin	1997–2000
Thomas Gold	1997–2000	Edward C. Stone	1999–2002
James E. Gunn	1997–2000	Joseph H. Taylor, Jr.	1999–2002

Moe Prize

Helen North	1997–2000	Bruce M. Metzger	1999–2002
Richard Herr	1999–2002		

Phillips Award

Vincent L. McKusick	1998–2001

Phillips Fund

Edward C. Carter II	1997–2000	Anthony F. C. Wallace	1997–2000
Eric P. Hamp	1997–2000	Regna Darnell	(non-member)

Slater Fellowship

John L. Heilbron	1999–2002	Daniel J. Kevles	1999–2002
Edward C. Carter II	1999–2002	Abraham Pais	1999–2002
Marshall Clagett	1999–2002	Noel M. Swerdlow	1998–2001
Gerald Holton	1997–2000		

Administrative Board, The Papers of Benjamin Franklin

Representatives of The Society	Yale University	Members-at-Large
Edward C. Carter II	Edmund S. Morgan, chairman	Robert Middlekauff
Robert C. Darnton	David B. Davis	Paul Le Clerc
Gordon Wood	John G. Ryden	Mary Maples Dunn
Barbara Oberg		

Advisory Committee, The Joseph Henry Papers

Representatives of American Philosophical Society	Smithsonian Institution	National Academy of Sciences
Charles C. Gillispie	Michael Heyan	Frederick Seitz
Herbert Friedman	Robert Hoffmann	Janice Goldblum

Representative to American Council of Learned Societies

Edward C. Carter II	Theodore Ziolkowski

Library Advisory Committee

Edward C. Carter II   1999–2002

Anthropology	Life Sciences	Linguistics
Ward H. Goodenough	Lily E. Kay	Ward H. Goodenough
David K. van Keuren	Joshua Lederberg	Eric P. Hamp
Anthony F. C. Wallace	Victor A. McKusick	Henry M. Hoenigswald

Mathematical and Physical Sciences
Charles C. Gillispie
Frederik L. Nebeker
William Stanton
Hatten S. Yoder, Jr.

Natural History and Geology
Charles C. Gillispie
Herman H. Goldstine
Noel M. Swerdlow
John A. Wheeler

PRESIDENT'S REPORT

Today marks the end of my six-year term. I have found it to be an exciting and significant period in my life, and can say unreservedly that I enjoyed every moment of it.

I assumed office at a sad time. My predecessor, Eliot Stellar, an extremely able and dedicated individual, was in the final stages of a fatal illness. Eliot was a wonderful person in very many ways. His performance as President made my job much easier, just by example.

One of my main concerns was the Society's finances. The Society does not charge dues; funds for our programs must come from the income produced by our endowments, gifts, donations and an annual giving campaign. The endowment was $59 million six years ago when I took office; it is now over $125 million. A result of a 5% spending rule, we were able to obtain approximately $5,000,000 from the endowment. The 5% Rule was one promulgated by the Society a number of years ago, and follows a similar rule adopted by most academic institutions. In any event, we have gone from $3.2 million of income per annum provided by the endowment to $5 million per year.

Much of our success in this area was accomplished by an outstanding Finance Committee. The members, I believe, are familiar to you, but I want to make special mention of Bill Eagleson, Chairman Emeritus of Mellon Bank, who is the Chairman of the Finance Committee. In addition to the increased income from the endowment, the annual giving campaign has been most successful. This past year, Dr. Paul Talalay did a magnificent job with annual giving, and we think Bill Golden will do the same this year.

During my tenure, we were also concerned about our physical plant. I am pleased to report that this facility, Franklin Hall, is now fully on-line. It is a splendid building, and we use it to the maximum. We purchased a new roof and a new state-of-the art temperature control system and fire protocol for the Library building. We are proceeding under the leadership of Bill Frederick to restore the Jefferson Garden. And, our work on Philosophical Hall is almost finished, and miracle beyond miracles, we are well within budget.

Shortly after commencing my stewardship, Dr. Herman Goldstine made it clear that he would be stepping down as the Executive Officer after serving 13 years. No one has contributed more to the well-being of the Society than Herman. He and I talked every day about the Society, and generally what had to be done next. However, good fortune smiled on us and we were able to attract an outstanding successor: Dr. Bearn has a sterling reputation as a scientist and an administrator. In addition, he is well versed regarding the affairs of the Society. He has closely paralleled Dr. Goldstine in his cooperation with me as President; I could not expect more unstinting support or friendship. The staff has been magnificent—Carl Miller, Annie Westcott, Nora Monroe, Carole LeFaivre-Rochester— are a few that I have worked with closely, frequently on a daily basis. But the entire staff has been outstanding, and I cannot express my appreciation more sincerely.

We made two successful foreign trips in the last few years. The first was to Rome where we were hosted by the Lincei, the oldest learned society in the Western World. The second was to Stockholm, where we were the guests of the Royal Swedish Academy of Sciences. Both meetings were outstanding and we are now planning on entertaining the Royal Society of London in the year 2001, here in the United States.

I believe our intellectual programs have been most interesting and stimulating. The Meetings Committee works diligently in planning our spring and fall get-togethers, and in attracting good speakers. It would be difficult to exceed the quality of the program for the Millennium Meeting.

The *Year Book* and the *Newsletter* have both been revised, and are now far more useful than they were.

The real key to the Society, of course, is the membership. Our members are carefully selected. We consider any nomination that any member submits to us; and each is pondered carefully. In the final analysis, though, the election is up to our membership. We have tried in the last six years to elect a more diverse group. I have always taken much pleasure in knowing that we elected as early as 1789, the great Russian scientist, Princess Dashkova, the first time any learned society elected a woman.

The Library continues to function in a most effective fashion. We have sought after collections headed by a marvelous scholar, Dr. Carter, and we continue to obtain considerable help for our Library from the Mellon Foundation.

You have heard Dr. Bearn explain our initiative in the field of humanities and I shall not repeat it. I have already told you about the bequest from the Paul Mellon Estate, and what we are trying to do next door, at 431 Chestnut Street.

I believe that the future of the Society is good. Indeed, its prospects are most encouraging. You have elected a very fine successor in Frank Rhodes, the President Emeritus of Cornell. Together with Dr. Bearn, they will be a wonderful team.

I cannot thank the Society too much for the support that I have received over these past six years. Someone recently asked me, "Why do you find the Society so attractive, you have so many other activities?" My answer was simply this:

Where can you find so many highly intelligent, open-minded people who are always civil in their discourse, and always courteous in their deportment. I feel honored to have had this opportunity to serve the Society and I thank you as sincerely as I can.

Arlin M. Adams

EXECUTIVE OFFICER'S REPORT

Before considering some of the highlights of the year, it should be noted that it was also a year of changing of the guard. For the last six years, Arlin Adams has served as our distinguished President. Indeed, all the highlights to be outlined below were undertaken during his term. His gracious, unostentatious leadership and the richness of his tenure will long remain. It can be said of Arlin, as was said by Plutarch of Tiberius, "We can picture him as a man who always maintained a certain seriousness of manner and with great goodwill towards his fellow man." Arlin's disciplined enthusiasm, sagely muted by an intense analytical mind, brought to all our events open discussion leading to thoughtful conclusions. His commitment and steadfastness during his six years of leadership encompassed a period of wise growth and institutional caution. While preserving our heritage, he has unstintingly supported new ventures. Fairness and democracy have been his hallmarks. Arlin Adams, adhering to our constitutional limitations, has now completed two terms and his sixth year as President. In a manner that bespoke the gentleness of his character, Arlin, at the close of our spring business meeting, quietly transferred the gavel to the hand of our new President, Frank Rhodes, former President of Cornell University. It is a matter of great satisfaction to the entire membership that Arlin Adams will continue to be active in the Society; he has already agreed to serve on the Finance Committee and will be a source of advice and wisdom for the Society for many years to come.

With gracious word and the warmest demeanor, Frank Rhodes endeared himself to the membership by his brief remarks. A six-year Presidency, replete with accomplishment and fond memories, has concluded, but now the Society enters its next years with a spirit of excitement and optimism. Frank Rhodes brings to our Society a remarkable mixture of grace and learning. Rising to their feet, the Society's members welcomed our new President with loud applause and with a feeling of great anticipation in the sure knowledge that in the coming years, building on the Presidency of Arlin Adams, the Society will achieve ever greater heights.

Among some notable steps taken during the last year, the Society was pleased to launch a fellowship in the humanities and social sciences, generously supported by the Mellon Foundation. There were 251 applicants in the Humanities section of the program and 119 in the Social Sciences. The humanities panel was ably chaired by Dr. Bernard Bailyn and the Social Sciences by Dr. Gardner Lindzey. Each section's panel selected seven winners. Successful applicants were drawn from 11 states and 13 institutions. The average age of those awarded fellowships was 47.

Another major undertaking during the last year has been the renovation of Philosophical Hall. While faithful to its historical character, the building has been completely renovated to make use of existing space to provide an elevator and offices for the staff, and to modify two rooms so that the treasures of the Society can be displayed to their advantage. The Society's curator, Henry Millon, has guided and directed the aesthetic aspects of this undertaking while Carl Miller has overseen the renovation with his usual care and diligence. We have been fortunate in having for this renovation, an architect, Arthur Jones of Bower Lewis Thrower, who was ever-sensitive to the historical nature of our Society and our building. It has been a great pleasure to work with him and his colleagues and it is our expectation that the building will be largely renovated by July 1999. The display cases are likely to be completed and installed by year's end.

A new program of outreach is in its early planning stages. A selected number of high school students, drawn principally from their last year in high school, will be offered an educational program, designed specifically for their needs, and drawing upon the singular talents of our membership. It is a matter of satisfaction that the Superintendent of Schools, Dr. David Hornbeck, is an enthusiastic supporter of the scheme. It is hoped to launch the program in the year 2000 or 2001.

It is a matter of record that annual fund raising reached an all-time high in 1998. $187,094 was raised with 40% of our members contributing. The success of the fund-raising is entirely due to the untiring efforts of Ann Westcott and Dr. Paul Talalay. During the coming year Ms. Westcott will again be leading the fund-raising under another of our distinguished members Mr. William Golden.

Although we are, at the time of writing, unsure of the details, we are enormously pleased and grateful to learn that our distinguished late member Mr. Paul Mellon has bequeathed to the Society a sum of money that will be at least $1.5 million and may be more, when the estate is finally settled.

A very significant event in the life of the Society was the purchase of 431 Chestnut Street. The building is next door to Benjamin Franklin Hall and can be easily modified so that access between the two buildings will be possible. The purchase of the building provides a great opportunity for expansion for the Society in the years ahead. Meanwhile, a number of possible immediate uses are under discussion.

The Millennium Meeting of the Society in April 1999 was generally regarded as an outstanding event in the history of the Society. The speakers, moderators and lead discussants at the meeting were exclusively members of the Society and included six speakers from abroad and six Nobel laureates. The publication of the papers will be a unique record of the breadth of the Society at the turn of the

Century. It was a meeting that attracted 475 attendees, requiring unusual logistical resourcefulness on the part of our staff, who ably shepherded members through the meeting's events.

For those members able to attend the Millennium Program in April, the meeting was the intellectual high point of the year. The carefully-crafted program, with speakers representing each class of the members fairly sparkled with their scholarship and insights and was testimony, once more, of the extraordinary accomplishments and intellectual fervor of the membership.

Alexander G. Bearn
Executive Officer

As of 31 July 1999, 825 members lived in 32 states and 25 foreign countries. There are 682 resident members and 143 foreign members. The largest number reside in California (136), Massachusetts (112), New York (99), New Jersey (82), Pennsylvania (59), and England (45). The regional distribution is Northeast 47.9 percent, West 17.2, foreign 17.2 percent, South 11.4 percent, and Midwest 6.3 percent.

Name, class of membership, and date of election appear on the first line, followed by the member's position, professional address, office telephone number (O), home telephone number (H), office fax number (O)(F), home fax number (H)(F), and e-mail address (E). Addresses preceded by "Home" are home addresses or professional/business addresses that differ from the one associated with the individual's position. Information below has been updated to 31 July 1999.

RESIDENT MEMBERS

Aarsleff, Dr. Hans   IV 1994
Professor of English, Emeritus
Princeton University
Home: 120 Longview Drive
Princeton, NJ 08540

Abeles, Dr. Robert Heinz   II 1999
Professor of Biochemistry, Emeritus
415 South Street, MS 009
Brandeis University
Waltham, MA 02453-2728
(781)736-2310 (O)
(781)736-2349 (F)
abeles@brandeis.edu (E)

Abelson, Dr. Philip Hauge   I 1961
Science Advisor, American Association
   for the Advancement of Science
1200 New York Avenue, N.W.
Washington, DC 20005
(202)326-6641 (O)

Abrahamson, Hon. Shirley S.   V 1998
Chief Justice
Wisconsin Supreme Court
P.O. Box 1688
Madison, WI 53701-1688
(608)266-1885 (O)
(608)222-9358 (H)
(608)261-8299 (F)

Abrams, Dr. Meyer Howard   IV 1973
Class of 1916
   Professor of English, Emeritus
Cornell University
Home: 378 Savage Farm Drive
Ithaca, NY 14850
(607)255-3428 (O)
(607)257-7012 (H)
(607)255-6661 (F)
mha5@cornell.edu (E)

Adams, Hon. Arlin Marvin   V 1979
Former U.S. Circuit Judge
Counsel
Schnader, Harrison, Segal and Lewis
1600 Market Street, Suite 3600
Philadelphia, PA 19103
Home: Apt. A33, Briar House
8302 York Road
Elkins Park, PA 19027
(215)751-2072 (O)
(215)884-1276 (H)
(215)972-7246 (F)

Adams, Dr. Frederick B., Jr.   III 1965
Director Emeritus
Pierpont Morgan Library
Home: 208 rue de Rivoli
75001 Paris, France
33-01-42-60-46-16 (H)

Adams, Dr. Robert McC.   IV 1974
Secretary Emeritus
The Smithsonian Institution
Adjunct Professor
Department of Anthropology
University of California
La Jolla, CA 92093-0532
Home: 9753 Keeneland Row
La Jolla, CA 92037
(619)678-0397 (H) California
(970)927-3380 (H) Colorado
(619)534-5946 (O)(F)
(619)678-0397 (H)(F)
rmadams@ucsd.edu (E)

Adler, Dr. Julius   II 1989
Professor Emeritus
Department of Biochemistry and Genetics
420 Henry Hall
University of Wisconsin
Madison, WI 53706
(608)262-3693 (O)
(608)262-3453 (F)
adlerlab@macc.wisc.edu (E)

Alberts, Dr. Bruce M.   II 1994
President
Professor of Biochemistry and Biophysics
National Academy of Sciences
2101 Constitution Avenue, N.W.
Washington, DC 20418
(202)334-2100 (O)
(202)338-4527 (H)
(202)334-1647 (F)
balberts@nas.edu (E)

Almond, Dr. Gabriel A.   III 1966
Professor Emeritus of Political Science
Stanford University
Home: 4135 Old Trace Road
Palo Alto, CA 94306
(650)497-2614 (O)
(650)941-2302 (H)
almond@leland.stanford.edu (E)

Altman, Dr. Sidney   II 1990
Sterling Professor of Biology
Department of Biology
402 Kline Biology Tower
P.O. Box 208103,
Yale University
New Haven, CT 06520-8103
Home: 71 Blake Road
Hamden, CT 06517
(203)432-3500/6 (O)
(203)432-5713 (F)
sidney.altman@qm.yale.edu (E)

Anderson, Dr. Don L.   I 1990
Eleanor and John R. McMillan
Professor of Geophysics
Seismological Laboratory
Mail Code 252–21
California Institute of Technology
Pasadena, CA 91125
(626)395-6901 (O)
(626)564-0715 (F)
dla@gps.caltech.edu (E)

Anderson, Dr. James G. I 1998
Philip S. Weld Professor of Atmospheric
  Chemistry
Department of Chemistry and Chemical
  Biology
12 Oxford Street
Harvard University
Cambridge, MA 02138
(617)495-5922 (O)
(617)495-4902 (F)
anderson@huarp.harvard.edu (E)

Anderson, Dr. Philip W. I 1991
Joseph Henry Professor Emeritus
Physics Department
Princeton University
Princeton, NJ 08544
(609)466-1497 (H)
(609)258-1006 (F)
pwa@pupgg.princeton.edu (E)

Annenberg, Hon. Walter H. V 1990
Former Ambassador to the
  Court of St. James's
Former Chairman of Triangle Publications
Former Chairman and Chief Executive
  Officer
St. Davids Center, Suite A-200
150 Radnor-Chester Road
St. Davids, PA 19087
Home [Winter]:
"Sunnylands," P.O. Box 98
Rancho Mirage, CA 92270
Home [Summer]:
Inwood, Llanfair Road
Wynnewood, PA 19096
(610)341-9396 (O)
(610)642-0560 (H)
(610)964-8688 (F)

Appleby, Dr. Joyce III 1994
Professor of History
University of California
Los Angeles, CA 90095
Home: 615 Westholme Avenue
Los Angeles, CA 90024
(310)825-3679 (O)
(310)470-8946 (H)
(310)206-9630 (F)
appleby@history.ucla.edu (E)

Arrow, Dr. Kenneth Joseph III 1968
Joan Kenney Professor of Economics
  Emeritus
Professor of Operations Research, Emeritus
Department of Economics
Stanford University
Stanford, CA 94305-6072
(650)723-9165 (O)
(650)725-5702 (F)
arrow@leland.stanford.edu (E)

Atkinson, Dr. Richard C. II 1980
President
Office of the President
1111 Franklin Street, 12th Floor
Oakland, CA 94607-5200
Home: 70 Rincon Road
Kensington, CA 94707
(510)987-9074 (O)
(510)528-9228 (H)
(510)987-9086 (F)
Richard.Atkinson@ucop.edu (E)

Augustine, Mr. Norman R. I 1997
Chairman of Executive Committee
Lockheed Martin Corporation
9826 Sorrel Avenue
Potomac, MD 20854
(301)897-6185 (O)
(301)897-6028 (F)

Austrian, Dr. Robert II 1987
John Herr Musser Professor
Chairman Emeritus
Department of Research Medicine
552 Johnson Pavilion
School of Medicine
University of Pennsylvania
Philadelphia, PA 19104-6088
Home: 250 South 17th Street
Philadelphia, PA 19103
(215)662-3186 (O)
(215)545-2333 (H)
(215)349-5111 (F)

Axelrod, Dr. Julius II 1995
Scientist Emeritus
National Institute of Mental Health
Building 36, Room 3A-15
9000 Rockville Pike
Bethesda, MD 20892
Home: 10401 Grosvenor Place, Apt. 1209
Rockville, MD 20852
(301)496-2639 (O)
(301)402-1748 (F)
axelrod@codon.nih.gov (E)

Ayala, Dr. Francisco José II 1984
Donald Bren Professor of Biological
    Sciences
Department of Ecology and Evolutionary
    Biology
321 Steinhaus Hall
University of California
Irvine, CA 92697-2525
Home: 2 Locke Court
Irvine, CA 92612
(949)824-8293 (O)
(949)856-1247 (H)
(949)824-2474 (O)(F)
(949)856-1016 (H)(F)
fjayala@uci.edu (E)

Babcock, Dr. Horace W. I 1966
Director Emeritus
Observatories of the Carnegie Institution
    of Washington
813 Santa Barbara Street
Pasadena, CA 91101
Home: Villa Santa Barbara, 267
227 Anapamu Street
Santa Barbara, CA 93101-2005
(805)965-9619 (H)

Bacher, Dr. Robert Fox I 1948
Professor Emeritus of Physics
California Institute of Technology
Home: Casa Dorinda
300 Hot Springs Road, #12
Montecito, CA 93108
(805)969-8668 (H)

Bailey, Dr. D. R. Shackleton IV 1977
Pope Professor Emeritus of the Latin
    Language and Literature
Harvard University
Home: 303 North Division
Ann Arbor, MI 48104
(734)665-8062 (H)

Bailey, Mr. Herbert Smith, Jr. V 1986
Former Director
Princeton University Press
Home: Fearrington Post 248
Pittsboro, NC 27312
(919)542-1229 (H)
p42bailey@aol.com (E)

Bailyn, Dr. Bernard III 1971
Adams University Professor, Emeritus
Department of History
Harvard University
Cambridge, MA 02138
(617)496-3066 (O), (617)496-8869 (F)

Baker, Dr. Herbert George   II 1986
Professor Emeritus of Integrative Biology
University of California
Home: 635 Creston Road
Berkeley, CA 94708
(510)642-7036 (O)
(510)524-2882 (H)
(510)643-6264 (F)

Baker, Dr. James Gilbert   I 1970
Optical Physicist and Astronomer
Research Associate
60 Garden Street
Harvard College Observatory, C-12
Cambridge, MA 02138
Home: 14 French Drive
Bedford, NH 03110-5717
(617)495-1693 (O)
(603)472-5860 (H)

Baker, Dr. Keith Michael   III 1997
J. E. Wallace Sterling Professor in the
    Humanities
Director, Stanford Humanities Center
Stanford University
Stanford, CA 94305-2024
(650)723-3052 (O)
(650)723-1895 (F)
kbaker@leland.stanford.edu (E)

Baker, Dr. William O.   I 1963
Former Chairman, AT&T Bell Labs
Rockefeller University
Andrew W. Mellon Foundation
Charter Trustee
Princeton University, Life Trustee
H. F. Guggenheim Foundation
Carnegie Mellon University
Overseer
School of Engineering and Applied Sciences
University of Pennsylvania
Home: Spring Valley Road
Morristown, NJ 07960
(973)377-1568 (H)

Baldeschwieler, Dr. J. D.   I 1979
J. Stanley Johnson Professor of Chemistry
Department of Chemistry
California Institute of Technology
P.O. Box 50065
Pasadena, CA 91115-0065
(626)395-6088 (O)
(626)568-0402 (F)
jb@cco.caltech.edu (E)

Baltimore, Dr. David   II 1997
President
California Institute of Technology
1200 E. California Boulevard
Mail Code 204–31
Pasadena, CA 91125
(626)395-6301 (O)
(626)449-9374 (F)
baltimo@caltech.edu (E)

Bard, Dr. Allen J.   I 1999
Professor and Hackerman
Welch Regents' Chair of Chemistry
Department of Chemistry and Biochemistry
University of Texas at Austin
Austin, TX 78712-1167
(512)471-3761 (O)
(512)471-0088 (F)
ajbard@mail.utexas.edu (E)

Barker, Dr. Clyde Frederick   II 1997
John Rhea Barton and Donald Guthrie
    Professor and Chairman
Four Silverstein Pavilion
3400 Spruce Street
University of Pennsylvania
Philadelphia, PA 19104
(215)662-2027 (O)
(610)649-5790 (H)
(215)349-5906 (F)
barker@mail.med.upenn.edu (E)

Barr, Dr. James   IV 1993
Distinguished Professor of Hebrew
   Bible, Emeritus
Vanderbilt University
Home: 1432 Sitka Court
Claremont, CA 91711
(909)621-4189 (H) California
44-01865–772741 (H) England

Barton, Dr. Jacqueline K.   I 1999
Arthur and Marian Hanisch Memorial
   Professor of Chemistry
Department of Chemistry, M/C 127–72
California Institute of Technology
Pasadena, CA 91125
(626)395-6075 (O)
(626)568-1724 (H)
(626)577-4976 (F)
jkbarton@its.caltech.edu (E)

Barzun, Dr. Jacques   IV 1984
University Professor
Provost Emeritus
Columbia University
Home: 18 Wolfeton Way
San Antonio, TX 78218-6045

Bass, Dr. George Fletcher   IV 1989
George T. and Gladys H. Abell Professor of
   Nautical Archaeology
Texas A & M University
Institute of Nautical Archaeology
P.O. Drawer HG
College Station, TX 77841-5137
(409)845-6694 (O)

Baumol, Dr. William J.   III 1977
Professor of Economics
C. V. Starr Center for Applied Economics
Princeton University
Department of Economics
269 Mercer Street
New York University
New York, NY 10003
(212)998-8943 (O)
(212)995-3932 (F)
baumolw@fasecon.econ.nyu.edu (E)

Bearn, Dr. Alexander Gordon II 1972
Professor Emeritus of Medicine
Cornell University Medical College
Adjunct Professor
The Rockefeller University
Executive Officer
American Philosophical Society
104 South Fifth Street
Philadelphia, PA 19106-3387
(215)440-3435 (O)
(215)925-2666 (H)
(215)440-3436 (O)(F)
(215)925-3337 (H)(F)
abearn@amphilsoc.org (E)

Becker, Dr. Gary Stanley   III 1986
University Professor of Economics and
   Sociology
Department of Economics
1126 East 59th Street
University of Chicago
Chicago, IL 60637
(773)702-8168 (O)
(773)702-8490 (F)
gbecker@midway.uchicago.edu (E)

Bedini, Mr. Silvio A.   III 1975
Historian Emeritus
Former Keeper of Rare Books
Former Deputy Director
National Museum of American History
Smithsonian Institution
Washington, DC 20560
Home: 4303 47th Street, N.W.
Washington, DC 20016-2449
(202)786-2695 (O), (202)362-6905 (H)
(202)357-4256 (F)
sbedini@compuserve.com (E)

Beitzel, Mr. George B.   V 1987
Former Senior Vice President and Director
IBM
Home: 29 King Street
Chappaqua, NY 10514-3432
(914)238-1049 (O), (914)238-3702 (H)
(914)238-8436 (F)
dotgulla@aol.com (E)

Bell, Dr. Daniel   III 1978
Henry Ford II Professor of Social Sciences
    Emeritus
Harvard University
American Academy of Arts and Sciences
Norton's Woods
136 Irving Street
Cambridge, MA 02138
Home: 65 Francis Avenue
Cambridge, MA 02138
(617)576-5036 (O), (617)547-8524 (H)
(617)576-5088 (F)

Bell, Dr. Whitfield J., Jr.   III 1964
Former Executive Officer
American Philosophical Society
Library of the American
    Philosophical Society
105 South Fifth Street
Philadelphia, PA 19106
(215)440-3420 (O)

Bellah, Dr. Robert N.   III 1996
Elliott Professor of Sociology Emeritus
Department of Sociology
University of California
Berkeley, CA 94720-1980
(510)845-4950 (H)

Bellow, Mr. Saul C.   V 1998
Author
Department of English
Boston University
147 Bay State Road
Boston, MA 02215

Benedict, Dr. Manson   I 1977
Institute Professor Emeritus
Massachusetts Institute of Technology
Home: 108 Moorings Park Drive, #B206
Naples, FL 34105
(941)262-0420 (H)

Benzer, Dr. Seymour   II 1962
James G. Boswell Professor of
    Neuroscience, Emeritus
Division of Biology 156–29
California Institute of Technology
Pasadena, CA 91125
(626)395-4963 (O)
(626)568-2781 (F)
benzer@caltech.edu (E)

Berenbaum, Dr. May R.   II 1996
Professor and Head of Department of
    Entomology
Department of Entomology
University of Illinois
Urbana, IL 61801
(217)333-7784 (O)
(217)244-3499 (F)
maybe@uiuc.edu (E)

Berg, Dr. Paul   II 1983
Robert W. and Vivian K. Cahill Professor
  in Cancer Research and Director
Beckman Center, B-062
Stanford University Medical School
Stanford, CA 94305
(650)723-6170 (O)
(650)725-4951 (F)
pberg@cmgm.stanford.edu (E)

Bergson, Dr. Abram   III 1965
George F. Baker Professor of Economics,
  Emeritus
Littauer Center
Harvard University
Cambridge, MA 02138
(617)495-2158 (O)
(617)484-9171 (H)
(617)495-8319 (F)

Bethe, Dr. Hans Albrecht   I 1947
Professor Emeritus of Physics
Newman Laboratory of Nuclear Studies
Cornell University
Ithaca, NY 14850
(607)255-4397 (O)
(607)254-4552 (F)
dusty@hepth.cornell.edu (E)

Bevington, Dr. David M.   IV 1986
Phyllis Fay Horton Professor in the
  Humanities
Department of English
1050 E. 59th Street
University of Chicago
Chicago, IL 60637
Home: 5747 S. Blackstone Avenue
Chicago, IL 60637
(773)702-9899 (O)
(773)288-7905 (H)
(773)702-2495 (F)
bevi@uchicago.edu (E)

Bhagwati, Dr. Jagdish N.   III 1995
Arthur Lehman Professor of Economics
  and Director
Department of Economics
Columbia University
New York, NY 10027

Biddle, Mr. James   V 1972
Former President
National Trust for Historic Preservation
Home: P.O. Box 158
Andalusia, PA 19020
(215)639-2077 (H)
(215)639-2078 (F)

Billington, Dr. James H.   III 1988
Librarian
Library of Congress
101 Independence Avenue, S.E.
Washington, DC 20540-1000
(202)707-5205 (O)
(202)707-1714 (F)
libofc@loc.gov (E)

Bing, Dr. Richard John   II 1995
Director of Experimental Cardiology and
  Scientific Development
Huntington Medical Research Institutes
University of Southern California
Home: 5344 Alta Canyada
La Canada, CA 91011
(626)397-5451 (O)
(818)790-7169 (H)
(626)795-5774 (F)

Bishop, Dr. J. Michael   II 1995
University Professor
Chancellor Designate
Box 0552
University of California
San Francisco, CA 94143
(415)476-3211 (O)
(415)476-6185 (F)

Bisson, Dr. Thomas Noel   IV 1975
Henry Charles Lea Professor of Medieval
  History
Harvard University
Cambridge, MA 02138
Home: 21 Hammond Street
Cambridge, MA 02138-1915
(617)495-5221 (O), (617)354-0178 (H)
(617)496-3425 (F)
tnbisson@fas.harvard.edu (E)

Black, Dr. Barbara Aronstein III 1991
George Welwood Professor of Legal History
Columbia University School of Law
435 West 116th Street, Box C21
New York, NY 10027
(212)854-5735 (O), (212)663-1931 (H)
(212)854-7946 (F)

Blackwell, Dr. David   I 1990
Professor of Statistics, Emeritus
University of California
Berkeley, CA 94720
(510)642-6446 (O), (510)845-1220 (H)
(510)642-7892 (F)
davidbl@stat.berkeley.edu (E)

Blau, Dr. Peter M.   III 1996
Robert Broughton Distinguished Research
  Professor
Department of Sociology
University of North Carolina
Chapel Hill, NC 27599-3210
(919)962-1007 (O), (919)929-7885 (H)
(919)962-7568 (F)
pmblau@gibbs.oit.unc.edu (E)

Blinder, Dr. Alan S.   III 1996
Gordon S. Rentschler Memorial Professor
  of Economics
Department of Economics
105 Fisher Hall
Princeton University
Princeton, NJ 08544-1021
(609)258-3358 (O)
(609)258-5398 (F)

Blobel, Dr. Günter   II 1989
John D. Rockefeller, Jr., Professor of Cell
  Biology
Investigator
Howard Hughes Medical Institute
The Rockefeller University
1230 York Avenue
New York, NY 10021-6399
Home: 1100 Park Avenue
New York, NY 10028
(212)327-8096 (O)
(212)369-3552 (H)
(212)327-7880 (O)(F)
(212)369-3552 (H)(F)
blobel@rockvax.rockefeller.edu (E)

Bloch, Dr. Herbert   IV 1958
Pope Professor of the Latin Language and
  Literature, Emeritus
Harvard University
Home: 524 Pleasant Street
Belmont, MA 02178-3201
(617)484-8731 (H)

Bloch, Dr. Konrad Emil   II 1966
Professor of Biochemistry, Emeritus
Department of Chemistry and Chemical
    Biology
12 Oxford Street
Harvard University
Cambridge, MA 02138
Home: 16 Moon Hill Road
Lexington, MA 02173
(617)495-4069 (O), (781)862-9076 (H)
(617)495-1792 (F)
bloch@chemistry.harvard.edu (E)

Bloembergen, Dr. Nicolaas   I 1982
Gerhard Gade University Professor,
    Emeritus
231 Pierce Hall, 39 Oxford Street
Division of Applied Sciences
Harvard University
Cambridge, MA 02138
Home: 3 Stonewall Road
Lexington, MA 02173
(617)495-3336 (O), (617)862-1565 (H)
(617)495-9837 (F)

Bloom, Dr. Floyd E.   II 1989
Chairman
Department of Neuropharmacology
The Scripps Research Institute
10550 North Torrey Pines Road
La Jolla, CA 92037
(619)784-9730 (O)
(619)784-8851 (O)(F)
(619)274-9754 (H)(F)
fbloom@scripps.edu (E)

Bloom, Dr. Harold   IV 1995
Sterling Professor of Humanities
Berg Professor of English
Yale University
Home: 179 Linden Street
New Haven, CT 06511-2407
(203)432-0029 (O)

Blumberg, Dr. Baruch S.   II 1986
Senior Advisor to the President
Fox Chase Distinguished Scientist
University of Pennsylvania
Fox Chase Cancer Center
7701 Burholme Avenue
Philadelphia, PA 19111
(215)728-3164 (O)
(215)728-5310 (F)
bs_blumberg@fccc.edu (E)

Blumstein, Dr. Sheila E.   IV 1999
Albert D. Mead Professor of Cognitive and
    Linguistic Sciences
Department of Cognitive and Linguistic
    Sciences
Box 1978
Brown University
Providence, RI 02912
(401)863-2849 (O)
(401)863-2255 (F)
sheila_blumstein@brown.edu (E)

Bober, Dr. Phyllis Pray   IV 1999
Leslie Clark Professor in the Humanities
    Emerita
Professor Emeritus of Classical and Near
    Eastern Archaeology
Department of History
Bryn Mawr College
Bryn Mawr, PA 19010
(610)896-8242 (H)

Bodde, Dr. Derk   IV 1961
Professor Emeritus of Chinese Studies
University of Pennsylvania
Home: 6300 Greene Street
Apt. W-404
Philadelphia, PA 19144
(215)848-4688 (H)

Bogorad, Dr. Lawrence   II 1985
Maria Moors Cabot Professor of Biology,
    Emeritus
Department of Molecular and Cellular
    Biology
The Biological Laboratories
16 Divinity Avenue
Harvard University
Cambridge, MA 02138
Home: 2 White Pine Lane
Lexington, MA 02421
(617)495-4292 (O)
(781)861-8374 (H)
(617)495-4292 (F)
bogorad@biosun.harvard.edu (E)

Bohannan, Dr. Paul J.   III 1970
Professor Emeritus of Anthropology
University of Southern California
Home: P.O. Box 877
Three Rivers, CA 93271
(209)561-3518 (O)
(209)561-3686 (F)
paulboh@aol.com (E)

Bok, Dr. Derek C.   V 1980
President Emeritus
Harvard University
Kennedy School of Government
79 John F. Kennedy Street
Cambridge, MA 02138
(617)495-1186 (O)
(617)495-1972 (F)

Bonner, Dr. John Tyler   II 1972
George M. Moffett Professor of Biology,
    Emeritus
Department of Ecology and Evolutionary
    Biology
Princeton University
Princeton, NJ 08544-1003
(609)258-3841 (O)
(609)258-1712 (F)
jtbonner@princeton.edu (E)

Boorstin, Dr. Daniel Joseph   III 1981
The Librarian of Congress Emeritus
Library of Congress
Washington, DC 20540
(202)707-1500 (O)

Booth, Dr. Wayne Clayson   IV 1992
George M. Pullman Distinguished Service
    Professor of English, Emeritus
The University of Chicago
Home: 5411 S. Greenwood Avenue
Chicago, IL 60615
(773)363-4085 (H)
(773)363-7204 (H)
(773)702-5846 (F)
wcbooth@midway.uchicago.edu (E)

Bouwsma, Dr. William James IV 1981
Sather Professor of History, Emeritus
Department of History
University of California
Berkeley, CA 94720
Home: 1530 La Loma
Berkeley, CA 94708
(510)549-9209 (H)
(510)643-5323 (F)

Bowen, Dr. William Gordon   III 1978
President
Andrew W. Mellon Foundation
140 East 62nd Street
New York, NY 10021
(212)838-8400 (O)
(212)888-4172 (F)

Böwering, Dr. Gerhard H.   IV 1994
Professor of Islamic Studies
Box 208287
Yale University
New Haven, CT 06520-8287
Home: 438 Sea Hill Road
North Branford, CT 06471
(203)432-0828 (O)
(203)432-7844 (F)
gerhard.bowering@yale.edu (E)

Bowersock, Dr. Glen Warren IV 1989
Professor of Ancient History
School of Historical Studies
The Institute for Advanced Study
Princeton, NJ 08540
(609)734-8353 (O)
(609)924-4689 (H)
(609)951-4462 (F)
gwb@ias.edu (E)

Boyer, Dr. Paul D. II 1998
Professor Emeritus
University of California
[November—May]
1033 Somera Road
Los Angeles, CA 90077-2625
[May—November]
Box 276
Thayne, WY 83127
(310)825-1466 (O)
(310)472-8848 (H)
(307)883-2567 (H)
(310)206-7286 (F)
pdboyer@ucla.edu (E)

Bradley, Hon. Bill V 1997
United State Senator from New Jersey,
  1979–1997
1661 Page Mill Road
Palo Alto, CA 94304
(650)494-2554 (O)

Braidwood, Dr. Robert J. IV 1966
Professor Emeritus of Old World Prehistory
Oriental Institute
University of Chicago
Home: 0454 East 700 North
La Porte, IN 46350
(219)778-2253 (H)

Branscomb, Dr. Lewis M. I 1970
Aetna Professor of Public Policy
Director of Science Technology and Public
  Policy Program
Harvard University
John F. Kennedy School of Government
79 John F. Kennedy Street
Cambridge, MA 02138
Home: 155 Mildred Circle
Concord, MA 01742
(617)495-1853 (O)
(508)369-1878 (H)
(617)495-8963 (F)

Brée, Dr. Germaine IV 1965
Kenan Professor of Humanities, Emerita
Wake Forest University

Brentano, Mr. Robert James IV 1996
Jane K. Sather Professor of History
University of California
Berkeley, CA
Home: 35 Roble Court
Berkeley, CA 94705
(510)642-1971 (O)
(510)849-1571 (H)
011-39-041-5229805 (H) Venice
(510)643-5323 (F)
history@NCBCMSA.berkeley.edu (E)

Breslow, Dr. Ronald I 1980
S. L. Mitchill Professor of Chemistry and
  University Professor
Department of Chemistry
566 Chandler Laboratory
Columbia University
New York, NY 10027
(212)854-2170 (O)
(212)854-2755 (F)
rb33@columbia.edu (E)

Brimmer, Dr. Andrew F.   III 1976
President, Brimmer and Company, Inc.
Economic and Financial Consultants
4400 MacArthur Boulevard, N.W.
Suite 302
Washington, DC 20007
(202)342-6255 (O)
(202)342-6283 (F)

Brombert, Dr. Victor H.   IV 1987
Henry Putnam University Professor of
    Romance and Comparative Literature
245 East Pyne
Department of Comparative Literature
Princeton University
Princeton, NJ 08544
Home: 187 Library Place
Princeton, NJ 08540
(609)258-4499 (O)
(609)258-1873 (F)

Brooks, Dr. Harvey   I 1961
Benjamin Peirce Professor of Technology
    and Public Policy
JFK School of Government
79 John Kennedy Street, L327, BCSIA
Harvard University
Cambridge, MA 02138
Home: 46 Brewster Street
Cambridge, MA 02138-2236
(617)495-1445 (O)
(617)354-7170 (H)
(617)354-7170 (F)
nora_o'neil@harvard.edu (E)

Brown, Dr. Donald David   II 1981
Professor of Biology
Johns Hopkins University
Department of Embryology
115 West University Parkway
Carnegie Institution of Washington
Baltimore, MD 21210
(410)467-1414 (O)
(410)243-6311 (F)
brown@mail1.ciwemb.edu (E)

Brown, Mr. J. Carter   V 1992
Chairman
Commission of Fine Arts
Chairman
Ovation-The Arts Network
1201 Pennsylvania Avenue, N.W.
Suite 621
Washington, DC 20004
(202)347-1906 (O)
(202)347-2107 (F)

Brown, Dr. Jonathan M.   IV 1988
Carroll and Milton Petrie Professor
    of Fine Arts
Institute of Fine Arts
New York University
Home: 71 Battle Road
Princeton, NJ 08540
(212)772-5842 (O)
(609)921-3834 (H)
(212)772-5807 (O)(F)
(609)924-9520 (H)(F)
nenuto@aol.com (E)

Brown, Dr. Michael S.   II 1987
Professor of Molecular Genetics
University of Texas Southwestern
Medical School
5323 Harry Hines Boulevard
Dallas, TX 75235-9046
(214)648-2179 (O)
(214)648-8804 (F)
mbrow1@mednet.swmed.edu (E)

Brown, Prof. Peter Robert L. IV 1995
Philip and Beulah Rollins Professor of
    History
Princeton University
Home: 138 Westcott Road
Princeton, NJ 08540
(609)258-4159 (O)
(609)683-5677 (H)
(609)258-5326 (F)

Bruner, Dr. Jerome　　　III 1982
University Professor of Psychology
Senior Research Fellow in Law
Vanderbilt Hall
40 Washington Square
New York University Law School
New York, NY 10012
Home: 200 Mercer Street
New York, NY 10012
(212)998-6463 (O)
(212)674-7816 (H)
(212)673-6118 (F)
jerome.bruner@nyu.edu (E)

Bullock, Dr. Theodore H.　　II 1970
Professor of Neurosciences, Emeritus
Department of Neurosciences 0201
School of Medicine
9500 Gilman Drive
University of California
La Jolla, CA 92093-0201
Home: 3028 Driscoll Drive
San Diego, CA 92117
(619)534-3636 (O)
(619)534-3919 (F)

Burbidge, Dr. E. Margaret　　I 1980
University Professor, Emeritus
Research Physicist
Center for Astrophysics and Space Sciences
9500 Gilman Drive
University of California, 0424
La Jolla, CA 92093
(619)534-4477 (O)
(619)534-7051 (F)
mburbidge@ucsd.edu (E)

Burke, Mr. James Edward　　V 1991
Chairman
Partnership for a Drug-Free America
Chairman of the Board and Chief Executive
  Officer Emeritus
Johnson & Johnson
100 Albany Street, Suite 200
New Brunswick, NJ 08901

Burkhardt, Dr. Frederick H.　　V 1983
President Emeritus
American Council of Learned Societies
Darwin Correspondence Project
Home: Box 1067
Bennington, VT 05201
(802)442-9573 (O)
(802)442-9573 (H)
(802)442-9573 (F)
fhb@sover.net (E)

Burns, Dr. James MacGregor　III 1971
Professor of Political Science
Woodrow Wilson Professor of Government
Stetson Hall
Department of Political Science
Williams College
Williamstown, MA 01267
(413)458-8607 (H)

Burris, Dr. Robert H.　　II 1979
W. H. Peterson Professor Emeritus of
  Biochemistry
Department of Biochemistry
433 Babcock Drive
University of Wisconsin
Madison, WI 53706-1544
(608)262-3042 (O)
(608)233-5932 (H)
(608)262-3453 (F)
burris@biochem.wisc.edu (E)

Bynum, Dr. Caroline　　IV 1995
University Professor
Department of History
Fayerweather Hall
Mail Code 2546
Columbia University
New York, NY 10027
Home: 410 Riverside Drive—Apt. 101
New York, NY 10025
(212)854-2414 (O)
(212)932-0602 (F)

Cairns, Dr. John, Jr.   II 1999
University Distinguished Professor of
  Environmental Biology Emeritus
Virginia Polytechnic Institute and State
  University
Department of Biology
1020 Derring Hall
Virginia Tech
Blacksburg, VA 24061
(540)231-7075 (O)
(540)231-9307 (F)
cairnsb@vt.edu (E)

Calabresi, Hon. Guido   III 1997
Former Dean
Sterling Professor of Law Emeritus
Professional Lecturer, Yale Law School
Circuit Judge
United States Court of Appeals
2nd Circuit
157 Church Street
New Haven, CT 06510-2030
(203)773-2291 (O)
(203)393-0008 (H)
(203)773-2401 (O)(F)
(203)393-1575 (H)(F)

Cameron, Dr. Alan   IV 1992
Charles Anthon Professor of Latin
  Language and Literature
Columbia University
Home: 450 Riverside Drive
New York, NY 10027
(212)854-4551 (O)
(212)662-9319 (H)
(212)854-7856 (F)

Cardona, Dr. George   IV 1997
Professor of Linguistics
Undergraduate Chairman
Department of Linguistics
619 Williams Hall
University of Pennsylvania
Philadelphia, PA 19104-6305
Home: 352 E. Second Street
Moorestown, NJ 08057
(215)898-7849 (O)
(215)573-2091 (F)
cardona@unagi.cis.upenn.edu (E)

Carrier, Dr. George Francis   I 1976
T. Jefferson Coolidge Professor of Applied
  Mathematics, Emeritus
Division of Applied Sciences
Room 311, Pierce Hall
Harvard University
Cambridge, MA 02138
(617)495-3788 (O)
(508)358-4876 (H)
(617)495-9837 (F)

Carter, Dr. Edward C., II   III 1983
Librarian
American Philosophical Society
105 South Fifth Street
Philadelphia, PA 19106
Home: 15 South Valley Forge Road
Wayne, PA 19087
(215)440-3404 (O)
(610)687-5192 (H)
(215)440-8579 (F)
ecarter@mail.sas.upenn.edu (E)

Carter, Hon. James Earl   V 1991
Former President of the United States
Chairman
Board of Trustees
Distinguished Professor
Emory University
Member
Carnegie Commission on Science,
    Technology, and Government
The Carter Center
One Copenhill
Atlanta, GA 30307
(404)420-5100 (O)
(404)331-0283 (F)

Casper, Mr. Gerhard   III 1996
President and Professor of Law
President's Office
Building 10
Main Quadrangle
Stanford University
Stanford, CA 94305-2060
(650)723-2481 (O)
(650)725-9520 (F)

Chance, Dr. Britton   II 1958
Eldridge Reeves Johnson University
    Professor Emeritus of Biophysics and
    Physical Biochemistry and Radiologic
    Physics
Department of Biochemistry and Biophysics
School of Medicine
D501 Richards Building
37th & Hamilton Walk
University of Pennsylvania
Philadelphia, PA 19104-6089
Home: 4014 Pine Street
Philadelphia, PA 19104
(215)898-4342/7159 (O)
(215)662-0354 (H)
(215)898-1806 (O)(F)
(215)382-2190 (H)(F)
chance@mail.med.upenn.edu (E)

Chandler, Dr. Alfred D., Jr.   III 1984
Isador Straus Professor of Business History,
    Emeritus
Harvard University
Home: 47 Nobadeer Avenue
Nantucket, MA 02554-2878
(617)495-6367 (O)
(617)547-9013 (H)
(617)495-8736 (F)

Chargaff, Dr. Erwin   II 1979
Professor Emeritus of Biochemistry,
    Emeritus
Columbia University
Home: 350 Central Park West
Apt. 13-G
New York, NY 10025-6503
(212)222-7994 (H)

Chern, Dr. Shiing-shen   I 1989
Professor Emeritus
University of California
Berkeley, CA
Home: 8336 Kent Court
El Cerrito, CA 94530
(510)232-4148 (H)
(510)232-4724 (F)

Cho, Dr. Alfred Y.   I 1996
Director
Semiconductor Research
Bell Laboratories
Lucent Technologies
Room 6H-422
600 Mountain Avenue
P.O. Box 636
Murray Hill, NJ 07974-0636
Home: 11 Kenneth Court
Summit, NJ 07901
(908)582-2093 (O)
(908)273-5628 (H)
(908)582-2043 (F)
ayc@lucent.com (E)

Choppin, Dr. Purnell W.   II 1988
President
Howard Hughes Medical Institute
4000 Jones Bridge Road
Chevy Chase, MD 20815-6789
(301)215-8550 (O)
(202)462-4483 (H)
(301)215-8558 (F)
choppinp@hhmi.org (E)

Chow, Dr. Gregory C.   III 1992
Former Director of the Econometric
  Research Program
Class of 1913 Professor of Political
  Economy
Department of Economics
205 Fisher Hall
Princeton University
Princeton, NJ 08544-1021
(609)258-4030 (O)
(609)258-5561 (F)
gchow@princeton.edu (E)

Christopher, Hon. Warren   V 1997
Former Secretary of State
Senior Partner
O'Melveny & Myers
1999 Avenue of the Stars, 7th Floor
Los Angeles, CA 90067-6035
(310)553-6700 (O)
(310)246-8470 (F)

Chu, Dr. Steven   I 1998
Theodore and Frances Geballe Professor
Department of Physics
Stanford University
Stanford, CA 94305
(650)723-3571 (O)
(650)723-9173 (F)
schu@stanford.edu (E)

Clagett, Dr. Marshall   IV 1960
Professor of the History of Science,
  Emeritus
School of Historical Studies
The Institute for Advanced Study
Princeton, NJ 08540
(609)734-8311 (O)
(609)921-9065 (H)
(609)924-8399 (F)

Coale, Dr. Ansley J.   III 1963
Senior Research Demographer Emeritus
Professor Emeritus
Economics and Public Affairs
Princeton University
Home: Apt. F113, Pennswood Village
1382 Langhorne-Newtown Road
Newtown, PA 18940-2401
(215)968-6815 (H)

Cocke, Dr. John   I 1995
Former Research Staff Member and former
  IBM Fellow
IBM Research
313 Pound Ridge Road
Bedford, NY 10506

Cohen, Dr. I. Bernard   III 1995
Victor S. Thomas Professor Emeritus of the
  History of Science
Harvard University
Home: 5 Stella Road
Belmont, MA 02478
(617)496-2944 (O)
(617)484-1221 (H)
(617)495-3344 (O)(F)
(617)484-1211 (H)(F)
ibcohen@fas.harvard.edu (E)

Cohen, Dr. Joel E.   V 1994
Professor of Populations
Columbia University
Professor and Head of the Laboratory of
  Populations
Rockefeller University
1230 York Avenue, Box 20
New York, NY 10021-6399
(212)327-8883 (O)
(212)327-7974 (F)
cohen@rockvax.rockefeller.edu (E)

Cohen, Dr. Paul Joseph   I 1972
Professor of Mathematics
Stanford University
Stanford, CA 94305

Cohn, Dr. Mildred   I 1972
Benjamin Rush Professor, Emerita
University of Pennsylvania School of
  Medicine
Home: 226 W. Rittenhouse Square
Apt. #1806
Philadelphia, PA 19103
(215)898-8404 (O)
(215)546-3449 (H)
(215)898-1806 (F)
cohn@mail.med.upenn.edu (E)

Cone, Prof. Edward Toner   IV 1991
Professor Emeritus, Princeton University
Home: 18 College Road West
Princeton, NJ 08540
(609)921-2609 (H)

Connor, Dr. W. Robert   V 1996
Director, National Humanities Center
7 Alexander Drive
Research Triangle Park, NC 27709-2256
(919)549-0661 (O)
(919)990-8535 (F)
connor@ga.unc.edu (E)

Constable, Dr. Giles   IV 1987
Professor
School of Historical Studies
The Institute for Advanced Study
Princeton, NJ 08540
(609)734-8308 (O)
(609)683-1262 (H)
(609)951-4488 (O)(F)
(609)497-1854 (H)(F)

Converse, Dr. Philip E.   III 1988
Director Emeritus
Center for Advanced Study in the
  Behavioral Sciences
University of Michigan
Home: 9 Haverhill Court
Ann Arbor, MI 48105
(734)996-0348 (H)
pconverse@umich.edu (E)

Cooper, Dr. Leon N   I 1973
Thomas J. Watson, Sr., Professor of Science
Brown University
Director
Institute for Brain and Neural Systems
Box 1843
Providence, RI 02912
(401)863-2172 (O)
(401)863-3494 (F)
leon_cooper@brown.edu (E)

Cotton, Dr. Frank Albert   I 1992
W. T. Doherty-Welch Foundation
Distinguished Professor of Chemistry
Department of Chemistry
Texas A & M University
College Station, TX 77843-3255
(409)845-4432/3727 (O)
(409)589-2501 (H)
(409)845-9351 (F)
cotton@tamu.edu (E)

Cowan, Dr. W. Maxwell   II 1987
Vice President
Chief Scientific Officer
Howard Hughes Medical Institute
4000 Jones Bridge Road
Chevy Chase, MD 20815-6789
Home: 6337 Windermere Circle
North Bethesda, MD 20852
(301)215-8803 (O)
(301)493-9097 (H)
(301)215-8828 (F)

Cox, Dr. Archibald   III 1980
Carl M. Loeb University
Professor, Emeritus
Harvard University
Cambridge, MA 02138
(617)495-3133 (O)
(617)495-1110 (F)

Craig, Dr. Gordon A.   III 1963
J. E. Wallace Sterling Professor of
    Humanities, Emeritus
Stanford University
Home: 451 Oak Grove Avenue
Menlo Park, CA 94025
(650)323-1380 (H)

Crawford, Dr. Bryce, Jr.   I 1971
Regents' Professor Emeritus
Department of Chemistry
5 Smith Hall
University of Minnesota
Minneapolis, MN 55455
Home: 1666 Coffman Street, Apt. 114
St. Paul, MN 55108-1326
(612)645-3128 (H)
(612)626-7541 (F)
crawford@chemsun.chem.umn.edu (E)

Cronbach, Dr. Lee J.   III 1967
Vida Jacks Professor of Education, Emeritus
Stanford University
Home: 850 Webster Street, #623
Palo Alto, CA 94301
(650)324-7417 (H)
ljc@leland.stanford.edu (E)

Cronin, Dr. James Watson   I 1999
University Professor Emeritus
University of Chicago
5825 S. Dorchester Avenue
Chicago, IL 60637
(773)702-7102 (O)
(773)702-6645 (F)
jwc@hep.uchicago.edu (E)

Cronkite, Mr. Walter   V 1994
Special Correspondent and Consultant
CBS
Chairman
The Cronkite Ward Company
CBS, Inc.
51 W. 52nd Street, Room 1934
New York, NY 10019
(212)975-3627 (O)
(212)288-9253 (H)
(212)975-1509 (F)

Cronon, Dr. William J.   III 1999
Frederick Jackson Turner Professor of
    History, Geography, and Environmental
    Studies
University of Wisconsin
Home: 2027 Chadbourne Avenue
Madison, WI 53705
(608)265-6023 (O)
(608)265-6024 (F)
wcronon@facstaff.wisc.edu (E)

Cropper, Dr. Elizabeth   IV 1998
Professor of History of Art
Director of Villa Spelman
Johns Hopkins University
3400 N. Charles Street
Baltimore, MD 21218
(410)516-7117 (O)
(410)235-7174 (H)
(410)516-5188 (F)
poussin@jhunix.hcf.jhu.edu (E)

Cross, Dr. Frank Moore, Jr.   IV 1971
Hancock Professor of Hebrew and Other
Oriental Languages Emeritus
Harvard University
Harvard Semitic Museum
6 Divinity Avenue
Cambridge, MA 02138
Home: 31 Woodland Road
Lexington, MA 02420-2015
(617)495-5757 (O)
(781)862-4173 (H)
(617)496-8904 (F)

Cross, Mr. Theodore L.   V 1995
Editor-in-Chief
('Business and Society Review')
Chairman
Hanover Publishers, Inc.
200 West 57th Street, 15th Floor
New York, NY 10019
(212)399-1080 (O)
(609)921-3661 (H)
(212)245-1973 (F)

Crow, Dr. James Franklin   II 1966
Professor Emeritus of Genetics
Department of Genetics
445 Henry Mall
University of Wisconsin
Madison, WI 53705
(608)263-4438 (O)
(608)262-2976 (F)
jfcrow@facstaff.wisc.edu (E)

Curtin, Dr. Philip   III 1995
Herbert Baxter Adams Professor of History
The Johns Hopkins University
Home: 42 Windermere Way
Kennett Square, PA 19348
(610)388-9839 (H)
(610)388-9839 (F)
curtin@jhu.edu (E)

D'Arms, Dr. John H.   V 1998
President
American Council of Learned Societies
228 East 45th Street
New York, NY 10017-3398
Home: 14 Sutton Place South
New York, NY 10022
(212)697-1505 ext. 121 (O)
(212)750-5350 (H)
(212)949-8058 (F)
jhdarms@acls.org (E)

d'Harnoncourt, Ms. Anne   V 1988
The George D. Widener Director and Chief
   Executive Officer
Office of the Director
Philadelphia Museum of Art
P.O. Box 7646
Philadelphia, PA 19101-7646
(215)684-7701 (O)
(215)232-4338 (F)

Dahl, Dr. Robert A.   III 1960
Sterling Professor Emeritus of Political
   Science
Department of Political Science
P.O. Box 208301
Yale University
New Haven, CT 06520-8301
Home: 17 Cooper Road
North Haven, CT 06473
(203)432-5267 (O)
(203)288-3126 (H)
(203)432-6196 (O)(F)
(203)288-0869 (H)(F)
robert.dahl@yale.edu (E)

Darnton, Dr. Robert Choate   III 1989
Davis Professor of European History
History Department
Princeton University
Princeton, NJ 08544
Home: 6 McCosh Circle
Princeton, NJ 08540
(609)258-4159 (O)
(609)258-5326 (F)
darnton@princeton.edu (E)

David, Dr. Edward E., Jr.   I 1979
President
EED Inc.
Box 435
Bedminster, NJ 07921
(908)234-9319 (O)
(908)781-0999 (H)
(908)234-2956 (F)
eddavid@media.mit.edu (E)

Davidson, Dr. Donald H.   IV 1985
Willis S. and Marion Slusser Professor of
    Philosophy
Philosophy Department
314 Moses Hall
University of California
Berkeley, CA 94720
(510)642-3309 (O)
(510)642-4164 (F)

Davis, Dr. David Brion   III 1983
Sterling Professor of History
Department of History
P. O. Box 208324
Yale University
New Haven, CT 06520-8324
(203)432-1370 (O)
(203)432-7587 (F)

deBary, Dr. William T.   IV 1999
John Mitchell Mason Professor Emeritus
    and Provost Emeritus
Special Service Professor
Columbia University
502 Kent Hall
New York, NY 10027
Home: 98 Hickory Hill Road
Tappan, NY 10983
(212)854-3671 (O)
(914)359-3699 (H)
(212)678-8629 (F)
wtdl@columbia.edu (E)

Debreu, Dr. Gerard   III 1984
University Professor and Class of 1958
Professor of Economics and of
    Mathematics, Emeritus
Department of Economics
University of California
Berkeley, CA 94720-3880

Degler, Dr. Carl N.   III 1985
Margaret Byrne Professor of American
    History, Emeritus
Stanford University
Home: 907 Mears Court
Stanford, CA 94305
(650)493-0745 (H)
(650)725-0597 (F)
degler@leland.stanford.edu (E)

Dempsey, Dr. Charles G.   IV 1998
Professor of Italian Renaissance and
    Baroque Art
Department of History of Art
The Johns Hopkins University
Baltimore, MD 21218
(410)516-7117 (O)
(410)235-7194 (H)
(410)516-5188 (F)
demps_c@jhunix.hcf.jhu.edu (E)

Dennard, Dr. Robert H.   I 1997
IBM Fellow
IBM T. J. Watson Research Center
P.O. Box 218
Yorktown Heights, NY 10598
(914)945-1371 (O)
(914)945-3623 (F)
dennard@us.ibm.com (E)

Diamond, Dr. Jared Mason   II 1988
Professor of Physiology
School of Medicine
University of California
Los Angeles, CA 90095-1751
(310)825-6177 (O)
(310)206-5661 (F)
jdiamond@mednet.ucla.edu (E)

Doniger, Dr. Wendy   IV 1996
Mircea Eliade Distinguished Service
    Professor of History of Religions
The Divinity School
1025 East 58th Street
University of Chicago
Chicago, IL 60637
(773)702-8239 (O)
(773)702-6048 (F)
don8@midway.uchicago.edu (E)

Doolittle, Dr. Russell F.   II 1992
Research Professor of Biology and
    Chemistry
Center for Molecular Genetics
9500 Gilman Drive
University of California
La Jolla, CA 92093-0634
Home: 2750 Nottingham Place
La Jolla, CA 92037
(619)534-4417 (O)
(619)534-4985 (F)
rdoolittle@ucsd.edu (E)

Doty, Dr. Paul Mead   II 1970
Mallinckrodt Professor of Biochemistry,
    Emeritus
Professor of Public Policy, Emeritus
Department of Biochemistry and
    Molecular Biology
79 J. F. Kennedy Street, Room P-26
Harvard University
Cambridge, MA 02138
Home: 4 Kirkland Place
Cambridge MA 02138
(617)495-1401 (O)
(617)864-6679 (H)
(617)496-4403 (O)(F)
(617)864-3739 (H)(F)
pauldoty@fas.harvard.edu (E)

Dove, Prof. Rita   V 1996
Commonwealth Professor of English
Department of English
219 Bryan Hall
University of Virginia
Charlottesville, VA 22903
(804)924-6618 (O)
(804)924-1478 (F)
rfd4b@virginia.edu (E)

Dowling, Dr. John Elliott   II 1992
Harvard College Professor
Maria Moors Cabot Professor of Natural
    Science
The Biological Laboratories
16 Divinity Avenue
Harvard University
Cambridge, MA 02138
(617)495-2245 (O)
(617)720-4522 (H)
(617)496-3321 (F)
dowling@fas.harvard.edu (E)

Drell, Dr. Sidney D.   I 1987
Senior Fellow, Hoover Institution
Professor Emeritus
Stanford Linear Accelerator Center (SLAC)
P.O. Box 4349
Stanford, CA 94309
(650)926-2664 (O), (650)325-0565 (H)
(650)926-4500 (F)
drell@slac.stanford.edu (E)

Dresselhaus, Dr. Mildred S.   I 1995
Institute Professor
Massachusetts Institute of Technology
Room 13–3005
77 Massachusetts Avenue
Cambridge, MA 02139-4307
(617)253-6864 (O), (781)643-1078 (H)
(617)253-6827 (F)
millie@mgm.mit.edu (E)

Drickamer, Dr. Harry G.   I 1983
Professor Emeritus of Chemistry
School of Chemical Sciences
600 S. Mathews
University of Illinois
Urbana, IL 61801-3792
Home: 304 E. Pennsylvania Avenue
Urbana, IL 61801
(217)333-0025 (O), (217)333-5052 (F)
drickame@aries.scs.uiuc.edu (E)

Dulbecco, Dr. Renato   II 1993
President Emeritus and Distinguished
   Research Professor
The Salk Institute
P.O. Box 85800
San Diego, CA 92186-5800
Home: 7525 Hillside Drive
La Jolla, CA 92037
(619)453-4100 ext. 1682 (O)
(619)458-9741 (F)

Duncan, Dr. Otis Dudley   III 1973
Professor of Sociology, Emeritus
University of California
Santa Barbara, CA
Home: 4523 Auhay Drive
Santa Barbara, CA 93110-1705
(805)964-3109 (H)

Dunlop, Dr. John T.   III 1972
Lamont University Professor, Emeritus
208 Littauer Center
Harvard University
Cambridge, MA 02138
(617)495-4157 (O)
(617)495-7730 (F)

Dunn, Dr. Mary Maples   V 1999
President Emeritus
Smith College
Director
The Schlesinger Library
Radcliffe College
Home: 174 Lexington Avenue
Cambridge, MA 02138
(617)495-8647 (O)
(617)491-4716 (H)
mdunn@radcliffe.edu (E)

Dunn, Dr. Richard Slator   III 1998
Roy F. and Jeannette P. Nichols Professor
   of American History Emeritus
University of Pennsylvania
Founder and Director
McNeil Center for Early American Studies
Home: 226 W. Rittenhouse Square
Apt. 1404
Philadelphia, PA 19103
(215)735-5586 (H)

Dyson, Mr. Freeman John   I 1976
Professor Emeritus
The Institute for Advanced Study
Princeton, NJ 08540
Home: 105 Battle Road Circle
Princeton, NJ 08540
(609)734-8055 (O)
(609)924-2152 (H)
(609)951-4489 (F)
dyson@ias.edu (E)

Dyson, Dr. Robert Harris, Jr.   V 1984
Formerly, The Charles K. Williams II
   Director of The University of
   Pennsylvania Museum
   of Archaeology and Anthropology
33rd and Spruce Streets
University of Pennsylvania Museum
Philadelphia, PA 19104
Home: 1343 Rose Glen Road
Gladwyne, PA 19035
(215)898-4127 (O)
(610)642-4907 (H)
(215)898-0657 (F)

Eagleson, Mr. William B., Jr.   V 1977
Chairman Emeritus
Mellon Bank Corporation
Home: 1241 Denbigh Lane
Radnor, PA 19087
(610)527-1126 (H)
(610)527-8370 (F)

Eastburn, Dr. David P.   V 1982
Former President
Federal Reserve Bank of Philadelphia
Home: 75 Short Road
Doylestown, PA 18901
(215)348-8495 (H)

Easton, Mr. Roger L.   I 1998
Former Head, Space Applications Branch
Naval Research Laboratory
Washington, DC 20375
Home: RR2 Box 920
Canaan, NH 03741-9309
(603)523-7532 (H)
easton@ncst.nrl.navy.mil (E)

Ebert, Dr. James David   II 1974
Professor of Biology
[December-May]
Department of Biology
The Johns Hopkins University
3400 N. Charles Street
Baltimore, MD 21218
(410)516-8773 (O), (410)366-6808 (H)
(410)516-8537 (F)
[June-November]
Marine Biological Laboratory
Woods Hole, MA 02543
Home: 85 Two Ponds Road
Falmouth, MA 02540
(508)548-3705 (O), (508)540-2709 (H)
(508)457-1924 (F)

Eccles, Viscountess (Mary Morley
   Crapo Hyde Eccles)   V 1978
Author, Scholar, Book Collector
Home: Four Oaks Farm
350 Burnt Mill Road
Somerville, NJ 08876
(908)725-0966 (H)
(908)725-9215 (F)

Edelman, Dr. Gerald Maurice   II 1977
Member and Chairman of the Department
   of Neurobiology, SBR 14
Scripps Research Institute
10550 North Torrey Pines Road
La Jolla, CA 92037
(619)554-3600 (O)
(619)554-6660 (F)

Edelman, Ms. Marian Wright V 1994
President
Children's Defense Fund
25 E Street N.W.
Washington, DC 20001
(202)662-3500 (O)
(202)662-3580 (F)

Edsall, Dr. John Tileston II 1955
Professor of Biochemistry Emeritus
Harvard University
Home: 985 Memorial Drive, Apt. 503
Cambridge, MA 02138-5769
(617)495-2314 (O)
(617)876-5007 (H)
(617)495-8308 (F)

Ehrlich, Dr. Paul R. II 1990
Bing Professor of Population Studies and
    Professor of Biological Sciences
Department of Biological Sciences
Stanford University
Stanford, CA 94305
(650)723-3171 (O)
(650)723-0998 (H)
(650)723-5920 (F)

Eisner, Dr. Thomas II 1986
Schurman Professor of Chemical Biology
W347 Mudd Hall
Cornell University
Ithaca, NY 14853-2702
(607)255-4464 (O)
(607)255-6186 (F)
tel4@cornell.edu (E)

Elliott, Sir John IV 1982
Regius Professor Emeritus of Modern
    History
University of Oxford, Oriel College
Home: 122 Church Way, Iffley
Oxford OX4 4EG, England
01865–716703 (H), 01865–777301 (F)

Emeneau, Dr. M. B. IV 1952
Professor of Sanskrit and General
    Linguistics, Emeritus
University of California
Home: 909 San Benito Road
Berkeley, CA 94707
(510)524-2444 (H)

Ernst, Dr. W. Gary I 1994
Professor
Department of Geological and
    Environmental Sciences
Stanford University
Stanford, CA 94305-2115
Home: One Sunhill
Portola Valley, CA 94028
(650)723-0185 (O), (650)851-2394 (H)
(650)725-7970 (F)
ernst@pangea.stanford.edu (E)

Fagles, Dr. Robert IV 1997
Poet and Arthur W. Marks '19·
    Professor of Comparative Literature
318 East Pyne
Princeton University
Princeton, NJ 08544
Home: 67 Lambert Drive
Princeton, NJ 08540
(609)258-4027 (O), (609)921-2879 (H)
(609)258-1873 (F)
fagles@princeton.edu (E)

Farnsworth, Prof. E. Allan   III 1994
Alfred McCormack Professor of Law
Columbia University
Columbia Law School
435 West 116th Street
New York, NY 10027
Home: 201 Lincoln Street
Englewood, NJ 07631
(212)854-2661 (O)
(201)568-2114 (H)
(212)854-7946 (F)
allan@law.columbia.edu (E)

Fefferman, Dr. Charles L.   I 1988
Herbert Jones University Professor,
   Mathematics
Princeton University
Home: 234 Clover Lane
Princeton, NJ 08540
(609)258-4205 (O)

Feldstein, Dr. Martin   III 1989
George F. Baker Professor of Economics
Harvard University
President
National Bureau of Economic Research
1050 Massachusetts Avenue
Cambridge, MA 02138
(617)868-3905 (O)
(617)868-7194 (F)
msfeldst@nber.org (E)

Fenno, Dr. Richard F., Jr.   III 1989
Kenan Professor of Political Science
Distinguished University Professor
Department of Political Science
University of Rochester
Rochester, NY 14627
(716)275-4294 (O)
(716)381-9205 (H)
(716)271-1616 (F)
rff1@troi.cc.rochester.edu (E)

Fisher, Dr. Michael E.   I 1993
Distinguished University Professor and
   Regents Professor
Institute for Physical Science and
   Technology
University of Maryland
College Park, MD 20742-2431
(301)405-4820 (O)
(301)587-3259 (H)
(301)314-9404 (F)

Fitch, Dr. Val L.   I 1995
James S. McDonnell Distinguished
   University Professor of Physics, Emeritus
Department of Physics
P.O. Box 708
Princeton University
Princeton, NJ 08544
(609)258-4374 (O)
(609)921-7345 (H)
(609)258-6360 (F)
vfitch@princeton.edu (E)

Folkman, Dr. Judah   II 1999
Julia Dyckman Andrus Professor of
   Pediatric Surgery
Professor of Cell Biology
Harvard Medical School
Children's Hospital
300 Longwood Avenue
Boston, MA 02115
(617)355-7661 (O)
(617)355-7662 (F)

Fong, Dr. Wen C.   IV 1992
Edwards S. Sanford Professor of Art
   History
Princeton University
Consultative Chairman
Asian Art Department
The Metropolitan Museum of Art, New York
Home: 83 Allison Road
Princeton, NJ 08540
(609)258-3732 (O)
(609)921-8364 (H)

Ford, Dr. Franklin L. III 1974
McLean Professor of Ancient and Modern
    History, Emeritus
Harvard University
Home: 1010 Waltham Street
Apt. C-557
Lexington, MA 02421-8093
(617)495-2545 (O)
(617)863-7256 (H)
(617)496-3425 (F)

Fox, Dr. Marye Ann I 1996
Office of the Chancellor
Box 7001
North Carolina State University
Raleigh, NC 27695-7001
(919)515-2191 (O)
(919)831-3545 (F)
chancellor@ncsu.edu (E)

Franklin, Dr. John Hope III 1973
John M. Manly Distinguished Service
    Professor, Emeritus
University of Chicago
James B. Duke Professor of History
Duke University
Home: 208 Pineview Road
Durham, NC 27707
(919)489-7513 (H)
(919)490-9789 (F)

Frauenfelder, Dr. Hans E. I 1981
Professor of Physics
Director
Center for Nonlinear Studies
Los Alamos National Laboratory
CNLS, MS B258
Los Alamos, NM 87545
Home: P.O. Box 854
Tesuque, NM 87574
(505)665-2547 (O)
(505)983-7512 (H)
(505)665-2859 (O)(F)
frauenfelder@lanl.gov (E)

Frederick, Mr. William H., Jr. V 1995
President
Private Gardens Incorporated
1454 Ashland Clinton School Road
Hockessin, DE 19707
Home: 1472 Ashland Clinton School Road
Hockessin, DE 19707
(302)656-2573 (O)
(302)656-6075 (H)

Fredrickson, Dr. Donald S. II 1985
Former Director
National Institutes of Health
Former President & CEO
Howard Hughes Medical Institute
Bethesda, MD 20892
Home: 6615 Bradley Boulevard
Bethesda, MD 20817
(301)469-8197 (O)
(301)365-0833 (H)
(301)469-8540 (F)
dsf@nlm.nih.gov (E)

Freedberg, Dr. David IV 1997
Professor of Art History
Department of Art History
Columbia University
New York, NY 10027
(212)854-4505 (O)
(212)854-7329 (F)
daf5@columbia.edu (E)

Friedman, Dr. Herbert I 1964
Chief Scientist Emeritus
Hulburt Center for Space Research
Naval Research Laboratory
Washington, DC 20375
Home: 2643 N. Upshur Street
Arlington, VA 22207
(202)767-3363 (O)
(703)243-5810 (H)
(202)404-7296 (F)

Friedman, Dr. Milton   III 1957
Paul Snowden Russell Distinguished Service
   Professor Emeritus of Economics
University of Chicago
Senior Research Fellow
Hoover Institution
Stanford, CA 94305-6010
(650)723-0580 (O)
(650)723-1687 (F)

Frieman, Dr. Edward A.   V 1990
Director Emeritus
Science Applications International Corp.
10260 Campus Point Drive
San Diego, CA 92121
Home: 6425 Muirlands Drive
La Jolla, CA 92037
(619)546-6657 (O)
(619)454-4864 (H)
(619)534-9859 (F)
efrieman@ucsd.edu (E)

Fruton, Dr. Joseph S.   I 1967
Eugene Higgins Professor Emeritus of
   Biochemistry
Professor Emeritus of the History of
   Medicine
L230 Sterling Hall of Medicine
333 Cedar Street
Yale University
New Haven, CT 06510
Home: 123 York Street
New Haven, CT 06511
(203)785-4340 (O)
(203)624-3735 (H)
(203)737-4130 (F)

Frye, Dr. Roland Mushat   IV 1975
Schelling Professor of English Literature,
   Emeritus
University of Pennsylvania
Home: 226 W. Valley Road
Wayne, PA 19087
(610)687-3195 (H)

Fuchs, Dr. Victor R.   III 1990
Henry J. Kaiser Jr. Professor Emeritus
Stanford University
Research Associate
National Bureau of Economic Research
Home: 796 Cedro Way
Stanford, CA 94305
(650)326-7639 (O)
(650)858-1527 (H)
(650)328-4163 (O)(F)
(650)858-1527 (H)(F)

Gajdusek, Dr. D. Carleton   II 1978
Adjunct Professor
Institute of Human Virology
Guest Scholar, C.N.R.S.
Institute Alfred Fessard
Avenue de la Terrasse
91198 Gif-sur-Yvette, Cedex
France
33-1-69-07-05-38 (F)

Galbraith, Dr. John Kenneth   III 1980
Paul M. Warburg Professor of Economics,
   Emeritus
206 Littauer Center
Harvard University
Cambridge, MA 02138
(617)495-2140 (O)
(617)496-1200 (F)

Gall, Dr. Joseph Grafton   II 1989
Professor of Developmental Genetics
American Cancer Society
Staff Member
Department of Embryology
Carnegie Institution of Washington
115 West University Parkway
Baltimore, MD 21210
Home: 107 Bellemore Road
Baltimore, MD 21210
(410)554-1217 (O)
(410)433-8205 (H)
(410)243-6311 (F)
gall@mail1.ciwemb.edu (E)

Gardner, Dr. David Pierpont   V 1989
President Emeritus
University of Utah
University of California
Hewlett Foundation
525 Middlefield Road, Suite 200
Menlo Park, CA 94025
(650)329-1070 (O), (650)329-9342 (F)

Gardner, Hon. Richard N.   V 1998
Of Counsel
Morgan, Lewis and Bockius LLP
Former Ambassador to Spain and Italy
Henry L. Moses Professor of Law and
    International Organization
Columbia Law School
435 W. 116th Street
Columbia University
New York, NY 10027
(212)309-6942 (O), (212)369-6022 (H)
(212)309-6273 (F)
gard6942@mlb.com (E)

Garwin, Dr. Richard Lawrence I 1979
IBM
Thomas J. Watson Research Center
P.O. Box 218
Yorktown Heights, NY 10598
(914)945-2555 (O), (914)723-5972 (H)
(914)945-4419 (F)
rlg2@watson.ibm.com (E)

Gates, Dr. Henry Louis, Jr.   V 1995
W.E.B. Du Bois Professor of the Humanities
Department of Afro-American Studies
12 Quincy Street
Harvard University
Cambridge, MA 02138-3804
(617)496-5468 (O), (617)868-3480 (H)
(617)496-2871 (F)

Gay, Dr. Peter   III 1987
Sterling Professor of History, Emeritus
Yale University
Home: 105 Blue Trail
Hamden, CT 06518
(212)930-9257 (O)
(203)288-6752 (H)
(212)930-0040 (O)(F)
(203)288-6752 (H)(F)
pgay@nypl.org (E)

Geertz, Dr. Clifford   IV 1972
Harold F. Linder Professor of Social Science
Institute for Advanced Study
Princeton, NJ 08540
(609)734-8251 (O)
(609)951-4457 (F)
geertz@ias.edu (E)

Gell-Mann, Prof. Murray   I 1993
Robert A. Milikan Professor of Physics,
    Emeritus
Sante Fe Institute
1399 Hyde Park Road
Sante Fe, NM 87505
(505)984-8800 (O)
(505)989-8781 (H)
(505)982-0565 (F)
mgm@santafe.edu (E)

Gibbons, Mr. John H.   V 1999
Senior Fellow
National Academy of Engineering
The National Academies
P.O. Box 379
The Plains, VA 20198
(540)253-9843 (O)
(540)253-5409 (H)
(540)253-5076 (H)(F)
jackgibbons@erols.com (E)

Gillispie, Dr. Charles C.   IV 1972
Dayton-Stockton Professor of History of
   Science, Emeritus
Department of History
Princeton University
Princeton, NJ 08544-1017
Home: 3 Morgan Place
Princeton, NJ 08540
(609)258-5528 (O), (609)921-7362 (H)
(609)258-5326 (F)

Gingerich, Dr. Owen   I 1975
Professor of Astronomy and of the History
   of Science
Harvard University and Smithsonian
   Astrophysical Observatory
Harvard-Smithsonian Center for
   Astrophysics
60 Garden Street
Cambridge, MA 02138
(617)495-7216 (O), (617)876-6556 (H)
(617)496-7564 (F)
ginger@cfa.harvard.edu (E)

Glaser, Dr. Donald A.   II 1997
Professor of Physics and Neurobiology
Graduate School
University of California
Home: 41 Hill Road
Berkeley, CA 94708
(510)642-7231 (O), (510)841-2563 (F)
glaser@socrates.berkeley.edu (E)

Glass, Dr. H. Bentley   II 1963
Professor Emeritus
SUNY, Stony Brook
Home: 1066 8th Street
Boulder, CO 80302
(303)443-3978 (H)

Gleason, Prof. Andrew Mattei I 1977
Hollis Professor of Mathematicks and
   Natural Philosophy, Emeritus
Harvard University
Home: 110 Larchwood Drive
Cambridge, MA 02138-3649
(617)495-4316 (O)
(617)864-5095 (H)
(617)864-7876 (F)
gleason@abel.math.harvard.edu (E)

Goetzmann, Dr. William H.   III 1999
Jack S. Blanton, Sr., Chair in History and
   American Studies
University of Texas at Austin
303 Garrison Hall
Austin, TX 78712
Home: 4802 Timberline Drive
Austin, TX 78746
(512)471-6171 (O)
(512)327-0606 (H)
(512)471-8834 (F)
goetzmann@mail.utexas.edu (E)

Goheen, Hon. Robert F.   V 1986
President Emeritus
Senior Fellow in Public and International
   Affairs
Woodrow Wilson School
Princeton University
Princeton, NJ 08540
Home: 1 Orchard Circle
Princeton, NJ 08540
(609)924-2751 (O)
(609)258-6385 (O)
(609)924-8110 (H)
(609)258-1985 (F)
rfgoheen@princeton.edu (E)

Gold, Dr. Thomas   I 1972
John L. Wetherill Professor Emeritus of
  Astronomy
Cornell University
Space Sciences Building
Ithaca, NY 14853
Home: 7 Pleasant Grove Lane
Ithaca, NY 14850
(607)257-6696 (O)
(607)257-7969 (F)

Goldberger, Dr. Marvin L.   I 1980
Dean of Natural Sciences
Professor of Physics
University of California
Home: 621 Mira Monte
La Jolla, CA 92037-6728
(619)534-6882 (O)
(619)456-2455 (H)
(619)534-5224 (F)
mgoldberger@ucsd.edu (E)

Golden, Mr. William T.   V 1982
Chairman Emeritus
American Museum of Natural History
Treasurer
American Association for the Advancement
  of Science
500 Fifth Avenue, 50th Floor
New York, NY 10005
Home: 730 Park Avenue
New York, NY 10110
(212)425-0333 (O)
(212)737-3227 (H)
(212)344-7897 (F)
wtg40wall@aol.com (E)

Goldhaber, Dr. Maurice   I 1972
Director Emeritus
Brookhaven National Laboratory
Physics Building 510A
P.O. Box 5000
Upton, NY 11973
(516)344-3494 (O)
(516)344-5820 (F)

Goldstein, Dr. Joseph L.   II 1987
Paul J. Thomas Professor and Chairman
Department of Molecular Genetics
The University of Texas
Southwestern Medical Center at Dallas
5323 Harry Hines Boulevard
Dallas, TX 75235-9046
(214)648-2141 (O)
(214)648-8804 (F)
jgolds@mednet.swmed.edu (E)

Goldstine, Dr. Herman Heine IV 1979
Executive Officer Emeritus
American Philosophical Society
Home: Beaumont
56 Pasture Lane
Bryn Mawr, PA 19010
(610)527-6715 (H)
(610)527-6714 (F)

Gomory, Dr. Ralph E.   I 1985
President
Alfred P. Sloan Foundation
630 Fifth Avenue, Suite 2550
New York, NY 10111-0242
Home: 260 Douglas Road
Chappaqua, NY 10514
(212)649-1649 (O)
(914)238-8522 (H)
(212)757-5117 (F)
gomory@sloan.org (E)

Goodenough, Dr. Ward H.   IV 1973
University Professor of Anthropology,
  Emeritus
Department of Anthropology
University of Pennsylvania
Philadelphia, PA 19104-6398
Home: 3300 Darby Road, #5306
Haverford, PA 19041-1072
(215)898-7461 (O)
(610)645-9057 (H)
(215)898-7462 (F)
whgooden@sas.upenn.edu (E)

Goodman, Dr. Corey S.　　II 1999
Investigator
Howard Hughes Medical Center
Professor of Neurobiology and Genetics
Department of Molecular and Cell Biology
Life Sciences Addition, Room 519
University of California
Berkeley, CA 94720-3200
(510)643-9949 (O)
(510)643-5548 (F)
goodman@uclink4.berkeley.edu (E)

Goodman, Dr. Leo A.　　III 1976
Class of 1938 Professor
Department of Sociology and Department
　of Statistics
University of California
Berkeley, CA 94720
Home: 38 Oakridge Road
Berkeley, CA 94705-2426
(510)642-4766 (O)
(510)843-6013 (H)
(510)642-0659 (F)

Goody, Dr. Richard M.　　I 1997
Mallinckrodt and Gordon McKay Professor
　Emeritus
Harvard University
Home: 101 Cumloden Drive
Falmouth, MA 02540-1609
(508)540-4437 (H)
(508)540-5970 (F)
rgoody@capecod.net (E)

Gossman, Dr. Lionel　　IV 1996
Professor
Department of Romance Languages and
　Literatures
201 East Pyne
Princeton University
Princeton, NJ 08544-5264
(609)258-4518 (O)
(609)258-4535 (F)
lgossman@princeton.edu (E)

Grabar, Dr. Oleg　　IV 1990
Professor Emeritus
School of Historical Studies
Institute for Advanced Study
Princeton, NJ 08540
(609)734-8310 (O)
(609)921-3860 (H)
(609)951-4462 (F)
grabar@ias.edu (E)

Grafton, Dr. Anthony　　IV 1993
Professor of History
Department of History
129 Dickinson Hall
Princeton University
Princeton, NJ 08544-1017
(609)258-4182 (O)
(609)258-5326 (F)
grafton@princeton.edu (E)

Graham, Dr. Loren R.　　III 1995
Professor of History of Science
Massachusetts Institute of Technology
Harvard University
Home: 7 Francis Avenue
Cambridge, MA 02138
(617)253-4092 (O)
(617)491-1616 (H)
(617)258-8118 (F)
lrg@mit.edu (E)

Graham, Dr. Patricia Albjerg　　V 1999
President
Spencer Foundation
Charles Warren Professor of the History of
　American Education
Graduate School of Education
420 Gutman
Harvard University
Cambridge, MA 02138
(617)496-4839 (O)
(312)337-7000 ext. 6519 (O)
(617)496-3095 (F)
(312)337-0282 (F)
patricia_graham@harvard.edu (E)

Grant, Dr. Peter R. II 1991
Class of 1877 Professor of Zoology
Department of Ecology and Evolutionary
  Biology
Princeton University
Princeton, NJ 08544-1003
(609)258-5156 (O)

Gray, Dr. Hanna H. V 1981
Harry Pratt Judson Distinguished Service
  Professor of History
Department of History
1126 East 59th Street
The University of Chicago
Chicago, IL 60637
(773)702-7799 (O), (773)702-4600 (F)
h-gray@uchicago.edu (E)

Greenawalt, Mr. Kent III 1992
University Professor
Columbia University
Columbia Law School
435 W. 116th Street
New York, NY 10027
(212)854-2637 (O), (609)924-4157 (H)

Greenberg, Dr. Joseph H. IV 1975
Professor of Anthropology, Emeritus
Stanford University
Home: 860 Mayfield Avenue
Stanford, CA 94305
(650)723-4824 (O)
josephg@csli.stanford.edu (E)

Greene, Dr. Jack P. III 1992
Andrew W. Mellon Professor in the
  Humanities
Department of History
The Johns Hopkins University
Baltimore, MD 21218
(410)516-7596 (O), (410)467-5104 (H)
(410)516-7586 (F)

Greenewalt, Dr. Crawford H., Jr.
  IV 1987
Professor of Classical Archaeology
Department of Classics
Dwinelle Hall 05303
University of California
Berkeley, CA 94720
Home: 2581 Virginia Street
Berkeley, CA 94709
(510)642-4218 (O)
(510)642-5304 (O)
(510)841-2191 (H)
(510)643-6984 (F)

Greengard, Dr. Paul II 1994
Vincent Astor Professor and Head of the
  Laboratory of Molecular
  and Cellular Neuroscience
Laboratory of Molecular and Cellular
  Neuroscience
The Rockefeller University

Greenough, Ms. Beverly Sills V 1979
Chairman
Lincoln Center for Performing Arts
Managing Director
Metropolitan Opera
Former Board President
New York City Opera Company
Home: 211 Central Park West
New York, NY 10024
(212)875-5110 (O)
(212)873-8585 (H)
(212)362-4174 (F)

Greenstein, Dr. Jesse L. I 1968
Lee A. DuBridge Professor Emeritus
California Institute of Technology
Home: 1763 Royal Oaks Drive
North B-5
Bradbury, CA 91010-1979
(626)305-2535 (H)
(626)357-9723 (F)

Gregorian, Dr. Vartan   V 1985
President
Carnegie Corporation of New York
437 Madison Avenue
New York, NY 10022
(212)371-3200 (O)
(212)223-8831(F)

Griffin, Dr. Donald R.   II 1971
Professor Emeritus
The Rockefeller University
Associate
Concord Field Station
Harvard University
Old Causeway Road
Bedford, MA 01730
Home: Apt. A-212
1010 Waltham Street
Lexington, MA 02173-8044
(617)275-1725 (O)
(617)863-2573 (H)
(617)275-9613 (F)
griffin@fas.harvard.edu (E)

Griffiths, Dr. Phillip A.   I 1992
Director
Institute for Advanced Study
Olden Lane
Princeton, NJ 08540
(609)734-8200 (O)
(609)683-7605 (F)
pg@ias.edu (E)

Gundersheimer, Dr. Werner   V 1998
Director
Folger Shakespeare Library
201 S. Capitol Street, S.E.
Washington, DC 20003
(202)675-0300 (O)
(202)675-0315 (F)
gundershei@folger.edu (E)

Gunn, Dr. James E.   I 1987
Eugene Higgins Professor
Department of Astrophysical Sciences
Princeton University
Princeton, NJ 08544
(609)258-3802 (O)

Gunther, Dr. Gerald   III 1981
William Nelson Cromwell Professor of
    Law, Emeritus
Stanford University School of Law
559 Nathan Abbott Way
Stanford, CA 94305-8610
Home: 858 Lathrop Drive
Stanford, CA 94305
(650)723-4477 (O)
(650)725-0253 (F)

Güterbock, Dr. Hans Gustav   IV 1977
Tiffany and Margaret Blake Distinguished
    Service Professor, Emeritus
Professor of Hittitology
Oriental Institute
University of Chicago
Home: 5834 South Stony Island Avenue
Chicago, IL 60637
(773)324-1733 (H)
(773)324-2910 (F)

Gutowsky, Dr. H. S.   I 1982
Research Professor of Chemistry, Emeritus
177 Noyes Laboratory, Box 25
600 S. Mathews Avenue
University of Illinois
Urbana, IL 61801-3602
Home: 202 W. Delaware Avenue
Urbana, IL 61801
(217)333-7621 (O)
(217)344-1104 (H)
(217)244-5484 (F)
humes@aries.scs.uiuc.edu (E)

Haas, Mr. John C.   V 1992
Former Chairman and Director
Rohm and Haas Company
Current Board Member
Balch Institute for Ethnic Studies
Temple University Hospital
Home: 330 N. Spring Mill Road
Villanova, PA 19085-1737
(215)592-2626 (O), (215)592-3044 (F)
mahhaa@rohmhaas.com (E)

Habicht, Dr. Christian   IV 1983
Professor Emeritus of Ancient History
School of Historical Studies
The Institute for Advanced Study
Princeton, NJ 08540
Home: 273 Western Way
Princeton, NJ 08540
(609)734-8341 (O), (609)924-8399 (F)
habicht@ias.edu (E)

Hackerman, Dr. Norman   I 1972′
President Emeritus, Rice University
Distinguished Professor Emeritus of
   Chemistry
The University of Texas at Austin
The Robert A. Welch Foundation
5555 San Felipe, Suite 1900
Houston, TX 77056-2727
Home: 2001 Pecos
Austin, TX 78703
(713)961-9884 (O), (512)472-5725 (H)
(713)961-5168 (F)
atmar@welch1.org (E)

Hackney, Dr. Sheldon   V 1988
Professor of History
Department of History
3401 Walnut Street, Room 352B
University of Pennsylvania
Philadelphia, PA 19104
Home: 2128 Pine Street
Philadelphia, PA 19103
(215)898-5912 (O)
(215)985-3122 (H)
(215)573-2089 (O)(F)
(215)985-3123 (H)(F)
shackney@history.upenn.edu (E)

Halperin, Dr. Bertrand I.   I 1990
Hollis Professor of Mathematicks and
   Natural Philosophy
Lyman Laboratory of Physics
Harvard University
Cambridge, MA 02138
Home: 11 Gray Street
Arlington, MA 02174
(617)495-4294 (O)
(617)496-2545 (F)
halperin@cmt.harvard.edu (E)

Hamburg, Dr. David A.   II 1983
President
Carnegie Corporation of New York
437 Madison Avenue
New York, NY 10022
(212)371-3200 (O)
(212)289-2898 (H)
(212)223-8831 (F)

Hamp, Dr. Eric Pratt   IV 1980
Robert Maynard Hutchins Distinguished
  Service Professor Emeritus of
  Linguistics, Psychology, Ancient
  Mediterranean World and Slavic
  Languages
Center for Balkan and Slavic Studies
University of Chicago
University of Schkodër
Home: 5200 South Greenwood Avenue
Chicago, IL 60615
(773)324-9170 (H)
(773)834-0924 (F)

Handlin, Dr. Oscar   III 1999
Carl M. Loeb University Professor Emeritus
Widener 783
Harvard University
Cambridge, MA 02138
Home: 18 Agassiz Street
Cambridge, MA 02140-2802
(617)495-7931 (O)
(617)661-3145 (H)
lilioscar@aol.com (E)

Happer, Dr. William   I 1998
Higgens Professor of Physics
Department of Physics
Princeton University
Princeton, NJ 08544
(609)258-4382 (O)
(609)921-1487 (H)
(609)258-2496 (F)
happer@pupgg.princeton.edu (E)

Hardin, Dr. Garrett   II 1974
Professor Emeritus of Human Ecology
University of California
Home: 399 Arboleda Road
Santa Barbara, CA 93110-2001
(805)967-1384 (H)
(805)967-2715 (F)
hardin@silcom.com (E)

Harper, Dr. Prudence Oliver   IV 1994
Curator in Charge
Department of Ancient Near Eastern Art
Metropolitan Museum of Art
1000 Fifth Avenue
New York, NY 10028
Home: 45 East 85th Street
New York, NY 10028
(212)570-3907 (O)
(212)650-2997 (F)

Harris, Dr. Cyril Manton   V 1987
Charles Batchelor Professor Emeritus of
  Electrical Engineering
Professor Emeritus of Architecture
Columbia University
Home: 45 Sutton Place South
New York, NY 10022
(212)223-5162 (H)
(212)223-5162 (F)

Harrison, Dr. Evelyn Byrd   IV 1979
Edith Kitzmiller Professor Emerita of the
  History of Fine Arts
Institute of Fine Arts
New York University
1 East 78th Street
New York, NY 10021
(212)772-5831 (O)
(212)535-5112 (H)

Harrison, Dr. Stephen Coplan   II 1997
Investigator
Howard Hughes Medical Institute
Professor of Biochemistry and Molecular
  Biology
7 Divinity Avenue
Harvard University
Cambridge, MA 02138
(617)495-4090 (O)
(617)495-9613 (F)
chadmin@crystal.harvard.edu (E)

Haskins, Dr. Caryl Parker   II 1955
Scientist, Author
1545 Eighteenth Street, N.W.
Washington, DC 20036
Home: 22 Green Acre Lane
Westport, CT 06880
(202)332-6880 (O)
(203)227-2428 (H)

Heckscher, Mr. Maurice   V 1964
Former Senior Partner
Duane, Morris & Heckscher
Home: Apt. G-318 Cathedral Village
600 E. Cathedral Road
Philadelphia, PA 19128
(215)984-8907 (H)

Heeschen, Dr. David Sutphin   I 1974
Former Director and Senior Scientist
National Radio Astronomy Observatory
520 Edgemont Road
Charlottesville, VA 22901
Home: 702 Copa d'Oro
Marathon, FL 33050
(804)296-0231 (O)
(305)289-0911 (H)

Heilbron, Dr. John L.   IV 1990
Professor of History and Vice Chancellor,
    Emeritus
Senior Research Fellow
Worcester College, Oxford
University of California
April House
Shilton near Burford
Oxon OX18 4AB
England
jlheilbron@ohst7.berkeley.edu (E)

Henkin, Dr. Louis   III 1986
University Professor Emeritus
Columbia University, School of Law
435 West 116th Street
New York, NY 10027
Home: 460 Riverside Drive
New York, NY 10027
(212)854-2634 (O)
(212)854-7946 (F)
henkin@law.columbia.edu (E)

Henrichs, Dr. Albert   IV 1998
Eliot Professor of Greek Literature
Harvard University
Home: 272 Concord Avenue
Cambridge, MA 02138-1338
(617)495-4027 (O)
(617)354-6310 (H)
(617)495-6720 (O)(F)
(617)354-6310 (H)(F)
henrichs@fas.harvard.edu (E)

Herbert, Dr. Robert L .   IV 1993
Professor of Fine Arts of the Alumnae
    Foundation
Mount Holyoke College
Department of Art
South Hadley, MA 01075-1499
(413)538-2243 (O)
(413)536-3864 (H)
(413)538-2167 (F)
rherbert@mhc.mtholyoke.edu (E)

Herr, Dr. Richard   III 1993
Professor of History Emeritus
University of California
Berkeley, CA 94720-2550
Home: 1541 Hawthorne Terrace
Berkeley, CA 94708
rherr@socrates.berkeley.edu (E)

Herring, Dr. Pendleton III 1948
President, Emeritus
Social Science Research Council
Home: 30 Castle Howard Court
Princeton, NJ 08540
(609)921-6951 (H)
epherring@aol.com (E)

Herschbach, Dr. Dudley I 1989
Frank B. Baird, Jr., Professor of Science
Department of Chemistry
12 Oxford Street
Harvard University
Cambridge, MA 02138
(617)495-3218 (O)
(617)495-4723 (F)
hbach@chemistry.harvard.edu (E)

Hesburgh, Rev. Theodore M. V 1974
Office of the President, Emeritus
University of Notre Dame
1315 Hesburgh Library
Notre Dame, IN 46556
(219)631-6882 (O)
(219)631-6877 (F)

Hewlett, Mr. William R. V 1981
Director Emeritus
Hewlett-Packard Company
1501 Page Mill Road
Palo Alto, CA 94304-1100
Home: 720 Los Trancos Road
Portola Valley, CA 94028
(650)857-2626 (O)
(650)852-8694 (F)

Hilgard, Dr. Ernest R. II 1969
Emeritus Professor of Psychology and
   Education
Department of Psychology
Building 420, Room 206
Stanford University
Stanford, CA 94305-2130
Home: 850 Webster Street, #518
Palo Alto, CA 94301-2837
(650)725-2415 (O), (650)725-5699 (F)
(650)322-4152 (H)

Hilleman, Dr. Maurice Ralph II 1997
Director
Merck Institute for Therapeutic Research
Merck & Co., Inc., (WP53C-350)
Sumneytown Pike at Broad Street
West Point, PA 19486
Home: 730 West Thomas Road
Erdenheim, PA 19118
(215)652-8913 (O)

Himmelfarb, Dr. Gertrude III 1986
Distinguished Professor of History, Emerita
Graduate School
City University of New York
Home: 2510 Virginia Avenue, N.W.
Apt. 1104N
Washington, DC 20037
(202)338-7207 (H)

Hindle, Dr. Brooke III 1982
Historian Emeritus
National Museum of American History
Smithsonian Institution
Home: 415 Russell Avenue, Apt. 808
Gaithersburg, MD 20877-2841
(301)216-5200 (H)

Hirschman, Dr. Albert O.   III 1963
Professor Emeritus
The Institute for Advanced Study
Princeton, NJ 08540
(609)734-8252 (O)
(609)921-1763 (H)
(609)924-8399 (F)

Hoenigswald, Dr. Henry M.   IV 1971
Professor of Linguistics, Emeritus
University of Pennsylvania
Home: 908 Westdale Avenue
Swarthmore, PA 19081
(610)543-8086 (H)
(215)573-2091 (F)
henryh@babel.ling.upenn.edu (E)

Hoffmann, Dr. Roald   I 1984
John A. Newman Professor of Physical
   Science
Baker Laboratory
Cornell University
Ithaca, NY 14853-1301
(607)255-3419 (O)
(607)255-5707 (F)

Hoffmann, Dr. Stanley   III 1981
Professor
Center for European Studies
27 Kirkland Street
Harvard University
Cambridge, MA 02138
(617)495-4303 (O)
(617)496-9015 (F)
shhoffm@fas.harvard.edu (E)

Holton, Dr. Gerald   III 1996
Mallinckrodt Professor of Physics
   Professor of History of Science, Emeritus
358 Jefferson Physical Laboratory
Harvard University
Cambridge, MA 02138
Home: 64 Francis Avenue
Cambridge, MA 02138
(617)495-4474 (O), (617)868-9003 (H)
(617)495-0416 (F)
holton@physics.harvard.edu (E)

Hopfield, Dr. John J.   I 1988
Professor of Molecular Biology
Lewis Thomas Labs
Princeton University
Princeton, NJ 08544-1014
(609)258-1239 (O)
hopfield@princeton.edu (E)

Hornig, Dr. Donald Frederick I 1967
Professor Emeritus
Harvard University
Brown University
Home: 16 Longfellow Park
Cambridge, MA 02138
(617)432-3226 (O), (617)492-0327 (H)
(617)432-4710 (F)
dhornig@hsph.harvard.edu (E)

Howell, Dr. F. Clark   II 1975
Emeritus Professor of Anthropology
Museum of Vertebrate Zoology
Valley Life Sciences Building
University of California
Berkeley, CA 94720
Home: 1994 San Antonio Street
Berkeley, CA 94707
(510)642-1393 (O), (510)524-6243 (H)
(510)643-8231 (F)

Hubel, Dr. David Hunter II 1982
John Franklin Enders University Professor
   of Neurobiology
Department of Neurobiology
220 Longwood Avenue
Harvard Medical School
Boston, MA 02115
(617)432-1655 (O)
(617)432-0210 (F)

Huxtable, Ms. Ada Louise V 1989
Architecture Critic
The Wall Street Journal
[November-June]
969 Park Avenue
New York, NY 10028
[June-November]
33 Neptune Road
Marblehead, MA 01945
(212)734-0985 (O) NY
(781)631-7854 (O) MA
(212)717-5405 (F) NY
(781)639-8046 (F) MA
alhwsj@tiac.net (E)

Imbrie, Dr. John II 1981
H. L. Dougherty Professor of
   Oceanography
Department of Geological Sciences
Brown University
Providence, RI 02912

Inkeles, Dr. Alex III 1972
Professor of Sociology, Emeritus
Stanford University
Senior Fellow
Hoover Institution
Lou Henry Hoover 239
Stanford, CA 94305
Home: 1001 Hamilton Avenue
Palo Alto, CA 9430
(650)723-4856 (O)
(650)723-1687 (F)
inkeles@hoover.stanford.edu (E)

Jameson, Dr. Michael H. IV 1973
Crossett Professor of Humanistic Studies,
   Emeritus
Professor of Classics
Stanford University
Home: 647 Glenbrook Drive
Palo Alto, CA 94306
(650)723-2581 (O)
(650)493-3940 (H)
(650)723-3235 (F)
michael.jameson@stanford.edu (E)

Jamieson, Dr. Kathleen Hall V 1997
Dean and Professor
3620 Walnut Street
Annenberg School for Communication
University of Pennsylvania
Philadelphia, PA 19104-6220
(215)898-7041 (O)
(215)898-2024 (F)
kjamieson@asc.upenn.edu (E)

Jefferson, Dr. Edward G. V 1985
Former Chairman of the Board and Chief
   Executive Officer
P.O. Box 4027
Greenville, DE 19807
(302)658-0388 (H)
(302)658-0504 (F)

Jencks, Dr. William P. II 1995
Gyula and Katica Tauber Professor of
   Biochemistry and Molecular
   Pharmacodynamics, Emeritus
Department of Biochemistry
415 South Street, MS 009
Brandeis University
Waltham, MA 02453-2728
(781)736-2315 (O)
(781)862-8875 (H)
(781)736-2349 (F)
jencks@binah.cc.brandeis.edu (E)

Johnson, Dr. Howard Wesley   V 1985
President Emeritus and Former Chairman
  of the Corporation
Massachusetts Institute of Technology
Room E15–405
77 Massachusetts Avenue
Cambridge, MA 02139
(617)253-0636 (O), (617)258-5539 (F)
hwj@mit.edu (E)

Jones, Dr. Christopher P.   IV 1996
George Martin Lane Professor of Classics
  and History
Department of Classics
Boylston Hall
Harvard University
Cambridge, MA 02138
(617)496-3823 (O), (617)496-6720 (F)
cjones@fas.harvard.edu (E)

Jorgenson, Dr. Dale W.   III 1998
Frederic Eaton Abbe Professor of
  Economics
Department of Economics
122 Littauer Center
Harvard University
Cambridge, MA 02138-3001
Home: 1010 Memorial Drive
Cambridge, MA 02138-4859
(617)495-4661 (O), (617)491-4069 (H)
(617)495-4660 (O)(F)
(617)491-4105 (H)(F)
djorgenson@harvard.edu (E)

Julesz, Dr. Bela   II 1995
State of New Jersey Professor of Psychology
  and Director
Laboratory of Vision Research
Home: 30 Valley View Road
Warren, NJ 07059
(908)445-6660 (O), (908)647-0753 (H)
(908)445-6715 (F)
julesz@cyclops.rutgers.edu (E)

Kadanoff, Dr. Leo P.   I 1997
John D. and Catherine T. MacArthur
  Professor of Physics and Mathematics
University of Chicago
James Franck Institute
5640 South Ellis Avenue
Chicago, IL 60637
(773)702-7189 (O)
(773)702-5863 (F)
L-Kadanoff@uchicago.edu (E)

Kamen, Dr. Martin David   I 1974
Professor Emeritus
University of California
Home: 300 Hot Springs Road
Casa Dorinda B-64
Montecito, CA 93108
(805)969-8850 (H)

Kandel, Dr. Eric R.   II 1984
University Professor
Columbia University College of Physicians
  and Surgeons
Senior Investigator
Howard Hughes Medical Institute
College of Physicians and Surgeons
Center for Neurobiology and Behavior
722 West 168th Street
New York, NY 10032
(212)305-4143 (O)
(212)960-2474 (F)
erk5@columbia.edu (E)

Kaplan, Mrs. Helene L.   V 1990
Of Counsel
Skadden, Arps, Slate, Meagher & Flom
919 Third Avenue, Room 29/72
New York, NY 10022
(212)735-2340/1 (O)
(212)735-2000/1 (F)

Karle, Dr. Isabella L.   I 1992
Senior Scientist
Code 6030
Laboratory for the Structure of Matter
Naval Research Laboratory
Washington, DC 20375-5341
Home: 6304 Lakeview Drive
Falls Church, VA 22041
(202)767-2624 (O), (702)256-0687 (H)
(202)767-6874 (F)

Karle, Dr. Jerome   I 1990
Chief Scientist
Code 6030
Naval Research Laboratory
Washington, DC 20375-5341
Home: 6304 Lakeview Drive
Falls Church, VA 22041
(202)767-2665 (O), (702)256-0687 (H)
(202)767-0953 (F)
williams@harker.nrl.navy.mil (E)

Karlin, Dr. Samuel   I 1995
Professor Emeritus of Mathematics
Stanford University
Stanford, CA 94305
(650)723-2204 (O), (650)473-9390 (H)
(650)725-2040 (F)
fd.zgg@forsythe.stanford.edu (E)

Karp, Dr. Richard M.   I 1994
Professor of Computer Science and
   Engineering and Adjunct Professor of
   Molecular Biotechnology
Department of Computer Science and
   English
Box 352350, 114 Sieg Hall
University of Washington
Seattle, WA 98195-2350
(206)543-4226 (O), (206)528-5585 (H)
(206)543-2969 (F)
karp@cs.washington.edu (E)

Kassebaum Baker, Hon. Nancy V 1996
United States Senator
Baker, Donaldson
Suite 800
800 Pennsylvania Avenue, N.W.
Washington, DC 20004
Home: Apt. #1107
700 New Hampshire Avenue, N.W.
Washington, DC 20037

Katz, Dr. Stanley N.   V 1996
Professor Emeritus
American Council of Learned Societies
Professor
446 Robertson Hall
Woodrow Wilson School
Princeton University
Princeton, NJ 08544-1013
Home: 152 Clover Lane
Princeton, NJ 08540
(609)258-5637 (O)
(609)921-7379 (H)
(609)258-1235 (F)
snkatz@wws.princeton.edu (E)

Katzenbach, Mr. Nicholas   V 1992
Home: 33 Greenhouse Drive
Princeton, NJ 08540-4802
(609)924-8536 (H)
(609)924-6610 (F)

Kaysen, Dr. Carl   III 1967
David W. Skinner Professor of Political
   Economy, Emeritus
Security Studies Program
Massachusetts Institute of Technology
292 Main Street (E38–603)
Cambridge, MA 02138
(617)253-4054 (O)
(617)253-9330 (F)

Kearns, Mr. David T.   V 1990
Former Chairman and CEO
Former Deputy Secretary of Education
Xerox Corporation
100 1st Stamford Place
Stamford, CT 06904-2340
(203)325-6240 (O)
(203)325-6445 (F)

Kellermann, Dr. Kenneth I.   I 1997
Chief Scientist
National Radio Astronomy Observatory
520 Edgemont Road
Charlottesville, VA 22903
(804)296-0240 (O)
(804)979-7146 (H)
(804)296-0385 (F)

Kelley, Dr. Donald Reed   III 1995
James Westfall Thompson Professor of
   History
Rutgers University
88 College Avenue
New Brunswick, NJ 08903-5059
(908)932-1228 (O)
(908)932-8708 (F)
dkelley@rci.rutgers.edu (E)

Kelley, Dr. William N.   V 1998
Dean, University of Pennsylvania School of
   Medicine
Chief Executive Officer
University of Pennsylvania Health System
21 Penn Tower
399 S. 34th Street
Philadelphia, PA 19104-4385
(215)898-5181 (O)
(610)520-9659 (H)
(215)898-5607 (F)
kelleyw@mail.med.upenn.edu (E)

Kelly, Dr. Thomas J.   II 1998
Boury Professor
Chairman
Department of Molecular Biology and
   Genetics
The Johns Hopkins University
School of Medicine
603 PCTB
725 N. Wolfe Street
Baltimore, MD 21205
(410)955-3292 (O), (410)955-0831 (F)
tkelly@jhmi.edu (E)

Kennan, Prof. George Frost   III 1952
Professor Emeritus
The Institute for Advanced Study
Olden Lane
Princeton, NJ 08540
Home: 146 Hodge Road
Princeton, NJ 08540
(609)734-8314 (O), (609)497-0521 (H)
(609)951-4453 (F)

Kennedy, Dr. Donald   II 1976
President Emeritus
Global Environment Forum/IIS
Encina Hall, Room 200
Stanford University
Stanford, CA 94305-6055
Home: 555 Coronado Avenue
Stanford, CA 94305
(650)725-2745 (O), (650)725-2592 (F)
hk.dxk@forsythe.stanford.edu (E)

Kennedy, Dr. Eugene Patrick   II 1993
Hamilton Kuhn Professor of Biological
   Chemistry Emeritus
Harvard University
Home: 221 Mount Auburn Street, #109
Cambridge, MA 02138
(617)432-1861 (O), (617)738-0516 (F)
eugene_kennedy@HMS.harvard.edu (E)

Kennedy, Dr. George A.   IV 1984
Paddison Professor of Classics, Emeritus
University of North Carolina
Colorado State University
Home: P.O. Box 271880
Fort Collins, CO 80527
(970)282-4395 (H)
(970)491-2160 (F)

Kennedy, Dr. Paul M.   III 1991
Dilworth Professor of History
Director
International Security Studies
Department of History
P.O. Box 208324
Yale University
New Haven, CT 06520-8324
(203)432-6244/6246 (O)
(203)432-6250 (F)
paul_kennedy@quickmail.yale.edu (E)

Kennedy, Dr. Randall LeRoy   III 1998
Professor of Law
Harvard Law School
Cambridge, MA 02138

Keohane, Dr. Nannerl O.   V 1994
President, Professor of Political Science
President's Office
207 Allen Building
Box 90001
Duke University
Durham, NC 27708-0001
(919)684-2424 (O)
(919)684-3050 (F)

Kety, Dr. Seymour S.   II 1975
Professor of Neuroscience, Emeritus
Harvard University Medical School
Home: 10 Longwood Drive, Apt. 252
Westwood, MA 02090
(617)855-3232 (O), (781)461-9264 (H)
(617)855-2778 (O)(F)
(781)320-0502 (H)(F)
skety@wjh.harvard.edu (E)

Kevles, Dr. Daniel J.   III 1996
Koepfli Professor of the Humanities
Division of the Humanities and Social
   Sciences, 228–77
California Institute of Technology
Pasadena, CA 91125
(626)395-4086 (O), (626)793-4681 (F)
kevles@cco.caltech.edu (E)

Khorana, Dr. Har Gobind   II 1973
Alfred P. Sloan Professor of Biology and
   Chemistry, Emeritus
77 Massachusetts Avenue, 18–509
Massachusetts Institute of Technology
Cambridge, MA 02139
(617)253-1871 (O), (617)253-0533 (F)

Kilbourne, Dr. Edwin D.   II 1994
Research Professor of Microbiology and
   Immunology
Basic Science Building, Room 315
New York Medical College
Valhalla, NY 10595
Home: 23 Willard Avenue
Madison, CT 06443
(914)594-4193 (O), (203)245-9349 (H)
(914)594-4176 (O)(F)
(203)318-0036 (H)(F)
kilbourn@ct1.nai.net (E)

Kindleberger, Dr. Charles P.   III 1987
Ford International Professor of Economics,
   Emeritus
Massachusetts Institute of Technology
Home: A 406 Brookhaven
1010 Waltham Street
Lexington, MA 02421
(781)863-2540 (H)

Kirch, Dr. Patrick Vinton   IV 1998
Class of 1954 Professor of Anthropology
Department of Anthropology
232 Kroeber Hall
University of California
Berkeley, CA 94720
(510)643-8346 (O)
(510)643-8557 (F)
Kirch@Qal.Berkeley.Edu (E)

Kitzinger, Dr. Ernst   IV 1967
Arthur Kingsley Porter University Professor
   Emeritus
Harvard University
Home: 14 Richmond Road
Oxford OX1 2JJ
England

Klein, Dr. Lawrence Robert   III 1970
Benjamin Franklin Professor of Economics,
   Emeritus
Department of Economics
3718 Locust Walk
University of Pennsylvania
Philadelphia, PA 19104-6297
Home: 1317 Medford Road
Wynnewood, PA 19096
(215)898-7713 (O)
(610)649-4947 (H)
(215)898-4477 (F)
(610)649-3178 (H)(F)
lrk@econ.ssc.upenn.edu (E)

Knauer, Dr. Elfriede Regina   IV 1999
Consulting Scholar, Mediterranean Section
University of Pennsylvania
Home: The Quadrangle, Apt. 3314
3300 Darby Road
Haverford, PA 19041-1070
(610)649-1857 (H)

Knoll, Dr. Andrew H.   II 1997
Professor of Biology
Harvard University
Botanical Museum
26 Oxford Street
Cambridge, MA 02138
(617)495-9306 (O), (617)495-5667 (F)
aknoll@oeb.harvard.edu (E)

Knopoff, Dr. Leon   I 1992
Research Professor of Physics and
   Geophysics
Institute of Geophysics and Planetary
   Physics
University of California
Los Angeles, CA 90095-1567
(310)825-1885 (O), (310)206-3051 (F)
knopoff@physics.ucla.edu (E)

Knowles, Dr. Jeremy R.   I 1988
Amory Houghton Professor of Chemistry
   and Biochemistry
Dean of the Faculty of Arts and Sciences
Faculty of Arts and Sciences
University Hall 5
Harvard University
Cambridge, MA 02138
Home: 7 Bryant Street
Cambridge, MA 02138
(617)495-1566 (O), (617)876-8469 (H)
(617)495-8208 (O)(F)
(617)496-2698 (H)(F)
jeremy_knowles@harvard.edu (E)

Knox, Dr. Bernard M. W.   IV 1985
Director Emeritus
Center for Hellenic Studies
Home: 13013 Scarlet Oak Drive
Darnestown, MD 20878
(301)869-3923 (H)
(301)869-3923 (F)

Knudson, Dr. Alfred G., Jr.   II 1991
Senior Member
Institute for Cancer Research
Fox Chase Cancer Center
7701 Burholme Avenue
Philadelphia, PA 19111
(215)728-3642 (O)
(215)732-8022 (H)
(215)728-3105 (F)

Koenen, Dr. Ludwig   IV 1991
H. C. Youtie Distinguished University
    Professor of Papyrology
Department of Classical Studies
2160 Angell Hall
435 S. State Street
University of Michigan
Ann Arbor, MI 48109
Home: 1312 Culver
Ann Arbor, MI 48103
(734)764-0362 (O)
(734)995-3956 (H)
(734)763-4959 (F)
koenen@umich.edu (E)

Kohn, Dr. Walter   I 1994
Research Professor of Physics
University of California
Santa Barbara, CA
Home: 236 La Vista Grande
Santa Barbara, CA 93103
(805)893-3061 (O)
(805)962-1489 (H)
(805)893-3307 (F)
kohn@physics.ucsb.edu (E)

Koop, Dr. C. Everett   V 1992
Senior Fellow
C. Everett Koop Institute at Dartmouth
McInerny Professor of Surgery
Dartmouth Medical School
Home: 3 Ivy Pointe Way
Hanover, NH 03755
(603)650-1450 (O)
(603)650-1452 (F)
cekoopinst@dartmouth.edu (E)

Kornberg, Dr. Arthur   II 1960
Professor of Biochemistry, Emeritus
School of Medicine
Stanford University
Stanford, CA 94305-5307
(650)723-6167 (O)
(650)723-6783 (F)

Koshland, Dr. Daniel E., Jr.   II 1988
Professor of the Graduate School
Department of Molecular and Cell Biology
329 Stanley Hall #3206
University of California
Berkeley, CA 94720-3206
(510)642-0416 (O)
(510)284-9697 (H)
(510)643-6386 (O)(F)
(925)299-6849 (H)(F)
dek@uclink4.berkeley.edu (E)

Krauskopf, Dr. Konrad Bates   I 1967
Professor of Geochemistry Emeritus
School of Earth Sciences
Stanford University
Stanford, CA 94305
Home: Pearce Mitchell Place #13
Stanford, CA 94305
(650)723-3325 (O)
(650)725-0979 (F)
konrad@pangea.stanford.edu (E)

Landau, Dr. Ralph   V 1996
Consulting Professor of Economics
Senior Fellow
Stanford Institute for Economic Policy
  Research
Stanford University
Listowel, Inc.
2 Park Avenue, Suite 1525
New York, NY 10016
(212)683-8660 (O)

Landes, Dr. David S.   III 1982
Coolidge Professor of History
Professor, Emeritus
Widener Library Study "U"
Harvard University
Cambridge, MA 02138
(617)495-4849 (O)
(617)354-6308 (H)
(617)495-7730 (F)

Lang, Dr. Mabel L.   IV 1971
Paul Shorey Professor of Greek, Emeritus
Department of Greek
Bryn Mawr College
Bryn Mawr, PA 19010
mlang@brynmawr.edu (E)

Langfitt, Dr. Thomas W.   V 1988
Senior Fellow
Wharton School of Pennsylvania
317 Vance Hall
University of Pennsylvania
Philadelphia, PA 19104
Home: 260 Beech Hill Road
Wynnewood, PA 19096
(215)573-4659 (O)
(610)642-0446 (H)

Lapidus, Dr. Ira M.   IV 1994
Former Professor of History and Chairman
Center for Middle Eastern Studies
Department of History
University of California at Berkeley
Berkeley, CA 94720
ilapidus@uclink4.berkeley.edu (E)

Lardy, Dr. Henry Arnold   II 1976
Vilas Professor of Biological Sciences,
  Emeritus
Institute for Enzyme Research
1710 University Avenue
University of Wisconsin
Madison, WI 53705
Home: 1829 Thorstrand Road
Madison, WI 53705
(608)262-3372 (O), (608)233-1584 (H)
(608)265-2904 (F)
lardy@enzyme.wisc.edu (E)

Lax, Dr. Peter D.   I 1996
Professor of Mathematics
New York University
Courant Institute of Mathematical Sciences
251 Mercer Street
New York, NY 10012
Home: 300 Central Park West
New York, NY 10024
(212)998-3232 (O), (212)362-9006 (H)
(212)995-4121 (F)
lax@cims.nyu.edu (E)

Lederberg, Dr. Joshua   II 1960
Former President
Sackler Foundation Scholar
1230 York Avenue
The Rockefeller University
New York, NY 10021-6399
(212)327-7809 (O), (212)327-8651 (F)
lederberg@mail.rockefeller.edu (E)

Lederman, Dr. Leon Max   I 1989
Pritzker Professor of Science
Illinois Institute of Technology
Fermi National Accelerator Laboratory
P.O. Box 500, M.S. 105
Batavia, IL 60510
(630)907-5911 (O), (630)840-4780 (H)
(630)907-5913 (F)
lederman@fnal.gov (E)

Lee, Dr. Tsung-Dao   I 1972
Enrico Fermi Professor of Physics
Department of Physics
Columbia University
New York, NY 10027

Leggett, Dr. Anthony J.   I 1991
MacArthur Professor and Professor of
   Physics
Loomis Laboratory of Physics
1110 W. Green Street
University of Illinois
Urbana, IL 61801
(217)333-2077 (O), (217)333-9819 (F)
tony@cromwell.physics.uiuc.edu (E)

Leighton, Dr. Alexander H.   IV 1950
Professor Emeritus of Social Psychiatry
Harvard School of Public Health
Dalhousie University
Home: 20 Chestnut Street
Boston, MA 02108
(617)523-5488 (O), (617)523-5488 (H)
(617)724-8301 (F)

Leonard, Dr. Nelson J.   I 1996
Reynold C. Fuson Professor Emeritus
University of Illinois
Faculty Associate
Department of Chemistry
Mail Code 164–30
California Institute of Technology
Pasadena, CA 91125
Home: 389 California Terrace
Pasadena, CA 91105
(818)395-6541 (O)
(818)792-7745 (H)
(818)564-9297 (O)(F)
(818)568-3749 (H)(F)

Leopold, Dr. Luna Bergere   I 1972
Emeritus Professor of Geology
Department of Geology and Geophysics
University of California
Home: 400 Vermont Avenue
Berkeley, CA 94707
(510)527-7046 (H)
(510)527-7046 (F)

Levi, Dr. Edward Hirsch   III 1978
President Emeritus and Glen A. Lloyd
   Distinguished Service Professor Emeritus
1116 East 59th Street
University of Chicago
Chicago, IL 60637
Home: 4950 Chicago Beach Drive
Chicago, IL 60615
(773)702-8588 (O)
(773)288-2555 (H)
(773)702-5846 (F)

Levi-Montalcini, Dr. Rita   II 1986
President
Institute of the Italian Encyclopedia
National Research Council, Guest Professor
Institute of Neurobiology
Viale Marx, 15
Rome 00137, Italy
Home: Viale di Villa Massimo 3
Rome 00161, Italy
39-6-86895043 (O), 39-6-44 23 14 89 (H)
39-06-86090370 (F)

Levy, Dr. Kenneth   IV 1988
Scheide Professor of Music History,
  Emeritus
Woolworth Music Center
Princeton University
Princeton, NJ 08544
(609)258-4241 (O), (609)924-3376 (H)
(609)258-6793 (F)
kenlevy@pucc.princeton.edu (E)

Lewalski, Dr. Barbara Kiefer IV 1986
William R. Kenan Professor of History and
  Literature and of English Literature
Department of English
Harvard University
Cambridge, MA 02138
(617)495-2533 (O), (401)831-7177 (H)
(617)496-8737 (F)

Lewis, Dr. Bernard, F.   IV 1973
Cleveland E. Dodge Professor of Near
  Eastern Studies, Emeritus
Department of Near Eastern Studies
Princeton University
Princeton, NJ 08544-1008
(609)258-5489 (O), (609)258-1242 (F)

Lewis, Dr. Edward B.   II 1990
Thomas Hunt Morgan Professor of Biology,
  Emeritus
Biology Division, 156–29
California Institute of Technology
  Pasadena, CA 91125
Home: 805 Winthrop Road
San Marino, CA 91108
(626)395-4941 (O)
(626)799-2325 (H)
(626)449-0756 (F)

Lin, Dr. Chia-Chiao   I 1978
Courtesy Professor of Florida State
  University
Institute Professor Emeritus
Department of Mathematics
77 Massachusetts Avenue
Massachusetts Institute of Technology
Cambridge, MA 02139
(617)253-1796 (O)

Lindzey, Dr. Gardner   II 1970
Director Emeritus
Center for Advanced Study in the
  Behavioral Sciences
202 Junipero Serra Boulevard
Stanford, CA 94305
Home: 1100 Sharon Park Drive
Menlo Park, CA 94025
(650)321-2052 (O)
(650)561-9111 (H)
(650)321-1192 (F)
gardner@casbs.stanford.edu (E)

Lipset, Dr. Seymour Martin   III 1982
Senior Fellow, The Hoover Institution
Stanford University
Hazel Professor of Public Policy
The Institute of Public Policy
Pohick Module, Room 22
Mail Stop 3C6
George Mason University
Fairfax, VA 22030-4444
Home: 900 North Stafford Street, #2120
Arlington, VA 22203
(703)993-2283 (O), (703)993-2284 (F)
slipset@gmu.edu (E)

Litz, Dr. A. Walton   IV 1991
Holmes Professor of Literature, Emeritus
22 McCosh Hall
Princeton University
Princeton, NJ 08544
(609)258-4060 (O), (609)921-8432 (H)
(609)258-1607 (F)

Llinás, Dr. Rodolfo, R.   II 1996
Chairman
550 First Avenue, Room 442
Department of Physiology and
   Neuroscience
New York University Medical Center
New York, NY 10016
(212)263-5415 (O), (212)888-2886 (H)
(212)689-9060 (F)
llinar@popmail.med.nyu.edu (E)

Lloyd-Jones, Sir Hugh   IV 1992
Regius Professor of Greek, Emeritus
University of Oxford
Home: 15 West Riding
Wellesley, MA 02482
(617)237-2212 (H), (617)237-2246 (F)
c/o m.lefkowitz@wellesley.edu (E)

Loeb, Dr. John Nichols   II 1998
Professor of Medicine
Department of Medicine
630 West 168th Street
Columbia University
New York, NY 10032
(212)305-9178 (O)

Longsworth, Mr. Charles R.   V 1990
Chairman Emeritus
Colonial Williamsburg Foundation
P.O. Box 567
Athol, MA 01331
(508)249-8401 (O)
(508)249-6850 (F)

Lovejoy, Dr. Thomas E.   II 1999
Counselor to the Secretary on Biodiversity
   and Environmental Affairs
Lead for Environment for Latin America
   and Caribbean
World Bank
Smithsonian Institution, 230
1000 Jefferson Drive, S.W.
Washington, DC 20560

Lubchenco, Dr. Jane   II 1998
Distinguished Professor of Zoology
Wayne and Gladys Valley Professor of
   Marine Biology
Department of Zoology
3029 Cordley Hall
Oregon State University
Corvallis, OR 97331-2914
(541)737-5337 (O)
(541)737-3360 (F)
lubchenj@bcc.orst.edu (E)

Lucas, Dr. Robert E., Jr.   III 1997
John Dewey Distinguished Service Professor
Department of Economics
1126 E. 59th Street
University of Chicago
Chicago, IL 60637
(773)702-8179 (O)
(773)702-8490 (F)
relucas@midway.uchicago.edu (E)

Luce, Dr. R. Duncan   III 1994
Distinguished Research Professor
Social Science Plaza
University of California
Irvine, CA 92612-4057
Home: 20 Whitman Court
Irvine, CA 92715-4057
(949)824-6239 (O)
(949)854-8203 (H)
(949)824-3733 (F)
rdluce@uci.edu (E)

Lyman, Dr. Richard W.   V 1998
President Emeritus
J.E. Wallace Sterling Professor in the
    Humanities Emeritus
Stanford University
Home: 101 Alma Street
Apt. 107–8
Palo Alto, CA 94301
(650)725-1497 (O)
(650)321-3503 (H)
(650)321-7663 (H)(F)
rlyman@leland.stanford.edu (E)

Ma, Mr. Yo-Yo   V 1999
Cellist
c/o ICM Artists
40 W. 57th Street
New York, NY 10019

McCarty, Dr. Maclyn   II 1981
Professor Emeritus
1230 York Avenue
The Rockefeller University
New York, NY 10021-6399
Home: 400 East 56th Street
New York, NY 10022-4147
(212)327-8158 (O)
(212)371-2631 (H)
(212)327-8960 (O)(F)
(212)371-3162 (H)(F)
mccartm@rockvax.rockefeller.edu (E)

MacCormack, Dr. Sabine G.   IV 1997
Mary Ann and Charles R. Walgreen
    Professor of Classical Studies
Department of Classical Studies
University of Michigan
Ann Arbor, MI 48109
Home: 1200 Brooks Street
Ann Arbor, MI 48103
(734)764-4499 (O)
(734)769-5766 (H)
(734)763-4959 (F)
sgm@umich.edu (E)

McCredie, Dr. James R.   IV 1986
Sherman Fairchild Professor of Fine Arts
    and Director
Institute of Fine Arts
New York University
Chairman, Managing Committee
American School of Classical Studies at
    Athens
Home: 30 Battle Road
Princeton, NJ 08540
(212)772-5805 (O)
(609)921-2662 (H)
(212)772-5807 (O)(F)
(609)683-4584 (H)(F)
jrm1@is2.nyu.edu (E)

MacDonald, Dr. Gordon J.   I 1963
Director
IIASA
A-2361 Laxenburg
Austria
43-2236-807-402 (O)
43-2236-73441 (H)
43-2236-807366 (F)
macdon@iiasa.ac.at (E)

McGhee, Hon. George Crews   V 1993
Former Government Official
Corporate Director
Washington, DC
Home: Farmer's Delight
36276 Mountville Road
Middleburg, VA 20117-3308
(540)687-3451 (H)
(540)687-3451 (F)

Mackey, Dr. George Whitelaw   I 1971
Professor of Mathematics
Harvard University
Home: 25 Coolidge Road
Cambridge, MA 02138

McKusick, Dr. Victor Almon   II 1975
University Professor of Medical Genetics
Johns Hopkins Hospital
1007 Blalock
600 N. Wolfe Street
Baltimore, MD 21287-4922
Home: 221 Northway
Baltimore, MD 21218
(410)955-6641 (O)
(410)955-4999 (F)
mckusick@peas.welch.jhu.edu (E)

McKusick, Hon. Vincent Lee   V 1986
Former Chief Justice
Maine Supreme Judicial Court
Pierce Atwood
One Monument Square
Portland, ME 04101-1110
Home: 1152 Shore Road
Cape Elizabeth, ME 04107
(207)791-1209 (O), (207)791-1350 (O)(F)
(207)799-1416 (H), (207)767-7309 (H)(F)
VMcKusick@PierceAtwood.com (E)

Mac Lane, Dr. Saunders   I 1949
Max Mason Distinguished Service
    Professor of Mathematics, Emeritus
Eckhart Hall
Department of Mathematics
5734 University Avenue
University of Chicago
Chicago, IL 60637
Home: 5712 Dorchester Avenue
Chicago, IL 60637
(773)702-7330 (O), (773)363-0099 (H)
(773)702-9787 (F)
saunders@math.uchicago.edu (E)

McNamara, Mr. Robert S.   V 1981
Former President
The World Bank
Home: 1350 I Street, N.W., Suite 500
Washington, DC 20005-3305
(202)682-3132 (O), (202)667-5550 (H)
(202)682-3130 (F)

McNeill, Dr. William Hardy   III 1977
Robert A. Millikan Distinguished Service
    Professor of History, Emeritus
University of Chicago
Home: P.O. Box 45
36 School House Road
Colebrook, CT 06021
(860)379-3509 (H)

McPherson, Dr. James M.   III 1991
George Henry Davis '86 Professor of
   American History
Princeton University
Home: 15 Randall Road
Princeton, NJ 08540
(609)258-4173 (O)
(609)258-5326 (F)

McPherson, Dr. Mary P.   V 1983
Vice President
Andrew W. Mellon Foundation
140 East 62nd Street
New York, NY 10021
(212)838-8400 (O)
(610)527-4967 (H)
(212)888-4172 (O)(F)
(610)527-5715 (H)(F)
mpm@mellon.org (E)

MacPherson, Dr. Robert   I 1999
Professor
School of Mathematics
Institute for Advanced Study
Princeton, NJ 08540
(609)734-8104 (O)
(609)924-8399 (F)
rdm@math.ias.edu (E)

Mahoney, Miss Margaret E.   V 1993
President
MEM Associates, Inc.
521 Fifth Avenue, Suite 1801
New York, NY 10175
Home: 65 E. 76th Street, Apt. 5B
New York, NY 10021
(212)297-0500 (O)
(212)297-2509 (F)

Marcus, Dr. Rudolph Arthur   I 1990
Arthur Amos Noyes Professor of Chemistry
Noyes Laboratory of Chemical Physics
Mail Code 127–72
California Institute of Technology
Pasadena, CA 91125
Home: 331 S. Hill Avenue
Pasadena, CA 91106-3405
(626)395-6566 (O)
(626)793-4661 (H)
(626)792-8485 (F)
ram@caltech.edu (E)

Marler, Dr. Peter R.   II 1983
Professor, Emeritus
Rockefeller University
Animal Communication Laboratory
Department of Animal Physiology
University of California
Davis, CA 95616-8761
(916)752-8531 (O)
(916)795-3320 (H)
(916)752-6049 (F)

Martin, Dr. John Rupert   IV 1985
Marquand Professor Emeritus
Department of Art & Archaeology
Princeton University
Princeton, NJ 08540
Home: 107 Mercer Street
Princeton, NJ 08540

Marty, Dr. Martin E.   IV 1994
Fairfax M. Cone Distinguished Service
   Professor Emeritus
University of Chicago
Home: 239 Scottswood
Riverside, IL 60546
(312)397-6401 (F)

Massey, Dr. Walter Eugene   V 1991
Director
Office of the President
Morehouse College
803 Westview Drive
Atlanta, GA 30314
Home: 6000 Estates Drive
Oakland, CA 94611
(404)215-2645 (O)
(404)659-6536 (F)

Matlock, Prof. Jack F., Jr.   V 1998
George F. Kennan Professor
Institute for Advanced Study
Olden Lane
Princeton, NJ 08540
Home: 63 Battle Road
Princeton, NJ 08540
(609)734-8303 (O)
(609)252-1953 (H)
(609)924-8399 (F)
matlock@ias.edu (E)

May, Dr. Georges   IV 1980
Sterling Professor of French, Emeritus
Yale University
Home: 177 Everit Street
New Haven, CT 06511-1306
(203)562-5535 (H)
(203)432-7975 (F)
georges.may@yale.edu (E)

Mayr, Dr. Ernst   II 1965
Alexander Agassiz Professor of Zoology,
   Emeritus
Museum of Comparative Zoology
26 Oxford Street
Harvard University
Cambridge, MA 02138
Home: Carleton-Willard Village
207 Badger Terrace
Bedford, MA 01730
(781)275-9777 (H)

Meinwald, Dr. Jerrold   I 1987
Goldwin Smith Professor of Chemistry
Department of Chemistry and Chemical
   Biology
Baker Laboratory
Cornell University
Ithaca, NY 14853-1301
(607)255-3301 (O)
(607)257-0035 (H)
(607)255-3407 (F)
circe@cornell.edu (E)

Mellink, Dr. Machteld J.   IV 1974
Professor of Classical and Near Eastern
   Archaeology, Emerita
Bryn Mawr College
Bryn Mawr, PA 19010-2899
Home: 264 Montgomery Avenue
Haverford, PA 19041-1531
(610)526-5339 (O)
(610)642-3896 (H)
(610)526-7479 (F)

Merton, Dr. Robert K.   III 1959
University Professor Emeritus
Columbia University
Home: 71 Hither Lane
East Hampton, NY 11937
(212)854-3103 (O)
(212)662-4040 (516)329-3071 (H)
(212)864-2128 (516)329-2626 (H)(F)
rm241@columbia.edu (E)

Meselson, Dr. Matthew S.   II 1981
Thomas Dudley Cabot Professor of the
   Natural Sciences
The Fairchild Biochemistry Building
7 Divinity Avenue
Harvard University
Cambridge, MA 02138
(617)495-2264 (O)
(617)496-2444 (F)
msm@wjh.harvard.edu (E)

Metzger, Dr. Bruce Manning IV 1986
Professor Emeritus of New Testament
Princeton Theological Seminary, CN 821
Princeton, NJ 08542-0803
Home: 20 Cleveland Lane
Princeton, NJ 08540
(609)924-4060 (H)
(609)924-2973 (F)

Meyerowitz, Dr. Elliot M. II 1998
Professor of Biology
Division of Biology 156–29
1200 East California Blvd.
California Institute of Technology
Pasadena, CA 91125
(626)395-6889 (O)
(626)449-0756 (F)
meyerow@cco.caltech.edu (E)

Meyerson, Dr. Martin V 1977
Emeritus President and University Professor
Office of the President Emeritus
University of Pennsylvania
225 Van Pelt Library/6206
Philadelphia, PA 19104
Home: 2016 Spruce Street
Philadelphia, PA 19103
(215)898-5577 (O)
(215)732-6116 (H)
(215)898-2379 (F)
meyerson@pobox.upenn.edu (E)

Michalowski, Dr. Piotr IV 1999
George G. Cameron Professor of Ancient
  Near Eastern Languages and
  Civilizations
Department of Near Eastern Studies
2068 Frieze Building
University of Michigan
Ann Arbor, MI 48109
(734)764-0314 (O)
(734)761-7647 (H)
(734)936-2679 (O)(F)
(734)665-6518 (H)(F)
piotrm@umich.edu (E)

Middlekauff, Dr. Robert L. III 1997
Preston Hotchkis Professor of History
Department of History
University of California
Berkeley, CA 94720-2550
(510)642-1971 (O)
(510)658-1198 (H)
(510)643-5323 (F)
rlmiddlek@juno.com (E)

Miller, Dr. George A. II 1971
James S. McDonnell Distinguished
  University Professor of Psychology,
  Emeritus
Green Hall
Princeton University
Princeton, NJ 08544
(609)258-5973 (O)
(609)924-8286 (H)

Miller, Mr. J. Irwin V 1979
Chairman
Executive Committee
Cummins Engine Company, Inc.
301 Washington Street
Columbus, IN 47202
Home: 2760 Highland Way
Columbus, IN 47201
(812)377-5488 (O)
(812)376-8567 (H)

Miller, Dr. Neal E. II 1968
Professor Emeritus
The Rockefeller University
Research Affiliate
Department of Psychology
P.O. Box 208205
Yale University
New Haven, CT 06520-8205
Home: 200 Leeder Hill Drive, #225
Hamden, CT 06517
(For Federal Express)
(203)432-4525 (O)
(203)288-8281 (H)
(203)432-7172 (O)(F)
(203)288-3789 (H)(F)

Millon, Dr. Henry Armand   IV 1989
Dean, Center for Advanced Study in the
   Visual Arts
National Gallery of Art
Washington, DC 20565
(202)842-6484 (O)
(202)842-6733 (F)
h-millon@nga.gov (E)

Milnor, Dr. John Willard   I 1965
Professor and Director
Institute for Mathematical Sciences
Mathematics Department
State University of New York at Stony
   Brook
Stony Brook, NY 11794
(516)632-7318 (O)
(516)751-5758 (H)
(516)632-7631 (F)

Mintz, Dr. Beatrice   II 1982
Senior Member
Institute for Cancer Research
Fox Chase Cancer Center
7701 Burholme Avenue
Philadelphia, PA 19111
(215)728-2479 (O)
(215)728-3574 (F)

Mooney, Dr. Harold A.   II 1995
Paul S. Achilles Professor of Environmental
   Biology
Department of Biological Sciences
Stanford University
Stanford, CA 94305
(650)723-1179 (O)
(650)723-9253 (F)
hmooney@jasper.stanford.edu (E)

Moore, Dr. Francis Daniels   II 1998
Mosley Professor of Surgery, Emeritus
Harvard Medical School
Surgeon-in-Chief, Emeritus
Countway Library of Medicine
10 Shattuck Street
Boston, MA 02115
Home: 10 Longwood Drive, Apt. 555
Westwood, MA 02090
(617)734-0420 (O)
(617)264-5293 (F)

Morawetz, Dr. Cathleen Synge I 1996
Samuel B. Morse Professor Emerita
Courant Institute of Mathematical Sciences
New York University
251 Mercer Street
New York, NY 10012
morawetz@cims.nyu.edu (E)
(212)998-3297 (O)
(212)995-4121 (F)

Morgan, Dr. Edmund Sears   IV 1964
Sterling Professor of History, Emeritus
Yale University
Home: 244 Livingston Street
New Haven, CT 06511
(203)777-1933 (H)

Morrison, Prof. Chloe A.   V 1994
Novelist and Robert F. Goheen Professor
Council of the Humanities
110 Dickinson Hall
Princeton University
Princeton, NJ 08544
(609)258-1070 (O)
(609)258-1071 (O)
(609)683-1865 (H)
(609)258-5095 (F)

Morrison, Dr. Philip   I 1974
Institute Professor Emeritus
Room 6-205
Massachusetts Institute of Technology
Cambridge, MA 02139
Home: 11 Bowdoin Street
Cambridge, MA 02138
(617)253-5086 (O)
(617)868-0234 (H)
(617)253-9798 (F)
philmorr@mit.edu (E)

Mosteller, Dr. Frederick   I 1961
Roger I. Lee Professor of Mathematical
   Statistics, Emeritus
Harvard University
Home: 28 Pierce Road
Belmont, MA 02174
(617)495-2583 (O)
(617)496-8057 (F)

Mountcastle, Dr. Vernon B.   II 1976
University Professor of Neuroscience,
   Emeritus
Johns Hopkins University School of
   Medicine
Home: 15601 Carroll Road
Monkton, MD 21111
(410)516-4271 (O)
(410)472-2514 (H)

Moyers, Mr. Bill D.   V 1995
Executive Director
Public Affairs TV, Inc.
356 W. 58th Street
New York, NY 10019-1804

Moynihan, Sen. Daniel P.   III 1968
United States Senator New York
464 Russell Senate Office Building
Washington, DC 20510-3201
(202)224-4451 (O)

Mumford, Dr. David   I 1997
Higgins Professor of Mathematics
Harvard University
University Professor
Box F
Brown University
Providence, RI 02912
(401)863-3441 (O), (401)863-1355 (F)

Munk, Dr. Walter Heinrich   I 1965
Professor Emeritus
Scripps Institution of Oceanography
University of California
9500 Gilman Drive
MC 0225
La Jolla, CA 92037
Home: 9530 La Jolla Shores Drive
La Jolla, CA 92037
(619)534-2883 (O), (619)534-6251 (F)
wmunk@ucsd.edu (E)

Nathan, Dr. David G.   II 1999
Richard and Susan Smith Professor of
   Medicine
Professor of Pediatrics
Harvard Medical School
President
Dana-Farber Cancer Institute
44 Binney Street, Suite 1628
Boston, MA 02115
(617)632-2155 (O), (617)632-2161 (F)
david_nathan@dfci.harvard.edu (E)

Nathans, Dr. Daniel   II 1985
University Professor
Howard Hughes Medical Institute
Johns Hopkins University School of
   Medicine
725 North Wolfe Street
Baltimore, MD 21205-2185
(410)955-8445 (O), (410)367-3280 (H)
(410)614-9460 (F)
dnathans@jhmi.edu (E)

Neel, Dr. James Van Gundia II 1965
Lee R. Dice Distinguished University
    Professor of Human Genetics, Emeritus
Professor of Internal Medicine, Emeritus
University of Michigan
Home: 2235 Belmont Road
Ann Arbor, MI 48104
(734)763-9311 (O)
(734)994-5933 (H)
(734)763-3784 (F)

Neufeld, Dr. Elizabeth F. II 1993
Professor and Chair
10833 Le Conte Avenue
School of Medicine
Department of Biological Chemistry
University of California
Los Angeles, CA 90024-1737

Neugebauer, Dr. Gerry I 1986
Robert B. Millikan Professor of Physics
California Institute of Technology
MS/320-47, Downs Laboratory
Pasadena, CA 91125

Neustadt, Dr. Richard Elliott III 1967
Douglas Dillon Professor Emeritus
The John F. Kennedy School of Government
Harvard University
79 John F. Kennedy Street
Cambridge, MA 02138
(617)495-1196 (O)
(617)496-6886 (F)

Newell, Dr. Norman Dennis II 1971
Professor Emeritus of Geology
Columbia University
Curator Emeritus
American Museum of Natural History
Invertebrate Department
Central Park West at 79th Street
New York, NY 10024-5192
Home: 135 Knapp Terrace
Leonia, NJ 07605
(212)769-5736 (O), (201)944-5596 (H)
(212)769-5783 (F)
newell@amnh.org (E)

Nierenberg, Dr. William Aaron I 1975
Director Emeritus
Scripps Institution of Oceanography
University of California at San Diego
Mail Code 0221
La Jolla, CA 92093-0221
Home: P.O. Box 927269
San Diego, CA 92192-7269
(619)534-6126 (O), (619)455-5330 (H)
(619)534-6023 (F)
wnierenberg@ucsd.edu (E)

Nirenberg, Dr. Louis I 1987
Professor
Courant Institute of Mathematical Sciences
New York University
251 Mercer Street
New York, NY 10012
(212)998-3192 (O), (212)724-1069 (H)
(212)995-4121 (F)
nirenl@cims.nyu.edu (E)

North, Dr. Helen F.   IV 1991
Centennial Professor of Classics, Emerita
Swarthmore College
Home: 604 Ogden Avenue
Swarthmore, PA 19081
(610)328-8165 (O)
(610)544-5863 (H)
(610)544-5863 (F)

Nottebohm, Dr. Fernando   II 1991
Professor
The Rockefeller University
Field Research Center
Tyrrel Road, RR 2, Box 38B
Millbrook, NY 12545
(914)677-3059 (O)
(914)677-6491 (F)
nottebo@rockvax.rockefeller.edu (E)

Nowell, Dr. Peter Carey   II 1993
Professor of Pathology
Pathology and Lab Medicine
Room M163
John Morgan Building
University of Pennsylvania School of
    Medicine
Philadelphia, PA 19104-6082
(215)898-8061 (O)
(610)566-7243 (H)
(215)898-4227 (F)
nowell@mail.med.upenn.edu (E)

Nussbaum, Dr. Martha C.   IV 1995
Professor of Law and Ethics
The University of Chicago
The Law School
1111 E. 60th Street
Chicago, IL 60637
(773)702-9494 (O)
(773)702-0730 (F)

O'Brien, Dr. Brian   I 1953
Consulting Physicist
Box 166
Woodstock, CT 06281
(203)928-7295 (H)

O'Connor, Justice Sandra Day V 1992
Associate Justice
Supreme Court of the United States
1 First Street, N.E.
Washington, DC 20543
(202)479-3151 (O)
(202)479-3478 (F)

O'Malley, Rev. John W.   IV 1997
Distinguished Professor of Church History
Weston Jesuit School of Theology
3 Phillips Place
Cambridge, MA 02138-3495
(617)492-1960 (O)
(617)492-5833 (F)
jomalley@WJST.edu (E)

Oakes, Mr. John Bertram   V 1986
Former Editor of the Editorial Page
Senior Editor
The New York Times
Home: 1120 Fifth Avenue
New York, NY 10128
(212)831-4543 (F)

Oberg, Dr. Barbara B.   III 1998
General Editor
The Papers of Benjamin Franklin
Department of History
129 Dickinson Hall
Princeton University
Princeton, NJ 08544
(609)258-3162 (O)
(609)430-0565 (H)
boberg@princeton.edu (E)

Oberman, Dr. Heiko A.   IV 1991
Regents' Professor of History
Late Medieval & Reformation Studies
Douglass 315
P.O. Box 210028
University of Arizona
Tucson, AZ 85721
(520)621-1284 (O)
(520)626-5444 (F)

Olsen, Mr. Kenneth H.   I 1999
Founder and Former President
Digital Equipment Corporation
Chairman
Advanced Modular Solutions, Inc.
60 Codman Hill Road
Boxborough, MA 01719
(978)266-9700 ext. 154 (O)
(978)266-1404 (F)
kolsen@mod.com (E)

Osterbrock, Dr. Donald E.   I 1991
Professor Emeritus of Astronomy and
   Astrophysics
Lick Observatory
University of California
Santa Cruz, CA 95064
Home: 120 Woodside Avenue
Santa Cruz, CA 95060
(831)459-2605 (O)
(831)427-2541 (H)
(831)426-3115 (F)
don@ucolick.org (E)

Ostriker, Dr. Jeremiah P.   I 1994
Charles A. Young Professor of Astronomy
Provost Professor
3 Nassau Hall
Princeton University
Princeton, NJ 08544
(609)258-3026 (O)
(609)924-5737 (H)
(609)258-0701 (F)
provost@princeton.edu (E)

Ostwald, Dr. Martin   IV 1993
William R. Kenan, Jr., Professor Emeritus
   of Classics
Swarthmore College
Professor Emeritus of Classical Studies
University of Pennsylvania
Home: 408 Walnut Lane
Swarthmore, PA 19081-1137
(610)543-6408 (H)
mostwal1@swarthmore.edu (E)

Owen, Dr. Ray D.   II 1984
Professor Emeritus of Biology
California Institute of Technology, 156–29
Pasadena, CA 91125
(626)395-4960 (O)
(626)449-0756 (F)

Pais, Dr. Abraham   I 1983
Detlev W. Bronk Professor of Physics,
   Emeritus
1230 York Avenue
Rockefeller University
New York, NY 10021
(212)327-8833 (O)
(212)753-3083 (H)
(212)327-7517 (F)

Palay, Dr. Sanford Louis   II 1997
Bullard Professor of Neuroanatomy,
   · Emeritus
Harvard Medical School
Distinguished Scientist-in-Residence
Boston College
Home: 78 Temple Road
Concord, MA 01742-1520
(978)369-0389 (H)

Palmer, Dr. Robert Roswell   III 1959
Professor of History, Emeritus
Yale University
Princeton University
Home: Pennswood Village #K205
1382 Newtown-Langhorne Road
Newtown, PA 18940-2401

Panofsky, Dr. Wolfgang K. H.   I 1985
Professor and Director Emeritus
Stanford Linear Accelerator Center
P.O. Box 4349
Stanford, CA 94309
Home: 25671 Chapin Avenue
Los Altos Hills, CA 94022
(650)926-3988 (O)
(650)948-6286 (H)
(650)926-2395 (F)
pief@slac.stanford.edu (E)

Paret, Dr. Peter   III 1988
Mellon Professor in the Humanities,
    Emeritus
Institute for Advanced Study
Princeton, NJ 08540
(609)734-8344 (O)
(609)683-5027 (H)
(609)951-4488 (F)

Parker, Dr. William N.   III 1994
Philip Golden Bartlett Professor of
    Economics and Economic History,
    Emeritus
Yale University
Home: 144 Edgehill Road
Hamden, CT 06517
(203)776-5944 (H)

Patrick, Dr. Ruth   II 1974
Senior Curator of Limnology and Honorary
    Chairman
Adjunct Professor
Academy of Natural Sciences
1900 Benjamin Franklin Parkway
Philadelphia, PA 19103
Home: 750 Thomas Road
Philadelphia, PA 19118
(215)299-1098/97 (O)
(215)233-0941 (H)
(215)299-1028 (F)

Paxton, Dr. Robert O.   III 1999
Mellon Professor of the Social Sciences
    Emeritus
Columbia University
Home: 460 Riverside Drive, Apt. 72
New York, NY 10027
(212)854-3659 (O)
(212)663-3396 (H)
(212)932-0602 (F)
ropl@columbia.edu (E)

Pei, Dr. Ieoh Ming   V 1981
Architect
Pei Cobb Freed and Partners
600 Madison Avenue
New York, NY 10022
(212)872-4010 (O)
(212)355-3797 (H)
(212)872-4222 (F)

Pelikan, Dr. Jaroslav Jan   IV 1978
Sterling Professor of History, Emeritus
Yale University
Home: 156 Chestnut Lane
Hamden, CT 06518-1604
(203)288-3030 (H)
(203)248-7402 (F)

Perlman, Mr. Itzhak   V 1997
Violinist, IMG Artists
420 West 45th Street
New York, NY 10036

Peters, Hon. Ellen Ash   V 1993
Senior Justice
Former Chief Justice
Connecticut Supreme Court
231 Capitol Avenue
Drawer N, Station A
Hartford, CT 06106
Home: 791 Prospect Avenue, B-5
W. Hartford, CT 06105
(860)566-3054 (O)
(860)232-2719 (H)
(860)566-8678 (F)

Piel, Dr. Gerard   V 1963
Former Editor and Publisher
Scientific American
Home: 1115 Fifth Avenue
New York, NY 10128
(212)534-7958 (H)
(212)348-2509 (F)

Pierce, Dr. John Robinson   I 1973
Visiting Professor of Music, Emeritus
Stanford University
Home: 4008 El Cerrito Road
Palo Alto, CA 94306
(650)493-5197 (H)

Pines, Dr. David   I 1988
Research Professor of Physics
Co-Director
Institute for Complex Adaptive Matter
Office of the President
University of California
Box 576
Tesuque, NM 87574
(505)667-5431 (O)
(505)984-3167 (H)
(505)984-3151 (F)
pines@cnls.lanl.gov (E)

Pingree, Dr. David   IV 1975
University Professor
Professor of the History of Mathematics
    and of Classics
Brown University
Box 1900
Providence, RI 02912
Home: 35 Halsey Street
Providence, RI 02906
(401)863-2101 (O)
(401)521-8952 (H)

Piore, Dr. Emanuel Rubin   I 1967
Former Director
Vice President and Chief Scientist
International Business Machines
    Corporation
Home: 2 Fifth Avenue, Apt. 7A
New York, NY 10011-8835
(212)260-9594 (H)

Pocock, Dr. John G. A.   IV 1994
Professor Emeritus of History
Johns Hopkins University
Home: 419 Wingate Road
Baltimore, MD 21210
(410)235-5035 (H)
(410)516-6364 (F)

Powell, General Colin L.   V 1998
U.S. Army, Retired
Chairman
America's Promise—The Alliance for Youth
Suite 767
909 N. Washington Street
Alexandria, VA 22314
(703)706-5986 (O)

Press, Dr. Frank   I 1973
Former President
National Academy of Sciences
Washington, DC 20418
Home: Suite #616 South
2500 Virginia Avenue, N.W.
Washington, DC 20037-1901
fpress@nas.edu (E)

Preston, Dr. Samuel H.   III 1992
Frederick J. Warren Professor
    of Demography
Dean, School of Arts and Sciences
116 College Hall
University of Pennsylvania
Philadelphia, PA 19104-6377
(215)898-7320 (O)
(215)898-0821 (F)

Price, Mr. Hugh B.   V 1995
President, National Urban League
120 Wall Street, 7th Floor
New York, NY 10005-3902
(212)755-2140 (F)

Prusiner, Dr. Stanley B.   II 1998
Professor of Neurology
Professor of Biochemistry
Box 0518
School of Medicine
Department of Neurology
University of California
San Francisco, CA 94143-0518
(415)476-4482 (O), (415)476-8386 (F)

Putnam, Dr. Hilary   IV 1999
Walter B. Pearson Professor of
   Mathematical Logic and Modern Math
Cogan University Professor
Department of Philosophy
Harvard University
Cambridge, MA 02138
Home: 116 Winchester Road
Arlington, MA 02174
(617)495-3921 (O), (617)495-2192 (F)
hputnam@fas.harvard.edu (E)

Putnam, Dr. Michael C. J.   IV 1998
W. Duncan MacMillan Professor of
   Classics
Department of Classics
Brown University
Providence, RI 02912-1856
Home: 26 Arnold Street
Providence, RI 02906
(401)863-2203 (O), (401)751-1217 (H)
(401)863-7484 (F)
michael_putnam@brown.edu (E)

Pye, Dr. Lucian W.   III 1976
Ford Professor Emeritus of Political Science
Department of Political Science, E53–451
Massachusetts Institute of Technology
Cambridge, MA 02139
(617)253-3379 (O), (617)484-8203 (H)
(617)258-6164 (F)
pye@mit.edu (E)

Quandt, Dr. Richard E.   III 1991
Hughes Rogers Professor of Economics,
   Emeritus
Economics Department
Fisher Hall
Princeton University
Princeton, NJ 08544-1021
(609)258-4005 (O)
(609)924-3933 (H)
(609)258-6419 (F)
quandt@pucc.princeton.edu (E)

Quine, Dr. Willard Van O.   IV 1957
Edgar Pierce Professor of Philosophy,
   Emeritus
Emerson Hall
Harvard University
Cambridge, MA 02138
Home: 38 Chestnut Street
Boston, MA 02108
(617)495-3913 (O)
(617)723-6754 (H)
(617)495-2192 (F)
drquine@aol.com (E)

Ramo, Dr. Simon   I 1971
Director Emeritus and Co-founder
TRW Inc.
9200 Sunset Boulevard, Suite 801
Los Angeles, CA 90069
(310)550-8360 (O)
(310)550-0258 (F)

Rampersad, Dr. Arnold   IV 1995
Woodrow Wilson Professor of Literature
Princeton University
Home: 235 Santa Teresa Lane
Stanford, CA 94305-8001
(650)723-4622 (O)
(650)566-1122 (H)
(650)566-1133 (F)
rampersad@stanford.edu (E)

Ramsey, Dr. Norman F.   I 1958
Higgins Professor of Physics, Emeritus
Lyman Laboratory
Harvard University
Cambridge, MA 02138
Home: 24 Monmouth Court
Brookline, MA 02146
(617)495-2864 (O), (617)277-2313 (H)
(617)496-5144 (F)
ramsey@physics.harvard.edu (E)

Rauch, Mr. R. Stewart   V 1957
Former Chairman
The Philadelphia Savings Fund Society
Home: 13 Pond Lane
Bryn Mawr, PA 19010-1771
(610)527-0293 (O)

Raven, Dr. Peter Hamilton   II 1988
George Engelmann Professor of Botany
Washington University
Director, Missouri Botanical Garden
P.O. Box 299
St. Louis, MO 63166-0299
Home: 2361 Tower Grove
St. Louis, MO 63110
(314)577-5111 (O), (314)577-9595 (F)
praven@nas.edu (E)

Rawls, Dr. John   IV 1974
Professor of Philosophy
Department of Philosophy
Harvard University
Cambridge, MA 02138

Reed, Mr. John Shepard   V 1998
Chairman and CO-CEO
Citigroup, Citicorp, Citibank
70 Independence Drive
Princeton, NJ 08540
(215)559-2732 (O), (609)924-4059 (H)
(212)559-1049 (F)

Reiner, Dr. Erica   IV 1982
John A. Wilson Distinguished Service
    Professor of Assyriology, Emerita
Oriental Institute
University of Chicago
1155 East 58th Street
Chicago, IL 60637
Home: 5447 Ridgewood
Chicago, IL 60615
(773)702-9550 (O)
(773)288-1274 (H)
(773)702-9853 (F)
e-reiner@uchicago.edu (E)

Rhoads, Dr. Jonathan Evans   II 1958
Professor of Surgery
Provost Emeritus
5014 Ravdin Courtyard Building
3400 Spruce Street
Hospital of University of Pennsylvania
Philadelphia, PA 19104
Home: 3300 Darby Road
Apt. 1201
Haverford, PA 19041
(215)662-2008 (O)
(610)642-3131 (H)
(215)349-5849 (F)

Rhodes, Dr. Frank H. T.   V 1991
President Emeritus
Professor of Geological Sciences
3104 Snee Hall
Cornell University
Ithaca, NY 14853
Home: 603 Cayuga Heights Road
Ithaca, NY 14850
(607)255-6233 (O)
(607)257-7112 (H)
(607)254-4780 (F)
mjw11@cornell.edu (E)

Rice, Dr. Stuart Alan   I 1986
Frank P. Hixon Distinguished Service
    Professor of Chemistry
The James Franck Institute
.5640 South Ellis Avenue
University of Chicago
Chicago, IL 60637
(773)702-7199 (O)
(773)667-2679 (H)
(773)702-5863 (O)(F)
(773)667-0454 (H)(F)
sarice@rainbow.uchicago.edu (E)

Rich, Dr. Alexander   II 1980
William Thompson Sedgwick Professor of
    Biophysics
Department of Biology, Room 68–233
77 Massachusetts Avenue
Massachusetts Institute of Technology
Cambridge, MA 02139-4307
Home: 2 Walnut Avenue
Cambridge, MA 02140
(617)253-4715 (O)
(617)547-1637 (H)
(617)253-8699 (F)

Richards, Dr. Frederic M.   II 1992
Sterling Professor, Emeritus
Department of Molecular Biophysics &
    Biochemistry
P.O. Box 208114
Yale University
New Haven, CT 06520-8114
Home: 69 Andrews Road
Guilford, CT 06437
(203)432-5620 (O)
(203)453-3361 (H)
(203)432-5175 (O)(F)
(203)453-4794 (H)(F)

Ridgway, Dr. Brunilde S.   IV 1993
Rhys Carpenter Professor of Archaeology,
    Emerita
Bryn Mawr College
Home: 601 W. Montgomery Avenue
Bryn Mawr, PA 19010
(610)526-5053 (O)
(610)525-7252 (H)
(610)526-7480/7479 (F)
bridgway@brynmawr.edu

Riesman, Dr. David   III 1974
Henry Ford II Professor of Social Sciences,
    Emeritus
Harvard University
Home: 299 Cambridge Street
Winchester, MA 01890
(617)495-3822 (O)
(617)729-3645 (H)
(617)729-0688 (F)
glazier@wjh.harvard.edu (E)

Ripley, Dr. S. Dillon, II   V 1980
The Secretary Emeritus
Smithsonian Institution
Home: 2324 Massachusetts Avenue
Washington, DC 20008
(202)232-3131 (H)

Robbins, Dr. Frederick C.   II 1972
University Professor Emeritus
Dean Emeritus
Epidemiology and Biostatistics
Room WG51
10900 Euclid Avenue
Case Western Reserve Medical School
Cleveland, OH 44106-4945
(216)368-3713 (O)
(216)321-2919 (H)
(216)368-3970 (F)

Roberts, Dr. John D.   I 1974
Institute Professor of Chemistry, Emeritus
California Institute of Technology

Rocher, Dr. Ludo   IV 1990
W. Norman Brown Professor of South
  Asian Studies
University of Pennsylvania
Home: The Dorchester #1506
226 W. Rittenhouse Square
Philadelphia, PA 19103
(215)898-7466 (O), (215)985-9340 (H)

Rockefeller, Mr. David   III 1959
Chairman
Rockefeller Group, Inc.
30 Rockefeller Plaza
Room 5600
New York, NY 10112
(212)649-5600 (O)

Rodgers, Dr. John   I 1986
Silliman Professor of Geology, Emeritus
P.O. Box 208109
Yale University
New Haven, CT 06520-8109
(203)432-3128 (O), (203)432-5668 (F)
ajs@hess.geology.yale.edu (E)

Rodin, Dr. Judith   V 1995
President
University of Pennsylvania
100 College Hall
Philadelphia, PA 19104-6380
(215)898-7221 (O), (215)898-3080 (H)
(215)898-9659 (F)
rodin@pobox.upenn.edu (E)

Rosen, Dr. Charles Welles   IV 1995
Professor of Music and Social Thought
101 West 78th Street
University of Chicago
New York, NY 10024
(212)877-8020 (H)

Rosenbluth, Dr. Marshall N.   I 1998
Professor Emeritus
Chief U.S. Scientist
University of California, San Diego
Home: 2311 via Siena
La Jolla, CA 92037
(619)612-5184 (O)
(619)546-8602 (F)
(619)459-0652 (H)

Rosenthal, Dr. Franz   IV 1961
Sterling Professor Emeritus of Near Eastern
  Languages
Yale University
Home: 80 Heloise Street
Hamden, CT 06517
(203)865-3952 (H)

Rosovsky, Dr. Henry   III 1987
Lewis P. and Linda L. Geyser University
  Professor Emeritus
Department of Economics
Loeb House, 17 Quincy Street
Harvard University
Cambridge, MA 02138
(617)495-4151 (O)
(617)495-9381 (F)
hrosovsky@harvard.edu (E)

Rostow, Dr. Walt W.   III 1983
Rex G. Baker, Jr., Professor of Political
  Economy, Emeritus
University of Texas at Austin
LBJ Presidential Library
2313 Red River Street
Austin, TX 78705
(512)471-4757 (O), (512)327-0436 (H)
(512)478-9104 (F)
rostow@eco.utexas.edu

Rowland, Dr. Frank Sherwood I 1995
Donald Bren Research Professor of
  Chemistry
Department of Chemistry
University of California
Irvine, CA 92697-2025
(714)824-6016 (O), (714)760-1333 (H)
(714)824-2905 (F)

Rowley, Dr. Janet D.   II 1993
Blum-Riese Distinguished Service Professor
  of Medicine and of Molecular Genetics
  and Cell Biology
5841 S. Maryland Avenue, MC 2115
University of Chicago
Chicago, IL 60637-1470
(773)702-6117 (O), (773)702-3002 (F)
jdrowley@mcis.bsd.uchicago.edu

Rubin, Dr. Vera C.   I 1995
Staff Astronomer
Carnegie Institution of Washington
Department Terrestrial Magnetism
5241 Broad Branch Road
Washington, DC 20015
(202)686-4370 ext. 4395 (O)
(202)966-3060 (H), (202)364-8726 (F)
rubin@gal.ciw.edu (E)

Rudenstine, Dr. Neil L.   V 1992
President and Professor of English
  Literature
President's Office
Massachusetts Hall
Harvard University
Cambridge, MA 02138
(617)495-1502 (O)
(617)495-1090 (H)
(617)495-8550 (F)

Ruderman, Dr. Malvin A.   I 1996
Centennial Professor of Physics
Department of Physics
538 W. 120th Street
Columbia University
New York, NY 10027
(212)854-3317 (O)
(212)677-7578 (H)
(212)932-3169 (F)

Russell, Dr. Elizabeth S.   II 1983
Senior Staff Scientist Emeritus
Jackson Laboratory
Home: Echo Lake
Mt. Desert, ME 04660
(207)288-3371 (O)

Ryskamp, Dr. Charles A.   IV 1995
Director Emeritus
Honorary Fellow
The Pierpont Morgan Library
The Frick Collection
Professor
Princeton University
Director's Visitor
Institute for Advanced Study
Princeton, NJ 08540

Sabloff, Dr. Jeremy Arac   IV 1996
The Williams Director
33rd and Spruce Streets
University of Pennsylvania Museum of
  Archaeology and Anthropology
Philadelphia, PA 19104-6324
(215)898-4050 (O)
(215)573-9369 (F)
jsabloff@ccat.sas.upenn.edu (E)

Salpeter, Dr. Edwin E.   I 1977
J. G. White Distinguished Professor of
  Physical Sciences
Center for Radiophysics and Space
  Research
612 Space Sciences Building
Cornell University
Ithaca, NY 14853-6801
(607)255-4937 (O)
(607)255-5907 (F)

Samuelson, Dr. Paul Anthony III 1958
Institute Professor Emeritus
E52–383C
Department of Economics
Massachusetts Institute of Technology
Cambridge, MA 02139
Home: 94 Somerset Street
Belmont, MA 02478
(617)253-3368 (O)
(617)253-0560 (F)

Sandage, Dr. Allan Rex   I 1995
Astronomer
Observatories of the Carnegie Institution of
  Washington
813 Santa Barbara Street
Pasadena, CA 91101
(818)304-0246 (O)
(818)285-5086 (H)
(818)795-8136 (F)
sandage@wiff06.OCIW.edu (E)

Saxon, Dr. David S.   V 1989
President Emeritus
University of California
Former Chairman
Massachusetts Institute of Technology
Department of Physics
Knudsen Hall, Room 2130J
405 Hilgard Avenue
University of California
Los Angeles, CA 90095-1547
(310)825-1654 (O)
(310)475-9537 (H)
(310)206-5668 (F)
saxon@physics.ucla.edu (E)

Scarf, Dr. Herbert Eli   III 1993
Sterling Professor of Economics
Cowles Foundation for Research in
  Economics
Box 208281
Yale University
New Haven, CT 06520-8281
(203)432-3693 (O)
(203)776-9197 (H)
(203)432-6167 (O)(F)
(203)787-3753 (H)(F)
herbert.scarf@yale.edu (E)

Schacht, Mr. Henry B.   V 1995
Director and Senior Advisor
E. M. Warburg, Pincus & Company, LLC
466 Lexington Avenue
New York, NY 10017-3147
(212)878-9379 (O)
(212)878-9356 (F)

Scheide, Mr. William H.   V 1994
Former President
Home: 133 Library Place
Princeton, NJ 08540
(609)924-0435 (H)

Schimmel, Dr. Paul   II 1999
Professor and Member
Beckman Center
10550 North Torrey Pines Road
The Skaggs Institute for Chemical Biology
The Scripps Research Institute
La Jolla, CA 92037
(858)784-8970 (O)
(858)784-8990 (F)
schimmel@scripps.edu (E)

Schlesinger, Prof. Arthur, Jr.   III 1987
Schweitzer Professor Emeritus in the
    Humanities
Box 540, 33 West 42nd Street
City University of New York
New York, NY 10036
Home: 455 East 51st Street
New York, NY 10022
(212)642-2060 (O)
(212)751-6898 (H)
(212)688-8399 (F)

Schopf, Dr. J. William   II 1985
Professor of Paleobiology
Department of Earth and Space Sciences
University of California
Los Angeles, CA 90095
(310)825-1170 (O)
(310)825-0097 (F)

Schrieffer, Dr. J. Robert   I 1975
Chief Scientist/Eminent Scholar Professor
Florida State University
Chief Scientist
National High Magnetic Field Lab.
1800 E. Paul Dirac Drive
Tallahassee, FL 32310
(904)644-3203 (O)
(904)644-5038 (F)
schrieff@magnet.fse.edu (E)

Scranton, Hon. William W.   V 1997
Former United States Ambassador to the
    United Nations
Former Governor of Pennsylvania
231 PNC Bank Building
201 Penn Avenue
Scranton, PA 18503
(570)961-7137 (O)
(570)563-1121 (H)
(570)961-6583 (F)

Scully, Dr. Vincent   V 1997
Sterling Professor Emeritus of the History
    of Art
Yale University
Home: 252 Lawrence Street
New Haven, CT 06511
(203)432-2667 (O)
(203)772-2934 (H)
(203)432-7462 (F)

Seamans, Dr. Robert C., Jr.   V 1975
Henry R. Luce Professor of Environment
    and Public Policy
Massachusetts Institute of Technology
Home: 675 Hale Street
Beverly Farms, MA 01915
(978)927-0212 (H)
(978)927-5354 (F)
seamansbob@aol.com (E)

Seitz, Dr. Frederick   I 1946
President Emeritus
The Rockefeller University
66th Street and York Avenue
New York, NY 10021-6399
(212)327-8423 (O)
(212)327-7559 (F)
seitz@rockvax.rockefeller.edu

Sen, Dr. Amartya Kumar   III 1997
Lamont University Professor
Professor of Economics and Philosophy
Harvard University
The Master's Lodge
Trinity College
Cambridge CB2 1TQ
England
44-1223-338412 (O)
44-1223-338500 (F)

Ševčenko, Dr. Ihor   IV 1978
Dumbarton Oaks Professor of Byzantine
  History and Literature, Emeritus
Harvard University
Home: 1 Longfellow Road
Cambridge, MA 02138-4737
(617)495-4027/496-6018 (O)
(617)496-6720 (O)(F)
(617)497-1371 (H)(F)
sevcenko@fas.harvard.edu (E)

Sewell, Dr. William Hamilton III 1979
Vilas Professor and Chancellor Emeritus
Sociology Department
1180 Observatory Drive
University of Wisconsin
Madison, WI 53706
(608)262-2859 (O)
(608)238-9983 (H)
(608)265-5389 (F)
sewell@ssc.wisc.edu (E)

Shannon, Dr. Claude E.   I 1983
Donner Professor of Science, Emeritus
Massachusetts Institute of Technology
Home: 5 Cambridge Street
Winchester, MA 01890
(617)729-4767 (O)

Shapiro, Dr. Harold T.   V 1990
President
One Nassau Hall
Princeton University
Princeton, NJ 08544
Home: 83 Stockton Street
Princeton, NJ 08540
(609)258-6100 (O)
(609)252-1208 (H)
(609)258-1615 (O)(F)
(609)683-8721 (H)(F)
hts@princeton.edu (E)

Shapiro, Mr. Irving S., Esq.   V 1980
Former Chairman and CEO of DuPont
  Company
Of Counsel, Skadden, Arps, Slate, Meagher
  and Flom LLP
P.O. Box 636
One Rodney Square
Wilmington, DE 19899-0636
Home: Box 3835
Greenville, DE 19807
(302)651-3010 (O)
(302)571-1939 (H)
(302)651-3001 (F)
isshapir@skadden.com

Shapiro, Dr. Irwin I.   I 1998
Timken University Professor
Harvard University
Director, Harvard-Smithsonian
  Center for Astrophysics
Mail Stop 45
60 Garden Street
Cambridge, MA 02138
(617)495-7100 (O)
(617)495-7300 (H)
(617)495-7105 (O)(F)
(617)495-7300 (H)(F)
ishapiro@cfa.harvard.edu (E)

Sharp, Dr. Phillip A.   II 1991
Institute Professor and Head
Department of Biology
Center for Cancer Research
Room E17–529B
77 Massachusetts Avenue
Massachusetts Institute of Technology
Cambridge, MA 02139-4307
(617)253-6421 (O)
(617)253-3867 (F)
sharppa@mit.edu (E)

Shatz, Dr. Carla Jo   II 1997
Chairman (as of April 1, 2000)
Harvard Medical School
Department of Neurobiology
220 Longwood Avenue
Boston, MA 02115
(617)432-2527 (O)
(617)432-3223 (F)
carla_shatz@hms.harvard.edu (E)

Shepard, Roger Newland   III 1999
Professor Emeritus
Department of Psychology, Bldg. 420
Stanford University
Stanford, CA 94305-2130

Shultz, Hon. George P.   V 1992
Jack Steele Parker Professor of International
   Economics, Emeritus
Professor Emeritus
Graduate School of Business
Distinguished Fellow
Hoover Institution
Stanford University
Stanford, CA 94305-6010
(650)725-3492 (O)
(650)723-5441 (F)

Simmons, Dr. Ruth J.   V 1997
President
College Hall 20
Smith College
Northampton, MA 01063
(413)585-2100 (O), (413)585-2123 (F)

Simon, Dr. Herbert A.   III 1959
University Professor of Computer Science
   and Psychology
Carnegie Mellon University
Home: 128 N. Craig Street, Apt. 504
Pittsburgh, PA 15213-2758
(412)268-2787 (O), (412)521-5825 (H)
(412)521-8431 (F)
has@cs.cmu.edu (E)

Simons, Dr. Elwyn LaVerne   II 1996
James B. Duke Professor of Biological
   Anthropology and Anatomy
Scientific Director
Duke University Primate Center
3705 Erwin Road
Durham, NC 27705-5000
Home: 3603 Stoneybrook Drive
Durham, NC 27705-2428
(919)419-9355 (O), (919)490-5394 (F)
esimons@acpub.duke.edu (E)

Simpson, Dr. John Alexander   I 1996
Arthur H. Compton Distinguished Service
   Professor of Physics
The University of Chicago
Enrico Fermi Institute and Department of
   Physics
933 East 56th Street
Chicago, IL 60637
(773)702-7670 (O), (773)643-0480 (H)
(773)702-6645 (F)
simpson@odysseus.uchicago.edu (E)

Simpson, Dr. William Kelly   IV 1983
Professor of Egyptology
Yale University
Curator of Egyptian and Ancient Near
  Eastern Art
Museum of Fine Arts
Home: 129 Katonah's Wood Road
Katonah, NY 10536
(203)436-1564 (O)
(914)232-4221 (H)
(203)436-1564 (O)(F)
(914)232-4754 (H)(F)
william.simpson@yale.edu

Sinfelt, Dr. John H.   I 1994
Senior Scientific Advisor Emeritus
Exxon Research and Engineering Company
Corporate Research Laboratories
Clinton Township
Route 22 East
Annandale, NJ 08801
(908)730-2596 (O)
(908)439-3603 (H)
(908)730-3198 (F)

Singer, Dr. I. M.   I 1985
Institute Professor
Department of Mathematics (2-387)
Massachusetts Institute of Technology
Cambridge, MA 02139
(617)253-5601 (O)
(617)253-4358 (F)

Singer, Dr. Maxine F.   II 1990
President
Carnegie Institution of Washington
1530 P Street, N.W.
Washington, DC 20005-1910
(202)387-6404 (O)
(202)387-8092 (O)(F)
(202)462-7395 (O)(F)

Siraisi, Dr. Nancy G.   IV 1997
Professor of History
City University of New York
695 Park Avenue
Hunter College
New York, NY 10021
(212)772-5492 (O)
(212)772-5545 (F)
nsiraisi@cuny.campus.mci.net (E)

Sizer, Dr. Theodore R.   V 1996
University Professor Emeritus
Chairman
Brown University
Coalition of Essential Schools
Box 1969
Providence, RI 02912
(401)863-7717 (O)
(978)456-3027 (H)
(401)863-1290 (F)

Sjöberg, Dr. Åke W.   IV 1980
Clark Research Professor of Assyriology,
  Emeritus
Curator-in-Charge, Emeritus
University Museum
University of Pennsylvania
Home: 215 S. Buck Lane
Haverford, PA 19041
(215)898-4129 (O)
(610)642-1675 (H)

Slichter, Dr. Charles Pence   I 1971
Research Professor of Physics
1110 West Green Street
University of Illinois
Urbana, IL 61801-3080
(217)333-3834 (O)
(217)352-8255 (H)
(217)244-7559 (O)(F)
(217)398-0166 (H)(F)
cps@physics.uiuc.edu (E)

Smelser, Dr. Neil Joseph   III 1976
Director
Center for Advanced Study in the
    Behavioral Sciences
75 Alta Road
Stanford, CA 94305
Home: 400 El Escarpado
Stanford, CA 94305
(650)321-2052 (O)
(650)321-1192 (F)
neil@casbs.stanford.edu (E)

Smith, Dr. Emil L.   II 1973
Professor of Biological Chemistry, Emeritus
Biological Chemistry
University of California, Los Angeles
Home: 10627 Le Conte Avenue
Los Angeles, CA 90024-3205
(310)825-6494 (O)
(310)474-2379 (H)
(310)206-5272 (F)

Smith, Mr. Robert Imbrie   V 1985
Former President & C.E.O.
The Glenmede Trust Company
The Pew Charitable Trust
Home: P.O. Box 1451
Stowe, VT 05672

Smyth, Dr. Craig Hugh   IV 1979
Professor Emeritus of Fine Arts
Harvard University
Former Director
Harvard Center for Italian
    Renaissance Studies
Institute of Fine Arts
New York University
Villa I Tatti
Florence
Home: P.O. Box 39
Cresskill, NJ 07626

Snyder, Dr. Solomon H.   II 1992
Distinguished Service Professor of
    Neuroscience
Pharmacology and Molecular Sciences,
    and Psychiatry
The Johns Hopkins University
School of Medicine
725 North Wolfe Street
Baltimore, MD 21205-2185
(410)955-3024 (O)
(410)889-7379 (H)
(410)955-3623 (F)
ssnyder@bs.jhmi.edu (E)

Solow, Dr. Robert Merton   III 1980
Institute Professor Emeritus
Department of Economics, E52-383B
Massachusetts Institute of Technology
Cambridge, MA 02139
(617)253-5268 (O)
(617)253-0560 (F)

Souter, Hon. David H.   V 1994
Associate Justice Supreme Court of the
    United States
1 First Street, N.E.
Washington, DC 20543
(202)479-3380 (O)
(202)479-2967 (F)

Sovern, Dr. Michael Ira   V 1999
President Emeritus and Chancellor Kent
    Professor of Law
435 West 116th Street, Box 20
Columbia University
New York, NY 10027
(212)854-7870 (O)
(212)854-3132 (F)

Sowell, Dr. Thomas   III 1998
Rose and Milton Friedman Senior Fellow
Hoover Institution
Stanford, CA 94305-6010

Spacks, Dr. Patricia Meyer   IV 1996
Edgar F. Shannon Professor
Department of English
219 Bryan Hall
University of Virginia
Charlottesville, VA 22903
(804)924-7105 (O), (804)924-1478 (F)
pms2b@virginia.edu (E)

Spence, Dr. Jonathan Dermot III 1992
Sterling Professor of History
History Department, H.G.S.
320 York Street
Yale University
New Haven, CT 06510
(203)432-0759 (O)

Squire, Dr. Larry Ryan   II 1998
Professor of Psychiatry, Neurosciences,
    and Psychology
University of California
San Diego and Research Career Scientist
San Diego Veterans Affairs Medical Center
VAMC (116A)
3350 La Jolla Village Drive
San Diego, CA 92161
(619)552-8585 (O), (619)552-7457 (F)
1squire@ucsd.edu (E)

Srinivasan, Dr. T. N.   III 1999
Samuel C. Park, Jr., Professor of Economics
Department of Economics
Economic Growth Center
P.O. Box 208269
27 Hillhouse Avenue
Yale University
New Haven, CT 06520-8269
(203)432-3630 (O), (203)432-3635 (F)
t.srinivasan@yale.edu (E)

Staden, Dr. Heinrich von   IV 1997
Professor of Classics and
    Comparative Literature
Institute for Advanced Study
School of Historical Studies
Olden Lane
Princeton, NJ 08540
(609)734-8306 (O)

Starzl, Dr. Thomas E.   II 1999
Professor of Surgery
Department of Surgery
3601 Fifth Avenue
Falk Clinic, 5C
University of Pittsburgh School
    of Medicine
Pittsburgh, PA 15213
(412)624-0115 (O)
(412)681-0780 (H)
(412)624-0192 (F)
mangan@med.pitt.edu (E)

Stassen, Dr. Harold Edward   III 1949
Home: Attention: Bruce LaBelle
220 South Robert Street
Suite 208
St. Paul, MN 55107
(612)457-5861 (O)

Stebbins, Dr. George Ledyard   II 1961
Professor of Genetics
University of California-Davis
Home: 341 West 8th Street
Davis, CA 95616
(916)753-2665 (H)

Steitz, Dr. Joan Argetsinger II 1992
Henry Ford II Professor of Molecular
  Biophysics and Biochemistry
Investigator
Howard Hughes Medical Institute
Yale University School of Medicine
BCMM-136C
295 Congress Avenue, Box 9812
New Haven, CT 06536-0812
(203)737-4418 (O)
(203)488-7875 (H)
(203)624-8213 (F)

Stella, Mr. Frank V 1999
Artist
17 Jones Street
New York, NY 10013

Stent, Dr. Gunther S. II 1984
Professor Emeritus of Neurobiology
Department of Molecular and Cell Biology
University of California
Berkeley, CA 94720-3200
Home: 145 Purdue Avenue
Berkeley, CA 94708
(510)642-5214 (O)
(510)526-7576 (H)
(510)643-6791 (F)
stent@uclink4.berkeley.edu (E)

Stern, Dr. Fritz III 1988
University Professor Emeritus
Columbia University
Home: 15 Claremont Avenue
New York, NY 10027
(212)666-2891 (H)
(212)316-0370 (F)

Stern, Mr. Isaac V 1995
Violinist
President
Carnegie Hall
c/o ICM Artists, Ltd.
40 West 57th Street
New York, NY 10019

Stiglitz, Dr. Joseph Eugene III 1997
Senior Vice President
Chief Economist
The World Bank
1818 H Street N.W., N6-043
Washington, DC 20433
(202)473-3774 (O)
(202)522-1158 (F)
jstiglitz@worldbank.org (E)

Stone, Dr. Edward C. I 1993
Director
Jet Propulsion Laboratory
Building 1800, Room 904
4800 Oak Grove Drive
Pasadena, CA 91109
(818)354-3405 (O)
(818)393-4218 (F)
edward.c.stone@jpl.nasa.gov (E)

Stork, Dr. Gilbert I 1995
Eugene Higgins Professor of Chemistry,
  Emeritus
Department of Chemistry
Havemeyer Hall
Box 3118
Columbia University
New York, NY 10027
(212)854-2178 (O)
(201)871-4032 (H)
(212)932-1289 (F)
gjs8@columbia.edu (E)

Strominger, Dr. Jack L. II 1994
Higgins Professor of Biochemistry
Department of Molecular and Cellular
  Biology
7 Divinity Avenue
Harvard University
Cambridge, MA 02138
(617)495-2733 (O)
(718)862-7731 (H)
(617)496-8351 (F)
jlstrom@fas.harvard.edu (E)

Strong, Mr. Maurice Frederick V 1993
Chairman, The Earth Council
255 Consumers Road, Suite 401
Toronto, Ontario M2J 5B6, Canada
(416)498-3150 (O)
(416)498-7296 (F)

Suppes, Dr. Patrick III 1991
Professor Emeritus
Stanford University
Home: 678 Mirada Avenue
Stanford, CA 94305-8475
(650)725-6030 (O)
(650)322-8409 (F)
suppes@ockham.stanford.edu (E)

Swerdlow, Dr. Noel M. IV 1988
Professor of Astronomy and Astrophysics
  and of History
Department of Astronomy
  and Astrophysics
5640 South Ellis Avenue
University of Chicago
Chicago, IL 60637
(773)702-7969 (O)
(312)943-0943 (H)
(773)702-8212 (F)
nms@oddjob.uchicago.edu (E)

Talalay, Dr. Paul II 1990
John Jacob Abel Distinguished Service
  Professor
Department of Pharmacology and
  Molecular Sciences
Johns Hopkins University
School of Medicine
725 N. Wolfe Street
Baltimore, MD 21205-2185
Home: 5512 Boxhill Lane
Baltimore, MD 21210
(410)955-3499 (O)
(410)323-0871 (H)
(410)502-6818 (F)
ptalalay@welchlink.welch.jhu.edu (E)

Taplin, Mr. Frank E., Jr. V 1987
Trustee, Environmental Defense Fund
Former President and Chief Executive
  Officer
Metropolitan Opera Association
Trustee Emeritus
Institute for Advanced Study
Home: 55 Armour Road
Princeton, NJ 08540
(609)924-4944 (H)
(609)924-7900 (H)
(609)924-4223 (F)

Tarjan, Dr. Robert E. I 1990
James S. McDonnell Distinguished
  University Professor of Computer Science
Chief Scientist
InterTrust Technologies, Inc.
Department of Computer Science
35 Olden Street
Princeton University
Princeton, NJ 08544
Home: 18 Lake Lane
Princeton, NJ 08540
(609)258-4797 (O)
(609)921-0132 (H)
(609)258-1771 (F)

Taruskin, Dr. Richard IV 1998
Professor of Music
Music Department
University of California
Berkeley, CA 94720

Taube, Dr. Henry I 1981
Professor of Chemistry, Emeritus
Stanford University
Stanford, CA 94305
(650)725-9344 (O)
(650)326-4662 (H)
(650)725-0259 (F)
hf.cp1@forsythe.stanford.edu (E)

Taylor, Dr. Joseph Hooten, Jr.   I 1992
James S. McDonnell Distinguished
    University Professor of Physics
Physics Department
Princeton University
Princeton, NJ 08544
(609)258-4368 (O)
(609)683-0571 (H)
(609)258-1124 (F)

Temkin, Dr. Owsei   IV 1958
William H. Welch Professor Emeritus of the
    History of Medicine
The Johns Hopkins University
School of Medicine
Home: 830 West 40th Street, HCC
Baltimore, MD 21211

Thompson, Dr. Homer A.   IV 1951
Professor Emeritus
The Institute for Advanced Study
Princeton, NJ
DO NOT SEND MAIL

Thompson, Dr. Richard F.   II 1999
Keck Professor of Psychology and
    Biological Sciences
Director, Neuroscience Program
3614 Watt Way, HNB 522
University of Southern California
Los Angeles, CA 90089-2520
Home: 28 Skysail Drive
Corona del Mar, CA 92625
(213)740-7350 (O)
(949)640-8920 (H)
(213)740-5687 (F)
thompson@neuro.usc.edu (E)

Thorne, Dr. Kip S.   I 1999
Feynman Professor of Physics
California Institute of Technology 130-33
Pasadena, CA 91125

Thorpe, Dr. James   IV 1982
Senior Research Associate
Duncaster T320
40 Loeffler Road
Bloomfield, CT 06002
Home: 1199 Arden Road
Pasadena, CA 91106
(626)405-2121 (O)
(626)405-0938 (H)

Tierney, Dr. Brian   IV 1990
Bryce and Edith M. Bowmar Professor,
    Emeritus
Cornell University
Home: 201 Willard Way
Ithaca, NY 14850
(607)255-8862 (O)
(607)272-5019 (H)
(607)255-0469 (F)
bt20@cornell.edu (E)

Tobin, Dr. James   III 1959
Sterling Professor Emeritus of Economics
Cowles Foundation for Research in
    Economics
Box 208281
Yale University
New Haven, CT 06520-8281
(203)432-3720 (O)
(203)432-6167 (F)

Townes, Dr. Charles H.   I 1960
University Professor
Department of Physics
Le Conte Hall
University of California
Berkeley, CA 94720
(510)642-1128/7686 (O)
(510)527-4860 (H)
(510)643-8497 (F)
cht@sunspot.ssl.berkeley.edu (E)

Treiman, Dr. Sam Bard   I 1999
Eugene Higgins Professor of Physics,
    Emeritus
Department of Physics
Princeton University
Princeton, NJ 08544

Truman, Dr. David Bicknell   III 1957
President Emeritus
Professor of Political Science, Emeritus
Mount Holyoke College
Home: 700 John Ringling Blvd.
Apt. N-312
Sarasota, FL 34236-1501
(941)361-7195 (H)
76375.2362@compuserve.com (E)

Tukey, Dr. John Wilder   I 1962
Donner Professor of Science and Professor
    of Statistics, Emeritus
Princeton University
Former Associate Executive Director
Research Information Services
AT & T Bell Laboratories
Home: P.O. Box 2043
Princeton, NJ 08543-2043
(609)258-4219 (O)
(609)924-5095 (H)
(609)258-1367 (F)
eo@math.princeton.edu (E)

Ulam, Dr. Adam B.   III 1989
Gurney Professor of History and
    Political Science
Director, Russian Research Center
Harvard University
1737 Cambridge Street
Cambridge, MA 02138
(617)495-4045 (O)
(617)495-8319 (F)

Vagelos, Dr. P. Roy   V 1993
Former Chairman and Chief Executive
    Officer
Merck and Company, Inc.
1 Crossroads Drive, Building A
Bedminister, NJ 07921
(908)658-3108 (O)
(908)719-9890 (H)
(908)658-9647 (F)

Van Allen, Dr. James Alfred   I 1961
Regent Distinguished Professor
Department of Physics and Astronomy
University of Iowa
Iowa City, IA 52242
Home: 5 Woodland Mounds Road
Iowa City, IA 52245
(319)335-1699 (O)
(319)335-1753 (F)
james-vanallen@uiowa.edu (E)

Vance, Mr. Cyrus R.   V 1993
Partner
Simpson, Thacher, and Bartlett
425 Lexington Avenue
New York, NY 10017-3954
(212)455-7190 (O)
(212)455-2502 (F)

Van Dusen, Mr. Lewis H., Jr.   V 1987
Of-Counsel
Former Senior Partner
Drinker, Biddle & Reath
One Logan Square
18th and Cherry Streets
Philadelphia, PA 19103-6996
Home: 750 Thomas Road
P.O. Box 4095
Philadelphia, PA 19118
(215)988-2869 (O)
(215)233-0941 (H)
(215)988-2757 (F)

Varmus, Dr. Harold E.   II 1994
Director
National Institutes of Health
9000 Rockville Pike
Bethesda, MD 20892
(301)496-2433 (O)
(301)402-2700 (F)

Vendler, Dr. Helen Hennessy IV 1992
A. Kingsley Porter University Professor
Department of English
Barker Center
12 Quincy Street
Harvard University
Cambridge, MA 02138
Home: 54 Trowbridge Street #B
Cambridge, MA 02138
(617)496-6028 (O)
(617)547-9197 (H)
(617)496-8737 (F)

Vermeule, Dr. Emily T.   IV 1972
Zemurray Stone-Radcliffe Professor of the
   Classics and Fine Arts
Harvard University
Home: 47 Coolidge Hill Road
Cambridge, MA 02138
(617)495-1734 (O)
(617)864-1879 (H)

Vogelstein, Dr. Bert   II 1995
Clayton Professor of Oncology
Howard Hughes Medical Institute
The Johns Hopkins Oncology Center
424 N. Bond Street
Baltimore, MD 21231
(410)955-8877 (O)
(410)955-0548 (F)

Vogt, Dr. Evon Zartman, Jr.   IV 1999
Professor of Anthropology, Emeritus
Peabody Museum
11 Divinity Avenue
Harvard University
Cambridge, MA 02138-2019
(617)495-2246 (O), (617)496-8041 (F)

Vogt, Dr. Peter K.   II 1991
Professor
The Scripps Research Institute
10550 N. Torrey Pines Road
La Jolla, CA 92037
Home: 7909 St. Louis Terrace
La Jolla, CA 92037
(619)784-9728 (O), (619)784-2070 (F)
pkvogt@scripps.edu (E)

Volcker, Mr. Paul A.   V 1998
Former Chairman
Board of Governors of the Federal Reserve
   System
Henry Kaufman Visiting Professor
Stern School of Business
610 Fifth Avenue, Suite 420
New York, NY 10020
(212)218-7878 (O), (212)249-6995 (H)
(212)218-7875 (O)(F)
(212)734-3951 (H)(F)

Vryonis, Dr. Speros, Jr.   IV 1974
Director and Alexander S. Onassis
   Professor
Speros Basil Vryonis Center for Hellenic
   Studies
3140 Gold Camp Drive, Suite 50
Rancho Cordova, CA 95670-6023
(916)631-9099 (O), (916)631-7175 (F)

Wake, Dr. David B. II 1996
Professor of Integrative Biology
Director, Museum of Vertebrate Zoology
3101 Valley Life Sciences Bldg., #3160
University of California
Berkeley, CA 94720-3160
(510)642-3567 (O)
wakelab@uclink4.berkeley.edu (E)

Wakeman, Dr. Frederic E., Jr. III 1998
Walter and Elise Haas Professor of Asian
  Studies
Institute of East Asian Studies
2223 Fulton Street, #2318
University of California
Berkeley, CA 94720-2318
(510)642-2809 (O)
(510)643-7062 (F)
jingcha@socrates.berkeley.edu (E)

Wallace, Dr. Anthony F. C. IV 1969
University Professor of Anthropology,
  Emeritus
University of Pennsylvania
Home: 614 N. Convent Road
Aston, PA 19014
(610)459-2922 (H)

Walzer, Dr. Michael III 1990
Professor of Social Science
School of Social Science
Institute for Advanced Study
Princeton, NJ 08540
(609)734-8253 (O)
(609)924-8316 (H)
(609)951-4457 (F)

Ward, Dr. Robert E. III 1973
Professor of Political Science, Emeritus
Stanford University
Home: 501 Portola Road, Box 8129
Portola Valley, CA 94028-7604
(650)424-4436 (H)
(650)424-4436 (F)

Wasserburg, Dr. Gerald J. I 1982
John D. MacArthur Professor of Geology
  and Geophysics
California Institute of Technology
Division of Geological and Planetary
  Sciences 170-25
Pasadena, CA 91125
Home: 1207 Arden Road
Pasadena, CA 91106
(626)395-6139 (O)
(626)449-7852 (H)
(626)796-9823 (F)
isotopes@gps.caltech.edu (E)

Watkins, Dr. Calvert IV 1975
Victor S. Thomas Professor of Linguistics
  and the Classics
Department of Linguistics
Boylston 314
Harvard University
Cambridge, MA 02138
Home: 10 Locke Street
Cambridge, MA 02140
(617)495-4054 (O)
(617)354-8294 (H)
(617)496-4447 (F)
watkins@fas.harvard.edu (E)

Watson, Dr. Bernard Charles V 1991
Presidential Scholar
Temple University
Home: 473 Copper Beech Circle
Elkins Park, PA 19027
(215)204-2523 (O)
(215)886-2048 (H)

Watson, Dr. James Dewey II 1977
President
Cold Spring Harbor Laboratory
P.O. Box 100
Cold Spring Harbor, NY 11724
(516)367-8310/8311 (O)
(516)367-8480 (F)

Wechsler, Dr. Herbert   III 1985
Harlan Fiske Stone Professor of
  Constitutional Law, Emeritus
Columbia University School of Law
179 East 70th Street
New York, NY 10021
(212)734-8088 (H)

Weigley, Dr. Russell Frank   III 1993
Distinguished University Professor
Department of History
1115 W. Berk Street
Temple University
Philadelphia, PA 19122-6089
Home: 327 S. Smedley Street
Philadelphia, PA 19103-6717
(215)204-8919 (O), (215)545-7499 (H)
(215)204-5891 (F)

Weinberg, Dr. Alvin M.   I 1977
Distinguished Fellow
Former Director
Oak Ridge Associated Universities
P.O. Box 117
Oak Ridge, TN 37831-0117
(423)576-3249 (O), (423)483-6045 (H)
(423)576-3643 (F)

Weinberg, Dr. Steven   I 1982
Josey Regental Professor of Science
Department of Physics
University of Texas
Austin, TX 78712
(512)471-4394 (O), (512)471-4888 (F)
weinberg@physics.utexas.edu (E)

Weisskopf, Dr. Victor F.   I 1966
Institute Professor Emeritus
Massachusetts Institute of Technology
Home: 20 Bartlett Terrace
Newton, MA 02459

Wells, Dr. Herman B   V 1964
University Chancellor
Owen Hall 100
Indiana University
Bloomington, IN 47405
(812)855-6647 (O)
(812)855-5642 (F)
hbwells@indiana.edu (E)

West, Dr. Cornel   V 1997
Professor of Afro-American Studies
Professor of the Philosophy of Religion
Du Bois Fellow
Harvard University
12 Quincy Street
Cambridge, MA 02138
(617)495-7868 (O)

Westheimer, Dr. Frank H.   I 1976
Loeb Professor of Chemistry, Emeritus
Harvard University
Cambridge, MA 02138
(617)495-4096 (O)
(617)495-1792 (F)
Westheimer@Chemistry.harvard.edu (E)

Wetherill, Dr. George W.   I 1998
Scientific Staff Member
Department of Terrestrial Magnetism
5241 Broad Branch Road, N.W.
Carnegie Institution of Washington
Washington, DC 20015-1305
(202)686-4370 ext. 4375 (O)
(202)244-3435 (H)
(202)364-8726 (F)
wetherill@eros.ciw.edu (E)

Wheeler, Dr. John Archibald   I 1951
Joseph Henry Professor of Physics, Emeritus
Ashbel Smith Professor
Jane and Roland Blumberg Professor
  (present)
University of Texas at Austin
Physics Department, Room 394
Princeton University
Princeton, NJ 08544-0708
Home: 1904 Meadow Lakes
Hightstown, NJ 08520
(609)258-5824 (O)
(609)426-6239 (H)
(609)258-6360 (F)
jawheeler@pupgg.princeton.edu (E)

Whipple, Dr. Fred Lawrence   I 1956
Director
Smithsonian Astrophysical Observatory
Former Phillips Professor of Astronomy
Harvard University
Home: 60 Garden Street
Cambridge, MA 02138-1516
(617)864-7383 (O)
(617)484-0988 (H)

White, Dr. Gilbert F.   III 1993
Gustavson Professor Emeritus of
  Geography
Institute of Behavioral Science
Campus Box 482
University of Colorado
Boulder, CO 80309-0482
(303)492-6311 (O)
(303)444-0169 (H)
(303)492-2151 (F)
gilbert.white@colorado.edu

White, Dr. Morton Gabriel   IV 1972
Professor Emeritus
The Institute for Advanced Study
Princeton, NJ 08540

White, Dr. Robert M.   I 1991
President Emeritus
National Academy of Engineering
Home: 5610 Wisconsin Avenue, Apt. 1506
Chevy Chase, MD 20815
(202)682-9331 (O), (301)652-4907 (H)
(202)682-9298 (O)(F)
(301)652-2901 (H)(F)
rwhite@theadvisorygroup.com (E)

Whitehead, Hon. John C.   V 1997
Former Chairman, Mellon Foundation
Chairman, Federal Reserve Bank
65 East 55 Street
New York, NY 10022
(212)755-3131 (O), (212)751-5924 (F)

Whitesides, Dr. George M.   I 1997
Mallinckrodt Professor of Chemistry
Department of History
12 Oxford Street
Harvard University
Cambridge, MA 02138
Home: 124 Grasmere Street
Newton, MA 02158
(617)495-9430 (O), (617)244-2140 (H)
(617)495-9857 (O)(F)
(617)630-8166 (H)(F)
gwhitesides@gmwgroup.harvard.edu (E)

Widom, Dr. Benjamin   I 1993
Goldwin Smith Professor of Chemistry
Department of Chemistry
Baker Laboratory
Cornell University
Ithaca, NY 14853-1301
Home: 204 The Parkway
Ithaca, NY 14850
(607)255-3363 (O), (607)257-7099 (H)
(607)255-4137 (F)
widom@vdwaals.chem.cornell.edu (E)

Wieschaus, Dr. Eric F.   II 1998
Investigator
Howard Hughes Medical Institute
Professor
Department of Molecular Biology
Washington Road
Princeton University
Princeton, NJ 08544
(609)258-5383 (O)
(609)258-1547 (F)
ewieschaus@molbiol.princeton.edu (E)

Wiesel, Dr. Torsten Nils   II 1982
President Emeritus and Director
The Shelby White and Leon Levy Center
   for Mind, Brain and Behavior
The Rockefeller University
1230 York Avenue
New York, NY 10021
(212)327-7093 (O)
(212)327-8988 (F)
wiesel@rockvax.rockefeller.edu

Wiles, Dr. Andrew J.   I 1997
Eugene Higgins Professor of Mathematics
Department of Mathematics
Fine Hall
Washington Road
Princeton University
Princeton, NJ 08544
(609)258-4197 (O)
(609)258-1367 (F)

Wiley, Dr. Don Craig   II 1996
Professor of Biochemistry and Biophysics
Department of Molecular and Cellular
   Biology
7 Divinity Avenue
Harvard University
Cambridge, MA 02138
(617)495-1808 (O)
(617)495-9613 (F)
wiley@xta10.harvard.edu (E)

Willey, Dr. Gordon R.   IV 1984
Bowditch Professor, Emeritus
Peabody Museum
Harvard University
Home: 25 Gray Gardens East
Cambridge, MA 02138
(617)495-3208 (O)
(617)354-1287 (H)

Williams, Dr. Robin M., Jr.   III 1967
Henry Scarborough Professor of Social
   Science, Emeritus
Visiting Professor
[January—June]
Department of Sociology
University of California
Irvine, CA 92697-5100
[July—December]
342 Uris Hall
Cornell University
Ithaca, NY 14853-7601
Home: 414 Oak Avenue
Ithaca, NY 14850-4800
(607)255-1416 (O)
(607)273-9119 (H)
(607)255-8473 (F)

Wilson, Dr. Edward O.   II 1976
Pellegrino University Research Professor
Museum of Comparative Zoology
Harvard University
26 Oxford Street
Cambridge, MA 02138-2902
(617)495-2315 (O), (617)495-1224 (F)
ewilson@oeb.harvard.edu (E)

Wilson, Dr. James Q.   III 1984
Collins Professor of Management
Graduate School of Management
University of California
Home: 32910 Camino de Buena Ventura
Malibu, CA 90265
(310)457-5260 (H)
(310)457-1351 (F)
jwilson@anderson.ucla.edu (E)

Wilson, Dr. Kenneth G.   I 1984
Youngberg Trustees Distinguished Professor
Department of Physics
174 W. 18th Avenue
Ohio State University
Columbus, OH 43210
(614)292-9396 (O)
(614)292-3221 (F)
kgw@pacific.ohio-state.edu (E)

Wilson, Dr. Robert R.   I 1969
Director Emeritus
Professor Emeritus
Newman Laboratory
Cornell University
Ithaca, NY 14853-5001
Home: 230 Savage Farm Drive
Ithaca, NY 14850-6502
(607)257-7625 (H)

Wilson, Dr. William Julius   III 1990
Malcolm Wiener Professor of Social Policy
The John F. Kennedy School of Government
Harvard University
79 John F. Kennedy Street
Cambridge, MA 02138
(617)496-4514 (O)
(617)496-9053 (F)

Winograd, Dr. Shmuel   I 1989
IBM Fellow
International Business Machines
Research Division
Thomas J. Watson Research Center
P.O. Box 218
Yorktown Heights, NY 10598
(914)945-2443 (O)
(914)945-3434 (F)
swin@watson.ibm.com (E)

Witkop, Dr. Bernhard   II 1999
National Institutes of Health
  Scholar, Emeritus
Home: 3807 Montrose Driveway
Chevy Chase, MD 20815-4701
(301)656-6418 (H), (301)402-0240 (F)

Witten, Dr. Edward   I 1993
Professor
School of Natural Sciences
Institute for Advanced Study
Princeton, NJ 08540
Home: 126 Clover Lane
Princeton, NJ 08540
(609)734-8021 (O), (609)683-0075 (H)
(609)924-8399 (F)

Wolfensohn, Mr. James David V 1997
President
The World Bank
1818 H Street, N.W.
Washington, DC 20433
(202)458-5120 (O), (202)522-3031 (F)

Wolman, Dr. Markley Gordon   I 1999
B. Howell Griswold, Jr., Professor of
  Geography and International Affairs
Department of Geography and
  Environmental Engineering
The Johns Hopkins University
Baltimore, MD 21218

Wood, Dr. Gordon S.   III 1994
University Professor and
  Professor of History
Department of History—Box N
Brown University
Providence, RI 02912
(401)863-2131 (O), (401)861-6643 (H)
(401)863-1040 (F)
gordon_wood@brown.edu

Woodward, Dr. C. Vann   III 1959
Sterling Professor of History, Emeritus
Yale University
Home: 83 Rogers Road
Hamden, CT 06517
(203)624-4534 (H)
(203)432-7587 (F)

Woolard, Mr. Edgar S., Jr.   V 1996
Former Chairman and Chief
    Executive Officer
DuPont
9000 DuPont Building
Wilmington, DE 19898
(302)774-1000 (O)

Woolf, Dr. Harry   V 1977
Professor-at-Large Emeritus
The Institute for Advanced Study
Princeton, NJ 08540
Home: 29 Sergeant Street
Princeton, NJ 08540
(609)734-8018 (O)
(609)497-1477 (H)
(609)951-4405 (F)

Wright, Dr. Gordon   III 1978
Bonsall Professor Emeritus of History
Stanford University
Home: 813 San Francisco Terrace
Stanford, CA 94305
(650)857-9292 (H)

Wyeth, Mr. Andrew   V 1967
Artist
"The Mill"
P.O. Box 155
Chadds Ford, PA 19317
(610)793-2861 (F)

Yang, Dr. Chen Ning   I 1964
Einstein Professor
Institute for Theoretical Physics
State University of New York
Stony Brook, NY 11794-3840
(516)632-7980 (O), (516)632-7954 (F)
chen.yang@sunysb.edu (E)

Yoder, Dr. Hatten S., Jr.   I 1979
Director Emeritus
Geophysical Laboratory
Carnegie Institution of Washington
5251 Broad Branch Road, N.W.
Washington, DC 20015-1305
Home: 6709 Melody Lane
Bethesda, MD 20817-3152
(202)686-2410 ext. 2461 (O)
(301)365-8758 (H)
(202)686-2419 (F)
yoder@gl.ciw.edu (E)

Zare, Dr. Richard N.   I 1991
Marguerite Blake Wilbur Professor in
    Natural Science
Department of Chemistry
Stanford University
Stanford, CA 94305-5080
(650)723-3062 (O), (650)725-0259 (F)
zare@stanford.edu (E)

Zewail, Dr. Ahmed H.   I 1998
Linus Pauling Professor of Chemistry and
    Professor of Physics
Director
NSF Laboratory for Molecular Sciences
California Institute of Technology
Mail Code 127–72
Pasadena, CA 91125
(626)395-6536 (O), (626)792-8456 (F)
(626)584-1222 (H)
zewail@cco.caltech.edu (E)

Ziolkowski, Dr. Theodore J.   IV 1984
Class of 1900 Professor of German and
  Comparative Literature
Princeton University
Home: 36 Bainbridge Street
Princeton, NJ 08540
(609)921-7567 (H)
(609)430-0209 (F)
tjz@princeton.edu (E)

Zuckerman, Dr. Harriet   III 1996
Professor Emerita
Columbia University
Senior Vice President
A. W. Mellon Foundation
140 E. 62nd Street
New York, NY 10021
(212)838-8400 (O)
(212)888-4172 (F)
hz@mellon.org (E)

FOREIGN MEMBERS

Aigrain, Dr. Pierre Raoul Roger
I 1981
Scientific Adviser to the President
Thomson SA
Cedex 67–92045 Paris La Défense France
Home: 56 Rue de Boulainvilliers
75016 Paris France
33-1-49-07-80-00 (O)
33-1-4525-8637 (H)

Allègre, Dr. Claude Jean   I 1992
Professor and Director of Laboratory of
   Geochemistry
Director of Institute of the Physics of the
   Earth
University of Paris VII, Lab.
Géochimie et Cosmochimie
Institut de Physique du Globe 4
Place Jussieu Tour 14/24, 75230 France
44-27-49-15 (O)
44-27-37-52 (F)
allegre@ipgp.jussieu.fr (E)

Arnold, Dr. Vladimir Igorevich I 1990
Professor
Moscow State University
Academy of Sciences U.S.S.R.
Steklov Institute of Mathematics
8, Gubkina Street
117966 Moscow GSP-1 Russia
7-095-132-4802 (H)
7-095-135-0555 (F)
arnold@genesis.mi.ras.ru (E)
[January-June]
Ceremade
Université Paris—Dauphine
Place du Maréchal de Lattre de Tassigny
75775 Paris Cedex 16e France
01-40-01-92-08 (H)
01-44-05-45-99 (F)
arnold@ceremade.dauphine.fr (E)

Atiyah, Sir Michael   I 1991
Former Master of Trinity College
Former President of Royal Society of
   London
Department of Mathematics
University of Edinburgh
Mayfield Road Edinburgh EH9 3JZ
England
Home: 3/8 West Grange Gardens
Edinburgh EH9 2RA England
44-0131-650-5086 (O)
44-0131-667-0898 (H)
44-0131-650-6553 (F)
atiyah@maths.ed.ac.uk (E)

Balandier, Dr. Georges   III 1976
Professor Emeritus of Sociology
Director of Studies, Associate Member
Académie Royale de Belgique
Académi d'Athenes
Université René Descartes
Sorbonne
Directeur d'Etudes à l'Ecole des Hautes
   Etudes en Sciences Sociales
54 Boulevard Raspaie
Paris 75006
Home: 13 rue de Square Carpeaux
75018 ParisFrance
33-1-544-39-79 (O)
33-1-46-27-05-22 (H)

Baldinger, Dr. Kurt   IV 1976
Professor of Romance Languages
Universität Heidelberg
Romanisches Seminar, D 69
Heidelberg 1, Seminarstrasse 3
Postfach Germany
Home: Höhenstrasse 24, 69118
Heidelberg-Ziegelhausen Germany
(0 62 21) 54 27 31 (O)
(0 62 21) 80 04 12 (H)

Beck, Dr. Hans-Georg   IV 1988
Professor Emeritus
University of Munich
Home: Findingerstr. 32, D-86923
Unterfinning Germany
49-08808-1248 (H)

Bergström, Dr. Sune   II 1984
Emeritus Professor of Biochemistry
Nobel Forum
Karolinska Institutet
Box 250, 17177 Stockholm Sweden
46-8-728-7801 (O)
46-8-611-85-87 (H)
46-8-611-17-33 (F)

Bessborough, Mary, Lady   V 1988
Chairman of The Friends of Benjamin
   Franklin House and The American
   Franklin Friends
Home: 4, Westminster Gardens
Marsham Street
London SW1P 4JA England
Home: Stansted Park
Rowlands Castle
Hampshire PO9 6DX England
44-071-828-5959 (O)
44-070-541-2223 (H)

Boardman, Sir John   IV 1999
Emeritus Professor of Classical
   Archaeology and Art
11 Park Street
University of Oxford Woodstock
Oxford OX20 1SJ England
44-01865 278084 (O)
44-01865 278082 (F)
ashm0053@esmine.ox.ac.uk (E)

Bodmer, Sir Walter F.   II 1989
Head of ICRF Cancer and Immuno-
   genetics Laboratory
Institute of Molecular Medicine
Principal, Hertford College
Catte Street
Oxford OX1 3BW England
44-01865-279405 (O)
44-01865-279437 (F)
walter.bodmer@hertford.ox.ac.uk (E)

Bohr, Dr. Aage   I 1965
Professor Emeritus
Niels Bohr Institute
University of Copenhagen
Blegdamsrej 17, 2100ø
Copenhagen Denmark
Home: Strandgade 34
1-Sal, 1401 Copenhagen Denmark
45-35-32-52-52 (O)
45-32-95-87-09 (H)

Booth, Sir Christopher   II 1981
The Harveian Librarian
The Royal College of Physicians
11 St. Andrews Place, Regents Park
London NW1 4LE England
Home: 9 Kent Terrace
London NW1 4RP England
44-71-935-1174 (O)
44-71-724-3379 (H)
44-71-487-5218 (F)

Borel, Dr. Armand   I 1985
Professor Emeritus
The Institute for Advanced Study
Princeton, NJ 08540
Home: 106 Battle Road Circle
Princeton, NJ 08540
(609)734-8108 (O), (609)951-4459 (F)
borel@math.ias.edu (E)

Bracher, Prof. Karl Dietrich III 1978
Professor Emeritus of Political Science and
 Contemporary History
Seminar für Politische Wissenschaft
University of Bonn
Home: Stationsweg 17
D-5300 Bonn 1 Germany
49-228-284358 (H)

Brenner, Dr. Sydney II 1979
Director, Molecular Sciences Institute
2168 Shattuck Avenue, 2nd Floor
Berkeley, CA 94704
Home: 3 Barton Square, Ely
Cambridgeshire England
44-01144-223-248011 (O)
44-01144-353-668012 (H)
44-01144-223-210136 (F)

Burkert, Dr. Walter IV 1987
Professor Ordinarius of Classics Emeritus
University of Zürich
Home: Wildsbergstrasse 8
CH-8610 Uster
Zürich Switzerland
41-00411-9403013 (H)
41-00411-9403013 (F)

Çambel, Prof. Halet IV 1979
Professor and Head (retired)
Istanbul University
Home: Birinci-cad. 212
Arnavutköy-Istanbul Turkey 80820
00-90-212-263-56-41 (H)
00-90-212-263-60-31 (F)

Casimir, Prof. Hendrik B. G. I 1971
Associate Professor of Physics, Emeritus
University of Leiden
Home: 5591 TT HEEZE
De Zegge 7 The Netherlands
31-0-40-2862233 (H)

Caspersson, Dr. Torbjörn II 1974
Karolinska Institutet
Department of Tumor Pathology
Karolinska Sjukhuset
S-104 01 Stockholm 60 Sweden

Chadwick, Dr. Henry IV 1982
Former Master of Peterhouse
Cambridge and Regius Professor
Cambridge, England
Home: 46 St. John Street
Oxford OX1 2HL England
44-1865–512814 (H)

Chagas, Dr. Carlos II 1968
Professor Emeritus
Federal University of Rio de Janeiro (UFRJ)
Instituto de Biofísica
Universidade Federal do Rio de Janeiro
 (UFRJ)
Centro de Ciências de Saude
Bloco "G" Cidade Universitária
Ilha do Fundão
21040 Rio de Janeiro RJ Brazil
Home: Rua Francisco Otaviano So
Copagadana, 22080
Rio de Janeiro RJ Brazil
55-021-590-5411 (O)
55-021-227-5009 (H)
55-021-280-8193 (F)

Cipolla, Dr. Carlo Manlio III 1981
Professor Emeritus
Scuola Normale Superiore, Pisa
University of California
Berkeley, CA

Cox, Sir David I 1990
Former Warden, Honorary Fellow
Nuffield College
Oxford OX1 1NF England
44-1865-278690 (O)
44-1865-278621 (F)
david.cox@nuf.ox.ac.uk (E)

Crick, Prof. Francis H. C.   II 1972
Distinguished Research Professor
The Salk Institute for Biological Studies
10010 N. Torrey Pines Road
La Jolla, CA 92037
(619)453-4100 (O)
(619)550-9959 (F)

Crozier, M. Michel   III 1975
Founder and Director
Center for the Sociology of Organizations
19 rue Amélie
75007 Paris France
45–75005 (O)

Dahrendorf, Lord Ralf   III 1977
Professor of Social Science
St. Anthony's College
Bankgesellschaft Berlin (UK) plc
1 Crown Court, Cheapside
London EC2V 6JP England
44 0171-572-6700 (O)
44 0171-572-6799 (F)

de Duve, Dr. Christian   II 1991
Emeritus Professor
Catholic University of Louvain
Belgium
Andrew W. Mellon Professor
The Rockefeller University
1230 York Avenue
New York, NY 10021-6399
(212)327-8149 or 32-2-762-3292 (O)
(212)724-8048 or 32-10-866628 (H)
(212)327-7974 or 32-2-764-7573 (F)

Devonshire, The Duke of   V 1996
Chatsworth
Bakewell
Derbyshire DE45 1PP England
44-01246–582204 (H)
44-01246–582937 (F)

Dunitz, Dr. Jack David   I 1997
Professor Emeritus
Swiss Federal Institute of Technology
Organic Chemistry Laboratory
ETH-Zentrum
CH-8092 Zürich Switzerland
411-632-2892 (O)
411-632-1109 (F)
dunitz@org.chem.ethz.ch (E)

Edzard, Dr. Dietz Otto   IV 1996
Professor
University of München
Institut für Assyriologie und Hethitologie
Geschwister Scholl-Platz
80539 München Germany
011-49-89-2180-3553 (O)
011-49-89-2180-2322 (F)

Eigen, Prof. Manfred   I 1968
Former Director
Professor Emeritus
Max Planck Institute for Biophysical
  Chemistry
Am Fassberg
37077 Göttingen Germany
49-551-201-1432 (O)
49-551-541146 (H)
49-551-201-1435 (F)

Eisenstadt, Dr. Shmuel   III 1973
Professor Emeritus
The Hebrew University of Jerusalem
c/o The Van Leer Jerusalem Institute
POB 4070
Jerusalem 91040 Israel
Home: 30 Radak Street
Jerusalem Israel
972-2-5605222 (O)
972-2-5619293 (F)

Esaki, Dr. Leo   I 1991
Office for Chairman
Tsukuba Convention Center
2-20-3 Takesono
Tsukuba
Ibaraki 305-0032 Japan
81-298-61-1200 (O)
81-298-61-1209 (F)
leoesaki@xb3.so-net.ne.jp (E)

Evans, Dr. John R.   V 1999
President Emeritus
University of Toronto
Chairman
Torstar Corporation
One Yonge Street
Toronto, Ontario M5E 1P6
Canada
(416)869-4015 (O)
(416)869-4802 (F)
jevans@thestar.ca (E)

Firth, Sir Raymond William   III 1965
Professor of Anthropology, Emeritus
University of London
Home: 33 Southwood Avenue
Highgate
London N6 5SA
England

Fischer, Dr. Wolfram   III 1995
Professor of Economic and Social History
   Emeritus
Freie Universität of Berlin
Hittorfstr. 2-4
D-14195 Berlin Germany
49-30-8383620 (O)
49-30-8311715 (H)
49-30-8382140 (O)(F)
49-30-84108138 (H)(F)
LS-Fischer@wiwiss.fu-berlin.de (E)

Frängsmyr, Dr. Tore   IV 1999
Research Professor in History of Science
History of Science Department
Box 256, SE-75105
Uppsala University
Uppsala Sweden
46-18-4711579 (O)
46-18-524795 (H)
46-18-108046 (F)
tore.frangsmyr@idehist.uu.se (E)

Fumaroli, Dr. Marc   IV 1997
Professor
Collége de France
11 place Marcelin-Berthelot
75231 Paris Cedex 05 France
011-33-1-44271109 (F)

Garin, Prof. Eugenio   IV 1972
President
Istituto Nazionale di Studi sul
   Rinascimento
Palazzo Strozzi
Piazza Strozzi, 50123
Florence
Home: 6 via Francesco Crispi
50129 Florence
Italy

Gol'danskii, Dr. Vitalii I.   I 1989
Director Emeritus
Advisor of Chemical Physics
Academy of Sciences of the U.S.S.R.
Ulitsa Kosygina 4
117334 Moscow V-334 Russia
007-095-137-35-45,939-72-02 (O)
007-095-137-34-50,135-11-36 (H)
007-095-938-2156 (F)
vig@chph.rc.ac.ru (E)

Gombrich, Sir Ernst H.   IV 1968
Professor Emeritus
The Warburg Institute
University of London
Home: 19 Briardale Gardens
London NW3 7PN England
44-0171-435-6639 (H)

Goodall, Dr. Jane   II 1988
Director
Gombe Stream Research Centre
Tanzania
Home: The Jane Goodall Institute
P.O. Box 14890
Silver Spring, MD 20911-4890
(301)565-0086 (O)
(301)565-3188 (F)

Grunberg-Manago, Dr. Marianne
     II 1992
Director of Research
Head Biochemistry Division
Institut de Biologie Physico-Chimique
Service de Biochimie
13, rue Pierre et Marie Curie
75005 Paris France
33-1-43-25-26-09 (O)
33-1-43-22-36-76 (H)
33-1-40-46-83-31 (F)

Gurdon, Sir John Bertrand   II 1983
Chairman
Wellcome CRC Institute
Tennis Court Road
Cambridge CB2 1QR England
Home: The Master's Lodge
Magdalene College
Cambridge CB3 0AG England
44-01223-332154 (O)
44-01223-332154 (H)
44-01223-363637 (F)

Habakkuk, Sir John   III 1966
All Souls College
Oxford OX1 4AL England
Home: 28 Cunliffe Close
Oxford OX2 7BL England
44-01865-279379 (O)
44-01865-556583 (H)
44-01865-279299 (F)

Hamilton, Dr. William D.   II 1999
Royal Society Research Professor
Zoology Department
South Parks Road
Oxford University
Oxford OX1 3PS England
Home: 28 Wytham Village
Oxford OX2 8QA England
44-01865-271210 (O)
44-01865-722981 (H)

Haskell, Prof. Francis   IV 1994
Professor Emeritus of the History of Art
Oxford University
Trinity College
Oxford OX1 3BH England
44-1865-278290 (O)
44-1865-515627 (H)
44-1865-316730 (F)

Havel, Pres. Václav   V 1995
President of Czech Republic
Kancelár prezidenta republiky
11908 Praha-Hradcany
Czech Republic

Hawking, Dr. Stephen William I 1984
Lucasian Professor of Mathematics
Silver Street
University of Cambridge
Cambridge CB3 9EW England
44-0223-351645 (O)
44-0223-351905 (H)

Hawkins, Dr. John David IV 1998
Professor of Ancient Anatolian Languages
School of Oriental and African Studies
University of London
London WC1H OXG England
44-0171-323-6291 (O)
44-0171-734-5409 (H)
44-0171-436-3844 (F)

Hölldobler, Dr. Bert II 1997
Professor of Zoology (Ordinarius)
Biozentrum of the University of Würzburg
Biozentrum, Zoologie II
Am Hubland
D-97074 Würzburg Germany
49-931-888-4307/8 (O)
49-931-467496 (H)
49-931-888-4309 (F)
bertholl@biozentrum.uni-wuerzburg.de (E)

Hoyle, Sir Fred I 1980
Former Plumian Professor of Astronomy
    and Experimental Philosophy
University of Cambridge
Home: 102 Admirals Walk
West Cliff Road
Bournemouth, Dorset BH2 5HF
England
44-0202–299550 (F)

Huber, Prof. Dr. Franz II 1986
Professor Emeritus
Max-Planck-Institute for Behavioral
    Physiology
D-82319, Seewiesen Germany
Home: Watzmannstr 16 D 82319
Starnberg Germany
49-08157–932335 (O)
49-08151–15630 (H)
49-08157–932209 (F)
huber@mpi-seewiesen.mpg.de (E)

Hulst, Dr. H. C. van de I 1960
Professor of Theoretical Astronomy,
    Emeritus
Huygens Observatory
Sterrewacht
P. O. Box 9513
2300 RA Leiden The Netherlands
31-071-5275834 (O)
31-071-131192 (H)
31-071-5275819 (F)

Hunger, Dr. Herbert IV 1980
Professor Emeritus
University of Vienna
Österreichische Akademie der
    Wissenschaften
A 1010 Vienna
Dr. Ignaz-Seipel-Platz 2
Austria
Home: Weissgerberlände 40
A1030 Vienna Austria
43-0222/51581/544 (O)
43-0222/7132662 (H)

Hunger, Prof. Hermann IV 1995
Associate Professor
University of Vienna
Institut für Orientalistik der Universität
    Wien
Universität Wien
Universitätsstrasse 7/V
A-1010 Wien I Austria
43-1-40103-2594 (O)
43-1-972-3622 (H)
43-1-402-0533 (F)
hermann.hunger@univie.ac.at (E)

Hutchison, Dr. W. Bruce V 1978
Editorial Director
Vancouver Sun
2250 Granville Street
Vancouver V6H 3G2 Canada
Home: 810 Rogers Avenue
Victoria, B.C. Canada

Huxley, Sir Andrew F.   II 1975
Former Master of Trinity College
Cambridge, CB2 1TQ England
Physiological Laboratory
University of Cambridge
Downing Street
Cambridge, CB2 3EG England
Home: Manor Field
1 Vicarage Drive
Grantchester
Cambridge CB3 9NG England
44-1223-338586 (O)
44-1223-840207 (H)
44-1223-840207 (F)

Inose, Dr. Hiroshi   I 1979
Director General
National Center for Science Information
   Systems
29–1 Otsuka 3-chome
Bunkyo-ku, Tokyo 112 Japan
Home: 39–9 Jingumae 5-chome
Shibuya-Ku, Tokyo 150 Japan
03-81-03-3942-6901 (O)
03-81-03-5468-7123 (H)
03-81-03-3942-6900 (F)

Ivanov, Dr. Vyacheslav V.   IV 1994
Professor
Slavic Languages and Literatures
University of California
Slavic Department
115 Kinsey Hall
Box 951502
Los Angeles, CA 90095-1502
(310)825-2676 (O)
(310)440-9081 (H)
(310)472-9434 (F)
ivanov@ucla.edu (E)

Jacob, Prof. François   II 1969
Professor Emeritus
Collège de France and Institut Pasteur
Départment de Biologie moléculaire
Institut Pasteur
25 rue du Docteur Roux
75724 Paris Cedex 15 France
(33 1) 45 68 84 87 (O)
(33 1) 40 61 31 16 (F)
fjacob@pasteur.fr (E)

Jermy, Dr. Tibor   II 1990
Director Emeritus
Plant Protection Institute
Hungarian Academy of Sciences
P.O. Box 102
Budapest H-1525 Hungary
Home: Pasaréti ut 66/a
Budapest H-1026 Hungary
(36)-1-176-9555 (O)
(36)-1-176-9729 (F)
h2370sze@ella.hu (E)

Jones, Dr. Alexander   IV 1998
Professor, Department of Classics
97 St. George Street
University of Toronto
Toronto, Ontario M5S 2E8 Canada
(416)978-0483 (O)
ajones@chass.utoronto.ca (E)

Jortner, Prof. Joshua   I 1990
Heinemann Professor of Chemistry
Tel-Aviv University
School of Chemistry
Campus Ramat Aviv, Tel-Aviv 69978
Israel
010-972-03-6408322 (O)
010-972-03-6955848 (H)
010-972-03-6415054 (F)
jortner@chemsg1.tau.ac.il (E)

Juan Carlos I, King of Spain   V 1992
c/o Excmo Sr. D. Sabino Fernandez Campo
El Jefe de la Casa de S.M. El Rey
Palacio de la Zarzuela
28071 Madrid Spain

Katchalski-Katzir, Prof. Ephraim
                                    II 1976
Former President of the State of Israel
Institute Professor
Department of Biological Chemistry
The Weizmann Institute of Science
P.O. Box 26
Rehovot 76100 Israel
972-8-9343947 (O)
972-8-9343525 (H)
972-8-9468256 (F)
bfkatzir@weizmann.weizmann.ac.il (E)

Kenny, Sir Anthony   V 1993
Warden
Rhodes House
Oxford
Secretary to the Rhodes Trust
Administrator for Rhodes Scholars
Oxford
Chairman of the Board
British Library
Rhodes House
Oxford OX1 3RG United Kingdom
44-865–270902 (O)
44-865–270914 (F)

Keynes, Dr. Richard Darwin   II 1977
Emeritus Professor
Physiological Laboratory
University of Cambridge
Downing Street
Cambridge CB2 3EG England
Home: 4 Herschel Road
Cambridge CB3 9AG England
44-1223-333840 (O)
44-1223-353107 (H)
44-1223-333840 (F)

Klein, Dr. George   II 1979
Head, Department of Tumor Biology
Microbiology and Tumorbiology Center
Karolinska Institutet
Box 280, 171 77
Stockholm Sweden
46-08-339877 (O)
46-8-7662001 (H)
46-8-330498 (F)

de Klerk, Mr. Frederik Willem V 1994
Deputy President South Africa
Leader, National Party
Private Bag X999
Cape Town 8000 South Africa
27-021-4014111 (O)
27-021-461-5877 (F)

Klug, Sir Aaron   II 1996
Director
Medical Research Council
MRC Laboratory of Molecular Biology
Hills Road
Cambridge, CB2 2QH England
44-1223-248011 (O)
44-1223-248959 (H)
44-1223-412231 (F)

Kornberg, Sir Hans   V 1993
University Professor
Professor of Biology
Boston University
Sir William Dunn Professor of Biochemistry
University of Cambridge
Master of Christ's College
Home: 134 Sewall Avenue, #2
Brookline, MA 02146
(617)353-4020 (O)
(617)739-6103 (H)
(617)353-5084 (O)(F)
(617)738-3378 (H)(F)
hlk@acs.bu.edu (E)

Landon, Mr. H. C. Robbins   V 1991
John Bird Professor of Music (retired)
University of Wales
Cardiff, Foncoussières, Rabastens
F-81800, Tarn France
33 5 63 40 61 45 (O)
33 5 63 33 76 36 (F)

Leclant, Prof. Jean   IV 1999
Professor Emeritus
Collège de France
Secrétaire Perpétuel Académie des
   Inscription et Belles Letteres
23 Quai de Conti
Palais de L'Institut de France
Paris 75006 France
01-44-41-43-10 (O), 01-43-26-96-75 (H)
01-44-41-43-11 (F)

Lee, Dr. Ho-Wang   II 1998
Director
Asan Institute for Life Sciences
388–1 Poongnap-dong, Songpa-ku
Seoul 138–736 Korea

Lehn, Dr. Jean-Marie Pierre   I 1987
Professor, Collège de France
11 Place Marcelin-Berthelot
75005 Paris France
Institut de Chimie
Université Louis Pasteur
1 rue Blaise Pascal
67000 Strasbourg France
33–44271360 (O), 33–88416056 (O)
33–44271356 (F), 33–88411020 (F)
lehn@chimie.u_strasbg.fr (E)

Leprince-Ringuet, Prof. Louis   I 1967
Former Professor of Nuclear Physics
Collège de France
Former Commissioner of Atomic Energy
Home: 86 rue de Grenelle
75007 Paris France
33-1-43-54-04-45 (O)

Le Rider, Dr. Georges Charles IV 1996
Professeur Au Collège de France
Membre de l'Institut de France
Collège de France
11 Place Marcelin Berthelot, F. 75231
Paris Cedex 05 France
33-1-4427-1269 (O)
33-1-4374-2988 (H)
33-1-4427-1019 (F)

Le Roy Ladurie, Prof. Emmanuel
   IV 1979
Professeur au Collège de France
Former Administrator General
Home: 88 rue d' Alleray
75015 Paris France
01-44-27-10-38 (O)
01-48-42-01-27 (H)
01-44-27-12-60 (F)

Lévi-Strauss, Prof. Claude   III 1960
Professor Emeritus
Lab d'Anthropologie Sociale
Collège de France
52 rue du Cardinal Lemoine
75005 Paris France
(19)44 27 17 31 (O)
(19)44 27 17 66 (F)

Levine, Dr. Raphael David   I 1996
Max Born Professor of Natural Philosophy
Department of Physical Chemistry
The Hebrew University
Jerusalem 91904 Israel
(972–2)6585260 (O)
(972–2)5637181 (H)
(972–2)6513742 (O)(F)
(972–2)5618721 (H)(F)
rafi@fh.huji.acil (E)

Lewis, Prof. Lord, of Newnham I 1994
Warden of Robinson College
Professor Emeritus
Robinson College
Grange Road
University of Cambridge
Cambridge, CB3 9AN England
011-44-1223-339120 (O)
011-44-1223-339962 (F)

Likhachev, Dr. Dmitri S.   IV 1992
Academician
Russian Academy of Sciences
Pushkin House
Enbankment Makaroff 4
St. Petersburg Russia
Home: Prospekt Svernika 34
16 St. Petersburg K-21 Russia
7-218-12-74 (O), 7-247-18-63 (H)

Lindauer, Prof. Martin   II 1976
Professor Emeritus
Theodor Boven-Institut
Zoölogisches Institut
Am Hübland
D-97074 Würzburg Germany
Home: Friesplatz 8, D-8000
Munchen 82 Germany
49-0931-888-4306 (O)
49-089-439-3473 (H)
49-0931-888-9309 (F)

Lovell, Sir Bernard   I 1974
Professor of Radio Astronomy, Emeritus
Former Director of the Experimental
  Station
University of Manchester
Nuffield Radio Astronomy Lab.
Jodrell Bank
Macclesfield, Cheshire SK11 9DN
England
Home: The Quinta
Swettenham, Nr. Congleton
Cheshire CW12 2LD England
44-01477-571321 (O)
44-01477-71254 (H)
44-01477–571618 (F)
je@ib.man.ac.uk (E)

Löwdin, Dr. Per-Olov   I 1983
Professor Emeritus
Uppsala University
Box 518, S-75120
Uppsala Sweden
Home: Quantum Theory Project
362 Williams Hall
University of Florida
Gainesville, FL 32611
46-18-517661 (O)
(904)392-6976 (O) (FL)
46-18-117159 (H)
46-18-502402 (F)
lowdin@dirac.kvac.uu.se (E)

Lundqvist, Dr. Stig   I 1985
Professor Emeritus
Chalmers University of Technology
Institute of Theoretical Physics
412 96 Göteborg Sweden
Home: Lövviksvägen 21
S-43655 Hovås Sweden
0-31-723196 (O)
0-31-282611 (H)
0-31-416984 (F)

Lüst, Dr. Reimar   I 1999
Professor Emeritus and Former President
Max Planck Society
Professor
University of Hamburg
Alexander von Humboldt Institute
Max Planck Institute for Meteorology
Bundesstrasse 15
D-20146 Hamburg Germany
49-40-41173-300 (O)
49-40-279-85-14 (H)
49-40-41173-390 (F)
luest@dkrz.de (E)

McLaren, Dr. Digby J.   I 1994
Past President
Royal Society of Canada
Past Director General
Geological Survey of Canada
Home: 670 420 Mackay Street
Ottawa
Ontario K1M 2C4 Canada
(613)742-3067 (H)

Maffei, Dr. Domenico   IV 1986
Professor Emeritus
University of Rome "La Sapienza."
Home: Via delle Cerchia, 19
53100 Siena Italy
39-577-45296 (H)

Mandela, Pres. Nelson R.   V 1994
Office of the President
Private Bag X83
Pretoria
South Africa 0001
27-012-326-2719 (F)

Mayer, Prof. Hans Eberhard   IV 1978
Professor Emeritus
University of Kiel
Historisches Seminar der Universität
D-24098 Kiel Germany
011-49-431-790728 (H)

Mayrhofer, Prof., Dr. Manfred
                IV 1992
Professor Emeritus
University of Vienna
A-1190 Wien
Bauernfeldgasse 9/2/6 Austria
43-0222–362500 (H)

Milsom, Dr. Stroud F. C.   III 1984
Fellow of St. John's College
Emeritus Professor of Law
Cambridge University England

Mitchell, Dr. Thomas Noel   V 1996
Provost
Trinity College
Provost's Office
Dublin 2 Ireland
3531-608-1558 (O)
3531-846-1492 (H)
3531-608-2303 (F)
provost@tcd.ie (E)

Mori, Dr. Wataru   V 1998
President
Japanese Association of Medical Sciences
2-28-16 Honkomagome
Bunkyo-ku, Tokyo (113-8621)
Japan
81-3-3946-2121 (O)
81-3-3941-5494 (H)
81-3-3946-6295 (F)
wmori@po.med.or.jp (E)

Morpurgo Davies, Dr. Anna   IV 1991
Professor of Comparative Philology
University of Oxford
England
Home: Sommerville College
Oxford OX2 6HD
England
44-1865-270690 (O)
44-1865-270620 (F)
anna.davies@some.ox.ac.uk (E)

Muti, Mr. Riccardo   V 1989
Laureate Conductor
The Philadelphia Orchestra
Music Director
La Scala
Home: 1420 Locust Street
Suite 400
Philadelphia, PA 19102
(215)893-1911 (O)
(215)893-1911 (H)

Nakane, Prof. Chie   III 1977
Professor of Social Anthropology Emeritus
The University of Tokyo
Hongo, Bunkyo-ku Tokyo
Japan
Home: 1404 Takanawa 4-24-55
Minato-ku Tokyo 108 Japan
81-03-3473-4321 (H)

Nicolaisen, Ms. A. Ida Benedicte
                                III 1999
Senior Research Fellow
Nordic Institute of Asian Studies
Borg'mester Godskesens Plads 4
2000 F. Denmark
(45)32-54-88-44 (O)
(45)32-96-25-30 (F)
nicolaisen@nias.ku.dk (E)

Nusslein-Volhard, Dr. Christiane
                                II 1995
Managing Director
Max-Planck-Institute für
  Entwicklungsbiologie
Abt. III (Genetik)
Spemannstr. 35
72076 Tübingen Germany
49-7071-601487 (O)
49-7071-601384 (F)
christiane.nuesslein-
  volhard.tuebingen.mpg.de (E)

Obolensky, Sir Dimitri   IV 1990
Professor Emeritus
Oxford University
Home: 29 Belsyre Court
Woodstock Road
Oxford OX2 6HU England
011-44-0865-56496 (H)

Odhiambo, Prof. Thomas R.   V 1992
Chief Executive Officer
The Industrial Technology and Engineering
  Trust (ITET)
P.O. Box 59900
Nairobi Kenya
254-2-571944 (O), 254-2-566383 (H)
254-2-884406 (F), 254-2-573029 (F)

Ogata, Dr. Sadako   V 1995
United Nations High Commissioner for
  Refugees
United Nations
Case postale 2500
Ch-1211 Geneva 2 Dépöt Switzerland
41-22-739-8100 (O)

Perrot, Mr. Jean J. F.   IV 1991
Honorary Director of Research C.N.R.S.
Home: 2, rue Emile Faguet
75014, Paris France
331-4545-0269 (H), 331-4540-4706 (H)
331-4541-0018 (F)

Perutz, Dr. Max Ferdinand   I 1968
Former Chairman
Medical Research Council Laboratory of
  Molecular Biology
Cambridge
Home: 42 Sedley Taylor Road
Cambridge, CB2 2PN England
44-01223-248011(O),44-01223-246041(H)
44-01223-213556 (F)

Peters, Sir (David) Keith　　II 1999
Regius Professor of Physic
School of Clinical Medicine
Addenbrooke's Hospital
University of Cambridge
Cambridge, CB2 2SP England
44-1223-336738 (O)
44-1223-336721 (F)
44-1223-356117 (H)
dkpl000@medschl.cam.ac.uk

Porter, Prof., Lord (George)　　I 1986
Chairman
Centre for Photomolecular Sciences
Departments of Chemistry and
　Biochemistry
Imperial College
London SW7 2AY England
44-0171-594-5786 (O)
44-0171-594-5812 (F)
g.porter@ic.ac.uk (E)

Rabin, Dr. Michael, O.　　I 1988
Professor of Computer Science
The Hebrew University of Jerusalem and
　Harvard University
Home: Aiken Computation Laboratory
Harvard University
Cambridge, MA 02138
(617)496-6294 (O)
(617)497-4006 (H)

Rao, Dr. C.N.R.　　I 1995
Albert-Einstein Research Professor
　and President
Chemistry & Physics of Materials Unit
Jawaharlal Nehru Centre for Advanced
　Scientific Research
Jakkur P.O.
Bangalore—560 064 India
91-80-8462761 (O)
91-80-8462750 (O)
91-80-3369410 (H)
91-80-8462766 (F)
cnrrao@jncasr.ac.in (E)

Rees, Sir Martin　　I 1993
Royal Society Research Professor
Cambridge University
Institute of Astronomy
Madingley Road
Cambridge, CB3 OHA England
44-223-337548 (O)
44-223-208948 (H)
44-223-337523 (F)

Regge, Dr. Tullio Eugene　　I 1982
Dipartimento di Fisica
Politecnico di Torino
Corso Duca degli Abruzzi, 24
10129 Torino Italy
39-011-564-73-52 (O)
39-011-660-32-75 (H)

de Riquer, Prof. Martin　　IV 1975
Professor of Romanic Literatures
Barcelona University
Home: Rosario 22–24
08017 Barcelona 17 Spain
34-3102349 (O)
34-2042485 (H)

Robertson, Sir Rutherford　　II 1971
Professor Emeritus & Former Director
Research School of Biological Sciences
Australian National University
Home: Unit 12
Linton Retirement Village
Glebe Street
Yass, NSW 2582 Australia
61-06-226-3093 (H)

Robinson, Hon. Mary　　V 1999
United Nations High Commissioner for
　Human Rights
Former President of Ireland
United Nations, Palais des Nations
CH-1211 Geneva 10 Switzerland
41 22 917 9240 (O)
41 22 917 9012 (F)
secrt.hchr@unog.ch (E)

de Romilly, Prof. Jacqueline   IV 1978
Professor Emeritus, Collège de France
Member Académie Française and Académie
  des Inscriptions et Belles Lettres
Home: 12 rue Chernoviz
75016 Paris France
33-01-42-24-59-07 (H)

Rosenberg, Dr. Pierre   IV 1997
President and Director
Musée du Louvre
39/36 Quai du Louvre
75038 Paris Cedex 01 France
33-01-40-20-50-09 (O)
33-01-40-20-54-42 (F)

Runciman, Hon. Sir Steven   IV 1965
Honorary Fellow
Trinity College
University of Cambridge
Home: Elshieshields, Lockerbie
Dumfriesshire DG11 1LY Scotland
44-01387-810280 (H)

Scarman, Lord Leslie George   V 1983
Former Lord of Appeal
House of Lords
Westminster
Home: 12 Monkton Manor
Monkton, Ramsgate
Kent CT12 4JT England
44-1843-822-455 (H)

Schäfer, Dr. Peter   IV 1997
Ronald O. Perelman Professor of Jewish
  Studies
Institut für Judaistik
Freie Universität Berlin
Department of Religion
Princeton University
Princeton, NJ 08540
(609)258-6008 (O)
49-30-838 5579 (F)
pschafer@zedat.fu-berlin.de (E)

Schweitzer, Dr. Pierre-Paul   III 1972
Honorary Inspector-General of Finances
France
Home: Route De Mon Idée 170
1253 Vandoeuvres Switzerland
41-22-750-1313 (H)

Sciama, Dr. Dennis W.   I 1980
Professor of Astrophysics
International School for Advanced Studies
Strada Costiera 11
34014 Trieste Italy
39-040-3787-475 (O)
39-040-3787-528 (F)
sciama@neumann.sissa.it (E)

Sela, Dr. Michael   II 1995
Institute Professor
Deputy Chairman Board of Governors
Department of Immunology
The Weizmann Institute of Science
Rehovot 76100 Israel
972-89-9466969 (O)
972-89-9471132 (H)
972-89-9468713 (F)
lisela@weizmann.weizmann.ac.il (E)

Serre, Dr. Jean-Pierre   I 1998
Professor Emeritus, Collège de France
3 rue d'Ulm
F-75005 Paris France
(33) 1 44271705 (O)
(33) 1 45533563 (H)
(33) 1 44271704 (F)
serre@dmi.ens.fr (E)

Skinner, Dr. Quentin R. D.   III 1997
Regius Professor of Modern History
University of Cambridge
Christ's College
Cambridge CB2 3BU England
44-01223-334974 (O)
44-01223-339557 (F)

Smith, Prof. John Maynard   II 1980
Professor of Biology
University of Sussex
Biology Building
Falmer, Brighton
Sussex BN1 9QG England
44-01273-606-755 (O)
44-01273-474-659 (H)

Spirin, Dr. Alexander S.   II 1997
Professor of Biochemistry and Molecular
   Biology
Director, Institute for Protein Research
Russian Academy of Sciences
142292 Pushchino
Moscow Region Russia
7(095)924-0493 (O)
7(095)137-3920 (H)
7(095)924-0493 (F)
spirin@sun.ipr.serpukhov.su (E)

Srinivas, Dr. Mysore N.   III 1974
J.R.D. Tata Visiting Professor
National Institute of Advanced Studies
Home: Arakeré
78A Benson Cross Road
Bangalore-560 046 India
91-3344351 (O), 91-5577038 (H)

Still, Dr. Carl-Otto   V 1990
President, Carl Still Corporation
Pittsburgh
Owner & Managing Director
Firma Carl Still GMBH & Co.
Home: Am Rosengarten 8
D-45657 Recklinghausen Germany
49-02361–925913 (O)
49-02361–14117 (H)
49-02361-181-444 (H)(F)
49-02361-925-917 (O)(F)

Thirsk, Dr. Joan   IV 1982
Former Reader in Economic History
University of Oxford
Home: 1 Hadlow Castle
Hadlow, Tonbridge
Kent TN11 OEG England
44-0732-850-708 (H)

Thomas, Sir John Meurig   I 1993
Professor of Chemistry
Royal Institution of Great Britain
The Master's Lodge
Peterhouse
University of Cambridge
Cambridge CB2 1QY England
44-01223–338200 (O)
44-01223–211362 (H)
44-01223–339200 (F)

Tobias, Dr. Phillip Vallentine   II 1996
Professor Emeritus
University of the Witwatersrand
Department of Anatomical Sciences
7 York Road, Parktown
Johannesburg 2193 South Africa
(027)(11) 647-2016 (O)
(027)(11)885-2748 (H)
(027)(11)643-4318 (F)
055pvts@chiron.wits.ac.za (E)

Todorov, Dr. Tzvetan   IV 1998
Directeur de recherches
CNRS
CRAL EHESS
105 Bd. Raspail
75006 Paris France
331-4548-2768 (O)
331-4549-9443 (F)

Vita-Finzi, Dr. Claudio   I 1997
Professor of Neotectonics
Department of Geological Sciences
Gower Street
University College
London WC1E 6BT England
Home: 22 South Hill Park
London NW3 2SB England
44 171 5042383 (O)
44 171 7944415 (H)
44 171 3887614 (F)
ucfbcvf@ucl.ac.uk (E)

Wehner, Dr. Rüdiger   II 1993
Full Professor
Department of Zoology
Winterthurerstrasse 190
University of Zürich
CH-8057, Zürich Switzerland
41 1 635-4831 (O)
41 1 635-5716 (F)
rwehner@zool.unizh.ch (E)

Wellesley, Arthur, The Duke
of Wellington   V 1993
Director
Massey Ferguson Holdings, Ltd.
Colonel-in-Chief
The Duke of Wellington's Regiment
Governor, Wellington College
Stratfield Saye House, Basingstoke
Hants RG27 OAS England
44-0256–882882 (O)
44-0256–882698 (F)

Wild, Dr. J. Paul   I 1962
Former Chairman and Chief Executive
Commonwealth Scientific and Industrial
   Research Organization
Home: 800 Avon Road
Ann Arbor, MI 48104
(734)663-8333 (H)
61-06-295-3473 (H) Australia
(734)761-1586 (F)

Wilson, Sir Robert   I 1996
Professor Emeritus
University College of London
Department of Physics and Astronomy
Gower Street
London WCIE 6BT England
44-0171-380-7154 (O)
44-0171-938-1373 (H)
44-0171-380-7145 (F)
rw@uk.uc.star (E)

Wright, Dr. Esmond   III 1991
Emeritus Professor of American History
University of London
Home: Radleigh House
Market Place
Masham
No. Yorks HG4 4EF England
44-071-387-5534 (O)
44-07-656-89277 (H)

Zeki, Dr. Semir   II 1998
Professor of Neurobiology
Co-Head
Wellcome Department of Cognitive
   Neurology
University College London
London WC1E 6BT England
44-171-380-7316 (O)
s.zeki@ucl.ac.uk (E)

zur Hausen, Dr. Harald   II 1998
Professor and Scientific Director
Deutsches Krebsforschungszentrum
(German Cancer Research Center)
Im Neuenheimer Feld 280
69120 Heidelberg Germany
49-6221-422850 (O)
49-6207-82286 (H)
49-6221-422840 (O)(F)
49-6207-82287 (H)(F)
zurhausen@dkfz-heidelberg.de (E)

CLASSIFIED LIST OF MEMBERS
AS OF 31 JULY 1999 *

CLASS I. MATHEMATICAL AND PHYSICAL SCIENCES

Astronomy: 25 Members

Babcock, Horace W.	Santa Barbara, CA	Neugebauer, Gerry	Pasadena, CA
Baker, James Gilbert	Cambridge, MA	Osterbrock, Donald E.	Santa Cruz, CA
Burbidge, E. Margaret	La Jolla, CA	Ostriker, Jeremiah P.	Princeton
Gingerich, Owen	Cambridge, MA	Rees, Sir Martin	Cambridge, England
Gold, Thomas	Ithaca, NY	Rubin, Vera C.	Washington, DC
Greenstein, Jesse L.	Bradbury, CA	Ruderman, Malvin	New York
Gunn, James E.	Princeton	Sandage, Allan Rex	Pasadena, CA
Heeschen, David S.	Marathon, FL	Shapiro, Irwin I.	Cambridge, MA
Hoyle, Sir Fred	Bournemouth, England	Stone, Edward C.	Pasadena, CA
Hulst, H.C. van de	Leiden, Netherlands	Whipple, Fred	Cambridge, MA
Kellermann, Kenneth I.	Charlottesville, VA	Wild, J. Paul	Ann Arbor, MI
Lovell, Sir Bernard	Macclesfield, England	Wilson, Sir Robert	London
Morrison, Philip	Cambridge, MA		

Chemistry and Chemical Biochemistry: 46 Members

Anderson, James G.	Cambridge, MA	Knowles, Jeremy R.	Cambridge, MA
Baker, William O.	Morristown, NJ	Lehn, Jean-Marie Pierre	Paris
Baldeschwieler, John D.	Pasadena, CA	Leonard, Nelson J.	Pasadena, CA
Bard, Allen J.	Austin, TX	Levine, Raphael David	Israel
Barton, Jacqueline K.	Pasadena, CA	Lewis, Lord, of Newnham	Cambridge England
Breslow, Ronald	New York		
Cotton, Frank Albert	College Station, TX	Löwdin, Per-Olov	Uppsala, Sweden
Crawford, Bryce, Jr.	Minneapolis	Marcus, Rudolph Arthur	Pasadena, CA
Drickamer, Harry G.	Urbana, IL	Meinwald, Jerrold	Ithaca, NY
Dunitz, Jack David	Switzerland	Perutz, Max Ferdinand	Cambridge England
Eigen, Manfred	Göttingen, Germany		
Fox, Marye Ann	Raleigh, NC	Porter, Lord George	London
Fruton, Joseph S.	New Haven	Rao, C.N.R.	Bangalore, India
Gol'danskii, Vitalli	Moscow	Rice, Stuart A.	Chicago
Gutowsky, H.S.	Urbana, IL	Roberts, John D.	Pasadena, CA
Hackerman, Norman	Houston	Rowland, Frank Sherwood	Irvine, CA
Herschbach, Dudley	Cambridge, MA	Stork, Gilbert	New York
Hoffmann, Roald	Ithaca, NY	Taube, Henry	Stanford
Hopfield, John J.	Princeton	Thomas, John Meurig	Cambridge, England
Hornig, Donald Frederick	Cambridge, MA	Westheimer, Frank H.	Cambridge, MA
Jortner, Joshua	Israel	Whitesides, George M.	Cambridge, MA
Kamen, Martin D.	Montecito, CA	Widom, Benjamin	Ithaca, NY
Karle, Isabella L.	Washington, DC	Zare, Richard N.	Stanford
Karle, Jerome	Washington, DC	Zewail, Ahmed H.	Pasadena, CA

* Names of members who have died since 1 January 1999 through 31 July 1999 have been removed; names of members elected April 1999 have been added.

Engineering: 17 Members

Augustine, Norman R.	Potamac, MD	Inose, Hiroshi	Tokyo
Benedict, Manson	Naples, FL	Olsen, Kenneth H.	Boxborough, MA
Carrier, George F.	Cambridge, MA	Pierce, John R.	Palo Alto
Cho, Alfred Y.	Murray Hill, NJ	Piore, Emanuel R.	New York
Cocke, John	Bedford, NY	Ramo, Simon	Los Angeles
David, Edward E., Jr.	Bedminster, NJ	Shannon, Claude	Winchester, MA
Dennard, Robert H.	New York	Sinfelt, John H.	Annandale, NJ
Dresselhaus, Mildred S.	Cambridge, MA	Tarjan, Robert E.	Princeton
Easton, Roger L.	Canaan, NH		

Mathematics: 30 Members

Arnold, Vladimir Igorevich	Moscow	Lin, Chia Chiao	Cambridge, MA
Atiyah, Sir Michael	Edinburgh, England	Mackey, George W.	Cambridge, MA
Blackwell, David	Berkeley	Mac Lane, Saunders	Chicago
Borel, Armand	Princeton	MacPherson, Robert	Princeton
Chern, Shiing-shen	El Cerrito, CA	Milnor, John W.	Stony Brook, NY
Cohen, Paul J.	Stanford	Morawetz, Cathleen Synge	New York
Cox, Sir David	Oxford, England	Mosteller, Frederick	Belmont, MA
Fefferman, Charles L.	Princeton	Mumford, David	Providence, RI
Gleason, Andrew M.	Cambridge, MA	Nirenberg, Louis	New York
Gomory, Ralph E.	New York	Rabin, Michael O.	Cambridge, MA
Griffiths, Phillip A.	Princeton	Serre, Jean-Pierre	Paris
Hawking, Stephen William		Singer, I. M.	Cambridge, MA
	Cambridge, England	Tukey, John W.	Princeton
Karlin, Samuel	Stanford	Wiles, Andrew J.	Princeton
Karp, Richard M.	Seattle, WA	Winograd, Shmuel	Yorktown Heights, NY
Lax, Peter D.	New York		

Physical Earth Sciences: 19 Members

Abelson, Philip Hauge	Washington, DC	McLaren, Digby J.	Ottawa
Allègre, Claude Jean		Munk, Walter H.	La Jolla, CA
	Place Jussieu Tour, France	Press, Frank	Washington, DC
Anderson, Don L.	Pasadena, CA	Rodgers, John	New Haven
Ernst, W. Gary	Stanford	Vita-Finzi, Claudio	London
Goody, Richard M.	Falmouth, MA	Wasserburg, Gerald J.	Pasadena, CA
Knopoff, Leon	Los Angeles	Wetherill, George W.	Washington, DC
Krauskopf, Konrad B.	Stanford	White, Robert M.	Chevy Chase, MD
Leopold, Luna B.	Berkeley	Wolman, Markley Gordon	Baltimore
MacDonald, Gordon J.	Austria	Yoder, Hatten S., Jr.	Washington, DC

Physics: 60 Members

Aigrain, Pierre Raoul Roger	Paris	Brooks, Harvey	Cambridge, MA
Anderson, Philip W.	Princeton	Casimir, Hendrik B.G.	Heeze, Netherlands
Bacher, Robert Fox	Montecito, CA	Chu, Steven	Stanford
Bethe, Hans A.	Ithaca, NY	Cooper, Leon N.	Providence, RI
Bloembergen, Nicolaas	Cambridge, MA	Cronin, James Watson	Chicago
Bohr, Aage	Copenhagen	Drell, Sidney D.	Stanford
Branscomb, Lewis M.	Cambridge, MA	Dyson, Freeman J.	Princeton

Esaki, Leo	Japan	Pines, David	Tesuque, NM
Fisher, Michael E.	College Park, MD	Ramsey, Norman F.	Cambridge, MA
Fitch, Val L.	Princeton	Regge, Tullio Eugene	Turin
Frauenfelder, Hans Emil	Tesuque, NM	Rosenbluth, Marshall N.	La Jolla, CA
Friedman, Herbert	Arlington, VA	Salpeter, Edwin E.	Ithaca, NY
Garwin, Richard L.	Yorktown Heights, NY	Schrieffer, J. Robert	Tallahassee, FL
Gell-Mann, Murray	Santa Fe, NM	Sciama, D.W.	Trieste
Goldberger, Marvin L.	La Jolla, CA	Seitz, Frederick, Jr.	New York
Goldhaber, Maurice	Upton, NY	Simpson, John Alexander	Chicago
Halperin, Bertrand I.	Cambridge, MA	Slichter, Charles	Urbana, IL
Happer, William	Princeton	Taylor, Joseph Hooten, Jr.	Princeton
Kadanoff, Leo P.	Chicago	Thorne, Kip S.	Pasadena, CA
Kohn, Walter	Santa Barbara, CA	Townes, Charles H.	Berkeley
Lederman, Leon	Batavia, IL	Treiman, Sam Bard	Princeton
Lee, Tsung-Dao	New York	Van Allen, James A.	Iowa City, IA
Leggett, Anthony J.	Urbana, IL	Weinberg, Alvin M.	Oak Ridge, TN
Leprince-Ringuet, Louis	Paris	Weinberg, Steven	Austin, TX
Lundqvist, Stig	Göteborg, Sweden	Weisskopf, Victor F.	Newton, MA
Lüst, Reimar	Bonn, Germany	Wheeler, John A.	Princeton
Nierenberg, William Aaron	San Diego, CA	Wilson, Kenneth G.	Columbus, OH
O'Brien, Brian	Woodstock, CT	Wilson, Robert R.	Ithaca, NY
Pais, Abraham	New York	Witten, Edward	Princeton
Panofsky, Wolfgang K. H.		Yang, Chen Ning	Stony Brook, NY
	Los Altos Hills, CA		

CLASS II. BIOLOGICAL SCIENCES

Molecular Biology and Biochemistry: 45 Members

Abeles, Robert Heinz	Waltham, MA	Kennedy, Eugene Patrick	Cambridge, MA
Adler, Julius	Madison, WI	Khorana, Har G.	Cambridge, MA
Alberts, Bruce	Washington, DC	Klug, Sir Aaron	Cambridge, England
Altman, Sidney	New Haven	Kornberg, Arthur	Stanford
Baltimore, David	Pasadena, CA	Koshland, Daniel E., Jr.	Berkeley
Berg, Paul	Stanford	Lardy, Henry Arnold	Madison, WI
Bergström, Sune	Stockholm	Levi-Montalcini, Rita	Rome
Bishop, J. Michael	San Francisco	Meselson, Matthew	Cambridge, MA
Bloch, Konrad E.	Cambridge, MA	Nathans, Daniel	Baltimore
Boyer, Paul D.	Los Angeles	Neufeld, Elizabeth F.	Los Angeles
Brown, Michael S.	Dallas	Rich, Alexander	Cambridge, MA
Burris, Robert H.	Madison, WI	Richards, Frederic M.	Guilford, CT
Chance, Britton	Philadelphia	Schimmel, Paul	La Jolla, CA
Cohn, Mildred	Philadelphia	Singer, Maxine F.	Washington, DC
Doolittle, Russell F.	La Jolla, CA	Smith, Emil L.	Los Angeles
Doty, Paul Mead	Cambridge, MA	Spirin, Alexander S.	Moscow
Edsall, John T.	Cambridge, MA	Steitz, Joan A.	New Haven
Glaser, Donald A.	Berkeley	Strominger, Jack L.	Cambridge, MA
Grunberg-Manago, Marianne	Paris	Talalay, Paul	Baltimore
Harrison, Stephen Coplan	Cambridge, MA	Watson, James D.	Cold Spring Harbor, NY
Jacob, François	Paris	Wiley, Don Craig	Cambridge, MA
Jencks, William P.	Waltham, MA	Witkop, Bernhard	Chevy Chase, MD
Katchalski-Katzir, Ephraim			
	Ramat Aviv, Israel		

Cellular and Developmental Biology: 10 Members

Blobel, Günter	New York	Ebert, James David	Baltimore
Bogorad, Lawrence	Cambridge, MA	Gurdon, John	Cambridge, England
Bonner, John T.	Princeton	Nusslein-Volhard, Christiane	
Brown, Donald David	Baltimore		Tübingen, Germany
Dulbecco, Renato	San Diego, CA	Russell, Elizabeth S.	Mt. Desert, ME
de Duve, Christian	New York		

Evolution and Ecology, Systematics, Population Genetics, Paleontology, and Physical Anthropology: 24 Members

Ayala, Francisco	Irvine, CA	Lubchenco, Jane	Corvallis, OR
Cairns, John	Blacksburg, VA	Mayr, Ernst	Cambridge, MA
Diamond, Jared M.	Los Angeles	Mooney, Harold A.	Stanford
Ehrlich, Paul R.	Stanford	Newell, Norman	New York
Eisner, Thomas	Ithaca, NY	Patrick, Ruth	Philadelphia
Grant, Peter R.	Princeton	Schopf, J. William	Los Angeles
Hamilton, William D.	Oxford, England	Simons, Elwyn LaVerne	Durham, NC
Hardin, Garrett	Santa Barbara, CA	Smith, John Maynard	Brighton, England
Haskins, Caryl P.	Washington, DC	Stebbins, George L.	Davis, CA
Howell, F. Clark	Berkeley	Tobias, Phillip Vallentine	South Africa
Knoll, Andrew H.	Cambridge, MA	Wake, David B.	Berkeley
Lovejoy, Thomas E.	Washington, DC	Wilson, Edward O.	Cambridge, MA

Medicine, Surgery, Pathology, and Immunology: 17 Members

Austrian, Robert	Philadelphia	Moore, Francis D.	Westwood, MA
Barker, Clyde Frederick	Philadelphia	Nathan, David G.	Boston, MA
Bearn, Alexander G.	Philadelphia	Nowell, Peter Carey	Philadelphia
Bing, Richard John	La Canada, CA	Peters, Sir (David) Keith	
Blumberg, Baruch S.	Philadelphia, PA		Cambridge, England
Booth, Sir Christopher	London	Rhoads, Jonathan E.	Philadelphia
Folkman, Judah	Boston, MA	Robbins, Frederick C.	Cleveland, OH
Fredrickson, Donald S.	Bethesda, MD	Sela, Michael	Rehovot, Israel
Loeb, John Nichols	New York	Starzl, Thomas E.	Pittsburgh

Microbiology, including Bacteriology, Virology, and Protozoology: 9 Members

Choppin, Purnell W.	Chevy Chase, MD	Prusiner, Stanley B.	San Francisco
Hilleman, Maurice Ralph	West Point, PA	Varmus, Harold	Bethesda, MD
Kilbourne, Edwin D.	Madison, CT	Vogt, Peter K.	Los Angeles
Lee, Ho-Wang	Seoul, Korea	zur Hausen, Harald	Heidelberg, Germany
McCarty, Maclyn	New York		

Physiology, Biophysics, and Pharmacology: 2 Members

Huxley, Sir Andrew F.	Cambridge, England	Keynes, Richard D.	Cambridge, England

Genetics: 18 Members

Bodmer, Walter F.	Oxford, England	Lewis, Edward B.	Pasadena, CA
Brenner, Sydney	Berkeley	McKusick, Victor Almon	Baltimore
Crow, James	Madison, WI	Mintz, Beatrice	Philadelphia
Gall, Joseph Grafton	Baltimore	Neel, James Van Gundia	Ann Arbor, MI
Glass, H. Bentley	Boulder, CO	Owen, Ray	Pasadena, CA
Goldstein, Joseph L.	Dallas	Rowley, Janet D.	Chicago
Kelly, Thomas J.	Baltimore	Sharp, Phillip A.	Cambridge, MA
Knudson, Alfred G.	Philadelphia	Vogelstein, Bert	Baltimore
Lederberg, Joshua	New York	Wieschaus, Eric F.	Princeton

Plant Sciences: 5 Members

Baker, Herbert	Berkeley	Raven, Peter	St. Louis
Jermy, Tibor	Budapest, Hungary	Robertson, Sir Rutherford	
Meyerowitz, Elliot M.	Pasadena, CA		Binalong, Australia

Neurobiology: 29 Members

Axelrod, Julius	Bethesda, MD	Kandel, Eric R.	New York
Benzer, Seymour	Pasadena, CA	Kennedy, Donald	Stanford
Bloom, Floyd	La Jolla, CA	Kety, Seymour S.	Westwood, MA
Bullock, Theodore H.	La Jolla, CA	Llinás, Rodolfo R.	New York
Chagas, Carlos	Rio de Janeiro	Mountcastle, Vernon B., Jr.	
Cowan, W. Maxwell	Chevy Chase, MD		Monkton, MD
Crick, Francis H.C.	La Jolla, CA	Palay, Sanford Louis	Concord, MA
Dowling, John E.	Cambridge, MA	Shatz, Carla J.	Boston
Edelman, Gerald M.	La Jolla, CA	Snyder, Solomon H.	Baltimore
Gajdusek, D. Carleton	France	Squire, Larry R.	San Diego, CA
Goodman, Corey S.	Berkeley	Stent, Gunther S.	Berkeley
Greengard, Paul	New York	Thompson, Richard F.	Los Angeles
Hubel, David H.	Boston, MA	Wehner, Rüdiger	Switzerland
Huber, Franz	Seewiesen, Germany	Wiesel, Torsten Nils	New York
Julesz, Bela	Warren, NJ	Zeki, Semir	London

Behavioral Biology, Psychology, Ethology, and Animal Behavior: 13 Members

Atkinson, Richard C.	Oakland, CA	Lindauer, Martin	Wurzburg, Germany
Berenbaum, May R.	Urbana, IL	Lindzey, Gardner	Stanford
Goodall, Jane	Silver Spring, MD	Marler, Peter R.	Davis, CA
Griffin, Donald R.	Bedford, MA	Miller, George A.	Princeton
Hamburg, David A.	New York	Miller, Neal E.	Hamden, CT
Hilgard, Ernest R.	Palo Alto	Nottebohm, Fernando	Millbrook, NY
Hölldobler, Bert	Wurzburg, Germany		

Not Assigned: 4 Members

Caspersson, Torbjörn	Stockholm	Imbrie, John	Providence, RI
Chargaff, Erwin	New York	Klein, George	Stockholm

CLASS III. SOCIAL SCIENCES

Anthropology, Demography, Psychology, and Sociology: 32 Members

Balandier, Georges	Paris	Luce, R. Duncan	Irvine, CA
Bell, Daniel	Cambridge, MA	Merton, Robert K.	New York
Bellah, Robert N.	Berkeley	Nakane, Chie	Tokyo
Blau, Peter M.	Chapel Hill, NC	Nicolaisen, A. Ida Benedicte	Denmark
Bohannan, Paul Jones	Three Rivers, CA	Preston, Samuel H.	Philadelphia
Bruner, Jerome	New York	Riesman, David	Winchester, MA
Coale, Ansley J.	Newtown, PA	Sewell, William	Madison, WI
Cronbach, Lee J.	Palo Alto	Shepard, Roger Newland	Stanford
Crozier, Michel	Paris	Simon, Herbert A.	Pittsburgh
Dahrendorf, Ralf	Oxford, England	Smelser, Neil Joseph	Stanford
Duncan, Otis D.	Santa Barbara, CA	Srinivas, Mysore N.	Bangalore, India
Eisenstadt, Shmuel	Jerusalem	Suppes, Patrick	Stanford
Firth, Sir Raymond William	London	White, Gilbert Fowler	Boulder, CO
Goodman, Leo A.	Berkeley	Williams, Robin M., Jr.	Ithaca, NY
Inkeles, Alex	Stanford	Wilson, William Julius	Cambridge, MA
Lévi-Strauss, Claude	Paris	Zuckerman, Harriet	New York

Economics: 36 Members

Arrow, Kenneth J.	Stanford	Kaysen, Carl	Cambridge, MA
Baumol, William J.	New York	Kindleberger, Charles P.	Lexington, MA
Becker, Gary S.	Chicago	Klein, Lawrence Robert	Wynnewood, PA
Bergson, Abram	Cambridge, MA	Lucas, Robert E.	Chicago
Bhagwati, Jagdish, N.	New York	Parker, William N.	Hamden, CT
Blinder, Alan S.	Princeton	Quandt, Richard E.	Princeton
Bowen, William G.	New York	Rockefeller, David	New York
Brimmer, Andrew	Washington, DC	Rosovsky, Henry	Cambridge, MA
Chow, Gregory C.	Princeton	Rostow, Walt W.	Austin, TX
Cipolla, Carlo M.	Italy	Samuelson, Paul	Cambridge, MA
Debreu, Gerard	Berkeley	Scarf, Herbert Eli	New Haven
Dunlop, John T.	Cambridge, MA	Schweitzer, Pierre-Paul	Paris
Feldstein, Martin	Cambridge, MA	Sen, Amartya Kumar	Cambridge, England
Friedman, Milton	Stanford	Solow, Robert M.	Cambridge, MA
Fuchs, Victor R.	Stanford	Sowell, Thomas	Stanford
Galbraith, John Kenneth	Cambridge, MA	Srinivasan, T. N.	New Haven
Hirschman, Albert Otto	Princeton	Stiglitz, Joseph Eugene	Washington, DC
Jorgenson, Dale W.	Cambridge, MA	Tobin, James	New Haven

History Since 1715: 54 Members

Adams, Frederick Baldwin, Jr.	Paris	Chandler, Alfred Dupont, Jr.	
Appleby, Joyce	Los Angeles		Cambridge, MA
Bailyn, Bernard	Cambridge, MA	Cohen, I. Bernard	Belmont, MA
Baker, Keith Michael	Stanford	Craig, Gordon	Menlo Park, CA
Bedini, Silvio A.	Washington, DC	Cronon, William J.	Madison, WI
Bell, Whitfield J., Jr.	Philadelphia	Curtin, Philip	Kennett Square, PA
Billington, James	Washington, DC	Darnton, Robert	Princeton
Boorstin, Daniel J.	Washington, DC	Davis, David	New Haven
Carter, Edward C., II	Philadelphia	Degler, Carl N.	Stanford

Dunn, Richard S.	Philadelphia	McNeill, William H.	Colebrook, CT
Fischer, Wolfram	Berlin, Germany	McPherson, James M.	Princeton
Ford, Franklin Lewis	Lexington, MA	Middlekauff, Robert	Berkeley
Franklin, John Hope	Durham, NC	Oberg, Barbara B.	Princeton
Gay, Peter	Hamden, CT	Palmer, Robert R.	Newtown, PA
Goetzmann, William H.	Austin, TX	Paret, Peter	Princeton
Graham, Loren R.	Cambridge, MA	Paxton, Robert O.	New York
Greene, Jack P.	Baltimore	Schlesinger, Arthur, Jr.	New York
Habakkuk, Sir John	Oxford, England	Skinner, Quentin Robert Duthie	
Handlin, Oscar	Cambridge, MA		Cambridge, England
Herr, Richard	Berkeley	Spence, Jonathan Dermot	New Haven
Himmelfarb, Gertrude	Washington, DC	Stern, Fritz	New York
Hindle, Brooke	Gaithersburg, MD	Ulam, Adam B.	Cambridge, MA
Holton, Gerald	Cambridge, MA	Wakeman, Frederic Evans, Jr.	Berkeley
Kelley, Donald Reed	New Brunswick	Weigley, Russell F.	Philadelphia
Kennan, George Frost	Princeton	Wood, Gordon S.	Providence, RI
Kennedy, Paul	New Haven	Woodward, C. Vann	Hamden, CT
Kevles, Daniel J.	Pasadena, CA	Wright, Esmond	Masham, England
Landes, David S.	Cambridge, MA	Wright, Gordon	Stanford

Jurisprudence and Political Science: 29 Members

Almond, Gabriel A.	Palo Alto	Hoffmann, Stanley	Cambridge, MA
Black, Barbara Aronstein	New York	Kennedy, Randall LeRoy	Cambridge, MA
Bracher, Karl D.	Bonn, Germany	Levi, Edward Hirsch	Chicago
Burns, James M.	Williamstown, MA	Lipset, Seymour Martin	Fairfax, VA
Calabresi, Guido	New Haven, CT	Milsom, Stroud F. C.	Cambridge, England
Casper, Gerhard	Stanford	Moynihan, Daniel P.	Washington, DC
Converse, Philip E.	Ann Arbor, MI	Neustadt, Richard E.	Cambridge, MA
Cox, Archibald	Cambridge, MA	Pye, Lucian W.	Cambridge, MA
Dahl, Robert A.	New Haven	Stassen, Harold E.	St. Paul, MN
Farnsworth, E. Allan	New York	Truman, David B.	Sarasota, FL
Fenno, Richard F., Jr.	Rochester	Walzer, Michael	Princeton
Greenawalt, Kent	New York	Ward, Robert E.	Portola Valley, CA
Gunther, Gerald	Stanford	Wechsler, Herbert	New York
Henkin, Louis	New York	Wilson, James Q.	Malibu, CA
Herring, Pendleton	Princeton		

CLASS IV. HUMANITIES

Archaeology: 20 Members

Adams, Robert McC.	La Jolla, CA	McCredie, James R.	Princeton
Bass, George F.	College Station, TX	Mellink, Machteld J.	Haverford, PA
Boardman, John Sir	Oxford, England	Perrot, Jean J.F.	Paris
Bober, Phyllis Pray	Bryn Mawr, PA	Ridgway, Brunilde Sismondo	
Braidwood, Robert J.	La Porte, IN		Bryn Mawr, PA
Çambel, Halet	Istanbul	Sabloff, Jeremy Arac	Philadelphia
Greenewalt, Crawford H., Jr.	Berkeley	Simpson, William Kelly	Katonah, NY
Harper, Prudence Oliver	New York	Thompson, Homer A.	Princeton
Harrison, Evelyn Byrd	New York	Vermeule, Emily D.T.	Cambridge, MA
Knauer, Elfriede Regina	Haverford, PA	Willey, Gordon R.	Cambridge, MA

Criticism: Arts and Letters: 12 Members

Abrams, Meyer Howard	Ithaca, NY	Kennedy, George A.	Ft. Collins, CO
Bevington, David M.	Chicago	Knox, Bernard M.W.	Darnestown, MD
Booth, Wayne Clayson	Chicago	Litz, A. Walton	Princeton
Brée, Germaine	Winston Salem, NC	Thorpe, James	Bloomfield, CT
Brombert, Victor H.	Princeton	Todorov, Tzvetan	Paris
Cone, Edward T.	Princeton	Vendler, Helen Hennessy	Cambridge, MA

Cultural Anthropology: 6 Members

Geertz, Clifford	Princeton	Leighton, Alexander H.	Boston, MA
Goodenough, Ward	Haverford, PA	Vogt, Evon Zartman	Cambridge, MA
Kirch, Patrick Vinton	Berkeley	Wallace, Anthony F.C.	Aston, PA

History of the Arts, Literature, Religion, and Science: 49 Members

Barzun, Jacques	San Antonio, TX	Kitzinger, Ernst	Oxford, England
Bloom, Harold	New Haven	Lang, Mabel L.	Bryn Mawr, PA
Böwering, Gerhard H.	New Haven	Levy, Kenneth	Princeton
Brentano, Robert J.	Berkeley	MacCormack, Sabine G.	Ann Arbor, MI
Brown, Jonathan M.	Princeton	Martin, John R.	Princeton
Brown, Peter Robert L.	Princeton	Marty, Martin E.	Riverside, IL
Bynum, Caroline	New York	May, Georges	New Haven
Chadwick, Henry	Oxford, England	Metzger, Bruce M.	Princeton
Clagett, Marshall	Princeton	Millon, Henry A.	Washington, DC
Cropper, Elizabeth	Baltimore, MD	Morgan, Edmund S.	New Haven
Cross, Frank M., Jr.	Cambridge, MA	Nussbaum, Martha Craven	Chicago
Dempsey, Charles G.	Baltimore, MD	O'Malley, John W.	Cambridge, MA
Doniger, Wendy	Chicago	Oberman, Heiko A.	Tucson, AZ
Fong, Wen C.	Princeton	Pelikan, Jaroslav J.	Hamden, CT
Frängsmyr, Tore	Sweden	Rampersad, Arnold	Stanford
Freedberg, David	New York	de Romilly, Jacqueline	Paris
Frye, Roland M.	Wayne, PA	Rosen, Charles Welles	New York
Fumaroli, Marc	Paris	Rosenberg, Pierre	Paris
Gillispie, Charles C.	Princeton	Ryskamp, Charles A.	Princeton
Goldstine, Herman H.	Bryn Mawr, PA	Schäfer, Peter	Princeton, NJ
Gombrich, Sir Ernst H.	London	Siraisi, Nancy G.	New York
Gossman, Lionel	Princeton	Sjöberg, Åke W.	Haverford, PA
Grabar, Oleg	Princeton	Smyth, Craig Hugh	Cresskill, NJ
Güterbock, Hans G.	Chicago	Spacks, Patricia Meyer	Charlottesville, VA
Haskell, Francis	Oxford, England	Staden, Heinrich von	Princeton
Heilbron, John L.	England	Swerdlow, Noel	Chicago
Herbert, Robert L.	South Hadley, MA	Taruskin, Richard F.	Berkeley
Jones, Alexander	Toronto	Temkin, Owsei	Baltimore
		Ziolkowski, Theodore	Princeton

History and Philology, East and West, through the 17th Century: 48 Members

Bailey, David R.S.	Ann Arbor, Michigan
Barr, James	Claremont, CA
Beck, Hans-Georg	Unterfinning, Germany
Bisson, Thomas N.	Cambridge, MA
Bloch, Herbert	Belmont, MA
Bodde, Derk	Philadelphia
Bouwsma, William J.	Berkeley
Bowersock, Glen W.	Princeton
Burkert, Walter	Zürich
Cameron, Alan	New York
Cardona, George	Moorestown, NJ
Constable, Giles	Princeton
deBary, William Theodore	New York
Elliott, Sir John	Oxford, England
Fagles, Robert	Princeton
Grafton, Anthony	Princeton
Habicht, Christian	Princeton
Henrichs, Albert	Cambridge, MA
Hunger, Herbert	Vienna
Jameson, Michael H.	Palo Alto
Jones, Christopher P.	Cambridge, MA
Koenen, Ludwig	Ann Arbor, MI
Lapidus, Ira M.	Berkeley
Leclant, Jean	Paris
Le Rider, Georges Charles	Paris
Le Roy Ladurie, Emmanuel	Paris
Lewalski, Barbara	Cambridge, MA
Lewis, Bernard	Princeton
Likhachev, Dmitri Sergeevich	Leningrad
Lloyd-Jones, Sir Hugh	Wellesley, MA
Maffei, Domenico	Siena
Mayer, Hans E.	Kiel, Germany
Michalowski, Piotr	Ann Arbor, MI
North, Helen F.	Swarthmore, PA
Obolensky, Sir Dimitri	Oxford
Ostwald, Martin	Swarthmore, PA
Pingree, David	Providence, RI
Pocock, John Greville Agard	Baltimore
Putnam, Michael C. J.	Providence, RI
Reiner, Erica	Chicago
de Riquer, Martin	Barcelona
Rocher, Ludo	Philadelphia
Rosenthal, Franz	Hamden, CT
Runciman, Sir Steven	Dumfriesshire, Scotland
Ševčenko, Ihor	Cambridge, MA
Thirsk, Joan	Tonbridge, England
Tierney, Brian	Ithaca, NY
Vryonis, Speros, Jr.	Rancho Cordova, CA

Linguistics: 14 Members

Aarsleff, Hans	Princeton
Baldinger, Kurt	Heidelberg, Germany
Blumstein, Sheila E.	Providence, RI
Edzard, Dietz Otto	München, Germany
Emeneau, Murray B.	Berkeley
Greenberg, Joseph H.	Stanford
Hamp, Eric P.	Chicago
Hawkins, John David	London
Hoenigswald, Henry M.	Swarthmore, PA
Hunger, Hermann	Vienna
Ivanov, Vyacheslav Vsevolodovich	Los Angeles
Mayrhofer, Manfred	Vienna
Morpurgo Davies, Anna	Oxford
Watkins, Calvert	Cambridge, MA

Philosophy: 6 Members

Davidson, Donald	Berkeley
Garin, Eugenio	Florence
Putnam, Hilary	Cambridge, MA
Quine, Willard V.	Cambridge, MA
Rawls, John	Cambridge, MA
White, Morton G.	Princeton

CLASS V. THE PROFESSIONS, ARTS, AND AFFAIRS

Creative Artists: 11 Members

Bellow, Saul	Boston, MA	Muti, Riccardo	Philadelphia
Dove, Rita	Charlottesville, VA	Perlman, Itzhak	New York
Eccles, Lady	Somerville, NJ	Stella, Frank	New York
Greenough, Beverly Sills	New York	Stern, Isaac	New York
Ma, Yo-Yo	New York	Wyeth, Andrew	Chadds Ford, PA
Morrison, Chloe Anthony	Princeton		

Physicians, Theologians, Lawyers, Jurists, Architects, and Members of Other Professions: 16 Members

Abrahamson, Shirley S.	Madison, WI	McKusick, Vincent L.	Portland, ME
Adams, Arlin M.	Philadelphia	O'Connor, Sandra Day	Washington, DC
Cohen, Joel E.	New York	Pei, Ieoh Ming	New York
Frederick, William H.	Hockessin, DE	Peters, Ellen Ash	Hartford, CT
Gardner, Richard N.	New York	Scarman, Leslie George, Baron of Quatt	
Heckscher, Maurice	Philadelphia		London
Kaplan, Helene L.	New York	Souter, David H.	Washington, DC
Katzenbach, Nicholas deB.	Princeton	Van Dusen, Lewis H., Jr.	Philadelphia
Koop, C. Everett	Bethesda, MD		

Administrators, Bankers and Opinion Leaders from the Public or Private Sectors: 108 Members

Annenberg, Walter H.	St. Davids, PA	Eastburn, David P.	Doylestown, PA
Bailey, Herbert S.	Pittsboro, NC	Edelman, Marian Wright	Washington, DC
Beitzel, G.B.	Chappaqua, NY	Evans, John R.	Toronto
Bessborough, Mary Countess of		Frieman, Edward A.	La Jolla, CA
	Hampshire, England	Gardner, David P.	Menlo Park, CA
Biddle, James	Andalusia, PA	Gates, Henry Louis, Jr.	Cambridge, MA
Bok, Derek C.	Cambridge, MA	Gibbons, John H.	The Plains, VA
Bradley, Bill	Palo Alto	Goheen, Robert F.	Princeton
Brown, J. Carter	Washington, DC	Golden, William T.	New York
Burke, James E.	New Brunswick, NJ	Graham, Patricia Albjerg	Cambridge, MA
Burkhardt, Frederick H.	Bennington, VT	Gray, Hanna H.	Chicago
Carter, James Earl	Atlanta, GA	Gregorian, Vartan	New York
Christopher, Warren	Los Angeles	Gundersheimer, Werner	Washington, DC
Connor, W. Robert		Haas, John C.	Villanova, PA
	Research Triangle Park, NC	Hackney, Sheldon	Philadelphia
Cronkite, Walter	New York	Havel, Václav	Czechoslovakia
Cross, Theodore L.	New York	Hesburgh, Theodore M.	Notre Dame, IN
D'Arms, John H.	New York	Hewlett, William R.	Palo Alto
d'Harnoncourt, Anne	Philadelphia	Hutchison, W. Bruce	Victoria, B.C.
Devonshire, The Duke of		Jamieson, Kathleen Hall	Philadelphia
	Derbyshire, England	Jefferson, Edward G.	Greenville, DE
Dunn, Mary Maples	Cambridge, MA	Johnson, Howard Wesley	Cambridge, MA
Dyson, Robert H., Jr.	Philadelphia	Juan Carlos I, King of Spain	Madrid
Eagleson, William B., Jr.	Radnor, PA	Kassebaum Baker, Nancy	Washington, DC

Katz, Stanley N.	Princeton	Rhodes, Frank H. T.	Ithaca, NY
Kearns, David T.	Stamford, CT	Ripley, S. Dillon	Washington, DC
Kelley, William N.	Philadelphia	Robinson, Mary	Switzerland
Kenny, Sir Anthony	Oxford, England	Rodin, Judith	Philadelphia
Keohane, Nannerl Overholser		Rudenstine, Neil L.	Cambridge, MA
	Durham, NC	Saxon, David S.	Los Angeles
de Klerk, Frederik Willem	South Africa	Schacht, Henry B.	New York
Kornberg, Sir Hans	Brookline, MA	Scheide, William H.	Princeton
Landau, Ralph	New York	Scranton, William W.	Scranton, PA
Langfitt, Thomas	Wynnewood, PA	Seamans, Robert C., Jr.	
Longsworth, Charles R.	Athol, MA		Beverly Farms, MA
Lyman, Richard W.	Palo Alto	Shapiro, Harold T.	Princeton
McGhee, George C.	Middleburg, VA	Shapiro, Irving S.	Wilmington, DE
McNamara, Robert S.	Washington, DC	Shultz, George P.	Stanford
McPherson, Mary Patterson	New York	Simmons, Ruth J.	Northampton, MA
Mahoney, Margaret E.	New York	Sizer, Theodore R.	Providence, RI
Mandela, Nelson Rolihlahi	South Africa	Smith, Robert I.	Stowe, VT
Massey, Walter Eugene	Atlanta, GA	Sovern, Michael I.	New York
Matlock, Jack F., Jr.	Princeton	Still, Carl-Otto	Germany
Meyerson, Martin	Philadelphia	Strong, Maurice Frederick	Toronto
Miller, J. Irwin	Columbus, IN	Taplin, Frank E.	Princeton
Mitchell, Thomas Noel	Dublin, Ireland	Vagelos, P. Roy	Bedminster, NJ
Mori, Wataru	Tokyo, Japan	Vance, Cyrus R.	New York
Morita, Akio	Tokyo, Japan	Volcker, Paul A.	New York
Moyers, Bill D.	New York	Watson, Bernard Charles	Elkins Park, PA
Oakes, John B.	New York	Wellesley, Arthur, Duke of Wellington	
Odhiambo, Thomas R.	Nairobi, Kenya		Basingstoke, England
Ogata, Sadako	Switzerland	Wells, Herman B	Bloomington, IN
Piel, Gerard	New York	West, Cornel	Cambridge, MA
Powell, Colin L.	Alexandria, VA	Whitehead, John C.	New York
Price, Hugh B.	New York	Wolfensohn, James David	Washington, DC
Rauch, R. Stewart	Bryn Mawr, PA	Woolard, Edgar S.	Wilmington, DE
Reed, John S.	Princeton	Woolf, Harry	Princeton

Scholars in the above fields: 4 Members

Harris, Cyril M.	New York	Landon, H. C. Robbins	Tarn, France
Huxtable, Ada Louise	New York	Scully, Vincent	New Haven

REPRESENTATION OF SUBJECTS

As of 31 December 1998

	Members	
	Resident	*Foreign*

CLASS I—MATHEMATICAL AND PHYSICAL SCIENCES

	Resident	Foreign
Astronomy	19	6
Chemistry and Chemical Biochemistry	33	12
Engineering	15	1
Mathematics	22	7
Physical Earth Sciences	15	3
Physics	49	9
	153	38
Total number in Class I	191	

CLASS II—BIOLOGICAL SCIENCES

	Resident	Foreign
Molecular Biology and Biochemistry	37	6
Cellular and Developmental Biology	7	3
Evolution and Ecology, Systematics, Population Genetics, Paleontology, and Physical Anthropology	19	2
Medicine, Surgery, Pathology, and Immunology	11	2
Microbiology, including Bacteriology, Virology, and Protozoology	7	2
Physiology, Biophysics, and Pharmacology	0	2
Genetics	1 6	2
Plant Sciences	3	2
Neurobiology	22	5
Behavioral Biology, Psychology, Ethology, and Animal Behavior	11	3
General	2	2
	135	31
Total number in Class II	166	

CLASS III—SOCIAL SCIENCES

	Resident	Foreign
Anthropology, Demography, Psychology, and Sociology	22	8
Economics	34	2
History Since 1715	48	4
Jurisprudence and Political Science	27	2
	131	16
Total number in Class III	147	

CLASS IV—HUMANITIES

Archaeology	15	2
Criticism: Arts and Letters	12	1
Cultural Anthropology	5	0
History of the Arts, Literature, Religion, and Sciences	47	8
History and Philology, East and West, through the 17th Century	36	12
Linguistics	6	7
Philosophy	4	1
	125	31
Total number in Class IV	156	

CLASS V—THE PROFESSIONS, ARTS, AND AFFAIRS

Creative Artists	8	1
Physicians, Theologians, Lawyers, Jurists, Architects, and Members of Other Professions	15	1
Administrators, Bankers and Opinion Leaders from the Public or Private Sectors	88	16
Scholars in the above fields	3	1
	114	19
Total number in Class V	133	

MEMBERSHIP CHANGES THROUGH 31 DECEMBER 1998*

	Members	
	Resident	*Foreign*
31 December 1997	630	133
Elected during 1998	41	8
Deceased during 1998	13	6
31 December 1998	658	135
85 Years of age and older	95	18
Under 85	563	117
Total	658	135

*Numbers supplied by Nora Monroe

GEOGRAPHICAL OR PROFESSIONAL
LOCATIONS OF MEMBERS *

Resident members living abroad are indicated by a bullet (•); foreign members living in the United States are indicated with two bullets (••).

RESIDENTS OF THE UNITED STATES

ARIZONA

Oberman, Heiko A.

CALIFORNIA

Adams, Robert McC.
Almond, Gabriel A.
Anderson, Don L.
Appleby, Joyce
Arrow, Kenneth J.
Atkinson, Richard C.
Ayala, Francisco José
Babcock, Horace W.
Bacher, Robert Fox
Baker, Herbert G.
Baker, Keith Michael
Baldeschwieler, John Dickson
Baltimore, David
Barr, James
Barton, Jacqueline K.
Bellah, Robert N.
Benzer, Seymour
Berg, Paul
Bing, Richard John
Bishop, J. Michael
Blackwell, David
Bloom, Floyd
Bohannan, Paul J.
Bouwsma, William J.
Boyer, Paul D.
Bradley, Bill
Brenner, Sydney••
Brentano, Robert J.
Bullock, Theodore H.

Burbidge, E. Margaret
Casper, Gerhard
Chern, Shiing-shen
Christopher, Warren
Chu, Steven
Cohen, Paul J.
Craig, Gordon A.
Crick, Francis H.C.••
Cronbach, Lee J.
Davidson, Donald
Debreu, Gerard
Degler, Carl N.
Diamond, Jared Mason
Doolittle, Russell F.
Drell, Sidney D.
Dulbecco, Renato
Duncan, Otis D.
Edelman, Gerald M.
Ehrlich, Paul R.
Emeneau, Murray B.
Ernst, W. Gary
Friedman, Milton
Frieman, Edward A.
Fuchs, Victor R..
Gardner, David Pierpont
Glaser, Donald A.
Goldberger, Marvin L.
Goodman, Corey S.
Goodman, Leo A.
Greenberg, Joseph H.
Greenewalt, Crawford H., Jr.
Greenstein, Jesse L.
Gunther, Gerald
Hardin, Garrett
Herr, Richard

*Names of members who have died since 1 January 1999 through 31 July 1999 have been removed; names of members newly elected in April 1999 have been added.

Hewlett, William R.
Hilgard, Ernest R.
Howell, F. Clark
Inkeles, Alex
Ivanov, Vyacheslav Vsevolodovich
Jameson, Michael H.
Kamen, Martin D.
Karlin, Samuel
Kennedy, Donald
Kevles, Daniel J.
Kirch, Patrick Vinton
Knopoff, Leon
Kohn, Walter
Kornberg, Arthur
Koshland, Daniel E., Jr.
Krauskopf, Konrad B.
Lapidus, Ira M.
Leonard, Nelson J.
Leopold, Luna B.
Lewis, Edward B.
Lindzey, Gardner
Luce, R. Duncan
Lyman, Richard W.
Marcus, Rudolph Arthur
Marler, Peter R.
Meyerowitz, Elliot M.
Middlekauff, Robert Lawrence
Mooney, Harold A.
Munk, Walter H.
Neufeld, Elizabeth F.
Neugebauer, Gerry
Nierenberg, William Aaron
Osterbrock, Donald E.
Owen, Ray D.
Panofsky, Wolfgang K. H.
Pierce, John R.
Prusiner, Stanley B.
Ramo, Simon
Rampersad, Arnold
Roberts, John D.
Rosenbluth, Marshall N.
Rowland, Frank Sherwood
Sandage, Allan Rex
Saxon, David S.
Schimmel, Paul
Schopf, J. William
Shepard, Roger Newland
Shultz, George P.
Smelser, Neil Joseph

Smith, Emil L.
Sowell, Thomas
Squire, Larry R.
Stebbins, George L.
Stent, Gunther S.
Stone, Edward C.
Suppes, Patrick
Taruskin, Richard F.
Taube, Henry
Thompson, Richard F.
Thorne, Kip S.
Townes, Charles H.
Vogt, Peter K.
Vryonis, Speros, Jr.
Wake, David B.
Wakeman, Frederic Evans, Jr.
Ward, Robert E.
Wasserburg, Gerald J.
Wilson, James Q.
Wright, Gordon
Zare, Richard N.
Zewail, Ahmed H.

COLORADO

Glass, H. Bentley
Kennedy, George Alexander
White, Gilbert Fowler

CONNECTICUT

Altman, Sidney
Bloom, Harold
Böwering, Gerhard H.
Calabresi, Guido
Dahl, Robert A.
Davis, David Brion
Fruton, Joseph S.
Gay, Peter
Kearns, David T.
Kennedy, Paul
Kilbourne, Edwin D.
McNeill, William H.
May, Georges
Miller, Neal E.
Morgan, Edmund Sears
O'Brien, Brian
Parker, William N.

Pelikan, Jaroslav J.
Peters, Ellen Ash
Richards, Frederic M.
Rodgers, John
Rosenthal, Franz
Scarf, Herbert Eli
Scully, Vincent
Spence, Jonathan Dermot
Srinivasan, T. N.
Steitz, Joan Argetsinger
Thorpe, James
Tobin, James
Woodward, C. Vann

DELAWARE

Frederick, William H.
Jefferson, Edward G.
Shapiro, Irving S.
Woolard, Edgar S.

DISTRICT OF COLUMBIA

Abelson, Philip Hauge
Alberts, Bruce
Bedini, Silvio A.
Billington, James
Boorstin, Daniel J.
Brimmer, Andrew F.
Brown, J. Carter
Edelman, Marian Wright
Gundersheimer, Werner
Haskins, Caryl P.
Himmelfarb, Gertrude
Karle, Isabella L.
Karle, Jerome
Kassebaum Baker, Nancy
Lovejoy, Thomas E.
McNamara, Robert S.
Millon, Henry Armand
Moynihan, Daniel P.
O'Connor, Sandra Day
Press, Frank
Ripley, S. Dillon, 2nd
Rubin, Vera C.
Singer, Maxine F.
Souter, David H.
Stiglitz, Joseph Eugene
Wetherill, George W.

Wolfensohn, James David
Yoder, Hatten S., Jr.

FLORIDA

Benedict, Manson
Heeschen, David S.
Schrieffer, J. Robert

GEORGIA

Carter, James Earl
Massey, Walter Eugene

ILLINOIS

Becker, Gary S.
Berenbaum, May R.
Bevington, David M.
Booth, Wayne Clayson
Cronin, James Watson
Doniger, Wendy
Drickamer, Harry G.
Gray, Hanna H.
Güterbock, Hans G.
Gutowsky, Herbert S.
Hamp, Eric P.
Kadanoff, Leo P.
Lederman, Leon M.
Leggett, Anthony J.
Levi, Edward Hirsch
Lucas, Robert E.
Mac Lane, Saunders
Marty, Martin E.
Nussbaum, Martha Craven
Reiner, Erica
Rice, Stuart A.
Rowley, Janet D.
Simpson, John Alexander
Slichter, Charles Pence
Swerdlow, Noel M.

INDIANA

Braidwood, Robert J.
Hesburgh, Theodore M.
Miller, J. Irwin
Wells, Herman B

IOWA

Van Allen, James A.

MAINE

McKusick, Vincent L.
Russell, Elizabeth S.

MARYLAND

Augustine, Norman R.
Axelrod, Julius
Brown, Donald David
Choppin, Purnell W.
Cowan, W. Maxwell
Cropper, Elizabeth
Dempsey, Charles G.
Ebert, James David
Fisher, Michael E.
Fredrickson, Donald S.
Gall, Joseph Grafton
Goodall, Jane••
Greene, Jack P.
Hindle, Brooke
Kelly, Thomas J.
Knox, Bernard M.W.
McKusick, Victor Almon
Mountcastle, Vernon B., Jr.
Nathans, Daniel
Pocock, John Greville Agard
Snyder, Solomon H.
Talalay, Paul
Temkin, Owsei
Varmus, Harold
Vogelstein, Bert
White, Robert M.
Witkop, Bernhard
Wolman, Markley Gordon

MASSACHUSETTS

Abeles, Robert Heinz
Anderson, James G.
Bailyn, Bernard
Baker, James Gilbert
Bell, Daniel
Bellow, Saul

Bergson, Abram
Bisson, Thomas N.
Bloch, Herbert
Bloch, Konrad E.
Bloembergen, Nicolaas
Bogorad, Lawrence
Bok, Derek C.
Branscomb, Lewis M.
Brooks, Harvey
Burns, James MacGregor
Carrier, George F.
Chandler, Alfred Dupont, Jr.
Cohen, I. Bernard
Cox, Archibald
Cross, Frank M., Jr.
Doty, Paul Mead
Dowling, John Elliott
Dresselhaus, Mildred S.
Dunlop, John T.
Dunn, Mary Maples
Edsall, John T.
Feldstein, Martin
Folkman, Judah
Ford, Franklin Lewis
Galbraith, John Kenneth
Gates, Henry Louis, Jr.
Gingerich, Owen
Gleason, Andrew M.
Goody, Richard M.
Graham, Loren R.
Graham, Patricia Albjerg
Griffin, Donald R.
Halperin, Bertrand I.
Handlin, Oscar
Harrison, Stephen Coplan
Henrichs, Albert
Herbert, Robert L.
Herschbach, Dudley
Hoffmann, Stanley
Holton, Gerald
Hornig, Donald Frederick
Hubel, David Hunter
Jencks, William P.
Johnson, Howard Wesley
Jones, Christopher P.
Jorgenson, Dale W.
Kaysen, Carl
Kennedy, Eugene Patrick

Kennedy, Randall LeRoy
Kety, Seymour S.
Khorana, Har G.
Kindleberger, Charles P.
Knoll, Andrew H.
Knowles, Jeremy R.
Kornberg, Sir Hans••
Landes, David S.
Leighton, A. H.
Lewalski, Barbara K.
Lin, Chia Chiao
Lloyd-Jones, Sir Hugh
Longsworth, Charles R.
Mackey, George W.
Mayr, Ernst
Meselson, Matthew S.
Moore, Francis D.
Morrison, Philip
Mosteller, Frederick
Nathan, David G.
Neustadt, Richard E.
O'Malley, John W.
Olsen, Kenneth H.
Palay, Sanford Louis
Putnam, Hilary
Pye, Lucian W.
Quine, Willard Van Orman
Rabin, Michael O.••
Ramsey, Norman F.
Rawls, John
Rich, Alexander
Riesman, David
Rosovsky, Henry
Rudenstine, Neil L.
Samuelson, Paul Anthony
Seamans, Robert C., Jr.
Ševčenko, Ihor
Shannon, Claude E.
Shapiro, Irwin I.
Sharp, Phillip A.
Shatz, Carla J.
Simmons, Ruth J.
Singer, I. M.
Solow, Robert M.
Strominger, Jack L.
Ulam, Adam B.
Vendler, Helen Hennessy
Vermeule, Emily D. T.
Vogt, Evon Zartman

Watkins, Calvert
Weisskopf, Victor F.
West, Cornel
Westheimer, Frank H.
Whipple, Fred
Whitesides, George M.
Wiley, Don Craig
Willey, Gordon R.
Wilson, Edward Osborne
Wilson, William Julius

MICHIGAN

Bailey, D. R. Shackleton
Converse, Philip E.
Koenen, Ludwig
MacCormack, Sabine G.
Michalowski, Piotr
Neel, James Van Gundia
Wild, J. Paul••

MINNESOTA

Crawford, Bryce, Jr.
Stassen, Harold E.

MISSOURI

Raven, Peter H.

NEW HAMPSHIRE

Easton, Roger L.
Koop, C. Everett

NEW JERSEY

Aarsleff, Hans
Anderson, Philip W.
Baker, William O.
Blinder, Alan S.
Bonner, John T.
Borel, Armand••
Bowersock, Glen W.
Brombert, Victor H.
Brown, Jonathan M.
Brown, Peter Robert L.
Burke, James E.

Cardona, George
Cho, Alfred Y.
Chow, Gregory C.
Clagett, Marshall
Cone, Edward T.
Constable, Giles
Darnton, Robert C.
David, Edward E., Jr.
Dyson, Freeman J.
Eccles, Lady
Fagles, Robert
Fefferman, Charles L.
Fitch, Val L.
Fong, Wen C.
Geertz, Clifford
Gillispie, Charles C.
Goheen, Robert F.
Gossman, Lionel
Grabar, Oleg
Grafton, Anthony
Grant, Peter R.
Griffiths, Phillip A.
Gunn, James E.
Habicht, Christian
Happer, William
Herring, Pendleton
Hirschman, Albert Otto
Hopfield, John J.
Julesz, Bela
Katz, Stanley N.
Katzenbach, Nicholas deB.
Kelley, Donald Reed
Kennan, George F.
Levy, Kenneth
Lewis, Bernard
Litz, A. Walton
McCredie, James R.
McPherson, James M.
MacPherson, Robert
Martin, John R.
Matlock, Jack F., Jr.
Metzger, Bruce M.
Miller, George A.
Morrison, Chloe Anthony
Oberg, Barbara B.
Ostriker, Jeremiah P.
Paret, Peter
Quandt, Richard E.
Reed, John S.

Ryskamp, Charles A.
Schäfer, Peter
Scheide, William H.
Shapiro, Harold T.
Sinfelt, John H.
Smyth, Craig H.
Staden, Heinrich von
Taplin, Frank E.
Tarjan, Robert E.
Taylor, Joseph Hooten, Jr.
Thompson, Homer A.
Treiman, Sam Bard
Tukey, John W.
Vagelos, P. Roy
Walzer, Michael
Wheeler, John A.
White, Morton G.
Wieschaus, Eric F.
Wiles, Andrew J.
Witten, Edward
Woolf, Harry
Ziolkowski, Theodore Joseph

NEW MEXICO

Frauenfelder, Hans Emil
Gell-Mann, Murray
Pines, David

NEW YORK

Abrams, Meyer Howard
Baumol, William
Beitzel, G. B.
Bethe, Hans A.
Bhagwati, Jagdish N.
Black, Barbara Aronstein
Blobel, Günter
Bowen, William G.
Breslow, Ronald
Bruner, Jerome
Bynum, Caroline
Cameron, Alan
Chargaff, Erwin
Cocke, John
Cohen, Joel E.
Cronkite, Walter
Cross, Theodore Lamont
D'Arms, John H.

de Bary, William Theodore
de Duve, Christian••
Dennard, Robert H.
Eisner, Thomas
Farnsworth, E. Allan
Fenno, Richard F., Jr.
Freedberg, David
Gardner, Richard N.
Garwin, Richard L.
Gold, Thomas
Golden, William T.
Goldhaber, Maurice
Gomory, Ralph E.
Greenawalt, Kent
Greengard, Paul
Greenough, Beverly Sills
Gregorian, Vartan
Hamburg, David A.
Harper, Prudence Oliver
Harris, Cyril M.
Harrison, Evelyn Byrd
Henkin, Louis
Hoffmann, Roald
Huxtable, Ada Louise
Kandel, Eric R.
Kaplan, Helene L.
Landau, Ralph
Lax, Peter D.
Lederberg, Joshua
Lee, Tsung-Dao
Llinás, Rodolfo R.
Loeb, John Nichols
Ma, Yo-Yo
McCarty, Maclyn
McPherson, Mary Patterson
Mahoney, Margaret E.
Meinwald, Jerrold
Merton, Robert K.
Milnor, John W.
Morawetz, Cathleen Synge
Moyers, Bill D.
Newell, Norman D.
Nirenberg, Louis
Nottebohm, Fernando
Oakes, John B.
Pais, Abraham
Paxton, Robert O.
Pei, Ieoh Ming
Perlman, Itzhak

Piel, Gerard
Piore, Emanuel R.
Price, Hugh B.
Rhodes, Frank H. T.
Rockefeller, David
Rosen, Charles Welles
Ruderman, Malvin
Salpeter, Edwin E.
Schacht, Henry B.
Schlesinger, Arthur, Jr.
Seitz, Frederick
Simpson, William Kelly
Siraisi, Nancy
Sovern, Michael I.
Stella, Frank
Stern, Fritz
Stern, Isaac
Stork, Gilbert
Tierney, Brian
Truman, David B.
Vance, Cyrus R.
Volcker, Paul A.
Watson, James D.
Wechsler, Herbert
Whitehead, John C.
Widom, Benjamin
Wiesel, Torsten Nils
Williams, Robin M., Jr.
Wilson, Robert R.
Winograd, Shmuel
Yang, Chen Ning
Zuckerman, Harriet

NORTH CAROLINA

Bailey, Herbert S., Jr.
Blau, Peter M.
Brée, Germaine
Connor, W. Robert
Fox, Marye Anne
Franklin, John Hope
Keohane, Nannerl Overholser
Simons, Elwyn LaVerne

OHIO

Robbins, Frederick C.
Wilson, Kenneth G.

OREGON

Lubchenco, Jane

PENNSYLVANIA

Adams, Arlin M.
Annenberg, Walter H.
Austrian, Robert
Barker, Clyde Frederick
Bearn, Alexander G.
Bell, Whitfield J., Jr.
Biddle, James
Blumberg, Baruch
Bober, Phyllis Pray
Bodde, Derk
Carter, Edward C., II
Chance, Britton
Coale, Ansley J.
Cohn, Mildred
Curtin, Philip
d'Harnoncourt, Anne
Dunn, Richard S.
Dyson, Robert Harris
Eagleson, William B., Jr.
Eastburn, David
Frye, Roland M.
Goldstine, Herman H.
Goodenough, Ward H.
Haas, John C.
Hackney, Sheldon
Heckscher, Maurice
Hilleman, Maurice Ralph
Hoenigswald, Henry M.
Jamieson, Kathleen Hall
Kelley, William N.
Klein, Lawrence Robert
Knauer, Elfriede Regina
Knudson, Alfred G.
Lang, Mabel L.
Langfitt, Thomas W.
Mellink, Machteld J.
Meyerson, Martin
Mintz, Beatrice
Muti, Ricardo••
North, Helen F.
Nowell, Peter Carey
Ostwald, Martin

Palmer, Robert R.
Patrick, Ruth
Preston, Samuel H.
Rauch, R. Stewart
Rhoads, Jonathan E.
Ridgway, Brunilde Sismondo
Rocher, Ludo
Rodin, Judith
Sabloff, Jeremy Arac
Scranton, William
Simon, Herbert A.
Sjöberg, Åke W.
Starzl, Thomas E.
Van Dusen, Lewis H., Jr.
Wallace, Anthony F. C.
Watson, Bernard Charles
Weigley, Russell F.
Wyeth, Andrew

RHODE ISLAND

Blumstein, Sheila E.
Cooper, Leon N.
Imbrie, John
Mumford, David
Pingree, David
Putnam, Michael C. J.
Sizer, Theodore R.
Wood, Gordon S.

TENNESSEE

Weinberg, Alvin M.

TEXAS

Bard, Allen J.
Barzun, Jacques
Bass, George F.
Brown, Michael S.
Cotton, Frank Albert
Goetzmann, William H.
Goldstein, Joseph L.
Hackerman, Norman
Rostow, Walt W.
Weinberg, Steven

VERMONT

Burkhardt, Frederick H.
Smith, Robert Imbrie

VIRGINIA

Cairns, John
Dove, Rita
Friedman, Herbert
Gibbons, John H.
Kellermann, Kenneth I.
Lipset, Seymour Martin
McGhee, George Crews
Powell, Colin L.

Spacks, Patricia Meyer

WASHINGTON

Karp, Richard M.

WISCONSIN

Abrahamson, Shirley Schlanger
Adler, Julius
Burris, Robert H.
Cronon, William J.
Crow, James F.
Lardy, Henry A.
Sewell, William Hamilton

FOREIGN RESIDENTS

AUSTRIA

Hunger, Herbert
Hunger, Hermann
MacDonald, Gordon J.•
Mayrhofer, Manfred

AUSTRALIA

Robertson, Sir Rutherford

BRAZIL

Chagas, Carlos

CANADA

Evans, John R.
Hutchison, W. Bruce
Jones, Alexander
McLaren, Digby J.
Strong, Maurice Frederick

CZECH REPUBLIC

Havel, Václav

DENMARK

Bohr, Aage
Nicolaisen, A. Ida Benedicte

ENGLAND

Atiyah, Sir Michael
Bessborough, The Countess of
Boardman, Sir John
Bodmer, Walter
Booth, Sir Christopher
Chadwick, Henry
Cox, David
Dahrendorf, Ralf
Devonshire, The Duke of
Elliott, John H.•
Firth, Sir Raymond W.
Gombrich, Sir Ernst H.
Gurdon, John Bertrand
Habakkuk, Sir John
Hamilton, William D.
Haskell, Francis
Hawking, Stephen William
Hawkins, John David
Heilbron, John L.•
Hoyle, Sir Fred
Huxley, Sir Andrew F.
Kenny, Sir Anthony

Keynes, Richard D.
Kitzinger, Ernst•
Klug, Sir Aaron
Lewis, Lord of Newnham
Lovell, Sir Bernard
Milsom, Stroud F. C.
Morpurgo Davies, Anna
Obolensky, Sir Dimitri
Perutz, Max F.
Peters, Sir (David) Keith
Porter, Professor Lord
Rees, Sir Martin
Scarman, Leslie George
Sen, Amartya Kumar•
Skinner, Quentin Robert Duthie
Smith, John M.
Thirsk, Joan
Thomas, John Meurig
Vita-Finzi, Claudio
Wellesley, Arthur, The Duke of
Wellington
Wilson, Sir Robert
Wright, Esmond
Zeki, Semir

FRANCE

Adams, Frederick Baldwin, Jr.•
Aigrain, Pierre
Allègre, Claude Jean
Balandier, Georges
Crozier, Michel
Fumaroli, Marc
Gajdusek, D. Carleton•
Grunberg-Manago, Marianne
Jacob, François
Landon, H. C. Robbins
Leclant, Jean
Lehn, Jean-Marie Pierre
Leprince-Ringuet, L.
Le Rider, Georges Charles
Le Roy Ladurie, Emmanuel
Lévi-Strauss, Claude
Perrot, Jean J. F.
de Romilly, Jacqueline
Rosenberg, Pierre
Serre, Jean-Pierre
Todorov, Tzvetan

GERMANY

Baldinger, Kurt
Beck, Hans-Georg
Bracher, Karl D.
Edzard, Dietz Otto
Eigen, Manfred
Fischer, Wolfram
Hölldobler, Bert
Huber, Franz
Lindauer, Martin
Lüst, Reimar
Mayer, Hans E.
Nusslein-Volhard, Christiane
Still, Carl-Otto
zur Hausen, Harald

HUNGARY

Jermy, Tibor

INDIA

Rao, C.N.R.
Srinivas, Mysore N.

IRELAND

Mitchell, Thomas Noel

ISRAEL

Eisenstadt, Shmuel N.
Jortner, Joshua
Katzir (Katchalski), Ephraim
Levine, Raphael David
Sela, Michael

ITALY

Cipolla, Carlo M.
Garin, Eugenio
Levi-Montalcini, Rita•
Maffei, Domenico
Regge, Tullio
Sciama, D.W.

JAPAN

Esaki, Leo
Inose, Hiroshi
Mori, Wataru
Morita, Akio
Nakane, Chie

KENYA

Odhiambo, Thomas R.

KOREA

Lee, Ho-Wang

NETHERLANDS

Casimir, Hendrik B.G.
Hulst, H.C. van de

RUSSIA

Arnold, Vladimir Igorevich
Gol'danskii, Vitalii I.
Likhachev, Dmitri Sergeevich
Spirin, Alexander S.

SCOTLAND

Runciman, Sir Steven

SOUTH AFRICA

de Klerk, Frederik Willem
Mandela, Nelson Rolihlahi
Tobias, Phillip Vallentine

SPAIN

Juan Carlos I, King of Spain
de Riquer, Martin

SWEDEN

Bergström, Sune
Caspersson, Torbjörn
Frängsmyr, Tore
Klein, George
Löwdin, Per-Olov
Lundqvist, Stig

SWITZERLAND

Burkert, Walter
Dunitz, Jack David
Ogata, Sadako
Robinson, Mary
Schweitzer, Pierre-Paul
Wehner, Rüdiger

TURKEY

Çambel, Halet

LIST OF PAST SOCIETY MEMBERS
FORMER RESIDENT MEMBERS

Before the union of the American Philosophical Society and the American Society into the American Philosophical Society held at Philadelphia for Promoting Useful Knowledge in 1769 (see Brief History of the Society, p. 289), there were members of both societies and members of either society. It is impossible to establish the date of election of many of these members. Accordingly, in the list below, those marked "A" were members of the two societies at the time of the union, "B" those who were members only of the American Philosophical Society, and "C" those who were members only of the American Society. Following each name is the year of election to membership in the American Philosophical Society.

A

Abbe, Cleveland	1871
Abbot, Charles, G.	1914
Abbot, Henry L.	1862
Abbott, Alexander C.	1897
Abbott, Charles C.	1889
Abbott, Helen C. de S. *See* Michael, Helen A.	
Abel, John J.	1915
Abercrombie, James	1796
Abert, J. J.	1832
Ackley, Gardner	1972
Adams, Charles F.	1880
Adams, Charles F.	1901
Adams, Edwin P.	1915
Adams, Herbert B	1886
Adams, James T.	1938
Adams, John	1780
Adams, John Q.	1818
Adams, Joseph Q.	1940
Adams, Roger	1935
Adams, Walter S.	1915
Adamson, John C.	1856
Addison, Alexander	1900
Adler, Cyrus	1900
Adrain, Robert	1812
Agassiz, Alexander	1875
Agassiz, Elizabeth	1869
Agnew, D. Hayes	1872
Aitken, Robert G.	1919

Albright, William F.	1929
Alderman, Edwin A.	1925
Alexander, James	B
Alexander, James	C
Alexander, James W.	1928
Alexander, John H.	1852
Alexander, Joseph A.	1845
Alexander, Stephen	1839
Alexander, William, claimed 6th Earl of Stirling	1770
Alison, Francis	B
Alison, Robert H.	1878
Allen, Andrew	B
Allen, Benjamin	1812
Allen, Charles E.	1922
Allen, Don C.	1958
Allen, George	1856
Allen, Harrison	1867
Allen, James	B
Allen, Joel A.	1878
Allen, John	B
Allen, W. H.	1858
Allen, William	B
Allibone, S. Austin	1865
Allison, Burgiss	1789
Allison, Joseph	1875
Allison, N. S.	1814
Alvarez, Luis Walter	1953
Ames, Charles G.	1881
Ames, Herman V.	1921
Ames, Joseph S.	1905

Anastos, Milton V.	1967	Bailey, Liberty H.	1896
Anderson, Alexander	1791	Baird, Absalom	1791
Anderson, Carl David	1938	Baird, Henry C.	1869
Anderson, George L.	1886	Baird, Henry M.	1884
Anderson, George W.	1869	Baird, Robert	1848
Anderson, Henry J.	1828	Baird, Spencer F.	1855
Anderson, James	B	Baker, Carlos Heard	1982
Anderson, M. B.	1867	Baker, John R.	1884
Andrews, Charles McL	1924	Baker, Newton D.	1936
Andrews, Donald H.	1933	Baker, William S.	1886
Andrews, E. B.	1871	Balch, Edwin S.	1899
Andrews, John	1786	Balch, Thomas W.	1901
Andrews, Roy C.	1927	Baldwin, Henry	1838
Anfinsen, Christian B.	1975	Baldwin, James M.	1897
Angell, James B.	1889	Baldwin, Matthias W.	1833
Angell, James R.	1924	Baldwin, Simeon E.	1910
Anthon, Charles E.	1868	Bancker, Charles N.	1825
Antill, Edward	A	Bancker, Gerard	1772
Appleton, William H.	1893	Bancroft, George	1841
Arbo, John	C	Bancroft, Wilder D.	1920
Armstrong, Edward C.	1932	Barber, Edwin A.	1881
Armstrong, Hamilton F.	1940	Barbour, Thomas	1937
Arthur, Joseph C.	1919	Barca, Calderon de la	1848
Ashburner, Charles A.	1880	Bard, Philip	1959
Ashhurst, John	1884	Bard, Samuel	C
Ashhurst, John	1928	Bardeen, John	1958
Ashhurst, Richard L.	1884	Barghoorn, Elso Sterrenberg	1978
Aspden, Matthias	B	Barker, George F.	1873
Astin, Allen V.	1958	Barker, Wharton	1884
Atkinson, George F.	1913	Barlow, Joel	1809
Atterbury, William W.	1916	Barnard, Chester I.	1943
Audubon, John J.	1831	Barnard, Edward E.	1903
Aydelotte, Frank	1923	Barnard, F. A. P.	1871
		Barnard, William T.	1887
B		Barnes, Albert	1855
		Barnsley, Thomas	B
Baade, Walter	1953	Barnwell, William	1802
Bache, Alexander D.	1829	Bartholow, Roberts	1880
Bache, Franklin	1820	Bartlett, Harley H.	1929
Bache, Hartman	1831	Bartlett, Paul D.	1978
Bache, R. Meade	1884	Bartlett, W. H. C.	1840
Bache, Thomas H.	1877	Barton, Benjamin S.	1789
Bache, William	1797	Barton, George A.	1911
Bacon, Thomas	B	Barton, Richard P.	1792
Baekeland, Leo H.	1935	Barton, Thomas	B
Baer, George F.	1898	Barton, W. P. C.	1813
Bailey, Irving W.	1926	Barton, William	1787
Bailey, J. W.	1852	Bartram, Isaac	C
Bailey, Joel	1770	Bartram, John	A

Bartram, Moses	C	Bers, Lipman	1980
Bartram, William	C	Bethune, George W.	1839
Barus, Carl	1903	Bettle, William	C
Bastin, Edson S.	1896	Betton, Samuel	1828
Bate, Walter J.	1966	Betton, Thomas F.	1857
Bateman, Harry	1924	Biddle, A. Sydney	1889
Bauer, Louis A.	1909	Biddle, Alexander	1888
Baugh, Albert C.	1946	Biddle, Arthur	1888
Baugh, Daniel	1899	Biddle, Cadwalader	1880
Bayard, James A.	C	Biddle, Clement	C
Bayard, John	1787	Biddle, Clement C.	1821
Bayard, Thomas F.	1897	Biddle, Craig	1877
Bayne-Jones, Stanhope	1944	Biddle, Edward	C
Baynton, John	1771	Biddle, George W.	1897
Beach, Frank Ambrose	1961	Biddle, James	B
Beach, Samuel	1789	Biddle, John	1863
Beadle, E. R.	1870	Biddle, John B.	1853
Beadle, George W.	1945	Biddle, John G.	1814
Beams, Jesse W.	1939	Biddle, Nicholas	1813
Beard, Charles A.	1936	Biddle, Owen	C
Beasley, Frederick	1814	Biddle, Thomas	1829
Beck, Charles F.	1845	Bigelow, Jacob	1818
Beck, James M.	1926	Biggs, John, Jr.	1951
Beck, T. Romeyn	1839	Billings, John S.	1887
Becker, Carl	1936	Bingham, William	1787
Becker, George F.	1907	Binney, Barnabas	1784
Beckley, John	1791	Binney, Horace	1808
Bedford, Nathaniel B.	1796	Binney, Horace	1869
Bee, Thomas	1781	Birch, A. Francis	1955
Beeson, Charles H.	1940	Bird, Robert M.	1853
Belknap, Jeremy	1784	Birge, Edward A.	1923
Bell, Alexander G.	1882	Birge, Raymond	1943
Bell, Eric T.	1937	Birkhoff, Garrett	1960
Bell, John	1832	Birkhoff, George D.	1921
Bell, Joseph S.	1882	Bispham, George T.	1895
Bement, Clarence S.	1895	Blackall, Eric	1971
Benbridge, Henry	1771	Blackwelder, Eliot	1939
Bendix, Reinhard	1977	Blackwell, Robert	1784
Benedict, Francis G.	1910	Blair, Andrew A.	1889
Benezet, John	C	Blair, Samuel	1797
Bennett, Charles E.	1913	Blair, Thomas S.	1866
deBenneville, James S.	1897	Blake, Francis G.	1950
Bensell, Charles	C	Blake, Robert P.	1944
Bentley, Gerald E.	1970	Blake, William P.	1870
Bentley, William	1811	Blakeslee, Albert F.	1924
Berkey, Charles P.	1928	Blalock, Alfred	1963
Berkner, Lloyd V.	1956	Blanckenhagen, Peter H. von	1985
Berle, Adolf A.	1965	Blanshard, Brand	1948
Berry, Edward W.	1919	Blasius, William	1875

Bleakley, John	1789	Brackett, Cyrus F.	1877
Blegen, Carl W.	1941	Bradford, Thomas	B
Bliss, Gilbert A.	1926	Bradford, William	1785
Blitzer, Charles	1988	Bradley, Wilmot H.	1963
Bloch, Felix	1965	Branner, John C.	1886
Blodget, Lorin	1872	Brashear, John A.	1902
Bloomfield, Leonard	1942	Brauer, Richard D.	1974
Bloomfield, Maurice	1904	Brearly, David	1789
Bloomfield, Morton Wilfred	1981	Breasted, James H.	1919
Blum, Jerome	1979	Breck, Samuel	1838
Boardman, George D.	1880	Breckinridge, Robert J.	1866
Boardman, Henry A.	1851	Bridenbaugh, Carl	1958
Boas, Franz	1903	Bridges, Robert	1844
Boas, George	1950	Bridgman, Percy W.	1916
Bôcher, Maxime	1916	Briggs, Isaac	1796
Bodian, David	1973	Briggs, Lyman J.	1935
Bogert, Marston T.	1909	Briggs, Robert	1863
Boker, George H.	1884	Brigham, Clarence S.	1955
Bollmann, Justus E.	1800	Bright, James W.	1914
Bolton, Herbert E.	1937	Bringhurst, James	1774
Boltwood, Bertram B.	1911	Bringhurst, Joseph	C
Bonbright, James C.	B	Brinton, Crane	1953
Bond, Phineas	B	Brinton, Daniel G.	1869
Bond, Thomas	B	Brinton, J. H.	1810
Bond, Thomas, Jr.	B	Brinton, John H.	1886
Bond, W. C.	1852	Britton, J. Blodget	1873
Bonner, Campbell	1938	Britton, Nathaniel L.	1928
Bonner, James	1966	Brock, Robert C. H.	1899
Bonnycastle, Charles	1840	Brockenbrough, John	1835
Bonwill, William G. A.	1885	Bronk, Detlev W.	1934
Booth, James C.	1839	Brooke, C. F. Tucker	1938
Bopp, Karl R.	1958	Brooke, Richard	1769
Borden, Simeon	1842	Brooks, Cleanth	1973
Bordley, John B.	1783	Brooks, Van Wyck	1939
Borie, Adolph E.	1872	Brooks, William K.	1886
Boring, Edwin G.	1945	Broughton, T. Robert. S.	1955
Boss, Lewis	1911	Brown, Amos P.	1901
Boulding, Kenneth E.	1960	Brown, Arthur E.	1879
Bowditch, Henry P.	1904	Brown, Ernest W.	1898
Bowditch, Nathaniel	1809	Brown, Harrison Scott	1966
Bowdoin, James	1787	Brown, Henry A.	1877
Bowen, Catherine D.	1958	Brown, James	1827
Bowen, Ira S.	1940	Brown, John N.	1959
Bowen, Norman L.	1930	Brown, John P.	1856
Bowen, Samuel	1769	Brown, Nathaniel B.	1867
Bowman, Isaiah	1923	Brown, Samuel	1800
Boyd, Julian P.	1943	Brown, W. Norman	1946
Boyé, Martin H.	1840	Brown, William	1780
Boys, William	1799	Brubaker, Albert P.	1895

Bruce, Archibald	1807	Calkins, Gary N.	1920
Brumbaugh, Martin G.	1908	Calvert, Philip P.	1918
Brush, Charles F.	1910	Calvin, Melvin	1960
Brush, George J.	1865	Camac, William	1874
Bryan, George	A	Campbell, Donald T.	1993
Bryant, Henry G.	1898	Campbell, Douglas H.	1910
Bryant, William	1774	Campbell, George	1837
Bryant, William L.	1935	Campbell, John L.	1875
Buchanan, George	1789	Campbell, William W.	1903
Buchanan, James	1846	Canby, William M.	1868
Buchanan, Norman S.	1956	Cannon, Annie J.	1925
Buck, Carl D.	1923	Cannon, Walter B.	1908
Buckley, Oliver E.	1942	Capps, Edward	1920
Buddington, Arthur F.	1931	Carey, Henry C.	1833
Bühler, Curt F.	1967	Carey, Mathew	1821
Bull, Marcus	1827	Carleson. *See* Von Carleson	
Bullock, Charles	1869	Carleton, Henry	1859
Bumpus, Hermon C.	1909	Carll, John F.	1875
Bumstead, Henry A.	1918	Carlson, Anton J.	1928
Bunche, Ralph J.	1950	Carmichael, Leonard	1942
Bundy, McGeorge	1991	Carmichael, William	1780
Burd, Edward	1785	Carnegie, Andrew	1902
Burgess, Warren R.	1942	Carpenter, Rhys	1935
Burk, Isaac	1884	Carrel, Alexis	1909
Burk, Jesse Y.	1884	Carson, Hampton L.	1880
Burns, Arthur F.	1947	Carson, John	1785
Burrough, Marmaduke	1833	Carson, Joseph	1844
Bush, John N. D.	1946	Carter, James C.	1895
Bush, Vannevar	1937	Carter, Landon	1769
Butler, Benjamin F.	1844	Carty, John J.	1921
Butler, Elmer G.	1948	Case, Ermine C.	1931
Butler, Nicholas M.	1938	Caskey, John Langdon	1967
Butler, William	1881	Cass, Lewis	1826
Butterfield, Lyman H.	1964	Cassatt, Alexander J.	1872
Butts. *See* De Butts		Cassin, John	1852
Byrd, Richard E.	1930	Castle, William Bosworth	1939
		Castle, William E.	1910
C		Castner, Samuel	1887
		Cather, Willa	1934
Cadbury, Henry J.	1949	Cathrall, Isaac	1796
Cadwalader, John	C	Cattell, J. McKeen	1888
Cadwalader, John	1867	Cattell, W. C.	1871
Cadwalader, John	1899	Chafee, Zechariah, Jr.	1946
Cadwalader, John	1926	Chalmers, Lionel	C
Cadwalader, Lambert	C	Chamberlain, Joseph P.	1940
Cadwalader, Thomas	A	Chamberlin, Rollin T.	1943
Cadwalader, Thomas	1825	Chamberlin, Thomas C.	1905
Caldwell, Charles	1796	Chance, Henry M.	1880
Caldwell, Samuel	B	Chandler, Charles F.	1875

Chandrasekhar, Subrahmanyan	1945	Clifford, Thomas	C
Chaney, Ralph W.	1943	Clinton, DeWitt	1814
Chapman, Frank M.	1921	Cloos, Ernst	1954
Chapman, Henry C.	1875	Cloud, Joseph	1806
Chapman, John	C	Cloud, Preston	1973
Chapman, Nathaniel	1807	Clymer, George	C
Chase, George H.	1929	Coates, Benjamin H.	1823
Chase, Pliny E.	1863	Coble, Arthur B.	1939
Chase, Thomas	1864	Cochran, Thomas C.	1953
Chauncey, Charles	1813	Cockerell, Theodore D. A.	1928
Chauvenet, William	1851	Coffin, John H. C.	1869
Cherniss, Harold Fredrik	1949	Coggeshall, Lowell Thelwell	1957
Chevalier, Peter	C	Coghill, George E.	1935
Cheves, Langdon	1821	Cohen, Joshua I.	1854
Chew, Benjamin	B	Cohn, Edwin J.	1949
Chew, Benjamin	1787	Colden, Cadwallader	B
Chew, John T.	1974	Cole, Fay-Cooper	1941
Chew, Samuel C.	1951	Coleman, James S.	1970
Cheyney, Edward P.	1904	Coleman, William	B
Childs, George W.	1886	Coleman, William	1988
Chinard, Gilbert	1932	Coles, Edward	1839
Chittenden, Russell H.	1904	Coles, Edward	1899
Choate, Joseph H.	1906	Colhoun, Samuel	1815
Christie, James	1908	Collin, Nicholas	1789
Church, John	1802	Collins, Zaccheus	1804
Clark, Alvan	1880	Collitz, Hermann	1902
Clark, Clarence H.	1889	Colwell, Stephen	1857
Clark, Daniel	1769	Comegys, Benjamin B.	1879
Clark, George R	1967	Commons, John R.	1936
Clark, John M.	1944	Compton, Arthur H.	1925
Clark, Joseph S.	1976	Compton, Karl T.	1923
Clark, William B.	1902	Comstock, John H.	1913
Clark, William M.	1939	Conant, James B.	1935
Clarke, Frank W.	1904	Conant, Kenneth John	1954
Clarke, Hans T.	1943	Condie, D. Francis	1835
Clarke, James F.	1874	Condon, Edward U.	1949
Clarke, John M.	1911	Conklin, Edwin G.	1897
Clarke, Thomas C.	1873	Conover, Samuel F.	1806
Clarkson, Gerardus	C	Conrad, Solomon W.	1822
Clarkson, Matthew	C	Conrad, Timothy A.	1865
Clay, Albert T.	1912	Converse, John H.	1898
Clay, Joseph	1799	Conyngham, John N.	1848
Claypole, Edward W.	1883	Conyngham, Redmond	1819
Cleaveland, Parker	1818	Cook, George H.	1864
Cleemann, Richard A.	1895	Cook, Gustavus W.	1934
Cleemann, Thomas M.	1885	Cook, Joel	1895
Cleland, Ralph E.	1932	Coolidge, William D.	1938
Cleveland, Charles D.	1865	Coombe, Thomas	A
Cleveland, Grover	1897	Coombe, Thomas, Jr.	1773

Cooper, James F.	1823	Currie, William	1792
Cooper, Myles	1769	Curti, Merle Eugene	1948
Cooper, Thomas	1802	Curtis, Cyrus H. K.	1930
Cope, Arthur C.	1961	Curtis, George W.	1892
Cope, Edward D.	1866	Curtis, Heber D.	1920
Cope, Thomas P.	1843	Curwen, John	1861
Copeland, Lammot duPont	1978	Cushing, Frank H.	1896
Coplin, W. M. Late	1911	Cushing, Harvey	1930
Coppée, Henry	1856	Cushing, Henry P.	1916
Cori, Carl Ferdinand	1947	Cushman, Robert E.	1949
Cori, Gerty T.	1948	Cutbush, James	1814
Cornelius, Robert	1862	Cutler, Manasseh	1785
Corner, George W.	1940	Cuyler, Theodore	1857
Corwin, Edward S.	1936		
Cottrell, Frederick G.	1938	**D**	
Cottrell, Leonard S.	1957		
Coues, Elliott	1878	D'Aligny, Henry F.	1870
Coulter, John M.	1915	DaCosta, J. M.	1866
Councilman, William T.	1918	DaCosta, John C.	1904
Courant, Richard	1953	Dahlgren, Ulric	1919
Courtenay, Edward H.	1835	Dall, William H.	1897
Cox, Allan	1984	Dallas, Alexander J.	1791
Cox, Jacob D.	1870	Dallas, George M.	1840
Cox, John	1789	Daly, Charles P.	1893
Coxe, Daniel	1772	Daly, Lloyd W.	1976
Coxe, Eckley B.	1870	Daly, Reginald A.	1913
Coxe, John	B	Damrosch, Walter J.	1939
Coxe, John R.	1799	Dana, Charles E.	1899
Coxe, Tench	1796	Dana, Edward S.	1896
Crafts, James M.	1916	Dana, James D.	1854
Craig, Isaac	1787	Danforth, Charles H.	1944
Cramp, Charles H.	1892	Daniels, Farrington	1948
Crane, Robert T.	1941	Darlington, William	1823
Crane, Thomas F.	1877	Darrach, William	1929
Craven, Wesley Frank	1976	Darrow, Karl Kelchner	1936
Crawford, J. P. Wickersham	1929	Davenport, Charles B.	1907
Creel, Herrlee G.	1983	Davidson, George	1866
Cremin, Lawrence Arthur	1984	Davidson, James	B
Cresson, Charles M.	1857	Davidson, Robert	1783
Cresson, John C.	1839	Davis, Arthur P.	1927
Cret, Paul P.	1928	Davis, Benjamin	C
Crew, Henry	1921	Davis, Bradley M.	1914
Crile, George W.	1912	Davis, Charles H.	1852
Crocker, William	1931	Davis, Charles Till	1998
Crosby, Sumner McKnight	1977	Davis, Hallowel	1965
Cross, Whitman	1915	Davis, Harvey N.	1935
Cross, Wilbur L.	1934	Davis, Isaac R.	1851
Crowell, Edward P.	1898	Davis, John	B
Culin, R. Stewart	1897	Davis, John	1811

Davis, John W.	1924	Dixon, Samuel G.	1892
Davis, Kingsley	1960	Dobson, Judah	1840
Davis, William M.	1899	Dobzhansky, Theodosius	1942
Davis, William M.	1883	Dodd, William E.	1936
Davisson, Clinton J.	1929	Dodds, Harold W.	1935
Day, Arthur L.	1912	Doisy, Edward A.	1942
Day, Charles	1925	Dolley, Charles S.	1886
Day, Edmund E.	1937	Donaldson, Henry H.	1906
Day, Frank M.	1899	Doolittle, Eric	1903
Day, William C.	1899	Dorr, Benjamin	1841
Day, William L.	1971	Dorsey, John S.	1814
Dearborn, Benjamin	1803	Dougherty, Thomas H.	1899
Deas, John	C	Douglas, James	1877
De Butts, Elisha	1821	Douglas, Lewis W.	1942
Debye, Peter	1936	Douglas, Paul H.	1952
De Garmo, Charles	1897	Douglass, Andrew E.	1941
De Lancey, Edward F.	1898	Downes, John	1843
De Lancey, James	B	Drake, Daniel	1818
De Lancey, William H.	1829	Draper, Daniel	1880
Delano, Frederic A.	1935	Draper, Henry	1877
Delaney, Sharp	1774	Draper, John W.	1844
Delmas, Gladys K.	1991	Drayton, William	1835
Demerec, Milislav	1952	Dreer, Ferdinand J.	1897
Demmé, C. R.	1840	Dresden, Arnold	1932
Dempster, Arthur J.	1932	Drexel, Anthony J.	1892
Denny, Harmar	1848	Drinker, Henry	C
De Normandie. *See* Normandie		Drinker, Henry	1951
Dercum, Francis X.	1892	Drinker, John	C
Derleth, Charles, Jr.	1936	Drown, Thomas M.	1875
Dethier, Vincent G.	1980	Dryden, Hugh L.	1950
Detwiler, Samuel R.	1940	Duane, Morris	1940
Dewees, William P.	1819	Duane, Russell	1906
Dewey, Bradley	1945	Duane, William	1921
Dewey, Chester	1863	Du Bois, Eugene F.	1940
Dewey, John	1911	Du Bois, Patterson	1880
De Witt, Simeon	1787	Du Bois, William E.	1844
Dick, James	C	Dubos, René Jules	1954
Dicke, Robert H.	1978	Dubourg, William	1806
Dickerson, Mahlon	1807	DuBridge, Lee A.	1942
Dickinson, James	B	Ducatel, Julius T.	1832
Dickinson, John	A	Duché, Jacob	A
Dickinson, John	1940	Duché, Jacob, Jr.	C
Dickson, Leonard E.	1920	Dudley, Charles B.	1879
Dickson, Samuel	1884	Dudley, Thomas H.	1880
Dickson, Samuel H.	1859	Duffield, Benjamin	1786
Dillingham, William H.	1843	Duffield, Edward	A
Dilworth, J. Richardson	1984	Duffield, George	1779
Dinsmoor, William B.	1933	Duffield, Samuel	B
Dixon, Roland B.	1926	Dugan, Raymond S.	1931

Duggar, Benjamin M.	1921	Einarsson, Stefán	1954
Dulaney, Daniel	B	Einstein, Albert	1930
Dunbar, Carl O.	1942	Eiseley, Loren C.	1960
Dunbar, William	1800	Eisenhart, Luther P.	1913
Duncan, Louis	1886	Elam, Samuel	1799
Dundas, James	1851	Elder, William	1872
Dunglison, Robley	1832	Eldridge, Samuel	C
Dunlap, John	1784	Eliot, Charles W.	1871
Dunlap, Thomas	1837	Ellet, Charles	1843
Dunlop, Robert G.	1990	Ellicott, Andrew	1785
Dunn, Gano	1924	Ellicott, Joseph	1770
Dunn, Leslie C.	1943	Elliot, A. Marshall	1895
Dunn, Nathan	1836	Elliot, Samuel	C
Dunning, George F.	1867	Elliot, Stephen	1819
Du Ponceau, Peter S.	1791	Elliott, Andrew	C
Du Pont, Francis I.	1930	Elmer, Jonathan	1774
Du Pont, Henry A.	1894	Elvehjem, Conrad A.	1947
Du Pont, Henry F.	1961	Elwyn, Alfred L.	1844
Du Pont, Irénée	1807	Ely, Theodore N.	1897
Du Pont, La Motte	1872	Emerson, Benjamin K.	1897
Du Pont, Pierre S.	1917	Emerson, Gouverneur	1833
Du Pont, Samuel F.	1862	Emerson, Ralph W.	1867
Durand, Elias	1854	Emerson, Rollins A.	1922
Durand, William F.	1917	Emlen, George	1827
Du Simitière, Pierre E.	C	Emmet, John P.	1838
Dutton, Clarence E.	1871	Emmet, William LeR.	1898
Du Vigneaud, Vincent	1944	Emmons, Samuel F.	1883
		Enders, John Franklin	1955
E		Engelman, George	1862
		Ericsson, John	1877
Earle, Pliney	1866	Erlanger, Joseph	1927
East, Edward M.	1916	Erskine, Robert	1780
Easton, Morton W.	1886	Esau, Katherine	1964
Eberle, John	1819	Espy, James P.	1835
Eckert, George N.	1852	Etting, Frank M.	1876
Eckfeldt, Jacob B.	1880	Ettinghausen, Richard	1976
Eckfeldt, Jacob R.	1844	Evans, Cadwalader	A
Eddy, H. Turner	1877	Evans, David	C
Edelstein, Ludwig	1954	Evans, Edmund C.	1859
Edgerton, Franklin	1935	Evans, Griffith C.	1941
Edgerton, Harold E.	1972	Evans, Rowland	C
Edison, Thomas A.	1896	Eve, Oswell	A
Edmunds, George F.	1895	Everett, Alexander H.	1831
Edsall, David L.	1906	Everett, Edward	1831
Edwards, Enoch	1787	Ewell, Marshall D.	1895
Eggan, Fred R.	1962	Ewing, John	B
Eglin, William C. L.	1926	Ewing, Maurice	1959
Eigenmann, Carl H.	1917	Eyring, Henry	1941

F

Fabricant, Solomon	1954	Ford, Guy S.	1939
Fainsod, Merle	1961	Ford, Paul L.	1898
Fairbank, John King	1969	Ford, Worthington C.	1922
Fairbank, William M.	1978	Fosdick, Raymond B.	1930
Farabee, William C.	1919	Foulke, John	1784
Faries, _____	B	Foulke, William P.	1854
Farlow, William G.	1905	Fowler, William Alfred	1962
Farmer, Ferdinand	B	Fox, Dixon R.	1935
Farnum, Joseph W.	1851	Fox, George	1784
Farrand, Livingston	1924	Fox, Herbert	1932
Farrand, Max	1928	Fox, Joseph	B
Fay, Sidney B.	1947	Foxcroft, John	A
Featherstonhaugh, George W.	1809	Foxcroft, Thomas	C
Feller, William	1966	Fraley, Frederick	1842
Fels, Samuel S.	1939	Fraley, Joseph C.	1880
Felton, Samuel M.	1854	Francis, J. W.	1844
Fenn, Wallace O.	1946	Francis, James B.	1865
Ferguson, William	1791	Francis, Thomas, Jr.	1954
Ferguson, William S.	1937	Francke, Kuno	1904
Fermi, Enrico	1939	Frank, Leonard G.	1875
Fernald, Merritt L.	1936	Frank, Tenney	1927
Fetter, Frank A.	1935	Frankfort, Henri	1948
Field, Robert P.	1890	Frankfurter, Felix	1939
Fieser, Louis F.	1941	Franklin, Benjamin	A
Findley, William	1789	Franklin, Edward C.	1912
Fine, Henry B.	1897	Franklin, William	A
Finley, Clement A.	1856	Franklin, William T.	1786
Finley, John H.	1919	Frantz, M. Alison	1973
Fisher, Irving	1927	Frazer, John F.	1842
Fisher, Joshua F.	1833	Frazer, Persifor	1872
Fisher, Sidney G.	1860	Frazer, Robert P.	1873
Fisher, Sidney G.	1897	Frazier, Benjamin W.	1896
Fisher, Thomas	C	Frazier, Charles H.	1905
Fisher, William R.	1840	Fred, Edwin Broun	1945
Fisk, James Brown	1960	Freeman, Douglas S.	1943
Flexner, Louis B.	1979	Freund, Paul A.	1966
Flexner, Simon	1901	Friebis, George	1889
Flint, Austin	1880	Friend, Albert M., Jr.	1952
Flint, Austin, Jr.	1880	Frieze, Henry S.	1884
Flory, Paul John	1973	Frost, Edwin B.	1909
Fluegel, J. G.	1853	Frost, Robert	1937
Foggo, Edward A.	1878	Fulbright, J. William	1953
Fooks, Paul	C	Fullerton, George S.	1890
Foote, Paul D.	1927	Fulton, John	1873
Forbes, Alexander	1931	Fulton, John F.	1949
Forbes, Stephen A.	1919	Fulton, Robert	1809
		Furness, Horace H.	1880
		Furness, Horace H.	1897

Furness, William H.	1840	Gilbert, Grove K.	1902
Furness, William H.	1897	Gildersleeve, Basil L.	1903
		Gill, Theodore N.	1867
G		Gilliss, J. Melville	1848
		Gilman, Daniel C.	1876
Gabb, William	1869	Gilmore, Myron	1972
Gale, Benjamin	A	Gilmore, Robert	1803
Gallatin, Albert	1791	Gilpin, Henry D.	1832
Galloway, Joseph	A	Gilpin, Joseph	1770
Gamble, Arch	1784	Gilpin, Joshua	1804
Gaposchkin, Cecilia P.	1936	Gilpin, Thomas	C
Garden, Alexander	A	Gilpin, Thomas	1814
Garnett, John	1802	Girardin, L. H.	1819
Garrett, Philip C.	1883	Glentworth, George	C
Garrison, Joseph F.	1884	Glueck, Nelson	1954
Gasser, Herbert S.	1937	Goddard, David Rockwell	1954
Gaston, William	1817	Goddard, Kingston	1857
Gates, Merrill E.	1886	Goddard, Paul B.	1840
Gates, Thomas S.	1930	Gödel, Kurt	1961
Gates, Thomas S., Jr.	1959	Godfrey, Thomas	B
Gatschet, Albert S.	1884	Godman, John D.	1825
Gauld, George	1774	Godon, Silvain	1809
Gay, Edwin F.	1932	Goethals, George W.	1913
Geddings, E.	1848	Goetze, Albrecht	1951
Gelb, Ignace Jay	1975	Goitein, Shelomo Dov	1970
Gellhorn, Walter	1965	Goldberg, Leo	1958
Genth, Frederick A.	1854	Goldsborough, Robert	1791
Genth, Frederick A.	1886	Goldsmith, Middleton	1879
George, Sidney	C	Gomberg, Moses	1920
Gerhard, Benjamin	1854	Gooch, Frank A.	1907
Gerhard, William W.	1843	Goodale, George L.	1893
Gerschenkron, Alexander	1970	Goode, George B.	1889
Gest, John M.	1921	Goodell, William	1877
Gest, William P.	1926	Goodfellow, Edward	1871
Giamatti, A. Bartlett	1982	Goodnow, Frank J.	1920
Giaque, William F.	1940	Goodpasture, Ernest W.	1943
Gibb, Sir Hamilton	1960	Goodrich, Carter	1946
Gibbs, George	1810	Goodrich, Herbert F.	1937
Gibbs, Josiah W.	1895	Goodspeed, Arthur W.	1896
Gibbs, Oliver W.	1854	Goodwin, Daniel R.	1861
Gibbs, William F.	1955	Goodwin, Harold	1892
Gibson, James	1807	Goodwin, W. W.	1895
Gibson, John	B	Gordon, George B.	1910
Gibson, John B.	1821	Gordon, Kermit	1971
Gibson, William	1820	Gorgas, William C.	1913
Gies, William J.	1915	Gorringe, Henry H.	1881
Gifford, Walter S.	1931	Gottschalk, Louis	1951
Gilbert, Cass	1934	Goudsmit, Samuel A.	1952
Gilbert, Felix	1969	Gould, A. A.	1849

Gould, Benjamin A.	1851	Guald, George	1770
Gowen, Franklin B.	1877	Guggenheim, William	1930
Graeme, Thomas	A	Guillou, Constant	1854
Graff, Frederic	1868	Gulick, Charles B.	1940
Graham, Clarence H.	1956	Gummere, Francis B.	1903
Graham, Evarts A.	1941	Gummere, John	1814
Graham, James D.	1840	Gummere, Samuel J.	1868
Grandgent, Charles H.	1929	Gutekunst, F.	1885
Grant, Ulysses S.	1868	Guyot, Arnold	1867
Grassi, C. F. A.	1796		
Graves, Frank P.	1927	**H**	
Gray, Asa	1848		
Gray, Elisha	1878	Haas, F. Otto	1967
Gray, George	1784	Hadley, Arthur T.	1902
Gray, George	1900	Hagen, Hermann A.	1886
Gray, Isaac	1781	Hagert, Henry S.	1875
Gray, James	1815	Hague, Arnold	1903
Grayson, William	1780	Haines, John S.	1873
Greely, Adolphus W.	1904	Haines, Reuben	1813
Green, Ashbel	1789	Haldeman, Samuel S.	1844
Green, Samuel A.	1893	Hale, Charles	1866
Green, Traill	1868	Hale, Edward E.	1870
Green, William H.	1863	Hale, George E.	1902
Greenaway, Emerson	1960	Hall, Asaph	1878
Greene, Evarts B.	1931	Hall, Charles E.	1875
Greene, S. Dana	1898	Hall, Charles M.	1898
Greene, William H.	1879	Hall, David	B
Greenewalt, Crawford H.	1954	Hall, Isaac H.	1893
Greenleaf, Simon	1848	Hall, James	1854
Greenman, Milton J.	1899	Hall, John E.	1814
Greenway, James	1794	Hall, Lyman B.	1885
Gregg, Alan	1944	Hallock, William	1908
Gregory, Henry D.	1889	Hallowell, A. Irving	1963
Gregory, Herbert E.	1923	Hallowell, Benjamin	1854
Gregory, William K.	1925	Hallowell, Edward	1851
Grier, Robert C.	1848	Hamilton, Alexander	1780
Griffith, J. P. Crozer	1907	Hamilton, James	B
Griffith, Robert E.	1828	Hamilton, William	1797
Griffith, Thomas W.	1838	Hammond, William A.	1859
Griffiths, Samuel P.	1785	Handler, Philip	1969
Grinnell, Henry	1853	Haney, John L.	1929
Grisby, Hugh B.	1856	Hanfmann, George M. A.	1970
Griscom, John	1836	Hanson, Howard	1950
Griscom, William W.	1881	Harbage, Alfred B.	1959
Griswold, Erwin N.	1955	Harbison, Frederick H.	1969
Gross, Samuel D.	1854	Harden, John W.	1873
Gross, Samuel W.	1885	Harding, George	1854
Grote, Augustus R.	1876	Harding, Robert	B
von Grunebaum, Gustave E.	1968	Hare, Charles W.	1815

Hare, J. I. Clark	1842	Hayden, Ferdinand V.	1860
Hare, Robert	1803	Hayes, Carlton J. H.	1940
Harkins, William D.	1925	Hayes, Isaac I.	1863
Harkness, Edward S.	1934	Hayes, Richard S.	1886
Harkness, William	1898	Hayford, John F.	1915
Harlan, Richard	1822	Hays, I. Minis	1886
Harlow, Harry F.	1957	Hays, Isaac	1830
Harnwell, Gaylord P.	1954	Hayward, Nathan	1937
Harper, Robert A.	1909	Hazard, Ebenezer	1781
Harrar, J. George	1962	Hazard, John N.	1972
Harris, Joseph S.	1887	Hazen, Charles D.	1923
Harris, Levett	1821	Hazlehurst, Henry	1889
Harris, Robert	C	Hazlehurst, Isaac	1851
Harris, Robert P.	1856	Heaton, Herbert	1945
Harris, Thomas	1828	Heckewelder, John	1797
Harris, William	1838	Heidelberger, Michael	1968
Harris, Zellig S.	1962	Heilprin, Angelo	1883
Harrison, Charles C.	1895	Heiser, Victor G.	1918
Harrison, George L.	1885	Heller, Walter Wolfgang	1975
Harrison, George R.	1950	Helmuth, J. H. C.	1784
Harrison, Joseph	C	Hembel, William	1813
Harrison, Joseph	1864	Hempel, Carl G.	1966
Harrison, Peter	C	Henderson, Andrew A.	1862
Harrison, Ross G.	1913	Henderson, C. Hanford	1896
Harshberger, John W.	1906	Henderson, Lawrence J.	1921
Hart, James M.	1877	Henderson, Robert	1927
Hart, John S.	1844	Henderson, Yandell	1935
Hartline, Haldan Keffer	1952	Hendricks, Sterling B.	1967
Hartranft, John F.	1876	Hendrickson, George L.	1932
Hartshorne, Edward	1858	Henry, Joseph	1835
Hartshorne, Henry	1863	Henry, William	C
Hartshorne, Joseph	1815	Herlihy, David	1990
Harvey, A. McGehee Harvey	1984	Herty, Charles H.	1917
Harvey, E. Newton	1929	Hess, Alfred F.	1931
Haskins, Charles H.	1921	Hess, Harry H.	1960
Hassler, Ferd. R.	1807	Hewett, Waterman T.	1893
Hastie, William H.	1972	Hewson, Thomas T.	1801
Hastings, A. Baird	1941	Hexter, Jack H.	1985
Hastings, Charles S.	1906	Heyward, Thomas, Jr.	1784
Hatcher, John B.	1897	Hibben, John G.	1912
Haupt, Herman	1871	Hicks, Gilbert	B
Haupt, Lewis M.	1878	Higginbotham, A. Leon, Jr.	1978
Haupt, Paul	1902	Hildebrand, Joel H.	1951
Haury, Emil W.	1969	Hildeburn, Charles R.	1897
Hauser, Philip M.	1965	Hilgard, Julius E.	1863
Haven, Samuel F.	1865	Hill, David J.	1910
Hawk, Philip B.	1915	Hill, George W.	1903
Haworth, Leland J.	1965	Hill, Hamilton A.	1882
Hay, John	1898	Hill, Henry	1771

Hill, Thomas	1863	Hopkinson, Joseph	1815
Hillebrand, William F.	1906	Hopkinson, Thomas	B
Hillegas, Michael	C	Hopper, Edward	1869
Hiller, Hiram M.	1897	Hoppin, J. M.	1893
Hilprecht, Hermann V.	1886	Horn, George H.	1869
Himes, Charles F.	1874	Horner, Inman	1886
Himili, John	C	Horner, William E.	1819
Hirst, Barton C.	1899	Horsfall, Frank L.	1956
Hisaw, Frederick L.	1940	Horsfield, Thomas	1829
Hitchcock, Charles H.	1870	Horsford, E. N.	1849
Hitchcock, Edward	1841	Horsmanden, Daniel	B
Hobbs, William H.	1909	Hosack, David	1810
Hocking, William E.	1943	Hotchkiss, Jedediah	1881
Hockley, Richard	B	Houckgeest, A. E. Van Braam	1797
Hockley, Thomas	1885	Hough, Franklin B.	1882
Hodge, Hugh	1796	Hough, George W.	1872
Hodge, Hugh L.	1832	Houston, Edwin J.	1872
Hodge, James T.	1864	Houston, Henry H.	1887
Hodgson, William B.	1830	Houston, William C.	1780
Hoebel, E. Adamson	1963	Houston, William V.	1949
Hoffman, Walter J.	1889	Hovland, Carl I.	1950
Hofstadter, Richard	1957	Howard, Leland O.	1911
Hofstadter, Robert	1986	Howe, Henry M.	1897
Hoge, John	1791	Howell, Joshua	C
Hoge, Jonathan	1786	Howell, William H.	1903
Holbrook, John E.	1839	Hrdlička, Aleš	1918
Holden, Edward S.	1897	Hubbard, Joseph S.	1852
Holland, James W.	1886	Hubble, Edwin P.	1929
Holland, Leicester B.	1931	Huber, Gotthelf C.	1912
Holland, William J.	1928	Hudson, Manley O.	1941
Hollingsworth, Levi	C	Huebner, Solomon S.	1930
Hollingsworth, Samuel L.	1856	Huggins, Charles B.	1962
Hollyday, Henry	B	Hughes, Charles E.	1926
Holmes, Abiel	1816	Hulett, George A.	1913
Holmes, Oliver W.	1880	Hummel, Arthur W.	1950
Holmes, William H.	1899	Humphrey, H. C.	1877
Holyoke, Edward A.	B	Humphrey, James E.	1892
Homans, George C.	1964	Humphreys, Andrew A.	1857
Home, Archibald	B	Humphreys, David	1804
Hooker, Nathaniel	B	Humphreys, Joshua	1789
Hooten, Earnest A.	1931	Humphreys, Samuel	1826
Hoover, Herbert	1918	Humphreys, William J.	1929
Hopkins, B. Smith	1927	Hunsaker, Jerome Clarke	1940
Hopkins, Edward W.	1908	Hunt, J. Gibbons	1876
Hopkins, Stephen	C	Hunt, Thomas S.	1861
Hopkins, William	C	Hunter, Richard S.	1895
Hopkinson, Edward, Jr.	1938	Hunter, Walter S.	1941
Hopkinson, Francis	A	Huntingdon, Samuel	1783
Hopkinson, John P.	1832	Huntington, Archer M.	1930

Huntington, Edward V.	1933	James, John F.	1848
Hurst, James Willard	1958	James, Joseph	1787
Hutchins, Thomas	1772	James, Thomas C.	1797
Hutchinson, Emlen	1898	James, Thomas P.	1857
Hutchinson, G. Evelyn	1956	Jameson, David	C
Hutchinson, James	1779	Jameson, J. Franklin	1920
Hutchinson, James H.	1884	Janowitz, Morris	1983
Hyatt, Alpheus	1895	Jarvis, Edward	1863
		Jarvis, Samuel F.	1820
I		Jastrow, Morris	1897
		Jay, John	1780
Iddings, Joseph P.	1911	Jayne, Henry LaB.	1898
Ingalls, David H. H.	1961	Jayne, Horace	1885
Ingersoll, Charles J.	1815	Jayne, Horace H. F.	1934
Ingersoll, Jared	1781	Jefferis, William W.	1882
Ingersoll, Joseph R.	1825	Jefferson, Thomas	1780
Ingersoll, R. Sturgis	1950	Jeffries, Zay	1948
Ingersoll, Ralph I.	1848	Jenkins, Charles F.	1944
Ingham, Samuel D.	1840	Jenks, John S.	1936
Ingham, William A.	1875	Jenks, Williams	1837
d'Invilliers, Edward V.	1893	Jennings, Herbert S.	1907
Irvin, David	1841	Jepsen, Glenn L.	1949
Irving, Washington	1829	Jessup, Philip C.	1939
Iselin, Columbus O'D.	1950	Jewett, Frank B.	1938
Ives, Frederick E.	1922	Johnson, Alba B.	1911
Ives, Herbert E.	1917	Johnson, Alvin S.	1942
Izard, George	1807	Johnson, Douglas	1920
Izard, Ralph	C	Johnson, Eldridge R.	1928
		Johnson, Emory R.	1915
J		Johnson, William	C
		Johnson, William	1810
Jackson, A. V. Williams	1909	Johnston, Francis	1787
Jackson, Chevalier	1919	Johnston, John	1876
Jackson, David	1792	Johnston, John	1946
Jackson, Dugald C.	1931	Jones, Charles C.	1881
Jackson, Isaac R.	1841	Jones, Harry C.	1910
Jackson, James	1818	Jones, Harry W.	1964
Jackson, Paul	C	Jones, Howard M.	1941
Jackson, R. M. S.	1863	Jones, Isaac	B
Jackson, Samuel	1823	Jones, Joel	1848
Jacobs, Benjamin	C	Jones, John	1769
Jacobs, Merkel H.	1930	Jones, John	1774
Jacobs, William S.	1802	Jones, Lewis R.	1925
Jacobsen, Thorkild	1962	Jones, Mary Ellen	1994
Jaeger, Werner	1944	Jones, Robert S.	B
James, Abel	C	Jones, Thomas P.	1831
James, Edmund J.	1884	Jones, Walter	1774
James, Edwin	1833	Jones, William	1805

Jordan, David S.	1905	Kidd, John	A
Jordan, Francis	1884	Kidder, Alfred V.	1934
Joslin, Elliott P.	1925	Kimball, Fiske	1943
Justice, George M.	1839	King, Clarence	1872
		King, Edward	1852
K		Kinnersley, Ebenezer	A
		Kinzel, Augustus B.	1963
Kac, Mark	1969	Kirk, Grayson	1954
Kane, Elisha K.	1851	Kirk, John F.	1864
Kane, Elisha K.	1883	Kirkbride, Joseph	B
Kane, John K.	1825	Kirkbride, Thomas S.	1851
Kane, Thomas L.	1856	Kirkpatrick, Ralph	1964
Kantorowicz, Ernst H.	1957	Kirkwood, Daniel	1851
Kármán, Theodore von	1941	Kirkwood, John G.	1944
Keane, John J.	1889	Kirtland, Jared P.	1875
Kearsley, John	B	Kistiakowsky, George B.	1940
Kearsley, John	C	Kittera, John W.	1793
Keasbey, Lindley M.	1899	Kittredge, George L.	1905
Keating, William H.	1822	Kline, John R.	1941
Keating, William V.	1854	Kluckhohn, Clyde K. M.	1952
Keefer, Chester S.	1951	Klüver, Heinrich	1965
Keen, Gregory B.	1897	Kneass, Strickland	1856
Keen, William W.	1884	Knight, Jacob B.	1878
Keeney, Barnaby C.	1965	Knox, Henry	1791
Keim, George DeB.	1882	Koenig, George A.	1874
Keiser, Edward H.	1898	Kofoid, Charles A.	1924
Keller, Harry F.	1900	Köhler, Wolfgang	1939
Kelley, Nicholas	1942	Kraeling, Carl H.	1958
Kelley, William D.	1884	Kraemer, Henry	1899
Kellogg, Frank B.	1931	Kramer, Paul Jackson	1971
Kellogg, Remington	1955	Kramer, Samuel N.	1949
Kellogg, Vernon	1920	Kraus, Charles A.	1939
Kelly, Mervin J.	1952	Krauth, Charles P.	1864
Kemmerer, Edwin W.	1932	Krieger, Leonard	1981
Kemp, James F.	1912	Kristeller, Paul Oskar	1974
Kendall, E. Otis	1842	Kroeber, Alfred L.	1941
Kendall, Edward C.	1951	Krout, John A.	1961
Kenderdine, Robert S.	1874	Krutch, Joseph W.	1953
Keniston, R. Hayward	1944	Kubler, George A.	1978
Kennedy, John P.	1853	Kuffler, Stephen W.	1978
Kennelly, Arthur E.	1896	Kuhn, Adam	A
Kent, James	1829	Kuhn, Hartman	1840
Kent, William	1848	Kuhn, Thomas S.	1974
Keppel, Frederick P.	1938	Kunkel, Louis O.	1942
Kerr, William C.	1872	Kunze, J. C.	1780
Kettering, Charles F.	1930	Kusch, Polykarp	1967
Key, V. O., Jr.	1956	Kuttner, Stephan George	1965
Keyes, Frederick G.	1938	Kuznets, Simon	1948

L

Labaree, Leonard W.	1962	Lee, Arthur	B
		Lee, Francis L.	B
Ladner, Gerhart B.	1972	Lee, Rensselaer Wright	1976
Lamb, Arthur B.	1936	Lee, Thomas J.	1862
Lambert, Preston A.	1904	Leech, Edward A.	1892
Lamberton, William A.	1899	Leeds, Morris E.	1940
Lamborn, Robert H.	1864	Lefschetz, Solomon	1929
Lamont, Thomas W.	1932	Legare, Hugh S.	1838
Lampland, Carl O.	1931	Le Gaux, Peter	1789
Lancaster, H. Carrington	1938	Lehman, Ambrose E.	1883
Land, Edwin Herbert	1957	Lehninger, Albert L.	1970
Landis, James McC.	1942	Leidy, Joseph	1849
Landreth, Burnet	1878	Leith, Charles K.	1926
Landsberger, Benno	1959	Leland, Waldo G.	1931
Landsteiner, Karl	1935	Lenher, Samuel	1964
Lane, Frederic Chapin	1955	Lenox, James	1854
Langer, William L.	1944	Lenthall, John	1843
Langley, Samuel P.	1875	Leonard, James B.	1897
Langmuir, Irving	1922	Leontief, Wassily	1951
Lanman, Charles R.	1906	Lérébours, Alexander	1796
Lapham, Increase A.	1874	Lerner, I. Michael	1969
Lardner, Lynford	B	Lesley, J. Peter	1856
La Roche, C. Percy	1873	Lesley, Joseph	1863
La Roche, René	1827	Leslie, Robert	1795
Lashley, Karl S.	1938	Lesquereux, Leo	1861
Latrobe, Benjamin H.	1799	Letchworth, Albert S.	1856
Latrobe, John H. B.	1854	Leuschner, Armin O.	1924
Lattimore, Owen	1943	Levene, Phoebus A.	1923
Lattimore, Richmond	1959	Leverett, Frank	1924
Laudise, Robert A.	1997	Levin, Harry	1961
Laurens, Henry	1772	Levis, Richard J.	1872
Laurens, John	1780	Lewis, Sir Arthur	1966
Lauristen, Charles C.	1954	Lewis, Clarence I.	1942
Law, Edward E.	1853	Lewis, Edwin O.	1946
Law, Philip H.	1879	Lewis, Elisha J.	1855
Lawes, John B.	1883	Lewis, Francis W.	1860
Lawrence, Ernest O.	1937	Lewis, G. Albert	1896
Lawrence, Jason O'B.	1823	Lewis, George W.	1944
Lawson, Andrew C.	1925	Lewis, Gilbert N.	1918
Lea, Arthur H.	1912	Lewis, Henry C.	1881
Lea, Henry C.	1867	Lewis, John F.	1909
Lea, Isaac	1828	Lewis, John F.	1960
Learned, Marion D.	1899	Lewis, Joseph J.	1881
Le Conte, John	1873	Lewis, Meriwether	1803
Le Conte, John E.	1851	Lewis, Warren H.	1943
Le Conte, John L.	1853	Lewis, Wilmarth S.	1957
Le Conte, Joseph	1873	Leyburn, John	1856
Le Conte, Robert G.	1905	Libbey, William	1897
		Libby, Willard F.	1954

Lilienthal, David Eli	1976	Loxley, Benjamin	B
Lillie, Frank R.	1916	Ludlow, James R.	1884
Lillie, Ralph S.	1937	Ludlow, John	1839
Lind, Samuel C.	1943	Ludlow, William	1884
Lindgren, Waldemar	1917	Lukens, Isaiah	1820
Lingelbach, William E.	1916	Lukens, Jesse	1772
Link, Arthur S.	1966	Lukens, John	A
Linton, M. Albert	1953	Lumiansky, Robert M.	1976
Lipmann, Fritz	1959	Luria, Salvador Edward	1964
Lippincott, J. Bertram	1921	Lusk, Graham	1924
Lippincott, J. Dundas	1899	Lydenberg, Harry M.	1939
Lippincott, Joshua B.	1869	Lyman, Benjamin S.	1869
Lippmann, Walter	1947	Lyman, Theodore	1918
Livezey, Thomas	C	Lynch, W. F.	1853
Livingston, Burton E.	1933		
Livingston, Edward	1825	**M**	
Livingston, Robert R.	1801		
Livingston, William	B	Mabery, Charles F.	1897
Lloyd, James	1771	MacAlister, James	1886
Lloyd, Morris	1963	McArthur, John	1875
Locke, John	1844	McCall, Charles A.	1771
Loeb, Jacques	1899	McCall, George A.	1854
Loeb, Leo	1910	McCall, Peter	1851
Loeb, Robert F.	1951	McCauley, Edward Y.	1881
Logan, George	1793	McCay, Leroy W.	1897
Logan, William	B	McClean, Arch	1772
Logan, William, Jr.	B	McClelland, George W.	1941
Long, C. N. Hugh	1949	McClenahan, Howard	1931
Long, Esmond R.	1940	McClintock, Barbara	1946
Long, Stephen H.	1823	McClune, James	1863
Longfellow, Samuel	1878	McClung, Clarence E.	1913
Longstreth, Miers F.	1848	McClure, Charles F. W.	1897
Longstreth, Morris	1878	McClurg, James	1774
Longwell, Chester R.	1948	McCollum, Elmer V.	1945
Loomis, Alfred L.	1930	McCook, Henry C.	1896
Loomis, Elias	1839	McCosh, James	1871
Lorimer, John	1769	McCrae, Thomas	1914
Lounsbury, Floyd Glenn	1987	McCrea, James	1910
Lovejoy, Arthur O.	1932	McCreath, Andrew S.	1879
Lovering, Joseph	1881	McCulloh, Richard S.	1846
Lovett, Edgar O.	1904	MacCurdy, George G.	1925
Low, Seth	1892	McDaniel, Walton B.	1917
Lowell, A. Lawrence	1909	MacDougal, Daniel T.	1916
Lowell, James R.	1883	McDowell, John	1807
Lowell, John	1787	McElroy, William D.	1971
Lowell, Percival	1897	McEuen, Charles	1843
Lowes, John L.	1934	McEuen, Thomas	1830
Lowie, Robert H.	1942	Macfarlane, James	1883
Lowrie, Walter H.	1859	Macfarlane, John M.	1892

McGregor, James II	1929	Marsh, George P.	1849
McHenry, James	1785	Marsh, Othniel C.	1868
McIlvaine, William	1826	Marshak, Robert E.	1983
McIlwain, Charles H.	1938	Marshall, E. K., Jr.	1948
MacInnes, Duncan A.	1942	Marshall, George C.	1946
MacIver, Robert M.	1942	Marshall, Humphry	C
McKean, Joseph B.	1824	Marshall, John	1830
McKean, Thomas	B	Marshall, John	1886
McKean, William V.	1877	Martin, Alexander	1797
McLane, Louis	1831	Martin, David	B
Maclaurin, Richard C.	1910	Martin, Edward	1933
Maclean, John	1806	Martin, Sydney E.	1962
MacLeish, Archibald	1976	Martin, William McChesney, Jr.	1972
MacLeod, Colin M.	1966	Martindale, Isaac C.	1880
Maclure, William	1799	Marvel, Carl S.	1945
McMaster, John B.	1884	Marvin, Charles F.	1916
McMath, Robert R.	1942	Mason, Andrew	1867
McMichael, Morton	1867	Mason, Edward S.	1954
McMillan, Edwin Mattison	1952	Mason, John Y.	1847
Macneven, William J.	1823	Mason, Otis T.	1899
MacNider, William deB.	1939	Mason, William P.	1896
McQuillen, John H.	1877	Mason, William S.	1928
McShane, Edward J.	1959	Mather, Frank J.	1940
MacVeagh, I. Wayne	1897	Mather, Joseph	C
Machlup, Fritz	1963	Matile, George A.	1856
Madison, James	1780	Matlack, Timothy	1780
Madison, James	1785	Matthew, William D.	1914
Magaw, Samuel	1784	Matthews, Albert	1899
Magie, William F.	1896	Mattingly, Garrett	1961
Magill, Roswell	1948	Maury, M. F.	1852
Mahan, Alfred T.	1897	May, Addison	1881
Maisch, John M.	1884	May, Joseph	1883
Mall, Franklin P.	1906	Mayall, Nicholas U.	1962
Mallery, Garrick	1882	Mayer, Alfred M.	1869
Mallet, John W.	1885	Mayer, Joseph E.	1970
Malone, Kemp	1945	Mayer, Maria G.	1964
Mangelsdorf, Paul C.	1955	Mayor, Alfred G.	1914
Manly, John M.	1912	Mead, Margaret	1977
Mann, Thomas	1942	Meade, George G.	1871
Mansfield, Ira F.	1878	Meade, William	1817
Mansfield, Jared	1816	Mease, James	1802
Marceau, Henri	1949	Meehan, Thomas	1871
March, Francis A.	1878	Meek, F. B.	1867
Marder, Arthur	1972	Meem, John	C
Margolis, Max L.	1927	Mees, Charles E. K.	1937
Mark, Edward L.	1907	Meigs, Arthur V.	1899
Marks, William D.	1878	Meigs, Charles D.	1826
Marschall, Frederick W. von	1771	Meigs, John F.	1852
Marsh, Benjamin V.	1864	Meigs, Josiah	1818

Meigs, Montgomery C.	1854	Milligan, George	1772
Meigs, William M.	1901	Milligan, Robert	1787
Meiss, Millard	1963	Millikan, Robert A.	1914
Mellon, Paul	1971	Mim. *See* Meem	
Melscheimer, Val	1795	Miner, Horace M.	1966
Meltzer, Samuel J.	1914	Minot, Charles S.	1896
Melville, George W.	1897	Minot, George R.	1935
Mendel, Lafayette B.	1916	Minto, Walter	1789
Mendenhall, Charles E.	1924	Mirsky, Alfred	1964
Mendenhall, Thomas C.	1899	Mitchel, Ormsby McK.	1853
Menzel, Donald H.	1943	Mitchell, Howard H.	1925
Mercer, Charles F.	1817	Mitchell, James T.	1890
Mercer, Henry C.	1895	Mitchell, John	B
Mercer, Hugh	C	Mitchell, John K.	1827
Meredith, William M.	1837	Mitchell, Maria	1869
Meredith, William T.	1813	Mitchell, S. Weir	1862
Meritt, Benjamin D.	1938	Mitchell, Samuel A.	1923
Merriam, C. Hart	1902	Mitchell, Wesley C.	1931
Merriam, Charles E.	1935	Mitchill, S. L.	1791
Merriam, John C.	1914	Modjeski, Ralph	1926
Merrick, John V.	1880	Moe, Henry A.	1943
Merrick, Samuel V.	1833	Monro, George	1789
Merrill, Elmer D.	1932	Montgomery, Deane	1958
Merrill, George P.	1923	Montgomery, James A.	1925
Merrill, Paul W.	1939	Montgomery, Thomas H.	1898
Merriman, Mansfield	1881	Montgomery, Thomas L.	1927
Messchert, Matthew H.	1873	Moore, Charles	A
Metz, Charles W.	1941	Moore, Clarence B.	1897
Michael, Helen Abbott	1887	Moore, Clifford H.	1928
Michelson, Albert A.	1902	Moore, Eliakim H.	1905
Mifflin, J. F.	1796	Moore, George F.	1920
Mifflin, Samuel	B	Moore, George T.	1905
Mifflin, Thomas	C	Moore, Gideon E.	1875
Miles, George C.	1966	Moore, J. Percy	1918
Miles, Samuel	C	Moore, James W.	1885
Miles, Walter R.	1944	Moore, John B.	1907
Milledoler, Philip	1840	Moore, Richard B.	1923
Miller, David H.	1928	Moore, Samuel	1805
Miller, Dayton C.	1919	Moore, Samuel P.	1771
Miller, E. Spencer	1857	Moore, Thomas	1809
Miller, Edward	1805	Moore, Wilbert E.	1958
Miller, Edward	1845	Mordecai, Alfred	1853
Miller, Gerrit S., Jr.	1927	Morehouse, George R.	1877
Miller, J. Imbrie	1870	Morell, John	1770
Miller, John A.	1915	Morey, Charles R.	1938
Miller, Leslie W.	1899	Morgan, Benjamin	1774
Miller, Perry	1956	Morgan, Benjamin R.	1813
Miller, Peter	C	Morgan, George	C
Miller, Samuel	1800	Morgan, John	C

Morgan, Marshall S.	1933	Murnaghan, Francis D.	1942
Morgan, Thomas H.	1915	Murphy, Robert C.	1946
Morgenthau, Hans J.	1961	Murray, Joseph	B
Morison, Samuel E.	1937	Murray, Joseph A.	1880
Morley, Edward W.	1903	Mütter, Thomas D.	1851
Morley, Frank	1897		
Morley, Sylvanus G.	1940	N	
Morris, Caspar	1851		
Morris, Ellwood	1843	Nagel, Ernest	1962
Morris, Harrison S.	1899	Nancarrow, John	1794
Morris, Israel W.	1899	Nassy, David	1793
Morris, J. Cheston	1883	Nauta, Walle J. H.	1971
Morris, Jacob G.	1851	Neill, John	1852
Morris, John	C	Neilson, William A.	1944
Morris, John	1786	Neugebauer, Otto E.	1947
Morris, John G.	1893	Neumann, John von	1938
Morris, John T.	1901	Newberry, J. S.	1867
Morris, Lawrence J.	1936	Newbold, William R.	1909
Morris, Robert	1786	Newcomb, Simon	1878
Morris, Robert H.	B	Newnan, John	1797
Morris, Roland S.	1922	Newton, Hubert A.	1867
Morrow, Dwight W.	1931	Neyes, Arthur A.	1911
Morse, Edward S.	1895	Nicholas, John S.	1946
Morse, Harmon N.	1903	Nichols, Edward L.	1904
Morse, Marston	1936	Nichols, Ernest F.	1906
Morse, Samuel F. B.	1848	Nichols, Francis	1803
Morton, Henry	1867	Nichols, Roy F.	1945
Morton, Henry J.	1857	Nichols, Starr H.	1872
Morton, Samuel G.	1828	Nicholson, John	1791
Morton, Thomas G.	1900	Nicklin, Philip H.	1829
Mosely, Philip E.	1950	Nicola, Lewis	C
Mosse, George L.	1997	Nicollet, J. N.	1842
Motley, John L.	1861	Nicolson, Marjorie Hope	1941
Moulton, Forest R.	1916	Niebuhr, Reinhold	1947
Moulton, Harold G.	1938	Niel, Cornelis Bernardus van	1948
Mower, T. G.	1844	Nier, Alfred O. C.	1953
Mudd, Emily Hartshorne	1993	Nipher, Francis E.	1907
Muhlenberg, Fred A.	1878	Nisbet, Robert A.	1973
Muhlenberg, Henry E.	1785	Nitze, William A.	1936
Muller, Hermann J.	1947	Noble, G. Kingsley	1933
Mulliken, Robert S.	1940	Nock, Arthur D.	1941
Mumford, Lewis	1941	Noguchi, Hideyo	1921
Munro, Dana C.	1901	Nolan, Thomas B.	1957
Munroe, Charles E.	1891	de Normandie, John A.	B
Murdock, Joseph B.	1886	Norris, George W.	1844
Murdock, Kenneth B.	1954	Norris, George W.	1922
Murgatroyd, John	C	Norris, George W.	1937
Murlin, John R.	1932	Norris, Isaac	1872

Norris, Joseph P.	1815	Otto, John M.	1769
Norris, William	1838	Outerbridge, Alexander E.	1880
Norris, William F.	1886		
North, Edward	1885	**P**	
Northrop, John Howard	1938		
Norton, William A.	1844	Packard, Alpheus S.	1878
Notestein, Frank W.	1945	Packard, David	1989
Notestein, Wallace	1946	Packard, Francis R.	1933
Nourse, Edwin G.	1952	Packard, John H.	1867
Novy, Frederick G.	1934	Page, John	1792?
Noyes, William A.	1914	Page, Mann	1785
Noyes, William A., Jr.	1947	Paine, Robert T.	1838
Nulty, Eugenius	1817	Paine, Thomas	1785
Nuttall, Thomas	1817	Painter, Sidney	1953
Nuttall, Zelia	1895	Painter, Theophilus S.	1939
		Palmer, William R.	1859
O		Pancoast, Henry S.	1898
		Pancoast, Joseph	1851
O'Neill, Eugene G.	1935	Pancoast, William H.	1883
Oberlin, John F.	C	Panofsky, Erwin	1943
Ochoa, Severo	1961	Pardee, Ario	1867
Ochs, Adolph S.	1931	Park, Roswell	1841
Odell, Jonathan	C	Parke, Thomas	1774
Ogburn, William F.	1940	Parker, George H.	1911
Okely, John	C	Parr, William	1771
Oliver, Andrew	C	Parrish, Dillwyn	1883
Oliver, Andrew	1773	Parrish, Joseph	1815
Oliver, Charles A.	1886	Parry, John Horace	1975
Oliver, James E.	1873	Parsons, Talcott	1960
Olivier, Charles P.	1932	Parsons, William	B
Olney, Richard	1897	Parvin, Theophilus	1885
Onsager, Lars	1959	Paschall, Isaac	C
Oppenheimer, J. Robert	1945	Paschall, John	C
Oppenheimer, Jane M.	1980	Paschall, Joseph	C
Ord, George	1817	Paschall, Stephen	
Ormandy, Eugene	1977	Paterson, William	1789
Ortmann, Arnold E.	1897	Paton, Steward	1914
Orton, Edward	1897	Patterson, C. Stuart	1885
Osborn, Frederick H.	1948	Patterson, Carlile P.	1880
Osborn, Henry F.	1887	Patterson, Edward	1900
Osborn, Henry S.	1867	Patterson, Ernest M.	1932
Osborne, Thomas B.	1921	Patterson, Lamar G.	1898
Osgood, Charles G.	1943	Patterson, Robert	1783
Osgood, William F.	1915	Patterson, Robert	1851
Osterhout, Winthrop J. V.	1917	Patterson, Robert M.	1809
Otis, George A.	1821	Patterson, Thomas L.	1853
Otolenge, Joseph	1771	Pattison, Robert E.	1893
Otto, John C.	1817	Patton, Francis L.	1897

Paul, J. Rodman	1899	Pettee, William H.	1898
Paulding, James K.	1839	Pettit, Charles	1779
Pauling, Linus C.	1936	Pettit, Henry	1895
Peale, Charles W.	1786	Peyre, Henri Maurice	1953
Peale, Franklin	1833	Pfaffmann, Carl	1964
Peale, Titian R.	1833	Phelps, Edward J.	1895
Pearce, Richard M.	1914	Phelps, William L.	1927
Pearl, Raymond	1915	Phillips, Francis C.	1899
Pearse, John B.	1875	Phillips, Henry	1877
Pearson, James	C	Phillips, Henry M.	1871
Pearson, Leonard	1908	Physick, Edmund	C
Pease, Calvin	1863	Physick, Philip S.	1802
Peck, William D.	1796	Pickering, Charles	1828
Peckham, Stephen F.	1897	Pickering, Edward C.	1896
Pecora, William T.	1970	Pickering, John	1820
Pegram, George B.	1947	Pickering, Tim	1795
Peirce, Benjamin	1842	Picot, Charles	1848
Peirce, Benjamin O.	1910	Piersol, George A.	1897
Peirce, C. Newlin	1878	Pilsbry, Henry A.	1895
Pemberton, Henry	1873	Pimentel, George C.	1985
Pemberton, Israel	B	Pinckney, C. C.	1789
Pemberton, James	B	Pinckney, Thomas	1797
Pender, Harold	1917	Pine, Robert E.	1786
Penington, Edward	C	Pirsson, Louis V.	1918
Penington, Edward	1808	Pittendrigh, Colin S.	1979
Penington, Edward	1875	Pitzer, Kenneth S.	1954
Penington, John	1791	Platt, Charles	1898
Penington, John	1839	Platt, Franklin	1874
Penn, John	B	Plitt, John	1823
Penn, Richard	B	Poinsett, Joel R.	1827
Penniman, Josiah H.	1901	Pollock, George	1813
Pennypacker, Samuel W.	1886	Pollock, James	1863
Penrose, Boies	1966	Poole, William	C
Penrose, Charles B.	1909	Porada, Edith	1978
Penrose, R. A. F.	1863	Porter, Keith R.	1977
Penrose, Richard A. F.	1905	Porter, Thomas C.	1864
Pepper, Edward	1886	Post, Chandler R.	1946
Pepper, George W.	1897	Post, Chr. F.	C
Pepper, O. H. Perry	1944	Potter, Alonzo	1844
Pepper, William	1851	Potter, David M.	1965
Pepper, William	1870	Pottle, Frederick Albert	1960
Pepper, William	1937	Potts, Jonathan	C
Perkins, Jacob	1819	Potts, Joseph D.	1892
Perkins, John	1774	Potts, Thomas	B
Perry, Ralph B.	1939	Potts, William J.	1885
Peter, Robert	1872	Pound, Roscoe	1940
Peters, Christian H. F.	1878	Powel, Samuel	C
Peters, Richard	B	Powel, Samuel	1855
Petersen, Howard C.	1954	Powell, John W.	1889

Power, Eugene B.	1975	Ratliff, Floyd	1972
Prescott, Albert B.	1898	Rau, Charles	1882
Prescott, William H.	1838	Ravdin, Isidor S.	1963
Preston, Thomas	1771	Ravenel, Mazijck P.	1901
Price, Don K.	1958	Rawle, Francis	C
Price, Eli K.	1854	Rawle, Francis	1898
Price, Eli K.	1916	Rawle, William	1786
Price, J. Sergeant	1867	Rawle, William	1841
Prime, Ebenezer	1769	Rawle, William B.	1899
Prime, Frederick	1875	Rawle, William H.	1887
Prince, John	1805	Ray, Gordon Norton	1977
Prince, John D.	1913	Raymond, Rossiter W.	1875
Pritchard, James B.	1973	Raynolds, William F.	1867
Pritchett, Henry S.	1899	Rea, Samuel	1913
Proctor, William	1847	Read, Charles	A
Proskouriakoff, Tatiana	1981	Read, Conyers	1934
Proud, Robert	B	Read, John M.	1863
Pryor, Thomas	A	Read, John M.	1867
Pugh, Evan	1862	Redfield, Robert	1947
Pumpelly, Raphael	1874	Redfield, W. C.	1844
Pupin, Michael I.	1896	Redick, David	1789
Purcell, Edward M.	1954	Redman, John	A
Purviance, Samuel	B	Reed, Henry	1838
Putnam, Frederick W.	1895	Reed, Henry	1886
Putnam, Herbert	1937	Reed, John	1848
		Reed, Joseph	B
Q		Reed, Joseph	1816
		Reed, T. B.	1877
Quincy, Edmund	1870	Reed, William B.	1856
Quincy, Josiah	1829	Reese, Charles L.	1922
Quinn, Arthur H.	1940	Reese, John J.	1852
		Reeves, Jesse S.	1934
R		Reeves, Samuel J.	1869
		Reid, Harry F.	1910
Rabi, Isidor Isaac	1941	Reischauer, Edwin Oldfather	1973
Raguet, Condy	1822	Reisner, George A.	1940
Ramsay, David	1803	Remington, Joseph P.	1899
Rand, B. Howard	1857	Remsen, Ira	1879
Rand, Edward K.	1925	Rennert, Hugo A.	1899
Rand, Theodore D.	1873	Renwick, James	1828
Randall, Clarence B.	1957	Repplier, Agnes	1928
Randall, F. A.	1878	Reston, James B.	1980
Randall, Samuel J.	1885	Revelle, Roger	1960
Randolph, Edmund	1791	Reynell, John	B
Randolph, Jacob	1833	Reynolds, Joel B.	1851
Randolph, Nathaniel A.	1884	Rhea, John	B
Randolph, Thomas M.	1794	Rhoades, Marcus M.	1962
Ransome, Frederick L.	1935	Rhoads, Charles J.	1921
Raper, Kenneth Bryan	1958	Rhoads, Edward	1868

Rhoads, Edward	1903	Rogers, James B.	1846
Rhoads, James E.	1893	Rogers, Lindsay	1941
Rhoads, Samuel	B	Rogers, Robert E.	1855
Rhoads, Samuel	1771	Rogers, Robert W.	1890
Rhoads, Samuel N.	1897	Rogers, William B.	1835
Rhodes, James F.	1910	Rogers, William B.	1880
Rice, Edwin W.	1928	Röhrig, F. L. Otto	1862
Richards, A. Newton	1935	Rolfe, John C.	1907
Richards, Benjamin W.	1839	Romans, Bernard	1774
Richards, Horace C.	1907	Romer, Alfred S.	1951
Richards, Theodore W.	1902	Rood, Ogden N.	1880
Richardson, Edgar P.	1969	Roosa, Robert V.	1966
Richardson, Joseph	B	Roosevelt, Theodore	1904
Riché, George I.	1885	Root, Elihu	1906
Richter, Curt P.	1959	Rosa, Edward B.	1912
Richter, Gisela M. P.	1942	Rosenbach, A. S. W.	1928
Richtmyer, Floyd K.	1935	Rosengarten, Adolph G.	1940
Ricketts, Palmer C.	1914	Rosengarten, George D.	1919
Riddle, Oscar	1926	Rosengarten, Joseph G.	1891
Ridgely, Charles	C	Rosenwald, Lessing J.	1947
Riley, Charles V.	1876	Ross, Andrew	1791
Rittenhouse, Benjamin	1789	Ross, James	1791
Rittenhouse, David	A	Ross, John	B
Rivers, Thomas M.	1942	Rossby, Carl-Gustaf A.	1946
Rives, William C.	1831	Rossi, Bruno B.	1959
Roach, William	1964	Rostovtzeff, Michael I.	1929
Robbins, William J.	1941	Rotch, A. Lawrence	1911
Roberts, George	C	Rothermel, Peter F.	1873
Roberts, George B.	1885	Rothrock, Joseph T.	1877
Roberts, Hugh	B	Rouelle, John	1792
Roberts, Joseph	1829	Rous, Peyton	1939
Roberts, Owen J.	1934	Rowe, Leo S.	1911
Roberts, Solomon W.	1843	Rowland, Henry A.	1896
Roberts, W. Milnor	1876	Royce, Josiah	1908
Roberts, Walter Orr	1973	Rubey, William W.	1952
Robertson, Howard P.	1940	Rudder, William	1878
Robins, James W.	1882	Rumsey, James	1789
Robinson, David M.	1936	Rumsey, William	B
Robinson, Fred N.	1944	Ruschenberger, W. S. W.	1849
Robinson, Geroid T.	1955	Rush, Benjamin	C
Robinson, Moncure	1833	Rush, James	1827
Robinson, Samuel	C	Rush, Richard	1817
Rockefeller, John D., Jr.	1931	Russell, Henry N.	1913
Rodgers, John R. B.	1787	Ruston, Thomas	1787
Roepper, W. T.	1871	Ruthven, Alexander G.	1931
Rogers, Ebenezer P.	1855	Ryberg, Inez S.	1963
Rogers, Fairman	1857	Ryder, John A.	1886
Rogers, Henry D.	1835		

S

Sachs, Paul J.	1947
Sachse, Julius F.	1894
Sadtler, Samuel P.	1874
Sagan, Carl	1995
St. Clair, Arthur	1780
St. John, Charles E.	1928
Sajous, Charles E.	1888
Salisbury, Harrison E.	1983
Sampson, Alden	1897
Sanders, Henry A.	1932
Sanders, Richard H.	1897
Sanderson, John	1840
Sansom, Joseph	1806
Sapir, Edward	1937
Sargent, Charles S.	1882
Sargent, Winthrop	1789
Sartain, John	1897
Sarton, George	1934
Sauer, Carl O.	1944
Sauveur, Albert	1919
Sawyer, John E.	1983
Saxton, Joseph	1837
Say, Thomas	1817
Scattergood, J. Henry	1931
Schaeffer, Fred. C.	1819
Schaeffer, George C.	1865
Schaeffer, J. Parsons	1927
Schäffer, Charles	1893
Schapiro, Meyer	1969
Schawlow, Arthur L.	1984
Schelling, Felix E.	1902
Schlesinger, Arthur M.	1941
Schlesinger, Frank	1912
Schmitt, Bernadotte E.	1942
Schmitt, Francis O.	1953
Scholander, Per F.	1962
Schoolcraft, Henry R.	1833
Schott, Charles A.	1863
Schramm, Jacob R.	1932
Schuchert, Charles	1913
Schultz, Adolph H.	1936
Schultz, Theodore W.	1962
Schurman, Jacob G.	1908
Schurz, Carl	1878
Schuyler, Robert L.	1942
Schwarzschild, Martin	1981

de Schweinitz, George E.	1912
Schweinitz, Lewis	1817
Scott, Charles F.	1898
Scott, James B.	1930
Scott, John M.	B
Scott, John M.	1815
Scott, John M.	1926
Scott, Lewis A.	1880
Scott, William B.	1886
Scribner, Charles, Jr.	1982
Scudder, Samuel H.	1878
Scull, William	C
Seaborg, Glenn T.	1952
Seares, Frederick H.	1917
Sears, Robert R.	1962
Sedgwick, William T.	1911
See, Thomas J. J.	1897
Segrè, Emilio Gino	1963
Seidensticker, Oswald	1870
Seiler, Carl	1879
Seiler, Emma	1870
Sellers, Charles C.	1979
Sellers, Coleman	1872
Sellers, Coleman	1899
Sellers, John	A
Sellers, William	1864
Sellin, Thorsten	1949
Sergeant, John	1813
Sergeant, Jonathan D.	1784
Sergeant, Thomas	1832
Serkin, Rudolf	1983
Setchell, William A.	1919
Setton, Kenneth M.	1952
Seybert, Adam	1797
Seybert, Henry	1824
Seymour, Charles	1939
Seymour, Thomas D.	1906
Shäffer, Charles	1893
Shaffer, Philip A.	1950
Shaler, William	1826
Shane, Charles D.	1955
Shannon, James A.	1967
Shapleigh, Waldron	1899
Shapley, Harlow	1922
Sharp, Benjamin	1886
Sharples, Philip P.	1881
Sharples, Stephen P.	1882
Sharpless, Isaac	1884

Sharswood, George	1851	Smith, Charles E.	1858
Sheafer, Peter W.	1863	Smith, Cyril Stanley	1955
Shear, Theodore L.	1939	Smith, Daniel B.	1829
Sheppard, Furman	1875	Smith, Edgar F.	1887
Sherwood, Andrew	1875	Smith, Erwin F.	1916
Shields, Charles W.	1877	Smith, Francis G.	1852
Shiell, Hugh	1781	Smith, George	1863
Shils, Edward A.	1980	Smith, George W.	1840
Shippen, Edward	B	Smith, Henry Nash	1981
Shippen, Edward	1868	Smith, Isaac	C
Shippen, Edward, Jr.	B	Smith, J. Lawrence	1857
Shippen, Joseph	B	Smith, James P.	1922
Shippen, Thomas L.	1793	Smith, John	A
Shippen, William	B	Smith, John R.	1800
Shippen, William, Jr.	B	Smith, Jonathan B.	B
Shklar, Judith N.	1990	Smith, Lloyd P.	1873
Shoemaker, Samuel	1769	Smith, Preserved	1937
Shope, Richard E.	1944	Smith, Rich. P.	1796
Shorey, Paul	1920	Smith, Richard S.	1864
Short, Charles W.	1835	Smith, Robert	B
Short, William	1804	Smith, Samuel	B
Shotwell, James T.	1936	Smith, Samuel H.	1797
Shryock, Richard H.	1944	Smith, Samuel S.	1785
Shull, George H.	1918	Smith, Stephen	1875
Shumard, Benjamin F.	1867	Smith, Theobald	1915
Shurtleff, Nathaniel B.	1857	Smith, Thomas	B
Sigerist, Henry E.	1945	Smith, Thomas P.	1799
Sigsbee, Charles D.	1899	Smith, William	B
Silliman, Benjamin	1805	Smith, William	B
Simmons, Howard E., Jr.,	1994	Smith, William	B
Simpson, George Gaylord	1936	Smith, William	1792
Sinclair, William J.	1923	Smith, William P.	B
Singer, Edgar A., Jr.	1925	Smith, William W.	1787
Singleton, Charles S.	1962	Smock, John C.	1897
Sinkler, Wharton	1900	Smyth, Albert H.	1887
Sinnott, Edmund W.	1939	Smyth, Charles H.	1908
Sioussat, St. George L.	1928	Smyth, Charles P.	1932
Skinner, Burrhus F.	1949	Smyth, Henry DeWolf	1947
Skinner, Henry	1922	Smyth, Herbert W.	1908
Slater, John C.	1940	Snell, George D.	1982
Slichter, Sumner H.	1946	Snowden, A. Loudon	1873
Slipher, Vesto M.	1921	Snyder, Monroe B.	1884
Smibert, Williams	C	Solis-Cohen, J.	1884
Smilie, John	1791	Solmsen, Friedrich	1966
Smith, A. Donaldson	1897	Sonmans, Peter	C
Smith, Albert H.	1878	Sonneborn, Tracy M.	1952
Smith, Allen J.	1907	Sontag, Raymond J.	1949
Smith, Aubrey H.	1860	Southard, Samuel L.	1831
Smith, Charles	1805	Spangler, Henry W.	1891

Sparks, Jared	1837	Stillman, Samuel	C
Speiser, Ephraim A.	1941	Stillwell, Lewis B.	1898
Spengler, Joseph J.	1954	Stirling, 6th Earl of.	
Sperry, Roger W.	1974	*See* Alexander, William	
Spicer, Edward H.	1974	Stock, Chester	1946
Spier, Leslie	1946	Stockard, Charles R.	1924
Spilhaus, Athelstan F.	1968	Stockton, Richard	B
Spitzer, Lyman, Jr.	1959	Stokes, Joseph, Jr.	1953
Spitzka, Edward A.	1908	Stokes, William A.	1872
Spoehr, Herman A.	1931	Stone, Frederick D.	1895
Spofford, Ainsworth R.	1873	Stone, Harlan F.	1939
Sprague, Oliver M. W.	1938	Stone, Lawrence	1970
Sproul, William C.	1920	Stone, Witmer	1913
Squibb, Edward R.	1897	Storer, D. Humphreys	1842
Squier, George O.	1917	Storrs, William L.	1848
Stadie, William C.	1947	Story, Joseph	1844
Stadler, Lewis J.	1941	Stouffer, Samuel A.	1952
Stakman, Elvin C.	1940	Stratton, Julius Adams	1956
Stallo, John B.	1881	Stratton, Samuel W.	1904
Stanley, Wendell M.	1940	Straus, Oscar S.	1917
Staughton, William	1808	Strawbridge, George	1877
Stebbins, Joel	1925	Strayer, Joseph Reese	1959
Stedman, Alexander	B	Streeter, George L.	1943
Stefansson, Vilhjalmur	1923	Strickland, William	1820
Steinhauer, Henry	1817	Strong, Theodore	1844
Steinmetz, Charles P.	1917	Strong, William	1866
Stellar, Eliot	1977	Struve, Otto	1937
Stengel, Alfred	1903	Stuart, George	1877
Stephens, Henry M.	1897	Stuart, John	1797
Stephens, John L.	1841	Stuart, Moses	1824
Stern, Curt	1954	Sturtevant, Alfred H.	1936
Stern, Otto	1946	Sturtevant, Edgar H.	1939
Sterrett, John R. S.	1908	Suits, C. G.	1951
Steuben, Friedrich W., Baron von		Sullivan, William	1838
	1780	Sullivant, William S.	1862
Stevens, Alexander H.	1848	Sully, Thomas	1835
Stevens, John	1789	Sulzberger, Mayer	1895
Stevens, S. Smith	1958	Sumner, Charles	1867
Stevens, Walter LeC.	1884	Sumner, Francis B.	1938
Stevens, William B.	1854	Suomi, Verner E.	1976
Stevenson, John J.	1877	Survilliers, Joseph B., Count de	1823
Stevenson, Sara Y.	1895	Sverdrup, Harald U.	1944
Stewart, Walter W.	1943	Swain, Joseph	1918
Stieglitz, Julius	1919	Swann, William F. G.	1926
Stigler, George J.	1955	Swasey, Ambrose	1919
Stiles, Ezra	B	Swift, Joseph G.	1814
Stiles, Joseph	C	Swindler, Mary H.	1943
Stille, Alfred	1852	Syle, E. W.	1884
Stillé, Charles J.	1867	Sylvester, J. J.	1877

Syng, Peter	C	Thompson, Heber S.	1884
Syng, Philip	B	Thompson, Margaret A.	1972
		Thompson, Oswald	1859
T		Thompson, Robert E.	1874
		Thompson, Stith	1947
Taft, William H.	1909	Thomson, Charles	C
Tait, Charles	1827	Thomson, Elihu	1876
Talcott, Andrew	1838	Thomson, Frank	1874
Taliaferro, William H.	1941	Thomson, James G.	1818
Taney, Roger B.	1844	Thomson, William	1880
Tanner, Henry S.	1829	Thorndike, Edward L.	1932
Tate, John T.	1941	Thorndike, Lynn	1939
Tatham, William	1897	Thorne, Samuel E.	1959
Tatham, William P.	1875	Thurston, Robert H.	1902
Tatlock, J. S. P.	1937	Thurstone, Louis L.	1948
Tatum, Edward L.	1957	Ticknor, George	1828
Taussig, Frank W.	1929	Tidyman, Philip	1825
Taussig, Helen B.	1973	Tilghman, Benjamin C.	1871
Taylor, Alonzo E.	1917	Tilghman, Benjamin C.	1902
Taylor, Archer	1951	Tilghman, James	B
Taylor, Deems	1934	Tilghman, Richard A.	1847
Taylor, Francis H.	1946	Tilghman, William	1805
Taylor, Frederick W.	1912	Tilghman, William M.	1870
Taylor, George W.	1961	Tilney, Frederick	1930
Taylor, Henry O.	1926	Tilton, James	1773
Taylor, Hugh S.	1928	Timoshenko, Stephen P.	1939
Taylor, Lily R.	1945	Titchener, Edward B.	1906
Taylor, Richard C.	1839	Tittmann, Otto H.	1906
Taylor, William B.	1877	Tolman, Edward C.	1947
Temin, Howard M.	1978	Tolman, Richard C.	1932
Tennent, David H.	1938	Toppan, Robert N.	1886
Tennent, Dr.	B	Torrey, John	1835
Terman, Frederick E.	1957	Totten, George M.	1851
Terman, Lewis M.	1953	Totten, Joseph G.	1836
Tesla, Nikola	1896	Tower, Charlemagne	1895
Thaxter, Roland	1912	Towne, John H.	1851
Thayer, M. Russell	1877	Townsend, Joseph B.	1868
Thayer, Russell	1875	Townsend, Washington	1882
Thayer, Sylvanus	1838	Tozzer, Alfred M.	1937
Thayer, William R.	1918	Trautwine, John C.	1844
Thayer, William S.	1924	Trautwine, William	1882
Thimann, Kenneth V.	1959	Trego, Charles B.	1843
Thomas, Allen C.	1884	Trelease, William	1903
Thomas, Charles Allen	1950	Trimble, Henry	1897
Thomas, Dorothy S.	1948	Troost, Gerard	1816
Thomas, Isaiah	1816	Trowbridge, Augustus	1911
Thomas, Lewis	1976	Trowbridge, John	1896
Thomas, Richard	1771	Trowbridge, William P.	1872
Thompson, Craig R.	1980	True, Frederick W.	1899

True, Rodney H.	1923	Vining, John	C
Trumbull, Henry C.	1884	Visscher, Maurice B.	1970
Trumbull, John	1792	Vlastos, Gregory	1989
Tucker, George	1837	Vose, George L.	1870
Tucker, J. Randolph	1895		
Tucker, Richard H.	1908	**W**	
Turner, George	1790		
Tuttle, David K.	1889	Wagley, Charles W.	1964
Tuve, Merle E.	1943	Wagner, Samuel	1885
Tweedy, John	C	Wagner, Tobias	1841
Tyler, Lyon G.	1889	Wahl, William H.	1874
Tyndale, Hector	1869	Walcott, Charles D.	1897
Tyson, James	1887	Wald, George	1958
Tyson, Job R.	1836	Walker, John	C
Tyson, Philip T.	1869	Walker, Sears C.	1837
Tyzzer, Ernest E.	1931	Wall, George	1785
		Wallace, Ellerslie	1884
U		Wallace, Henry A.	1943
		Waln, Lewis	1846
Uhlenbeck, George E.	1957	Waln, Nicholas	C
Uhler, William M.	1858	Walsh, Robert	1812
Ulam, Stanislaw Marcin	1967	Walter, Thomas U.	1839
Urey, Harold C.	1935	Ward, Lester F.	1889
		Ward, Robert DeC.	1922
V		Warden, David B.	1809
		Ware, Lewis S.	1881
Vaillant, George C.	1943	Ware, Nathaniel A.	1823
Vanderkemp, F. A.	1805	Warfield, Ethelbert D.	1897
Vanderkemp, John J.	1840	Waring, William	1793
Van Doren, Carl	1942	Warren, Charles	1939
Van Hise, Charles R.	1909	Warren, Charles H.	1928
Van Slyke, Donald D.	1938	Warren, Earl	1956
Vanuxem, Lardner	1822	Warren, Gouverneur K.	1867
Van Vleck, John H.	1939	Warren, John C.	1818
Vauclain, Samuel M.	1899	Warren, Robert B.	1949
Vaughan, John	1784	Warren, Robert Penn	1962
Vaughan, Samuel	1784	Warren, Shields	1963
Vaughan, Samuel, Jr.	1786	Washburne, E. A.	1863
Vaughan, T. Wayland	1923	Washington, Bushrod	1805
Vaughan, Victor C.	1909	Washington, George	1780
Vaux, George	1897	Washington, Henry S.	1922
Vaux, Richard	1884	Waterhouse, Benjamin	1791
Vaux, Roberts	1819	Waters, Nicholas B.	1792
Vaux, William S.	1859	Watkins, Franklin	1967
Veblen, Oswald	1912	Watson, James C.	1878
Venable, Francis P.	1905	Watson, Thomas J., Jr.	1984
Vere, Scheele de	1885	Watts, Stephen	A
Vethake, Henry	1831	Way, Nicholas	1773
Viner, Jacob	1942	Wayland, Francis	1838

Wayland, Herman L.	1890	White, David	1921
Wayne, Anthony	1780	White, Israel C.	1878
Wayne, Henry C.	1858	White, Lynn, Jr.	1968
Wayne, Isaac	1840	White, William	C
Weaver, Warren	1944	Whitehead, Alfred N.	1926
Webb, James	C	Whitfield, J. Edward	1905
Webber, Sam	1804	Whitfield, Robert P.	1898
Webster, Arthur G.	1906	Whitman, Charles O.	1899
Webster, Daniel	1837	Whitman, Walter G.	1959
Webster, David L.	1922	Whitman, William E.	1865
Webster, Noah	1827	Whitmore, Frank C.	1943
Weed, Lewis H.	1942	Whitney, George	1880
Weil, Edward H.	1885	Whitney, Hassler	1947
Weimer, Albert B.	1927	Whitney, Josiah D.	1863
Weiner, Myron	1999	Whitney, William D.	1863
Weiss, Paul	1953	Whitney, Willis R.	1931
Weitzmann, Kurt	1964	Whittier, John G.	1870
Welch, William H.	1896	Whittlesey, Chauncey	B
Wellek, René	1969	Wickham, John	1835
Wells, Richard	C	Wiesner, Jerome B.	1969
Welsh, Herbert	1884	Wigner, Eugene P.	1944
Welsh, John	1867	Wilcocks, Alexander	B
Wertenbaker, Thomas J.	1941	Wilcocks, Alexander	1864
West, Francis	1854	Wilder, Burt G.	1878
West, Samuel	B	Wiley, Harvey W.	1904
West, William	B	Wilkes, Charles	1843
Westergaard, Harald M.	1942	Wilkinson, James	1798
Westermann, William L.	1944	Wilks, Samuel S.	1948
Wetherill, Charles M.	1851	Willard, Joseph	1804
Wetherill, John P.	1827	Willcox, Joseph	1895
Wetherill, John P.	1878	Williams, Alfred H.	1949
Wetherill, Samuel P.	1933	Williams, Carroll Milton	1969
Wetmore, Alexander	1930	Williams, Edward H.	1897
Weyl, Hermann	1935	Williams, Edwin B.	1955
Wharton, Charles H.	1786	Williams, Henry J.	1833
Wharton, George M.	1840	Williams, John Henry	1942
Wharton, Henry	1880	Williams, Jonathan	1787
Wharton, Isaac	C	Williams, Robert R.	1942
Wharton, Joseph	1869	Williams, Samuel	1772
Wharton, Samuel	C	Williams, Talcott	1888
Wharton, Thomas	C	Williamson, Hugh	B
Wharton, Thomas I.	1830	Williamson, Robert S.	1870
Wheatley, Charles M.	1879	Willier, Benjamin H.	1955
Wheaton, Henry	1829	Willing, Thomas	B
Wheeler, Samuel	1795	Willis, Bailey	1905
Wheeler, William M.	1916	Willis, Henry	1890
Whipple, George H.	1938	Williston, Samuel W.	1918
Whitaker, Arthur P.	1952	Willits, Joseph H.	1938
White, Andrew D.	1869	Wilson, Alexander	1813

Wilson, E. Bright	1946	Woodward, Robert S.	1902
Wilson, Edmund B.	1888	Woodworth, Robert S.	1936
Wilson, Edwin B.	1917	Woolley, Stephen	C
Wilson, George G.	1936	Woolsey, Theodore D.	1871
Wilson, Harold A.	1914	Wootten, J. E.	1874
Wilson, Henry V. P.	1932	Workman, Benjamin	1785
Wilson, James	C	Workman, James	1821
Wilson, James C.	1885	Wormley, Theodore G.	1878
Wilson, James P.	1814	Worral, James	C
Wilson, John A.	1954	Worrall, James	1884
Wilson, Joseph M.	1874	Worthen, Amos H.	1863
Wilson, Robert E.	1957	Wright, Arthur W.	1896
Wilson, Thomas B.	1852	Wright, Frederick E.	1914
Wilson, William P.	1887	Wright, James	A
Wilson, Woodrow	1897	Wright, Louis Booker	1948
Winchell, Alexander	1865	Wright, Quincy	1943
Winlock, Herbert E.	1939	Wright, Sewall	1932
Winsor, Henry	1862	Wright, William H.	1935
Winsor, Justin	1893	Wu, Chien-Shiung	1981
Winthrop, James	1809	Wurts, Alexander J.	1899
Winthrop, John	B	Wurts, Charles S.	1881
Winthrop, Robert C.	1880	Wyckoff, Ambrose B.	1886
Winthrop, Thomas L.	1837	Wylie, Samuel B.	1806
Wireman, Henry D.	1887	Wyman, Jeffries	1866
Wissler, Clark	1924	Wynkoop, Benjamin	C
Wistar, Caspar	1787		
Wistar, D.	C	**Y**	
Wistar, Isaac J.	1893		
Wister, Caspar	1859	Yarnall, Ellis	1880
Wister, Charles J.	1811	Yeatman, Pope	1920
Wister, Owen	1897	Yerkes, Robert M.	1936
Wister, Owen J.	1866	Yost, Charles W.	1975
Witherspoon, John	1769	Young, Charles A.	1874
Witmer, Lightner	1897	Young, Donald R.	1945
Wittkower, Rudolf	1971	Young, James T.	1933
Wolf, Edwin, 2d	1974	Young, Owen D.	1929
Wolff, Robert Lee	1963	Young, Rodney S.	1965
Wolfgang, Marvin E.	1975	Youtie, Herbert C.	1957
Wolfson, Harry A.	1956		
Wolman, Leo	1941	**Z**	
Wood, George B.	1829		
Wood, Horatio C.	1866	Zane, Isaac	C
Wood, Richard	1879	Zariski, Oscar	1951
Wood, Robert W.	1908	Zeleny, John	1915
Wood, Stuart	1899	Zentmayer, Joseph	1873
Woodhouse, James	1796	Zinsser, Hans	1937
Woodring, Wendell P.	1953	Zirkle, Raymond	1960
Woodward, Henry	1874	Zworykin, Vladimir Kosma	1948
Woodward, Robert B.	1962		

FORMER FOREIGN MEMBERS

Following each name there is a notation of the country of the member as per the following table:

A	Austria	In	India
Ar	Argentina	Ir	Ireland
Au	Australia	Is	Israel
B	Belgium	J	Japan
Br	Brazil	L	Lebanon
C	Canada	M	Mexico
Ch	China	N	Netherlands
Co	Colombia	No	Norway
Cz	Czechoslovakia	NZ	New Zealand
D	Denmark	P	Portugal
E	England	Pa	Panama
Eg	Egypt	Pe	Peru
F	France	Po	Poland
Fi	Finland	R	Russia
G	Germany	S	Sweden
Gr	Greece	Sc	Scotland
Gu	Guatemala	Sp	Spain
H	Hungary	Sw	Switzerland
I	Italy	W	West Indies

As in the case of former resident members, the date of election is given with the exception of members elected before the union of the two Societies in 1769 (see Brief History of the Society, p. 289). In each such case there is an "A," "B," or "C" indicating that the member was a member of both Societies before the union, or a member only of the American Philosophical Society, or of the American Society.

This list is as accurate as it was possible to determine at this time. There are a number of question marks and blanks for names. Items in doubt are enclosed in brackets. Further study of the list will be made and anyone who can point out any inaccuracies or supply answers to the questions should do so. The same applies to the list of Former Resident Members.

A

Abrahamson, Joseph N. B. V.   D 1829
Acland, Sir Henry   E 1873
Adam, Lucien   F 1886
Adams, Charles   W 1775

Adams, Frank D.   C 1916
Adams, John C.   E 1848
Adelung, Friedrich   R 1818
Adet, Pierre A.   F 1796
Adrian, Edgar D.   E 1938
Adrian, Lord Richard.   E 1987
   See Hume, Richard, Baron

Adye, Stephen	E 1772	Banks, Sir Joseph	E 1787
Afzelius, Peter	S 1821	Barbé-Marbois, François, Marquis de
Agardh, Charles A.	S 1835		F 1780
Agassiz, Louis	Sw 1843	Barbeu-Dubourg, Jacques	F 1775
Airy, Sir George B.	E 1879	Barcena, Mariano	M 1877
Åkerman, Richard	S 1876	Barclay, Robert	E 1787
Alaman, Lucas	M 1851	Barnes, Thomas	E 1787
Albers, Johann A.	G 1819	Barrande, Joachim	A 1862
Albrecht, Paul	G 1886	Bartlett, Sir Frederic C.	E 1945
Alcantara, Pedro	P 1876	Barton, Sir Derek H. R.	E 1978
Alexandroff, Paul	R 1946	Bastian, Adolph	G 1886
Alfvén, Hannes Olof G.	S 1971	Baumhauer, Eduard H. von	N 1877
Allen, Alfred H.	E 1898	Beattie, James	Sc 1786
Alonso, Amado	Ar 1942	Beaufort, Francis	E 1840
Alonso, Dámaso	Sp 1962	Beazley, Sir John D.	E 1943
d'Alverny, Marie-Thérèse	F 1974	Becquerel, Henri	F 1902
Amaldi, Edoardo	I 1961	Bedford, Paul	W C
Anderson, James	E 1791	Bédier, Joseph	F 1937
Anderson, James	Sc 1794	Belcher, Jonathan	C C
Andrada e Silva, José B. de	Br 1822	Bell, Sir Harold I.	E 1941
Andreani, Paolo, Conte	I 1792	Bell, Sir Lowthian	E 1876
Andrewes, Sir Christopher H.	E 1955	Beneš, Edvard	Cz 1939
Angelis, Pedro de	Ar 1840	Bennett, John H.	Sc 1849
Angeviller, Charles C.		Bergius, Peter	S B
Labillarderie, comte d'	F 1784	Bergmann, Torbern	S 1773
Annemours, Charles F. A.		Berlin, Sir Isaiah	E 1975
Le Paulmier, chevalier d'	F 1783	Bernard, Claude	F 1860
Archer, Thomas C.	Sc 1876	Berthelot, Marcelin	F 1895
Arfwedson, Charles D.	S 1853	Bertholff, Frederick E. F.,
Argyll, Duke of.		Baron de Beelen	B 1785
See Campbell, George Douglas		Bertin, Georges	F 1895
Armstrong, Sir William G.	E 1874	Berzelius, John J.	S 1820
Aron, Raymond C. F.	F 1966	Bessborough, The Earl of	E 1988
Arrhenius, Svante A.	S 1911	Bessel, Friedrich W.	G 1840
Arthaud, Charles	W 1789	Bessemer, Sir Henry	E 1894
Augustus Frederick, Duke of Sussex		Best, Charles H.	C 1950
	E 1832	Bigsby, John J.	E 1825
Auwers, George F. J. A.	G 1912	Billé, Steen	D 1832
Avebury, 1st Baron.		Birch, Samuel	E 1869
See Lubbock, Sir John		Bischoff, Bernhard	G 1989
		Bischoff, Theodore L. W.	G 1860
		Bittel, Kurt	G 1984
B		Blackmore, William	E 1869
		Blackwell, Thomas E.	C 1863
Babinger, Franz	G 1964	Blades, William	E 1882
Baeyer, Adolf von	G 1910	Blagden, Sir Charles	E 1789
Baker, William	E 1787	Blainville. See Ducrotay de Blainville
Balbo, Prospero, Conte	I 1831	Blanchet, Francis	C 1801
Balfour, Arthur J.	E 1917	Blum, J. Reinhard	G 1882
Ball, Sir Robert S.	E 1891		

Ceselli, Luigi	I 1869	Cuñat, Joanne B.	Sp 1796
Chabas, François J.	F 1869	Curie, Marie Sklodowska	F 1910
Chadwick, Sir James	E 1948	Curtius, Ernst	G 1895
Charencey, Hyacinthe, Comte de		Curtius, Georg	G 1886
	F 1886	Cuthbert, Ross	C 1809
Charles, Jacques A. C.	F 1786		
Chastellux, François J., Marquis de		**D**	
	F 1781		
Chernyshev, Theodosy	R 1897	Dainton, Lord Frederick Sidney	
Chevalier, Michel	F 1852		E 1991
Christison, Robert	Sc 1841	Dale, Sir Henry H.	E 1939
Churchill, Sir Winston S.	E 1951	Dalman, John W.	S 1827
Clark, Sir James	E 1845	Dannefeld, C. Juhlin	S 1876
Clark, Sir W. E. Le Gros	E 1960	Dantas Pereira, José M.	P 1828
Clay, Sir Henry	E 1947	Darboux, Gaston	F 1902
Cochrane, Archibald, 9th		Darwin, Charles	E 1869
Earl of Dundonald	Sc 1795	Darwin, Sir Charles G.	E 1952
Coleridge, Sir John D., 1st Baron		Darwin, Erasmus	E 1792
	E 1884	Darwin, Francis	E 1909
Collins, William H.	C 1932	Darwin, George H.	E 1898
Collyer, William B.	E 1823	Dashkov, Catherine, Princess	R 1789
Condorcet, M. J. A. N.		Daubenton, Louis J. M.	F 1775
Caritat, Marquis de	F 1775	Daubeny, Charles G. B.	E 1838
Constant. *See* Estournelles de Constant		Daubrée, Gabriel A.	F 1863
Cook, Arthur B.	E 1944	Daux, Georges	F 1953
Copland, Douglas B.	Au 1948	Davenport, Sir Samuel	Au 1876
Copland, James	E 1845	David, Christian G. N.	D 1863
Coquebert de Montbret,		Davidson, Thomas	E 1866
Charles E., Baron	F 1823	Davy, Humphry	E 1810
Cora, Guido	I 1886	Dawkins, William B.	E 1880
Correa da Serra, José F.	P 1812	Dawson, Sir John W.	C 1862
Coste, Jean F.	F 1783	Deabbate, Gaspard	I 1823
Coupigny, André F. de	F 1793	Degrassi, Attilio	I 1958
Courcelle, Pierre	F 1968	Delage, Yves	F 1905
Court de Gébelin, Antoine	F 1783	Delambre, Jean B. J.	F 1803
Craigie, Sir William A.	E 1942	Delesse, Achille E.O.J.	F 1863
Crawford, Adair, Earl of	E 1785	Deleuze, Joseph P. F.	F 1817
Crell, Lorenz	G 1786	Delgada. *See* Rada y Delgada	
Crelle, August L.	G 1853	Delitzsch, Friedrich	G 1904
Crèvecoeur, Michael G. St. J. de		De Sanctis, Gaetano	I 1946
	F 1789	Des Cloizeaux, Alfred L. O. L.	F 1878
Croce, Benedetto	I 1944	Desmarest, Anselme G.	F 1819
Crookes, Sir William	E 1886	Desmoulins, Charles	F 1861
Crosse, John G.	E 1837	Desor, Edouard	Sw 1862
Crowther, Geoffrey	E 1953	Destutt de Tracy, Antoine L. C.,	
Crum, Walter E.	E 1944	Comte	F 1806
Cruz, Fernando	Sp 1889	Deveze, Jean	F 1796
Cullen, William	Sc A	Deville, Henri St. C.	F 1860
Cumont, Franz V. M.	B 1940	Dewar, James	E 1899

Freiré, Cypriano R.	P 1796	Goodsir, John	Sc 1849
Frerichs, Friedrich T. von	G 1862	Göppert, Heinrich R.	G 1862
Freyre, Gilberto de Mello	Br 1962	Gorter, Cornelis J.	N 1970
Frisch, Ragnar A.	No 1970	Gråberg af Hemso, Jakob, Grefve	
Froude, James A.	E 1862		S 1826
Frye, Northrop	C 1976	Granchain [de Sémerville, Comte?]	
Furet, François	F 1989		F 1786
Fuss, Nicholas	R 1818	Grandpré, Jacques M. le F. de	F 1796
		Granit, Ragnar	S 1954
G		Greg, Sir Walter W.	E 1945
		Gregorio, Antonio,	
Gage, Thomas	E B	Marquis de	I 1888
Galbraith, Vivian H.	E 1948	Gregory, Caspar R.	G 1891
Galvez, Mariano	Gu 1836	Grimaldi, Giuseppi C.,	
Garbier, Thibert	F 1786	Marquis de Pietracatella	I 1846
Garcia, Godofredo	Pe 1943	Grimm, Jacob	G 1863
Gardiner, Sir Alan H.	E 1943	Grivel, Guillaume	F 1786
Gardiner, Valentine	E C	Grosche, John G.	R 1791
Gardner, Dame Helen	E 1982	Grove, Sir George	E 1895
Gardoqui, Diego de	Sp 1789	Gruner, Louis	F 1869
Gardoqui, Francis de	Sp 1789	Gubernatis, Angelo de	I 1886
Garnett, Richard	E 1901	Guichen, L. U. de Bouexic,	
Gasparin, Alphonse, Comte de	F 1864	Comte de	F 1785
Gastelier, René G.	F 1786	Guillemard, John	E 1797
Gaugain, Jean M.	F 1873	Guizot, François P. G.	F 1840
Gauss, Karl F.	G 1853	Gützlaff, Karl	G 1839
Gayangos, Pascual de	Sp 1861		
Gébelin. *See* Court de Gébelin		**H**	
Geikie, Sir Archibald	E 1880		
Geikie, James	Sc 1876	Haeckel, Ernst	G 1885
Gellner, Ernest Andre	E 1993	Hahn, John D.	N 1770
Gérard de Rayneval,		Haidinger, Wilhelm K. von	A 1855
Conrad A.	F 1779	Haighton, John	E 1810
Gérome, J. Léon	F 1895	Hakakian Bey, T.	Eg 1869
Gibbons, Thomas	E 1775	Hale, Horatio E.	C 1872
Giglioli, Enrico H.	I 1901	Hall, Marshall	E 1853
Gill, Sir David	E 1910	Hamilton, William J.	E 1862
Gill, John	Ir C	Hammer-Purgstall, Jos. von	A 1817
Gilson, Etienne	F 1948	Hampe, Roland	G 1979
Giraldez, Joachim P. C.	P 1827	Hamy, Ernst, T. J.	F 1891
Gladstone, William E.	E 1881	Hardy, Godfrey H.	E 1939
Glaisher, James	E 1895	Harvey, William H.	Ir 1860
Glazebrook, Richard T.	E 1895	Hauer, Franz von	A 1874
Gloucester, Archibald	W 1771	Hawes, William	E 1805
Gloxin, Benjamin	F 1791	Heckscher, Eli F.	S 1940
Godoy, Manuel, Prince	Sp 1804	Heer, Oswald	Sw 1862
Gonzales, Francisco A.	Sp 1831	Heim, Roger	F 1959
Gooch, George P.	E 1939	Heinitz, Friedrich A. von	G 1789
Good, John M.	E 1811	Heisenberg, Werner	G 1937

Helmholtz, Hermann L. F. von			**I**	
	G	1873		
Henry, Thomas	E	1786	Im Thurn, Sir Everard F.	Sc 1885
Hermelin, Samuel G.	S	1785	Ingenhousz, Jan	A 1786
Herschel, Sir John F. W.	E	1854	Innis, Harold A.	C 1948
Herschel, Sir William	E	1785	Irvine, Sir James C.	Sc 1933
Hertzsprung, Ejnar	N	1941		
Herzberg, Gerhard	C	1972	**J**	
Hewson, William	E C			
Heymans, Corneille J. F.	B	1962	Jacobsson, Per	S 1957
Heyse, Paul	G	1895	Jaeger, G. Friedrich von	G 1860
Hilbert, David	G	1932	Jahn, Gustav A.	G 1848
Hill, Archibald V.	E	1938	James, Hugh	W 1785
Himsworth, Sir Harold	E	1972	Jamineau, Isaac	E C
Hindemith, Paul	Sw	1962	Janet, Pierre	F 1940
Hinshelwood, Sir Cyril N.	E	1963	Jannet, Claudio	F 1881
Hirn, Gustav A.	G	1886	Jardine, Sir William	Sc 1845
Hjort, Johan	No	1939	Jaudenes, José de	Sp 1796
Hochstetter, Ferdinand von	A	1869	Jebb, Sir Richard C.	E 1904
Hodge, Sir William	E	1964	Jenner, Edward	E 1804
Hodgkin, Sir Alan L.	E	1967	Jerne, Neils Kaj	F 1979
Hofmann, August W. von	G	1862	Joffre, Joseph J. C.	F 1918
Holland, Sir Henry	E	1846	Johannsen, Wilhelm L.	D 1916
Holland, Samuel	E	1775	Johnson, Sir William	E B
Hooker, Sir Joseph D.	E	1869	Jomard, Edme F.	F 1829
Hooker, Sir William J.	E	1862	Jones, H. Spencer	E 1942
Hopf, Heinz	Sw	1962	Jones, William	E 1801
Hopkins, Sir Frederick G.	E	1937	Julien, Stanislas	F 1843
Hormayr, Joseph, Baron von	A	1820	Jullien, Marc A.	F 1830
Houssay, Bernardo A.	Ar	1944	Jusserand, Jean A. A. J.	F 1907
Hovelacque, Abel	F	1886		
Hu Shih	Ch	1936	**K**	
Huck, Richard	E C			
Huggins, Sir William	E	1895	Kaegi, Werner	Sw 1976
Humboldt, F. H. Alexander,			Kankrin, Egor, Count	R 1843
Baron von	G	1804	Kapteyn, Jacobus C.	N 1907
Humboldt, Wilhelm, Baron von			Karpinsky, Alexander	R 1897
	G	1822	Kastler, Alfred	F 1976
Hume, Richard, Baron.			Kaup, Johann J.	G 1862
See Adrian, Lord			Kazem Beg, Alexander	R 1862
Hunfalvy, Paul	H	1886	Keith, Sir Arthur	E 1931
Hunter, John	E	1787	Keith, Arthur B.	Sc 1935
Hüpsch von Lontzen,			Keller, Ferdinand	Sw 1863
J. W. K. A., Baron	G	1790	Kelvin, Lord. *See*	
Hutchins, Joseph	W C		Thomson, Sir William	
Huxley, Thomas H.	E	1869	Kenyon, Sir Frederic G.	E 1937
Hyde de Neuville, Jean G., Baron			Kiepert, Heinrich	G 1886
	F	1829	Kiernan, Francis	E 1849
Hyrtl, Joseph	A	1860	Kihara, Hitoshi	J 1965

King, Charles W.	E	1882
Kirchhoff, Gustav R.	G	1864
Kirwan, Richard	E	1786
Kitasato, Shibasaburo	J	1914
Klaproth, Heinrich J.	G	1824
Klingstädt, Timotheus M., Baron von	R	1773
Knight, William A.	E	1898
Kohlrausch, Friedrich W. G.	G	1909
Kolbe, Hermann	G	1874
Kolmogorov, Andrei Nikolayevich	R	1961
Koninck, Laurent G. de	B	1882
Kopp, Hermann	G	1882
Kosciusko, Thaddeus	Po	1785
Kramers, Hendrik A.	N	1942
Krauss, Friedrich S.	A	1889
Krautheimer, Richard	I	1965
Krebs, Sir Hans A.	E	1960
Krogh, August	D	1941
Krusenstern, Ivan	R	1824
Kupffer, Adolf T. von	R	1847

L

Labouderie, Jean	F	1833
Lacordaire, Théodore	B	1856
Ladoucette, Jean C. F., Baron de	F	1842
Lafayette, Gilbert Motier, Marquis de	F	1781
La Forest, Antoine R. C. M., Comte de	F	1792
La Luzerne, Anne C. de	F	1780
Lambert, Guillaume	B	1872
La Métherie, Jean C. de	F	1817
Lanciani, Rodolfo	I	1897
Lane, Timothy	E	1772
Langlès, Louis M.	F	1819
Lanjuinais, Jean D., Comte	F	1819
Lankester, Edwin R.	E	1903
Larmor, Sir Joseph	E	1913
La Rochefoucauld d'Enville, Louis A., Duc de	F	1786
La Rochefoucauld-Liancourt, François A. F. de	F	1796
Larocque, A. J.	F	?1796
Larrey, Dominique J., Baron	F	1831
Lartêt, Edouard	F	1869

Lasteyrie du Saillant, Charles P., Comte de	F	1807
Latreille, Pierre A.	F	1819
Laue, Max F. T. von	G	1949
Lauth, Franz J.	G	1872
Laval, John, Count	R	1825
Lavoisier, Antoine L.	F	1775
Lawrence, Sir William	E	1823
Lebert, Hermann	G	1862
Leclerc, Georges L. *See* Buffon, Comte de		
Le Comte, F. H.	F	1796
Leemans, Conrad	N	1886
Legge, James	E	1895
Leland, Charles G.	E	1890
Leloir, Luis F.	Ar	1963
Lemaître, Abbé Georges	B	1945
Le Moine, Sir James MacP.	C	1889
Lenhossek, Josef von	H	1885
Lennox, Charles, 3d Duke of Richmond	E	1787
Leonhard, Karl C. von	G	1836
Leopoldo II, Grand Duke of Tuscany	I	1843
Lepsius, Karl R.	G	1845
Leray, Jean	F	1959
Le Roux, _____	F	1775
Le Roy, Jean B.	F	1773
Le Roy, Julien D.	F	1786
Leroy-Beaulieu, Paul	F	1881
Leslie, Charles R.	E	1837
Lesseps, Matthew	F	1820
Lesueur, Charles A.	F	1817
Letombe, Philippe J.	F	1802
Lettsom, John C.	E	1787
Levasseur, Pierre E.	F	1886
Le Veillard, Louis G.	F	1786
Leverrier, Urbain J. J.	F	1847
Levi-Civita, Tullio	I	1940
Lewis, Sir Aubrey J.	E	1961
Lewis, Samuel S.	E	1882
Liebig, Justus von	G	1862
Lighthill, Sir James	E	1970
Linant de Bellefonds Bey	Eg	1869
Linderstrom-Lang, Kaj U.	D	1951
Lindley, John	E	1862
Lindsay, David R. A., Earl of Crawford	Sc	1954
Linnaeus, Carolus	S	1769

Moore, Henry	E 1980		Nordenskjöld, Nils O. G.	S 1905
More, Samuel	E 1774		Nordmark, Zacharias	S 1822
Moreau de Saint Méry,			Nys, Ernest	B 1908
Médéric L. E.	F 1789			
Morelli, Domenico C.	I 1836		**O**	
Morinière, Noël de la	F 1818			
Morlot, Charles A.	Sw 1864		Occhialini, Giuseppe	F 1975
Mortillet, Gabriel de	F 1895		Oersted, Hans C.	D 1829
Morton, Charles	W 1771		Olrik, Christian	D 1856
Moruzzi, Giuseppe	I 1961		Olsen, Peter B.	D 1802
Mosely, Benjamin	W 1775		Onnes, Heike K.	N 1914
Mozard, Theo. C.	F 1797		Oort, Jan H.	N 1957
Much, Matthaeus	A 1886		Oppert, Jules	F 1891
Müller, Friedrich	A 1886		Osler, Sir William	E 1885
Müller, Friedrich M.	E 1863		Ostwald, Wilhelm	G 1912
Müller, Johannes P.	G 1846		Otto, Louis G., Comte	F 1787
Münter, Friederich	D 1830		Ovchinnikov, Yuri A.	R 1977
Muoni, Damiano	I 1880		Owen, Sir Francis P.C.	E 1876
Muralt, Alexander von	Sw 1978		Owen, Richard	E 1845
Murchison, Sir Roderick I.	E 1860			
Murray, Sir James A. H.	E 1881		**P**	
Murray, Johann A.	G 1791			
Murray, John	Sc 1819		Page, Sir Denys	E 1963
Murray, Sir John	Sc 1911		Paget, Sir James	E 1854
Mustoxidi, Andreas	Gr 1843		Painlevé, Paul F.	F 1918
Mynors, Roger	E 1985		Palisot de Beauvois, Ambroise	
Myrdal, Alva	S 1982		M. F. J., Baron de	F 1792
Myrdal, Gunnar	S 1982		Pallas, Peter S.	R 1791
			Palmieri, Luigi	I 1873
N			Parieu, Esquirou de	F 1871
			Parker, William	E 1785
Nadaillac, Jean F. A.			Parkes, Samuel	E 1822
du Pouget, Marquis de	F 1886		Pasteur, Louis	F 1885
Nagy, Charles	H 1833		Patterson, William	Ir 1798
Nairne, Edward	E 1770		Pavlov, Ivan	R 1932
Nansen, Fridtjof	No 1897		Paykull, Gustav	S 1801
Napier, John T.	Sc 1886		Peacock, George	E 1842
Naumann, Karl F.	G 1869		Pearson, Alexander	E 1824
Navarrete, Martin F.	Sp 1831		Pedersen, Johannes	D 1949
Naxera, Manuel	M 1836		Pedersen, Peder	D 1822
Newenham, Sir Edward	Ir 1787		Pekeris, Chaim L.	Is 1974
Niemcewicz, Julian U.	Po 1798		Peñafiel, Antonio	M 1886
Nikitin, Serge	R 1886		Penck, Albrecht F. K.	G 1908
Nilsson, Martin P.	S 1939		Penfield, Wilder G.	C 1950
Nilsson, Sven	S 1869		Penn, Granville	E 1836
Noël, Nicolas	F 1786		Pennant, Thomas	E 1791
Nöldeke, Theodor	G 1906		Penney, Lord William	E 1973
Nordenfalk, Carl	S 1970		Perceval, Robert	Ir 1785
Nordenskjöld, Nils A. E.	S 1876		Percival, Thomas	E 1786

Rokitanšky, Karl	A	1862
Rokkan, G. Stein	No	1978
Rolleston, George	E	1869
Rollett, Hermann	A	1885
Rönne, Ludwig P.M. von	G	1842
Roscoe, Sir Henry E.	E	1903
Rose, Heinrich	G	1860
Rosny, Léon L. L. P. de	F	1882
Ross, Sir William D.	E	1947
Rossi, Giovanni B. di	I	1873
Rougé, Olivier C. C. de	F	1869
Roume de St. Laurent, Philippe R.		
	F	1802
Rousseau de Happencourt, Karl C.		
	A	1893
Roux de Rochelle, Jean B. G.	F	1836
Roxburgh, William	Sc	1802
Rozier, Jean F.	F	1775
Rumford, Count. *See*		
Thompson, Benjamin		
Rumiantzov, Nicholas, Count	R	1825
Rümker, Karl L. C.	G	1839
Runnström, John	S	1953
Rutherford, Sir Ernest		
(later Lord Rutherford)	E	1904
Rütimeyer, Ludwig	Sw	1869

S

Sabine, Sir Edward	E	1841
Sakharov, Andrei D.	R	1978
Sakharov, Vasily	R	1853
Salam, Abdus	E	1992
Salazar, José M.	Co	1828
Sanchez, Jesus	M	1886
Sandberger, K. L. Fridolin von		
	G	1866
Sandiford, William	W	B
Santarem, Manuel F. de		
Barros e Sousa, Visconde de	P	1833
Saussure, Henri L. F. de	Sw	1873
Sauvy, Alfred L.	F	1974
Saville, Sir George	E	C
Saxe-Weimar, Karl Bernhard,		
Duke of	G	1830
Say, Jean-Baptiste L.	F	1872
Scandella, Giambattista	I	1798
Schiaparelli, Giovanni V.	I	1901
Schimper, Wilhelm P.	G	1866
Schinz, Carl	G	1864

Schlegel, Gustave	N	1899
Schorlemmer, Carl	E	1878
Schulze, Gottlob E.	G	1822
Schumacher, Heinrich C.	D	1823
Schuster, Sir Arthur	E	1913
Schwann, Theodor	B	1863
Sclater, Philip L.	E	1873
Sechhi, Angelo	I	1860
Sedgwick, Adam	E	1860
Selwyn, Alfred R. C.	C	1874
Sélys-Longchamps,		
Michael E., Baron de	B	1873
Séquard, Charles E. Brown.		
See Brown-Séquard		
Sergi, Giuseppe	I	1885
Sève de Bar, Edouard	F	1882
Sewell, Jonathan	C	1830
Shewell, Oliver, Baron	E	1949
Siebold, Carl T. E. von	G	1869
Siemens, Charles W.	E	1877
Silva, José B. de Andrada.		
See Andrada e Silva		
Siméon, Rémi	F	1886
Simpson, Sir James Y.	Sc	1863
Singer, Charles	E	1958
Six, James	E	1784
Small, Alexander	E	1773
Smith, Goldwin	C	1865
Smith, Sir James E.	E	1796
Snellen, Herman	N	1894
Somerville, Mary F.	E	1869
Sonnenfels, Joseph von	A	1817
Soulavie, Jean L. G.	F	1786
Span, James	Ir	C
Sparman, Anders	S	1790
Spemann, Hans	G	1937
Spence, George	W	1787
Spencer, Herbert	E	1883
Stamp, Josiah Charles, 1st		
Baron of Shortlands	E	1940
Stanhope, Charles, 3d Earl,		
Lord Mahon	E	1774
Stanhope, Philip H.,		
5th Earl, Lord Mahon	E	1854
Stanhope, Philips, 2nd Earl,		
Lord Mahon	E	1774
Stanley, Edward	E	1854
Steenstrup, Johann J. S.	D	1862
Stein, Sir M. Aurel	E	1939
Steinsky, Franz A.	A	1789

Vallancey, Charles | Ir 1780
Vallarta, Manuel S. | M 1954
Valltravers, Rodolph | G 1792
Van Berckel, Peter J. | N 1784
Van Hove, Leon | Sw 1980
Vanquelin, Louis N. | F 1811
Van't Hoff, Jacobus H. | G 1904
van Zeeland, Paul | B 1942
Vater, Johann S. | G 1817
Vaughan, Benjamin | E 1786
Vaughan, Petty | E 1842
Vaughan, William | E 1830
Vaux. *See* Cadet de Vaux
Vaux, George | E 1787
Venturi, Lionello | I 1947
Vergennes, Charles G., Comte de
F 1784
Verneuil, P. Edouard P. de | F 1860
Vinogradov, Ivan M. | R 1942
Viollet le Duc, Eugène E. | F 1875
Virchow, Rudolf | G 1862
Vogt, Karl C. | Sw 1869
Volney, Constantin F.
Chasseboeuf, Comte de | F 1797
Volpicelli, Paolo | I 1861
Volterra, Vito | I 1914
Vossion, Louis P. | F 1890
Vries, Hugo de | N 1903

W

Waals, Johannes D. van der | N 1916
Wace, Alan J. B. | E 1945
Wagner, Andreas | G 1860
Wagner, Rudolf von | G 1877
Waldeyer, Wilhelm | G 1904
Walker, John | Sc 1790
Wallace, Alfred R. | E 1873
Wallenstein, Jules de | R 1830
Ward-Perkins, John B. | E 1981
Warner, Ashton | W A
Warner, Samuel | W C
Warner, Thomas | W C
Warville, Jean P. Brissot de.
See Brissot de Warville
Washington, John | E 1839
Wedgwood, Dame Veronica | E 1969
Weil, André | F 1995

Weil, Gustav | G 1886
Weisbach, Albin | G 1885
Weismann, August | G 1906
West, Benjamin | E C
Westwood, John O. | E 1883
Wetterstedt, Gustavus, Count | S 1821
White, Michael James Denham
Au 1978
White, Thomas | E 1787
Whitefoord, Caleb | E 1790
Whitehurst, John | E 1786
Whittaker, Sir Edmund T. | Sc 1944
Wied-Neuwied, Maximilian
A. P., Prinz von | G 1845
Wieland, Theodor | G 1979
Wigglesworth, Vincent B. | E 1982
Wilkins, Sir Hubert | E 1930
Wilson, Sir Daniel | C 1863
Wilson, J. Tuzo | C 1971
Wöhler, Friedrich | G 1862
Woodward, Sir Llewllyn | E 1949
Worsaae, J. J. A. | D 1869
Wrangel, Charles M. | S B
Wright, William | W 1774
Wright, William A. | E 1900
Wundt, Wilhelm | G 1895
Wylie, Sir James | R 1821

Y

Yarrel, William | E 1830
Young, John Z. | E 1973
Yukawa, Hideki | J 1963

Z

Zach, Franz X. von | G 1798
Zantedeschi, Francesco | I 1851
Zecchinelli, Giovanni M. | I 1827
Zel'dovich, Yakov Borisovich | R 1979
Zimmerman, Eberhard A. W. von
G 1794
Zuckerman, Lord. Zuckerman of
Burnham Thorpe, Solly, Baron
E 1965

DEATHS OF MEMBERS

		Year of
1999	(Through 31 July 1999)	Election
Bate, Walter J., in Boston, MA, on 26 July, aet. 81		1966
Blitzer, Charles, in Washington, DC, on 19 February, aet. 87		1988
Cochran, Thomas C., in Haverford, Pa, on 2 May, aet. 97		1953
Herzberg, Gerhard, in Ottawa, Canada, on 3 March, aet. 94		1972
Ingalls, Daniel H. H., in Hot Springs, VA, on 17 July, aet. 83		1961
Kristeller, Paul Oskar, in New York City, on 7 June, aet. 94		1974
Leontief, Wassily, in New York, on 5 February, aet. 93		1951
McElroy, William D., in San Diego, CA, on 17 February, aet. 82		1971
Mellon, Paul, in Upperville, VA, on 1 February, aet. 91		1971
Mosse, George L., in Madison, WI, on 22 January, aet. 80		1997
Ratliff, Floyd, in Santa Fe, New Mexico, on 13 June, aet. 80		1972
Schawlow, Arthur L., in Palo Alto, CA, on 28 April, aet. 77		1984
Seaborg, Glenn T., in Lafayette, CA, on 25 February, aet. of 86		1952
Stone, Lawrence, in Princeton, NJ, on 16 June, aet. 79		1970
Weiner, Myron, in Moretown, VT, on 3 June, aet. 68		1999

The market value of each fund, as of 31 December 1998, appears in brackets at the end of its listing.

Arlin M. and Neysa Adams Fund

In 1996 Arlin and Nessa Adams contributed $6,000 to the Society, the income, less 10 percent which is to be added to the principal, to be expended for the support of symposia, colloquia, seminars and lectures. [$23,585.]

Balch International Law Library Fund

Founded in 1911 by Thomas Willing Balch, Esq., of Philadelphia with an initial gift of securities valued at about $700, increased by later gifts to about $1,600, as a memorial to his father for his part in bringing about the submission of the Alabama Claims to the Geneva Tribunal. A part of the income to be used to purchase books relating to the law of nations and such other uses, when thought advisable, as may promote the study of that science, not less than one-half of the income to be added annually to the principal. [$256,583]

Boyé Library Fund

Bequest of approximately $1,900 by Professor Martin Boyé of Coopersburg, Pennsylvania, a member of the Society, who died 5 March 1909. By resolution of the Society, December 1910, the income to be expended in the purchase of books, preferably on chemistry and geology. [$53,145]

Carl and Roberta A. Bridenbaugh Fund

In 1996 the Society was bequeathed $50,000 from the Roberta A. Bridenbaugh estate. In addition to this bequest, the Society also received the remainder interest of Dr. Bridenbaugh's participation in the Pooled Life Income Fund, an amount totaling $52,000. The new fund's principal and income will support general uses and purposes of the Society. [$487,685].

Brush Fund

Gift of $10,000 by Charles Francis Brush, LL.D., of Cleveland, Ohio, 24 November 1914. Income to be used for the general purposes of the Society. [$153,947]

Carlier Library Fund

Bequest of $5,000 by Auguste Carlier of Paris, a member of the Society, who died 16 March 1890. The income, less 10 percent which is to be added to the principal, to be expended for the purchase of books for the Library. [$271,549]

Carnegie Library Fund

Gift of $100,000 by the Carnegie Corporation in 1931. The income to be used for the maintenance of the Library. [$734,389]

Daland Fund

Bequest of the residuary estate of Dr. Judson Daland of Philadelphia, who died 14 August 1937, amounting to approximately $220,000. The income, less 10 percent which is to be added annually to the principal, to be used by the Society to promote research in clinical medicine. [$5,146,793]

Delmas Library Fund

Bequest of $250,000 by the estate of Gladys K. Delmas of New York in 1992. The income to be allocated for "library activities." [$529,863]

Delmas Publications Fund

Bequest of $250,000 by the estate of Gladys K. Delmas of New York in 1992. An additional $25,000 was added in 1995. The income to be allocated for the "publication of the Society's books, periodicals and articles which appear in the Society's various journals." [578,363]

Franklin Hall (Formerly Annex [NEH])

Established in 1983 by a grant of $16,666 from the National Endowment for the Humanities, which amount was part of a larger grant for the renovation of the Annex. The income to be used for the maintenance of the Annex, now called Franklin Hall. [$154,495]

Herman H. Goldstine Fund for Research in the History of Science

Established in 1995 with an anonymous gift of $100,000 to be given over a three-year period. The income to be used in support of research in the history of science or related fields. Ten percent of the annual income is to be added to principal. [$167,367]

Grantees' Fund

Established in 1983 by gifts of former recipients of the Society's research grants and to be increased by their future contributions. Income from the fund to be used for research grants. [$38,208]

Crawford H. Greenewalt Fund

Through the generosity of Mr. Crawford H. Greenewalt of Wilmington, Delaware, $200,000 was made available for the Andrew W. Mellon Foundation challenge grant to support the operation of the Library Conservation Department. The balance of $55,000 from Mr. Greenewalt's remainder interest in the Society's Pooled Life Income Fund was designated by Council for the Library's new environmental system. [$393,801]

Johnson Fund

Established in 1937 when Eldridge Reeves Johnson removed the restriction on his 1929 gift of $500,000 to a building fund. In 1957 all previous restrictions were removed and the income made available for general purposes of the Society. [$6,358,816]

Lashley Fund

Gift of $65,000 by Karl Spencer Lashley in 1957. Income to be used for an award to be made from time to time in recognition of useful and significant work in neurobiology. [$1,091,199]

H. C. Lewis Fund

The bequest of Henry Carvill Lewis. Although he died in 1888, his bequest did not come to the Society until 1974. At that time it was worth approximately $7,600. Income to be awarded periodically, together with a certificate, as a prize to a person who, in the opinion of the Council of the Society, has made during the year prior to the year of the award a valuable contribution to knowledge. [$143,630]

J. F. Lewis Fund

Gift of $10,000 made by Mrs. John F. Lewis in 1935 in memory of her husband. The income to be used each year as an award to the American citizen who shall announce at any general or special meeting of the Society, and publish among its papers, some truth which the Council shall deem worthy of the award, medicine and surgery excepted. [$599,415]

Lindback Fund

Established in 1982 by a grant of $50,000 from the Christian R. and Mary F. Lindback Foundation. Income, less 10 percent which is to be added to the principal, is for general purposes of the Library, "including the purchase of books, manuscripts or other items, and for increasing the utilization of the Library by scholars." [$205,567]

Magellanic Fund

Gift of 200 guineas by John Hyacinth de Magellan, of London, in 1786, for a gold medal to be awarded from time to time under prescribed terms, to the author of the best discovery or most useful invention relating to navigation, astronomy, or natural philosophy (mere natural history only excepted). Any surplus of interest remaining to be used for such purposes as may be authorized under the Society's Charter and Laws. By resolution of the Society, December 1899, the unexpended annual income, less 10 percent which is to be added to the principal, may be used for the purchase of books relating to those departments of science in which the premium is offered. [$276,867]

Mellon Fund

Grant of $300,000 made in 1972 by the Andrew W. Mellon Foundation, the income to be used "to facilitate use of the Library's collections by qualified scholars." Special programs in research and bibliography of kinds contemplated by the donor may be drafted annually by the Librarian and staff and reviewed by the Committee on Library. [$1,130,924]

Mellon VI Fund

Matching grant by the Andrew W. Mellon Foundation begun in 1992 and scheduled to continue until 1994 when a total foundation award of $750,000 was received. The income to be used for the operation of the Library Conservation Department. [$2,035,821]

Members Endowment Fund

In 1994 the Society started a conscientious effort to increase its endowment. Various members have contributed to this Fund in an on-going manner, providing that both principal and income be available for the general purposes of the Society. [$141,177]

Members International Fund
[$99,202]

Michaux Fund

Bequest of 92,000 francs by François André Michaux, a member of the Society, who died at Vauréal, France, 23 October 1855, to contribute to the progress of agriculture and silviculture in the United States. By resolution of the Society, April, 1996, the income, less 10 percent reserved for investment, to be used for the maintenance of the Thomas Jefferson Garden, the purchase of books and manuscripts for the Library, and the publication of books on horticulture and/or for research grants in ecology, plant biology, and soil science. [$837,790]

Henry Allen and Edith Monroe Moe Fund

Established in 1977 by a gift of $15,000 by Mrs. Moe in memory of Dr. Moe, President of the Society, 1959–70, and so named by action of the Council of the Society. The income is for the support of the Society's research and publications programs, as the Council may direct. [$138,704]

Henry Allen Moe Prize in the Humanities Fund

Established in 1982 by a gift of $37,500 by Mrs. Moe, to endow a prize in memory of her husband, to be presented annually to the author of the best paper in humanities or jurisprudence read to the Society. [$169,315]

Neugebauer Fund

Gift of $58,434.68 by Dr. Otto Neugebauer of Princeton, New Jersey in 1989 in memory of his daughter, Margot Neugebauer. The income, less 10 percent which is to be added annually to the principal, to be used for publications. [$141,822]

Osterhout Library Fund

A bequest of approximately $49,600 of Dr. Marian Irwin Osterhout, who died in 1973, in memory of her husband, Winthrop J. V. Osterhout, a member of the Society, and herself. The income to be used by the Society from time to time for the maintenance and operation of the Library. [$311,952]

Penrose Fund

Bequest of one-half of the residuary estate of Dr. Richard A. F. Penrose, Jr., of Philadelphia, a member of the Society, who died 31 July 1931, amounting to approximately $3,900,000. By the terms of the will this bequest to be considered an endowment fund, the capital to be properly invested and the income only to be used. [$73,407,025]

Phillips Fund

Bequest of his residuary estate, approximately $3,400 by Henry Phillips, Jr., Esq., of Philadelphia, who died 6 June 1895, to which were added on 5 October 1903 two bequests to him, approximately $7,500 from the estate of his aunt, Emily Phillips, and approximately $42,300, being an interest in the residuary estate of his uncle, Henry M. Phillips. Income to be used for the purchase of books and manuscripts on archaeology and philology, and to support research on North American linguistics and ethnohistory. [$1,529,406]

Phillips Prize Fund

The gift on 5 October 1888, of $5,000 by Miss Emily Phillips, of Philadelphia, in memory of her brother. Income to be used in the awarding of the Henry M. Phillips Prize for the best essay of real merit on the science and philosophy of jurisprudence. In addition, Henry M. Phillips grants are to be provided to persons to finance and support the research and, when deemed appropriate, the publication of distinguished papers, books and treatises in the field of law and jurisprudence. [$643,847]

Proskouriakoff Fund

Bequest of 30 percent of the residuary estate and of the trust of Miss Tatiana Proskouriakoff, of Cambridge, Mass., a member of the Society, who died 30 August 1985, amounting to approximately $100,443, principal and income to be available for the general purposes of the Society. [$277,941]

Jonathan E. Rhoads Lecture Fund

Established in 1996 through contributions from members of the Society, the College of Physicians of Philadelphia, and the Department of Surgery of the Hospital of the University of Pennsylvania. The income less 10 percent which is to be added to the principal to be expended for an annual lecture in the field of medicine. Part of the contributions was used to strike a special medal to be given to invited speakers. [$114,344]

Seybert Library Fund

Bequest of $2,000 by Henry Seybert, Esq., of Philadelphia, who died 3 March 1883. In 1949 $1,000 was added to the principal by the Society. By resolution of the Society, November 1909, the income to be expended for the purchase of books. [$78,862]

John C. Slater Library Research Fund

Proposed in 1981 by Rose Slater in memory of her husband, a member of the Society, and created after her death (1983) by a gift from Dr. Slater's children, Charles R. and John F. Slater, and Louise Slater Huntington. The income is primarily to promote scholarship in the history of modern physics (since 1900) and generally the history of science, by means of research grants, acquisition of pertinent materials, and the publication of scholarly investigations. [$318,253]

Stefansson Fund

Gift of $10,000 by Mrs. Evelyn Stefansson Nef of Washington, D.C. in 1991 in memory of her late husband, Vilhajalmur Stefansson. A second gift of $10,000 added in 1992. The income, less 10 percent which is to be added annually to the principal, to be used for the acquisition of library materials in the field of exploration, particularly polar exploration. [$64,845]

Tilghman Library Fund

Bequest of $200 by Chief Justice William Tilghman, of Philadelphia, President of the Society, who died 30 April 1827. Income to be expended for the purchase of books. [$36,923]

University Extension—Jayne Fund

Established 17 December 1946, by order of the Court of Common Pleas of Philadelphia dissolving the Corporation of the American Society for the Extension of University Teaching and awarding the remaining property of the corporation including that received from the Jayne Memorial Fund, and from any other source, to the American Philosophical Society, to be used for the promotion of university teaching, including, inter alia, arranging for lectures, publications, and research in the fields of the sciences, literature, and the arts. This fund by action of the Society is held as a memorial to Henry LaBarre Jayne, an officer and supporter of the American Society for the Extension of University Teaching, and a former Treasurer of the American Philosophical Society. The fund thus established consisted of securities and cash appraised at about $34,000. [$1,469,241]

Whitfield Fund

Bequest of the residuary estate of James Edward Whitfield, of Philadelphia, who died 4 November 1930, amounting to approximately $42,000. This fund was left "absolutely and in fee." Ten percent of the income is added to the principal annually and the balance applied to general purposes of the Society. [$625,437]

TRUST FUNDS

Haney Fund

Established in 1960 with income from the John Louis Haney Fund administered by the trustees of the estate of John Louis Haney, who died 28 December 1959, a portion of the income from which is to come each year to the Society to "constitute a revolving book fund for publishing desirable books with some commercial possibilities in either Class III (social sciences) or Class IV (humanities) of the Society's activities."

Hays Fund

I. Minis Hays, Librarian of the Society, 1897–1922, who died in 1925, made the Society residual legatee of the income of a trust fund administered by the First Pennsylvania Bank. The income became available to the Society in 1973. Under the will one-half of the annual income may be used to create and maintain a revolving fund of $25,000 for that purpose; a sum of $600 is to be applied annually to the cost of luncheons at the Annual Meetings; the balance may be used toward the expenses of the Library, the cost of publication of the Society's *Proceedings* and *Transactions*, or as grants for research.

Hays-Bradford Fund

Annie Bradford, a relative of I. Minis Hays, created a trust which provided that at the death of Dr. Hays the income should be used for the same purposes designated by the will of I. Minis Hays as set forth above. By action of Orphans Court of Philadelphia, the Hays-Bradford Fund has been incorporated into the Hays Fund, effective September 30, 1996.

IN ADDITION TO HONORING excellence in the sciences, humanities, arts, professions, and public service by election to membership, the Society sponsors eight special awards. A hand-illuminated certificate accompanies all awards.

BENJAMIN FRANKLIN MEDAL FOR DISTINGUISHED ACHIEVEMENT IN THE SCIENCES [1]

To mark the two hundredth anniversary of the birth of Benjamin Franklin in 1906, the United States Congress authorized a commemorative medal, to be designed by Augustus and Louis St. Gaudens. One copy in gold was presented, "under the direction of the President of the United States," to the Republic of France; and of the one hundred and fifty copies struck in bronze one hundred were for distribution as the President might direct, and fifty were given to the American Philosophical Society for its use. Subsequently additional medals were minted for the Society. The medal is the Society's highest award for the sciences or humanities.

Recipients:

1985	Charles Brenton Huggins	1993	Sir Michael Atiyah
1986	Helen Brooke Taussig (posthumously)	1993	Barbara McClintock (posthumously)
1987	Samuel Noah Kramer	1993	Emily H. Mudd
1987	Otto Neugebauer	1993	Ruth Patrick
1988	Sune Bergström	1993	Chen Ning Yang
1988	Jonathan E. Rhoads	1995	Ernst Mayr
1989	John A. Wheeler	1996	Victor A. McKusick
1990	Crawford H. Greenewalt	1997	Herman H. Goldstine
1990	Britton Chance	1998	Edward O. Wilson
1990	James B. Pritchard	1999	Frederick Robbins
1991	Lyman Spitzer	1999	Phillip Sharp

BENJAMIN FRANKLIN GOLD MEDAL

Republic of France

---

[1] *Until 1993 this award was known as the Benjamin Franklin Award for Distinguished Achievement in the Humanities or the Sciences. In 1993 at the time of the 250th anniversary of the founding of the Society, the Thomas Jefferson Medal for Distinguished Achievement in the Arts, Humanities or Social Sciences was created.*

Benjamin Franklin Medal

This medal, which is described above, was given from 1937 to 1983, for especially noteworthy contributions to the Society.

Recipients:

1937 William Lyon Phelps	1947 Douglas S. Freeman
1939 Eduard Benes	1949 William E. Lingelbach
1940 Edward S. Corwin	1979 George W. Corner
1941 Hugh S. Taylor	1982 Julia A. Noonan
1943 James B. Conant	1983 Whitfield J. Bell, Jr.
1945 Arthur H. Compton	

Benjamin Franklin Award for Distinguished Public Service

Established in 1987 to honor exceptional contributions to the general welfare, this award comprises a citation and the privilege of attending all meetings of the Society.

Recipients:

1987 Margaret Lady Thatcher	1994 Linus Pauling
1988 Thomas J. Watson, Jr.	1995 William T. Golden
1988 Former Chief Justice	1996 Edmund Nelson Carpenter II
Warren Earl Burger	1997 William T. Scranton
1989 Paul Mellon	1998 Alan Greenspan
1992 Thurgood Marshall	1999 George Mitchell
1993 Walter H. Annenberg	

Thomas Jefferson Gold Medal

In 1993, the United States Congress praised the APS as "the oldest learned society in the United States and one of the principal scholarly and scientific bodies in the world" and honored the Society and its third president, Thomas Jefferson, for "devotion to learning" by authorizing the minting of the Thomas Jefferson Medal.

King Juan Carlos I on behalf of Spain in recognition
of its democratic accomplishments

Thomas Jefferson Medal for Distinguished Achievement in the Arts, Humanities, or Social Sciences

1993 Bernard Bailyn
1993 Warren E. Burger
1993 John Hope Franklin
1993 Peter Paret
1993 Hanna H. Gray
1993 Daniel Patrick Moynihan

1994 Arthur S. Link
1995 George F. Kennan
1996 Homer A. Thompson
1997 Roland M. Frye
1998 Albert O. Hirshman
1999 Daniel Boorstin

Karl Spencer Lashley Award

Established by a gift from Karl Spencer Lashley, a distinguished neurobiologist and member of the Society. The income is to be used for an award of up to $15,000, to be made in recognition of work in the field of neurobiology.

Recipients:

1959 Rafael Lorente de No
1960 Heinrich Klüver
1961 Edgar Douglas, Lord Adrian
1962 Philip Bard
1963 Alexander Forbes
1964 Walle H. J. Nauta
1965 Giuseppe Moruzzi
1966 Hans-Lukas Teuber
1968 Theodore H. Bullock
1969 Elizabeth C. Crosby
1970 Horace Winchell Magoun
1971 Sir Wilfrid Le Gros Clark
1972 Paul P. MacLean
1973 Jonas Szentágothai
1974 Vernon B. Mountcastle, Jr.
1975 Paul Weiss
1976 Roger Walcott Sperry
1977 David Hunter Huber
1977 Torsten Nils Wiesel
1978 Victor Percey Whittaker
1979 Brenda Milnor

1980 Curt P. Richter
1982 Herbert H. Jasper
1983 Edward V. Evarts
1984 W. Maxwell Cowan
1985 David Bodian
1986 Pasko Rakic
1987 Louis Sokoloff
1988 Seymour Benzer
1989 Bela Julesz
1989 Gian Franca Poggio
1990 Viktor Hamburger
1991 Sanford L. Palay
1992 Seymour Kety
1993 Paul Greengard
1994 Robert H. Wurtz
1995 Larry Squire
1996 Patricia Goldman-Rakic
1996 Mortimer Mishkin
1997 Marcus Raichle
1997 Michael Posner
1999 Michael Merzenich

JOHN FREDERICK LEWIS AWARD

Established by a gift from Mrs. John F. Lewis. [The endowment is described above.] Since 1981 the award has recognized the best book published by the Society in a given year. It provides $2,500 to the recipient; the balance goes to the Society to support publication of the book.

Recipients:

1937 Ralph E. Cleland	1971 Paul Weiss
1938 Arthur J. Dempster	1972 Thomas Gold
1939 Henry Norris Russell	1973 Neal A. Weber
1940 Earle Radcliffe Caley	1974 George F. Kennan
1941 George Howard Parker	1975 Frederick A. Pottle
1943 George Gaylord Simpson	1976 Owen Gingerich
1944 Samuel Noah Kramer	1977 Choh Hao Li
1946 Enrico Fermi	1978 Lois Wladis Hoffman
1949 (1948) Donald R. Young	1979 Roland Mushat Frye
1949 Wallace O. Fenn	1981 Marshall Clagett
1950 Sewall Wright	1984 Kenneth M. Setton
1951 Joseph J. Spengler	1985 William Roach
1952 Otto Neugebauer	1986 Maija Jansson
1953 Bart J. Bok	1987 Darwin H. Stapleton
1954 Robert Livingston Schuyler	1988 Paul M. Lloyd
1955 John C. Trever	1989 Marshall Clagett
1956 Gerald T. Robinson	1990 Kenneth M. Setton
1957 Kenneth M. Setton	1990 Joseph S. Fruton
1958 Jesse W. Beams	1991 William O. Oldson
1959 Frank Lappin Horsfall, Jr.	1992 Irma Corcoran
1960 G. Ledyard Stebbins	1993 David Gilman Romano
1961 Crawford H. Greenewalt	1994 Maija Jansson and Paul
1962 E. Wyllys Andrews	Bushkovitch
1963 Edwin Bidwell Wilson	1994 Barbara Nevling Porter
1964 E.A. Speiser	1995 Herbert Kaplan
1965 Robert D. Dripps	1995 Corinne Comstock Weston
1966 William J. Robbins	1996 Joseph R. McElrath, Jr.
1967 Millard Meiss	1997 Russell McCormmach
1968 Adolf A. Berle, Jr	1998 Whitfield J. Bell, Jr.
1969 Herbert L. Ratcliffe	1998 M. W. Daly
1970 Elizabeth M. Ramsey	1999 Francesca Rochberg

MAGELLANIC PREMIUM

The premium consists of the medal and an award of $2,000. The Magellanic Premium is the nation's oldest medal for scientific achievement. [The endowment is described below.]

Recipients:

1790 Francis Hopkinson	1956 Karl von Frisch
1792 Robert Patterson	1959 Charles Stark Draper
1792 William Thornton	1960 Stuart William Seeley
1794 Nicholas Collin	1961 Edward L. Beach
1804 William Mugford	1966 W. H. Pickering
1804 Benjamin Smith Barton	1971 Paul M. Muller
1807 John Garnett	1971 William J. Sjogren
1809 James Humphreys, Jr.	1975 Ralph A. Alpher
1820 Josiah Chapman	1975 Robert Herman
1823 James Ewing	1980 Martin Lindauer
1825 Charles D. Brodie	1984 J. Frank Jordan
1836 James P. Espy	1988 George C. Weiffenbach
1864 Pliny Earle Chase	1988 William H. Guier
1887 Lewis M. Haupt	1990 Joseph H. Taylor
1922 Paul R. Heyl	1992 Edward C. Stone
1922 Lyman J. Briggs	1994 Gordon Pettengill
1952 James G. Baker	1997 Roger L. Easton
1953 Philip Van Horn Weems	1997 Bradford W. Parkinson

HENRY ALLEN MOE PRIZE IN THE HUMANITIES

The prize is $2,500 to the recipient; the balance goes to the Society to assist publication of the *Proceedings* in which the paper appears.

Recipients:

1982 Jerome Blum	1990 Henry M. Hoenigswald
1982 Rensselaer W. Lee	1991 Ada Louise Huxtable
1984 M. Alison Frantz	1992 Crawford Greenewalt, Jr.
1984 Edmund S. Morgan	1993 John Larner
1985 Alfred J. Rieber	1994 Bernard Bailyn
1986 Diane Ravitch	1995 James McPherson
1987 Robert R. Palmer	1996 Christian Habicht
1988 Nicholas DeB Katzenbach	1997 Jaroslav Pelikan
1988 Theodore J. Ziolkowski	1998 Gerhard Böwering
1989 Roland M. Frye	1999 Anthony Grafton

Henry M. Phillips Prize

[The endowment is described above.] The prize is $5,000. In 1993, the Society specified that this award in jurisprudence would recognize the most important publication in the field within a five-year period. The first award using this definition covered the years 1986–1990.

Recipients:

1895	George H. Smith	1957	Catherine Drinker Bowen
1900	W. G. Hastings	1960	Roscoe Pound
1912	Charles H. Burr	1962	Karl N. Llewellyn
1921	Quincy Wright	1974	John Rawls
1935	Lan L. Fuller	1976	Wolfgang Friedmann
1942	Edward S. Corwin	1980	Willard Hurst
1942	Harry W. Jones	1985	Samuel Edmund Thorne
1950	Philip C. Jessup	1986–90	Ronald Dworkin
1955	Edmond Cahn	1997	Joel Feinberg

Jacques Barzun Prize in Cultural History

Established by a gift from Roger L. Williams, Professor Emeritus of History, Laramie Wyoming in 1993 in honor of Jacques Barzun.

1993	Roger Chickering	1996	Dianne Satchko Macleod
1993	John J. O'Malley, S.J.	1997	Jeffrey F. Hamburger
1994	C. Stephen Jaeger	1997	Arnold Lewis
1994	James H. Johnson	1998	Maryanne Cline Horowitz
1995	Caroline Walker Bynum	1998	Philip D. Morgan

DEVELOPMENT REPORT

1998 Annual Fund:

The Annual Fund continued to grow in 1998 and achieved a new high with more than $187,000 raised. This amount exceeds the total raised in 1997 by $55,000, a remarkable increase of 41%. Unlike a number of comparable organizations, the APS does not charge its members dues and has not since the early 1930s. Consequently, the Society is dependent upon the generosity of its members and friends to support its mission. Of the Society's 790 members, 277 contributed to the 1998 Fund. While this represents 35% of the membership, it is well below the 100% level of participation desirable for the Society's continued financial stability. Forty-three friends of the APS provided support, bringing the total number of Fund contributors to 320, an increase of 46 over the 1997 total.

We greatly appreciate the strong chairmanship provided by Paul Talalay who was ably supported by Fund Committee members Arlin M. Adams, Alexander G. Bearn, Vincent L. McKusick, Helen F. North, Jaroslav Pelikan, Solomon H. Snyder and Lewis H. Van Dusen, Jr. Expectations for the continued success of the Fund remain justifiably high with William T. Golden's agreement to serve as the 1999 Chairman. As he assumes this important Society effort, Mr. Golden is confident that an increasing number of members and friends of the Society will realize the fundamental role they can and must play in its support. An ambitious 1999 Fund goal of $250,000 has been established. Your personal support of the Annual Fund is always greatly appreciated and wholly tax deductible. It is with sincere gratitude that on the following pages we acknowledge the generous participants in the 1998 Annual Fund.

International Fund:

To increase the number of Foreign members able to participate in its biannual meetings, the Society created the International Fund in early 1998. Now approaching $100,000, the income from this endowment fund affords the partial reimbursement of travel expenses incurred by Foreign members invited to speak at Society meetings. The benefits of this Fund were readily apparent at the Society's April 1999 Commemoration of the Millennium which was greatly enhanced by the papers delivered by five Foreign members representing three different countries. Your tax deductible contributions in support of this effort are gratefully encouraged so that we may continue to enjoy the scholarship, wisdom and collegiality of our Foreign members.

Publications Support:

Greatly impressed by the scholarship of the papers presented at the Society's Commemoration of the Millennium, friend of the Society John M. Templeton, Jr. pledged $10,000 to help support their publication and circulation. In making this pledge, he issued a challenge to other Society members and friends to match his gift and thereby assure a publication of the highest caliber. Several individuals have generously accepted this challenge and over $30,000 has been raised. If you would like to support the publication of the Millennium papers, contributions may be sent to the attention of the Executive Officer. It is anticipated that this volume will be available early in the year 2000.

DONOR LIST

Millennial Circle—$10,000 and Over

Mary, Lady Bessborough
Lee J. Cronbach

William Kelly Simpson

Century Circle—$5,000 to $9,999

Anonymous
Alexander G. Bearn
Theodore L. Cross
William T. Golden

Ernest & Roxanne Greene
Solomon & Elaine Snyder
Paul & Pamela Talalay
Lewis H. Van Dusen, Jr.

Franklin's Circle—$2,500 to $4,999

Walter H. Annenberg
Glen W. Bowersock
Ralph E. Gomory
Crawford H. Greenewalt, Jr.
Elizabeth Harvey

William R. Hewlett
Edward G. Jefferson
Franz Rosenthal
John C. Whitehead

Sustaining Donors—$1,000 to $2,499

Arlin & Neysa Adams
Robert & Bobbie Austrian
James E. Burke
Edmund N. Carpenter II
William & Cantor Eagleson, Jr.
Elizabeth Ettinghausen
Emily Huggins Fine
Herman & Ellen Goldstine
Kathleen Hall Jamieson
Helene Kaplan

C. Everett Koop
Ralph Landau
Edward B. Lewis
Margaret E. Mahoney
Maclyn & Marjorie McCarty
Mary Patterson McPherson
Martin Meyerson
J. Irwin Miller
Ruth Patrick
Gerard & Eleanor Piel

Simon Ramo
R. Stewart Rauch
Rohm & Haas Company
Betty E. Stellar

Frank E. & Peggy Taplin, Jr.
Peter K. Vogt
James D. Wolfensohn

Supporting Donors—$500 to $999

Bruce & Betty Alberts
Clyde F. & Dode Barker
Cummins & Susan Catherwood, Jr.
Purnell W. Choppin
Edward Toner Cone
Hans & Verena Frauenfelder
William H. Frederick, Jr.
David P. Gardner
Charles C. Gillispie
Andrew M. Gleason
Robert F. Goheen
Hanna H. Gray
Alex Inkeles
Edward H. Levi
James Robert McCredie

Vincent L. McKusick
Bruce M. Metzger
Helen F. North
Sanford L. Palay
Jaroslav Pelikan
Jonathan E. Rhoads
Marie A. Richards
Frederick C. Robbins
John & Edith Roberts
John A. Simpson
Patrick Suppes
Charles H. Townes
P. Roy Vagelos
Torsten Nils Wiesel
Edgar S. Woolard, Jr.

Standing Donors—$250 to $499

Hans Aarsleff
Paul Berg
Barbara Aronstein Black
Frederick H. Burkhardt
Gerhard Casper
Ansley J. Coale
Robert H. Dennard
Paul Doty
David & Sandy Eastburn
Roger & Barbara Easton
James Ebert
Franklin Ford
Herbert & Gertrude Friedman
Roland & Jean Frye
Christian Habicht
Maurice Heckscher
Nicholas deB. Katzenbach

Mabel Louise Lang
Henry Lardy
Charles Longsworth
Walter Eugene Massey
George Crews McGhee
Francis Moore
Ellen Ash Peters
Michael C. J. Putnam
Frederick Seitz
William & Elizabeth Sewell
Maxine F. Singer
Joan A. Steitz
Noel M. Swerdlow
Sir John Meurig Thomas
Nonna D. Wellek
Theodore & Yetta Ziolkowski

Contributing Donors—$100 to $249

Seymour & Shirley Abrahamson
Gus & Valla Amsterdam
Joyce Appleby
Julius & Sally Axelrod
Herbert & Elizabeth Bailey, Jr.

Silvio A. Bedini
Robert Bellah
Jane Bendix
Hans & Rose Bethe
Jean Frantz Blackall

Alan & Madeline Blinder
Herbert Bloch
Floyd E. Bloom
Baruch S. Blumberg
Elinor W. Bodian
Lawrence & Rosalyn Bogorad
Gerhard H. Böwering
Robert & Linda Braidwood
Harvey Brooks
Jonathan M. Brown
Jerome Bruner
Robert Burris
Caroline W. Bynum
Edward C. Carter II
Alfred & Fay Chandler
John R. Clarke
F. Albert Cotton
Elizabeth Cropper
John & Maria Teresa D'Arms
Robert Choate Darnton
Edward E. David, Jr.
Charles Dempsey
Lois E. Dethier
Renato Dulbecco
Richard & Mary Dunn
Christian de Duve
Robert H. Dyson, Jr.
W.G. Ernst
E. Allan Farnsworth
Jack & Dorothy Foltz
Barbara Frankel
Joseph S. Fruton
Joseph Grafton Gall
Richard E. Garwin
H. Bentley Glass
Ward H. Goodenough
Richard M. Goody
Loren R. Graham
Robert Kent Greenawalt
Paul Greengard
Beverly Sills Greenough
Jesse L. Greenstein
Vartan & Clare Gregorian
Werner & Karen Gundersheimer
Prudence O. Harper
Cyril & Ann Harris
Evelyn B. Harrison
Caryl P. Haskins
Robert L. Herbert

Richard Herr
Theodore M. Hesburgh
Ruth M. Hexter
A. Leon Higginbotham, Jr.
Brooke Hindle
Albert O. Hirschman
Henry M. Hoenigswald
Nancy Hofstadter
Berthold & Friederike Hölldobler
Donald F. Hornig
Franz & Lore Huber
Hiroshi Inose
Michael Jameson
Howard & Elizabeth Johnson
Isabella Karle
Jerome Karle
Samuel Karlin
Stanley N. Katz
Ephraim Katzir
Carl Kaysen
Edwin D. Kilbourne
Charles P. Kindleberger
Ernst Kitzinger
Leon Knopoff
Alfred G. Knudson, Jr.
Ludwig & Margret Koenen
Mara Schiff Kohn
Hans Kornberg
Konrad B. Krauskopf
Betty P. Kusch
Thomas & Carolyn Langfitt
Peter & Anneli Lax
Alexander H. Leighton
Luna & Barbara Leopold
Raphael David Levine
Bernard Lewis
John Nichols Loeb
Jane Lubchenco
R. Duncan Luce
Richard & Elizabeth Lyman
Rudolph A. Marcus
John R. Martin
Martin E. Marty
Ernst Mayr
Victor A. McKusick
William H. McNeill
James M. McPherson
Machteld J. Mellink
Florence Menzel

George A. Miller
Henry A. Millon
Cathleen S. Morawetz
Toni Morrison
Vernon B. Mountcastle
Walter H. Munk
Louis Nirenberg
Peter C. Nowell
Barbara Oberg
Peter Paret
Eric G. Pearson
Max F. Perutz
David Pingree
Lucian Pye
Richard E. Quandt
Erica Reiner
Alexander Rich
Frederic M. Richards
Brunilde Sismondo Ridgway
Michael & Carole Rochester
Julius & Julie Rosenwald, II
Edwin E. Salpeter
Herbert Eli Scarf
Arthur L. Schawlow

Isadore & Joan Scott
Vincent Scully
Ihor Ševčenko
Elwyn & Friderun Simons
Åke W. Sjöberg
Charles P. Slichter
Emil L. Smith
Murphy D. Smith
Craig & Barbara Smyth
Emily V. Smyth
E. C. Stone
Gilbert Stork
Owsei Temkin
James Thorpe
John W. Tukey
Helen Vendler
David & Marvalee Wake
Zdzislawa Walaszek-Coleman
Anthony F.C. Wallace
Herbert Wechsler
Steven & Louise Weinberg
Benjamin Widom
Robin M. Williams, Jr.
Robert R. Wilson

Donors—Less than $100

Meyer & Ruth Abrams
James Barr
Jacques Barzun
Richard John Bing
Ruth C. Birkhoff
Thomas Bisson & Margaretta Bisson
Derk & Galia Bodde
Sir Walter F. Bodmer
James MacGregor Burns
Guido Calabresi
Edwin Chargaff
Janice G. Cloud
Thomas C. Cochran
Dietz O. Edzard
Peter R. Grant
Gerald Gunther
Norman Hackerman
Eric Hamp
Susan L. Hazard
Samuel Heiman
Pendleton Herring
Kenneth I. Kellermann

George A. Kennedy
Daniel & Bettyann Kevles
Ira M. Lapidus
Martin Lindauer
Edmund S. Morgan
Norman D. Newell
Martin Ostwald
Ray D. Owen
Jeanne Pimentel
E.R. Piore
Charles A. Ryskamp
Jeremy & Paula Sabloff
Robert C. Seamans, Jr.
Donald & Betty Sheehan
Nancy G. Siraisi
Robert Imbrie Smith
Fritz Stern
Catherine N. Stratton
James Tobin
Margaret B. Van Dusen
Gilbert F. White
Robert M. White

MEETINGS OF THE SOCIETY

Autumn General Meeting
13–14 November 1998

SYMPOSIUM
THE GLOBALIZATION OF THE WORLD ECONOMY
Gerard Piel, Moderator

JAMES TOBIN
   Financial Globalization
ROBERT KUTTNER
   Can the Global Economy be a Mixed Economy?
JAMES K. GALBRAITH
   Inequality: A Global View
LANCE TAYLOR
   Globalization, Liberalization, Distribution, and Growth: Developing and Transition Economies

PAPERS READ

RONALD BRESLOW
   Extending Nature
SISSELA BOK
   Useful Knowledge, Ethics, and Science
DAVID EASTBURN
   Vive le Dilettante!
FREDERICK SEITZ
   First Use of Crystal Rectifiers in Wireless
BERNHARD WITKOP
   The Unknown Paul Ehrlich: The "Magic Bullet" Revisited
A. JAMES HUDSPETH
   How the Ear's Works Work
WHITFIELD J. BELL, JR.
   Founders and Foundations of the Society
JANE LUBCHENCO
   Entering the Century of the Environment: Rethinking Priorities
JOSEPH KERMAN
   Music and Politics: The Case of William Byrd (1540–1623)

MARTIN W. DALY
Sir Reginald Wingate and the British Empire in the Middle East
GÜNTER BLOBEL
Rebuilding Dresden's Historic Center

AWARDS

ARNOLD LEWIS
The Jacques Barzun Prize in Cultural History in recognition for his book, *An Early Encounter with Tomorrow: Europeans, Chicago's Look, and the World's Columbian Exposition.*
JEFFREY F. HAMBURGER
The Jacques Barzun Prize in Cultural History in recognition of his book, *Nuns as Artists: The Visual Culture of a Medieval Convent.*
MICHAEL I. POSNER
The Karl Spencer Lashley Award for his pioneering contributions to the imaging of the human brain.
MARCUS E. RAICHLE
The Karl Spencer Lashley Award for his pioneering contributions to the imaging of the human brain.
WHITFIELD J. BELL, JR.
The John Frederick Lewis Award in recognition of his book, *Patriot-Improvers: Biographical Sketches of Members of the American Philosophical Society, 1743–1769.*
MARTIN W. DALY
The John Frederick Lewis Award in recognition of his book, *The Sirdar: Sir Reginald Wingate and the British Empire in the Middle East.*
GERHARD BÖWERING
The Henry Allen Moe Prize in the Humanities in recognition of a paper read to the Society in November 1995 entitled, "The Concept of Time in Islam."
EDWARD O. WILSON
The Benjamin Franklin Medal for Distinguished Achievement in the Sciences in recognition of the great contributions this scientist has made through his research on ants to a better understanding of their societal relationships. Using exact methods he has produced a new understanding of the processes which produce man's creative achievements by subjecting them to the rigorous analyses used in studying the physical and chemical characteristics of ants and other species.
ALBERT O. HIRSCHMAN
The Thomas Jefferson Medal for Distinguished Achievement in the Arts, Humanities, or Social Science in recognition of his pioneering work in development economies, a work full of compassion for those living in adversity; the man of letters who uncovered the moral and psychological preconditions for the rise of capitalism; the foe of totalitarianism who in the 1940s helped scores

of refugees in Europe escape the Nazis; the deeply learned and adventurous scholar who is always prepared to cross borders in search of new ground.

RECOGNITION OF FIFTY YEARS OR MORE SOCIETY MEMBERSHIP

ROBERT F. BACHER
Class I, 1948
HANS A. BETHE
Class I, 1947

PENDLETON HERRING
Class III, 1948
FREDERICK SEITZ
Class I, 1946

Annual General Meeting
21–24 April 1999

COMMEMORATION OF THE MILLENNIUM

PAUL A. VOLCKER
After Dinner Remarks
JONATHAN E. RHOADS
A Toast to the Society in the New Millennium
ALEXANDER G. BEARN
Welcome

PAPERS READ

CLASS I: MATHEMATICAL AND PHYSICAL SCIENCES
Charles H. Townes, Moderator

STEVEN WEINBERG
The Laws of Nature
WOLFGANG K. H. PANOFSKY, *Discussant*
SIR MARTIN REES
Our Concept of the Cosmos: Progress, Prospects and Mysteries
FREEMAN J. DYSON, *Discussant*
PETER D. LAX
Mathematics and Computing
CHARLES L. FEFFERMAN, *Discussant*
RICHARD M. GOODY
Global Warming: Does Science Matter?
JAMES G. ANDERSON, *Discussant*
MAX F. PERUTZ
Molecular Biology of Huntington's Disease
JEROME KARLE, *Discussant*

CLASS II: BIOLOGICAL SCIENCES
Purnell W. Choppin, Moderator

PAUL L. BERG
  Scientists and The Public: An Ambivalent Partnership
  HAROLD T. SHAPIRO, *Discussant*
BERT VOGELSTEIN
  Cancer: The Revolution and The Challenge
  ALFRED G. KNUDSON, JR., *Discussant*
CARLA J. SHATZ
  Wiring the Brain: Dynamic Interplay Between Nature and Nurture
  JOHN E. DOWLING, *Discussant*
ERIC R. KANDEL
  Genes, Synapses and Long-term Memory
  VERNON B. MOUNTCASTLE, *Discussant*

CLASS III: SOCIAL SCIENCES
Charles P. Kindleberger, Moderator

LOUIS HENKIN
  Individual Rights and National Sovereignty
  KENT GREENAWALT, *Discussant*
ALAN S. BLINDER
  Economics Becomes a Science, Or Does It?
  ANDREW F. BRIMMER, *Discussant*
WILLIAM J. BAUMOL
  A Millennium of Economics in Twenty Minutes: Toward Useful Knowledge
  JOSEPH E. STIGLITZ, *Discussant*
JOEL E. COHEN
  Our Parents, Our Children: Population in the 20th and 21st Centuries
  SAMUEL H. PRESTON, *Discussant*

CLASS IV: HUMANITIES
Jaroslav Pelikan, Moderator

SIR JOHN ELLIOTT
  Reconstructing the Past
  ANTHONY GRAFTON, *Discussant*
HENRY A. MILLON
  Art and Architectural History in the 20th Century
  DAVID FREEDBERG, *Discussant*
WENDY DONIGER
  *More Than One Millennium: The Perennial Return
  of the History of Religions*
  HERMANN HUNGER, *Discussant*

MARC FUMAROLI
The Advantages of Singularity in an Era of Globalization
GLEN W. BOWERSOCK, *Discussant*

CLASS V: THE PROFESSIONS, ARTS AND AFFAIRS
Arlin M. Adams, Moderator

HANNA HOLBORN GRAY
One Hundred Years of the Renaissance
WILLIAM J. BOUWSMA, *Discussant*
DEREK BOK
*Fairness, Equal Opportunity, and the Admission of Minorities
to Universities*
DAVID GARDNER, *Discussant*
NANCY KASSEBAUM BAKER
Challenges of Health Care in Democratic Societies
FRANCISCO J. AYALA, *Discussant*
SHELDON HACKNEY
Democracy and Culture
JOHN H. D'ARMS, *Discussant*

AWARDS

FREDERICK ROBBINS
The Benjamin Franklin Medal for Distinguished Achievement in the Sciences
in recognition of the discovery with his colleagues in 1949 that viruses could
be grown in tissue culture. This work enabled the development of vaccines for
poliomyelitis and measles and altered the field of virology for all time.
PHILLIP SHARP
The Benjamin Franklin Medal for Distinguished Achievement in the Sciences
in recognition of his work on the biology of tumor viruses which led to his discovery that genes contain nonsense segments that are edited out by cells in the
course of utilizing genetic information. This landmark achievement, known as
RNA splicing, altered the course of molecular biology.
DANIEL BOORSTIN
The Thomas Jefferson Medal for Distinguished Achievement in the Arts, Humanities, or Social Sciences in recognition of a distinguished American historian whose career has included the publication of no less than twenty major
studies, several of them multi-volumed; more than a decade of vigorous and effective service as Librarian of Congress; editorial duty with a variety of scholarly journals; not to mention frequent lecturing in Asia and Europe as well as
in this country; and trusteeship of scholarly and cultural organizations.
ALAN GREENSPAN
The Benjamin Franklin Award for Distinguished Public Service in recognition
of his leadership and his work as Chairman of the Federal Reserve Board.

Their wise formation and skillful execution of monetary policy has contributed significantly to the longest period of prosperity in the United States on record. (Presented in March, 1999)

GEORGE MITCHELL

The Benjamin Franklin Award for Distinguished Public Service in recognition of his distinguished service as United States Senator, Majority Leader of the Senate, and more recently, as trusted facilitator of the fragile dialogue that holds hope of bringing peace to Northern Ireland. (Presented in March, 1999)

RECOGNITION OF FIFTY YEARS SOCIETY MEMBERSHIP

SAUNDERS MAC LANE
Class I, 1949

REPORTS ON COUNCIL AND BUSINESS MEETINGS

COUNCIL
NOVEMBER 13, 1998

The Council met at 10:00 a.m. in the Library Board Room. Present were: Arlin M. Adams, President, Bernard Bailyn, Alexander G. Bearn, Edward C. Carter II, Britton Chance, Purnell W. Choppin, Theodore L. Cross, Val L. Fitch, Herbert Friedman, Owen Gingerich, Robert F. Goheen, Loren R. Graham, Victor A. McKusick, Mary Patterson McPherson, Martin Meyerson, Henry A. Millon, Helen F. North, Ruth Patrick, Jonathan E. Rhoads, Morton G. White, Shmuel Winograd, and Hatten S. Yoder, Jr.; also present (by invitation) was Carl F. Miller, recorder.

Minutes. The minutes of the Council meeting of April 23, 1998 were approved as distributed. The minutes of the Executive Committee meetings of July 28 and October 27, 1998 were ratified as distributed.

Financial Matters. (1) Third Quarter Statement. The unrestricted funds schedule showed total revenues to be less than one percent below the target of 75%, while total expenses were nearly 5% under budget. The net result of this condition was an estimated surplus in excess of $300,000. When the Fall Meeting expenses as well as other fourth quarter expenditures are realized, this interim surplus will be reduced to a level consistent with budget expectations.

The restricted funds schedule reflected a balanced condition. Generally accepted accounting principles require that restricted revenue be recognized as corresponding expenses materialize. Accordingly, revenue and expenses equaled one another as shown in the zero balance.

(2) 1999 Budget. Dr. Bearn presented the new year budget. The financial plan continues the 5% spending rule and its application to a three-year moving average of the endowment's (mid-year) market values. Using the period 1996–1998, the 1999 budget has an average endowment value of $93.8 million, an increase of nearly $15 million over the 1998 average. In applying the stated spending rule to the three-year average, an endowment income of $4.69 million results. (When this calculation is adjusted for the restricted funds' reinvestment requirement, the resulting figure becomes $4.61 million.). This level of income is 18.9% more than the current year, representing an increase of $733,000. Total revenue for 1999 exceeds the current (1998) budget by a somewhat smaller margin of 14.1%. This reduction in the rate of increase results primarily from lower estimates for gifts and grants and deferred (restricted) revenue.

Total revenue for 1999 trails total expenses by nearly $254,000 when the Special Purposes Fund is included, whereas total revenue exceeds expenditures by $286,000 when the same special fund is excluded from consideration. When you continue this fund's exclusion, program allocations within the expense budget (of $5.4 million) are as follows: Research—25%, Publications—16%, Meetings/Membership—16%, and Library— 43%. These allocations entail the apportioning of Administration expenses—which now include Development expenses —and Franklin Hall expenditures according to their respective relationships to the four programs.

When the budget is separated into unrestricted and restricted activity two different patterns develop. The unrestricted activity largely determines the total budget because it accounts for approximately 80% of total revenue and 73% of total expenses—and 81% of each when the Special Purposes Fund is excluded. As a result, program allocations are very similar to the overall budget except for Research where a divergence normally arises. Accordingly, unrestricted program allocations are as follows: Research—21%, Publications—18%, Meetings/Membership—18%, and Library— 43%. Lastly, the unrestricted budget is projecting an estimated surplus in excess of $258,000. (It should be noted that in realizing this surplus amount, the spending rule is, in effect, lowered to 4.7%. Equally important, too, is the fact that an endowment loan payment of $167,000 is incorporated in the document. This repayment amount is based on a maximum borrowing of $2 million from the endowment, which is being amortized over 30 years at a 5% interest rate.)

The restricted budget plays a somewhat minor role in the overall financial picture, accounting for about 20% of total revenue and total expenditures. Nevertheless, its funds do influence two areas in particular—viz. research and the library—where 87% are utilized. More specifically, restricted program allocations are as follows: Research—45%, Publications—8%, Meetings/Membership—5%, and Library—42%. Finally, a modest surplus of $28,000 is projected.

The final type of activity, viz. the Special Purposes Fund, is normally excluded from most of the budget analysis because the component funds intentionally expend principal as well as income. However, the recent Mellon Foundation award of nearly $1 million for the new humanities research initiative has enhanced appreciably the Fund's relevance in the total budget. With the Fund's total value exceeding $1.7 million, some $614,000 is scheduled for expenditure in the new year, representing about 10% of total budgeted expenses. Some 53% of the scheduled expenditure is associated with the research program, while 45% is slated to provide support for the Library and some 2% for Publications.

In ratifying the 1999 budget, the Council asked that the curatorial allowance be increased to $30,000 and directed any unrestricted surplus realized at year end be applied to the endowment loan for Philosophical Hall renovations.

(2) Philosophical Hall Renovation Project. Dr. Bearn reported that the renovation project started last month and is scheduled for substantial completion in mid-April 1999. [Subsequent to this report, several developments arose requiring that the completion date be delayed until June.]

(3) New Humanities Program. Dr. Bearn announced that the Andrew W. Mellon Foundation was pleased to award nearly $1 million for the new humanities research program proposed last spring. The Society's commitment over the three-year period is $370,000, eighty percent of which is already accounted for in the 1998 and 1999 budgets. Dr. Bearn also mentioned that each of the two evaluation committees would have a minimum of two non-Society members.

Membership Dues. Dr. Bearn proposed the reinstatement of dues for the resident membership. The rationale for this proposal is the need for the membership to demonstrate a broad-based commitment to the Society, an aspect not evident in the current annual giving solicitation. Increasingly, more individuals, as well as corporations and foundations, are questioning the absence of membership dues, not as a major source of revenue but as a sign of genuine support and interest. Dr. Bearn reviewed the experiences of several sister institutions, noting in particular that the existence of dues had no adverse effect on their fund-raising activities.

An extended and comprehensive discussion followed. The consensus of the Council favored reinstatement of dues and ratified *in principle* the Executive Committee's recommendation. Dr. McPherson was asked to chair a committee consisting of Messrs. Meyerson and William B. Eagleson, Jr. to develop the details for implementing this action.

The Laws—Finance Committee. As chairman of the Finance Committee, Mr. Eagleson requested that service on this Committee be consistent with the provisions governing the other standing committees. He questioned the effectiveness of the current practice—electing chairman and members annually and indefinitely—and suggested that term limitation for both chairman and committee members be established. Mr. Eagleson will prepare a statement to accomplish this change and submit it to the Executive Committee for review.

Defined Benefit Plan. The Society's legal counsel has prepared a restatement of the pension plan to bring the program into compliance with Federal regulations. Following a review of the document's major points, the Council ratified the plan's restatement as submitted.

Awards. (1) Benjamin Franklin Award for Distinguished Public Service. The

Franklin Committee nominated former Senate Majority Leader, George Mitchell, for his outstanding service and contributions to public life.

(2) Benjamin Franklin Medal for Distinguished Achievement in the Sciences. The Franklin Committee proposed two Nobel Laureates in medicine for the 1999 award. The first is Dr. Frederic Robbins, who is credited with the development of the measles vaccine, and the second is Dr. Philip Sharp, who is distinguished *inter alia* for his studies of gene splicing.

(3) Thomas Jefferson Medal for Distinguished Achievement in the Arts, Humanities, or Social Sciences. The Jefferson Committee recommended Dr. Daniel J. Boorstin for his profound writing and outstanding contributions in American history.

Following the recommendations of the award committees, the nominees were unanimously ratified.

(4) Honoraria for Franklin Award, Franklin Medal, and Jefferson Medal Recipients. The Council agreed that granting honoraria to the recipients of these awards was proper and should be implemented immediately. The appointment of a committee was also approved to determine the appropriate amount to be given in each instance.

Fund Raising. Dr. Bearn reported that the 1997 Annual Fund achieved an all-time high in contributions, totaling more than $132,000. Of the Fund's 275 contributors, 230 were resident members who accounted for 86% of total gifts. The 1998 solicitation has a goal of $150,000, representing a 14% increase over the prior year. Dr. Paul Talalay is directing the current campaign.

Committee Reports. The chairmen of the standing committees presented brief written summaries of their reports. The Council with appreciation received all of these statements. The full reports will appear in the *Year Book.*

There being no further business the Council adjourned at 4:35 p.m. The next meeting of the Council will be held on Thursday, April 22, 1999 in the Library.

BUSINESS MEETING
NOVEMBER 14, 1998

President Arlin M. Adams called the meeting to order at 3:30 p.m. Approximately 60 members were in attendance. Mr. Adams read the roll of members whose deaths were reported since the last meeting, those present standing as a mark of respect. Dr. Henry A. Millon was welcomed as the Society's new Curator of Fine Arts, succeeding Dr. Jonathan M. Brown. The minutes of the Annual General Meeting of April 24, 1998 were approved as distributed.

Mr. Adams reviewed the various actions of Council. In general, these actions involved finances, a new research initiative, Philosophical Hall renovations, membership dues, the Laws, the pension plan, and awards. The financial issues focused on the third quarter statement and the 1999 budget.

The new research initiative marks a new departure for this Society activity. Combining a generous grant from the Andrew W. Mellon Foundation with Society funds, this three-year experimental program will provide funding for the latter six months of a faculty member's full year sabbatical. Fourteen awards will be made annually based on the decisions of two committees, one focusing on the humanities and the other on the social sciences.

Renovations began last month in Philosophical Hall. The installation of an elevator, expanded and improved office facilities, compliance with the provisions of the Americans with Disabilities Act and a modernized kitchen are the focal points of the renovation project. Funding for this work is through the Society's endowment; the loan will be amortized over 30 years at a 5% interest rate.

Dues for the resident membership was ratified *in principle* with a special committee—consisting of Dr. Mary Patterson McPherson as chairperson, and Messrs. William B. Eagleson, Jr. and Martin Meyerson—charged with working out the details. At this point an extended discussion occurred with Dr. Bearn emphasizing that dues should be viewed as a demonstration of interest and commitment by the resident membership and not as a revenue measure. Other comments lamented the loss of a distinctive Society tradition and suggested a more aggressive annual fund campaign to achieve greater membership support. In the end the consensus of opinion was to await the special committee's report.

As chairman of the Finance Committee, Mr. Eagleson requested that service on this committee be brought into conformance with the other standing committees. Instead of the chairman and members elected annually and indefinitely, he asked that term limitations be established. A statement to accomplish this objective will be prepared for the Executive Committee's review.

The defined benefit pension plan was restated to bring the program into compliance with federal regulations. This action entailed no change in benefit calculations or participation status.

In conclusion four award recipients were ratified for the Franklin Award and Medal and the Jefferson Medal. Also, a special committee was authorized to determine an appropriate honorarium for each of these awards. (A full description of the Council's deliberations is recorded in the Council minutes for November 13, 1998. It should also be noted that all of these actions were presented at the Business Meeting for *informational purposes only*.)

The 1997 annual giving program reached a new high with total gifts of

$132,219 received from 275 contributors. The 1998 solicitation has a goal of $150,000. Under Dr. Paul Talalay's chairmanship, the new campaign is also striving to increase substantially the number of supporters.

Mr. Adams discussed briefly some of the joint meeting ventures under consideration. An invitation has been extended to the Royal Society of London to meet in 2001 in Philadelphia. Other European scholarly and scientific organizations are also being considered for succeeding years.

Under new business a question about qualifications for Class I membership was raised; the matter was referred to the Class I Membership Committee and the Advisory Committee on Election of Members for resolution.

The final order of business was the Committee reports. Printed reports of the Standing Committees were available for the membership to examine. (A complete rendering of these reports will be printed in the *Year Book*.)

During this meeting 109 members and 225 guests were in attendance.

COUNCIL
APRIL 22, 1999

The Council met at 10:00 a.m. in the Library Board Room. Present were: Arlin M. Adams, President, Alexander G. Bearn, Edward C. Carter II, Britton Chance, Purnell W. Choppin, Mildred Cohn, William B. Eagleson, Jr., Val L. Fitch, Herbert Friedman, Owen Gingerich, Robert F. Goheen, Loren R. Graham, Gardner Lindzey, Victor A. McKusick, Vincent L. McKusick, Henry A. Millon, Helen F. North, Ruth Patrick, Jaroslav J. Pelikan, Jonathan E. Rhoads, Morton G. White, and Hatten S. Yoder, Jr.; also present (by invitation) were: Lawrence Bogorad, Andrea B. Nicotera, and Carl F. Miller, recorder.

Minutes. The minutes of the Council meeting of November 13, 1998 were approved as distributed. The minutes of the Executive Committee meetings of February 23 and March 22, 1999 were ratified as distributed.

Financial Matters. (1) Audit Report for 1998. Judge Adams expressed his pleasure with the audit process and the fact that the report contained an unqualified opinion. The only matter of concern related to the Society's objets d'art and their safekeeping. While a program has already been set up for the monitoring of the Library's printed and manuscript collections, the auditors—with the Audit Committee's unanimous approval—have urged the Executive Office to extend the monitoring activity to include the objets d'art. Dr. Henry A. Millon, the Society's Curator for the Fine Arts, is well aware of this need and very supportive of its accomplishment. [Subsequent to this meeting, Dr. Millon agreed to prepare a set of monitoring procedures for the Audit Committee's approval. Implementation of the expanded monitoring program is scheduled during the late summer or early fall.]

(2) Revised 1999 Budget. Dr. Bearn reported that the success of the Millennium Meeting fully utilized the original estimated operating surplus of approximately $258,000. This development generated mixed feelings among the Committee. While all were well pleased with the meeting's impending success, there was concern about the loss of the projected surplus. Mr. Eagleson recommended that the executive office take appropriate steps to recapture these funds and not permit them to be lost. Several options were suggested to accomplish this objective: solicitation of funds, cut or freeze expenses, implementation of mandatory dues, elimination of the 1999 Fall Meeting, and establishment of a quota system for meeting attendance. Although these choices did not generate much enthusiasm, the Committee believed that some action was required to recapture this money and to view the Millennium Meeting as a special affair and not as a precedent, cost-wise, for future gatherings. Mr. Eagleson also suggested that the budget for 2000 contain an estimated surplus equal to the amount originally projected for 1999 as well as demonstrating the recapturing of the lost 1999 surplus.

(3) Philosophical Hall Renovations. The completion date is scheduled for June. An estimate for the new exhibit areas has not been finished, but the completion of these two rooms will not prevent the staff from returning to the Hall on a timely basis. [Subsequent to this meeting , the date of August 14 was established as the time for returning to the Hall. This date occurs one day before the expiration of the lease with the Public Ledger Building.]

Dr. Millon reported on the progress of designing the exhibition areas in the two north meeting rooms. He has met with Mr. Stephen Saitas, an exhibit designer from New York, and with the architect and contractor for the renovation project. Colors, lighting, furnishings, and security—including the type of sprinkler system to be installed—have all been discussed at least preliminarily as well as the primary functions of each room. Present plans call for this part of the renovation project to be completed by the fall of the year.

(4) 431 Chestnut Street. Judge Adams reviewed his negotiations to obtain the property located at 431 Chestnut Street. The final agreed-upon price is $1.625 million, with a $200,000 deposit immediately and the balance due at time of settlement on January 10, 2000. The Finance Committee has already authorized that funds— totaling $2.325 million—be set aside in a Vanguard money market account for the purchase of the building, for immediate repairs and subsequent renovations.

(5) Reappointment of the Auditors. The accounting firm of Howe, Keller &

Hunter was retained for 1999 to conduct quarterly reviews and the year-end auditing work. The Council also requested that a surprise audit be undertaken from time to time.

(6) Membership Dues Report. Messrs. William B. Eagleson, Jr. and Martin Meyerson joined with Dr. Mary P. McPherson, as chairperson, to examine and resolve the dues issue approved in principle by Council last November. Mr. Eagleson reported that as a result of the Committee's findings, the following statement was drafted and unanimously recommended to Council for adoption: the Society anticipates that resident members will take seriously their membership and responsibilities and, accordingly, contribute $100 or more each year to further the aims of the Society. Following a brief discussion, the Council approved the proposal and directed that it be implemented by the Executive Office.

After this action was concluded, Dr. Goheen urged the executive office to continue the Annual Giving program in conjunction with the dues initiative in order to maximize the Society's fund-raising opportunities.

Report of the Committee on Nomination of Officers. Dr. Chance presented the slate of nominees for selected officer and councilor positions. Each individual was contacted and agreed to serve if elected. The slate was approved and recommended to the membership for ratification at the Business Meeting. The Council expressed its appreciation to Dr. Chance and his Committee for a job well done.

Advisory Committee on the Election of Members. Each Class Committee chairman, or designated representative, presented a report containing brief sketches of the academic or professional careers of each resident and foreign nominee. Each Class Committee was permitted to recommend seven resident nominees and three foreign candidates. Classes I through IV each submitted seven resident nominees with Class V presenting six candidates. In terms of foreign nominees, Classes I, III and V each nominated one candidate, while Class II submitted two nominees and Class IV presented three candidates. In addition to the foregoing candidates, one Interclass nominee, three TNG nominees and one Council nominee were also presented. The several reports elicited minimal discussion. Following each presentation, Council approved the nominees and recommended their election by the membership at the Business Meeting.

Executive Officer's Report. (1) APS Sabbatical/Research Fellowship Program. The new research program is generously supported in large part by the Andrew W. Mellon Foundation. Some 250 applications were received in the humanities and near 120 applications in the social sciences. Each section awarded 7 fellowships with the chosen scholars representing 11 states and 13 institutions. The average age of the humanities fellows was 48, while the social science fellows averaged 45. Dr. Lindzey also commented briefly on the social science section and its awardees.

(2) Aspiring Young Scholars Program. A successful meeting was held on April 5 with Dr. David Hornbeck, Superintendent of the Philadelphia Public Schools, and his assistant. An estimated date of March 2000 was projected for the inaugural program. A draft proposal for funding from the Pew Charitable Trusts has been written and will be submitted shortly to the foundation for its review.

(3) Millennium Meeting. The special spring meeting will be the most widely attended Society function with some 480 people expected to be present. The roster of speakers and discussants is very appealing and promises to provide an unusual "intellectual feast." The accompanying expense, however, is of some concern, and as indicated above requires the executive office to reassess the whole budget process.

(4) Paul Mellon Bequest. The Society has been notified of Mr. Mellon's intended bequest; between $1.5 million and $2.5 million will be given to the Society. Because the money is for general purposes, no specific activity or use has been designated to date for its support.

Fund Raising. Dr. Bearn reported that the 1998 solicitation was the most successful drive to-date, raising more than $180,000. The new-year campaign will be chaired by Mr. William T. Golden and has set $250,000 as its goal.

Herman H. Goldstine Portrait. Dr. Bearn reported that Dr. Goldstine has approved the initial sketch and that the finished work is scheduled for the fall. Fifteen thousand dollars has been budgeted for the portrait and another $1,000 for the frame.

Awards. (1) Jacques Barzun Prize. The Barzun Committee has nominated co-recipients for the 1999 prize. Dr. Maryanne Cline Horowitz has been nominated for her work, entitled *Seeds of Virtue and Knowledge,* while Dr. Philip D. Morgan has been selected for his study, *Slave Counterpoint.*

(2) John Frederick Lewis Award. The Lewis Committee has chosen Dr. Francesca Rochberg for the 1999 award in recognition of her monograph, entitled *Babylonian Horoscopes.*

(3) Karl Spenser Lashley Award. The Lashley Committee has recommended Dr. Michael Merzenich for the 1999 award for his contributions to the plasticity of the cortical representation of the body surface.

(4) Henry Allen Moe Prize. The Moe Committee has designated Dr. Anthony Grafton for the 1999 prize as a result of his paper, "Girolamo Cardano and the Tradition of Classical Astrology," which appeared in the September 1998 issue of the *Proceedings.*

Following these presentations, the Council unanimously ratified all of the award nominees.

Judge Adams also mentioned that all of the award and prize amounts are being reviewed by a committee chaired by Dr. Robert Austrian. Following its investigation, the Committee will submit to Council its findings and recommendations in this important activity of the Society.

Joint Meeting with the Royal Society of London. Tentative plans are underway for the Society to host a meeting in 2001 with the Royal Society.

The Laws-Finance Committee. The revisions were reviewed that were approved by the Executive Committee at its February meeting. The new provisions—establishing term limits and a procedure to replace members unable to complete their terms—were viewed favorably by Council and were ratified, accordingly. Notice of these changes had also been mailed to all members qualified to vote so that the new provisions could be considered at the Business Meeting.

Expression of Appreciation. The Council unanimously expressed its sincere appreciation to Judge Adams for his outstanding leadership and dedicated service to the Society. During his six years as president, the Society grew in many ways. The membership was expanded to include new disciplines, the programs were broadened to engage both academic and non-academic communities, the facilities were improved and enlarged, and the financial foundation for all of these activities realized a dramatic increase. While these accomplishments reflected the services of various people, very few presidencies ever witnessed so many significant developments.

In response, Judge Adams expressed his appreciation to the Council and the membership for bestowing on him the honor of the presidency. The privilege of holding this distinguished position will always be cherished and remain a very special part of his professional career. And notwithstanding the many demands that were placed upon him during these years, he was pleased to say that he thoroughly enjoyed the occasion and the opportunity to work with the membership and the staff.

There being no further business to discuss the meeting was adjourned at 4:45 p.m. The next meeting of the Council is scheduled for Friday, November 12, 1999.

BUSINESS MEETING
APRIL 23, 1999

President Arlin M. Adams called the meeting to order at 3:30 p.m. Approximately 130 members were in attendance. Mr. Adams read the roll of members whose deaths have been reported since the last meeting, those present standing as a mark of respect. The minutes of the Annual Autumn Meeting of November 14, 1998 were approved as distributed.

The next order of business was the election of officers and councilors. The nominees were recommended by the Committee on Nomination of Officers, and were reviewed earlier by Council. On motion duly moved and seconded, the following people were unanimously elected for the term of 1999–2002.

President	Frank H.T. Rhodes
Vice President	Victor A. McKusick
Secretary	Helen F. North
Secretary	Baruch S. Blumberg
Councilors	
Class I	Rudolph A. Marcus
Class II	Thomas Eisner
(Succeeding A. McGehee Harvey (dec.)	Günter Blobel
Class III	Bernard Bailyn
Class IV	Martin Ostwald
Class V	Theodore L. Cross

The election of new members followed. President Adams presented the official ballot to the members, noting that Council, as required, had reviewed and approved the document. The ballot contained the nominees for both resident and foreign membership. After their examination of the ballot, the members, upon motion properly moved and seconded, unanimously approved all of the nominees. The following people were elected.

RESIDENT

Class I
Allen J. Bard, Austin, TX
Jacqueline K. Barton, Pasadena, CA
James Watson Cronin, Chicago, IL
Robert D. MacPherson, Princeton, NJ
Kenneth H. Olsen, Boxborough, MA
Kip S. Thorne, Pasadena, CA
Samuel Bard Treiman, Princeton, NJ
Markley Gordon Wolman, Baltimore, MD

Class II
Robert Heinz Abeles, Waltham, MA
John Cairns, Jr., Blacksburg, VA
Moses Judah Folkman, Cambridge, MA
Corey S. Goodman, Berkeley, CA
Thomas E. Lovejoy, Washington, D.C.
David G. Nathan, Cambridge, MA
Paul Schimmel, La Jolla, CA

Thomas E. Starzl, Pittsburgh, PA
Richard F. Thompson, Los Angeles, CA
Bernhard Witkop, Bethesda, MD

CLASS III

William Cronon, Madison, WI
William H. Goetzmann, Austin, TX
Oscar Handlin, Cambridge, MA
Robert Owen Paxton, New York, NY
Roger Newland Shepard, Stanford, CA
T.N. Srinivasan, New Haven, CT
Myron Weiner, Cambridge, MA

CLASS IV

Sheila E. Blumstein, Providence, RI
Phyllis Pray Bober, Bryn Mawr, PA
William Theodore de Bary, New York, NY
Elfriede Regina Knauer, Philadelphia, PA
Piotr Michalowski, Ann Arbor, MI
Hilary Putnam, Cambridge, MA
Evon Zartman Vogt, Jr., Cambridge, MA

CLASS V

Mary Maples Dunn, Cambridge, MA
John H. Gibbons, Washington, D.C.
Patricia Albjerg Graham, Cambridge, MA
Yo-Yo Ma, New York, NY
Michael Ira Sovern, New York, NY
Frank Stella, New York, NY

FOREIGN

Class I
Reimar Lüst, Hamburg, Germany

Class II
William D. Hamilton, Oxford, England
Keith Peters, Cambridge, England

Class III
A. Ida Benedicte Nicolaisen, Copenhagen, Denmark

Class IV
John Boardman, Oxford, England
Tore Frängsmyr, Uppsala, Sweden
Jean Leclant, Paris, France

Class V
John R. Evans, Toronto, Canada
Mary Robinson, Geneva, Switzerland

The election of the Committee on Finance followed. The nominees were: William B. Eagleson, Jr., Chairman, Arlin M. Adams, Theodore L. Cross, David P. Eastburn, Robert F. Goheen, Herman H. Goldstine, Martin Meyerson, Jonathan E. Rhoads, and Lewis H. Van Dusen, Jr. Upon motion properly made and seconded, the nominees were unanimously elected.

The status of the Hays bequest was reviewed as were its various provisions directing the use of its funds. A resolution embodying these expenditure guidelines, which Council approved the previous day, was then presented to the membership for its ratification. Upon motion duly made and seconded, the membership ratified the resolution as submitted.

President Adams then reviewed highlights of the Council meeting (held the previous day). Formal actions involved financial matters, changes in the Laws, and prizes and awards. Other matters addressed were the new Sabbatical Program in the Humanities, the Young Scholars Program, the Herman H. Goldstine portrait, fund raising activities, and preliminary plans for a joint meeting in 2001 with the Royal Society of London. (A full description of the Council's deliberations is recorded in the Council minutes for April 22, 1999. It should also be noted that except for the proposed changes to the Laws, all of these issues were presented at the Business Meeting for *informational purposes only.*)

At this point, Judge Adams introduced the changes to the Laws, which were approved and recommended by Council. The changes applied to the Finance Committee, establishing term limits and a process enabling the president to appoint successors for those members unable to serve their full terms. Upon motion duly made and seconded, the proposed revisions to the Laws were ratified.

In his final presidential report, Mr. Adams reviewed the highlights of his six years in office. He noted that this period has been both exciting and memorable in many respects. While his service began at both a time of sadness—Dr. Eliot Stellar's untimely death—and celebration—the Society's 250th anniversary meeting— fortunately the latter was the portent of what lie ahead. One of Judge Adams's principal areas of interest has been the endowment and the Society's general finances. Since the spring of 1993 when his service commenced, Mr. Adams noted that the endowment has doubled in size to an amount in excess of $120 million. He praised the Finance Committee for its contribution to this development and especially two of its chairmen—Mr. William B. Eagleson, Jr. and Dr. Edward G. Jefferson—for their outstanding service and dedication. The chairmen and committee members of the annual giving program were also complimented for their commitment and contribution to the Society's financial success. The regular budget has reflected this improved condition as it grew from $3.2 million to more than $5.5 million. This dramatic growth was both a stimulus and response to new and expanded programs among the academic community and the local community as well.

The Society's physical plant has also received significant attention during this period. Library Hall has had an extensive renovation of its mechanical equipment and exterior surfaces. Philosophical Hall is currently undergoing its most substantial renovation since the 1940s with the installation of an elevator and facilities in compliance with the Americans with Disabilities Act. The Jefferson Garden, too, is in the midst of a major rejuvenation program, which promises to make it a valuable asset to the Society and an attractive sight for visitors to the National Park.

Mr. Adams also praised the two executive officers, who have served during his tenure. Both Dr. Herman H. Goldstine and Dr. Alexander G. Bearn have provided the Society with excellent leadership, prudent management, and expanded program activities. He complimented the Librarian, Dr. Edward C. Carter II, for his administration of an outstanding library program. He also praised the Hall and Library staffs in general for their dedication and devotion to the Society's goals and welfare.

He concluded his remarks by observing than in the end the *membership is the key and is the Society*. Without the members there would be no Philosophical Society nor the prestigious recognition of scholarly and scientific achievement which it has performed and fostered since its founding in the 18th century.

At this point, Judge Adams presented the Jefferson gavel to his successor, Dr. Frank H. T. Rhodes. Upon his receiving this symbol of order and intellectual achievement, Dr. Rhodes praised his predecessor for his many contributions over the past six years, saluted and thanked him for his untiring and generous service, and complimented him for the style and values he cherished for the Society and exhibited in the presence of his colleagues.

The final order of business was the Committee reports. Printed reports of the Standing Committees were available for the membership to examine. [A complete rendering of these reports will be printed in the *Year Book*.]

During this meeting 216 members and 256 guests were in attendance.
American Philosophical Society

REPORT OF THE COMMITTEE ON FINANCE

The Committee on Finance is charged with the custody, control and management of the Society's securities and other investments. Currently, eight professional managers assist the Committee in managing the investments which are divided among the Society's endowment, the I. Minis Hays trust, the pension trust, and the pooled life income funds.

Endowment

Two primary considerations govern the management of the endowment:
* The need to preserve, and if possible to enhance, the real purchasing power of principal;
* The need to manage the fund with that degree of prudence appropriate for funds of this character.

These requirements are reflected in an investment policy that seeks to maximize the long term total return of the portfolio through a combination of income and capital appreciation consistent with sound investment practices. A long time horizon characterizes endowment investment. This, together with an investment objective defined in terms of total return and the discipline of a prudent spending policy, permits the Society to maintain a heavy weighting in equities in order to capture the premium return historically provided by common stocks.

In spite of the unusual degree of volatility of securities markets during 1998, the endowment achieved a total return of 18.4% for the 12 months ending March 31, 1999, placing it in the 98th percentile of the fund universe with which we compare ourselves. A return of 5.2% was realized in the quarter ended March 31, 1999 on which date the fund's securities had a value of $121.5 million. (In addition, $1.5 million was owed to the Endowment by the Building Fund.) This compares with a market value of $98.6 million at the beginning of 1998 and $116.8 million at the end of that year.

The strong performance of the endowment results primarily from its above average equity exposure (currently near 80%), and from the persistent market strength of domestic "core" equities which are managed by 1838 Investment Advisors. Since realignment of the managers' responsibilities in mid-1997, core equities have appreciated at an annual rate in excess of 35% and now represent about 60% of the endowment's total value. The other asset classes and their relative sizes are Fixed Income (about 21%), Small and Medium Cap Domestic

Equity, and International Equity (each 10% or less). There have been no changes in the Society's roster of investment managers since 1997.

The Committee continues to weigh carefully the risks in maintaining a relatively high equity exposure at a time when valuations are historically high and market volatility is pronounced.

We have concluded that, for a fund with the characteristics of the Society's endowment, under-exposure to equities presents a greater risk over the long term than does a policy of maintaining positions through the market cycle.

I. Minis Hays Trust

This trust, managed by First Union Bank, had a value at March 31, 1999 of $4.7 million. It is to provide income to the Society in perpetuity, thus clothing it with characteristics of endowment, and is invested entirely in equities reflecting an investment policy aimed at growth in principal.

Recent changes in Pennsylvania law governing charitable trusts may permit the use of a total return policy and a spending rule in the Hays Trust. This matter is now under review by the trustees and by the Committee.

Pension Trust

The Society's Pension Trust which is managed by PNC Bank had a value of $2.2 million at March 31, 1999. A moderately conservative investment policy is reflected in the 65% equity position, and in the total return which is significantly below that of the endowment. Consideration is being given to termination of this defined benefit plan, and its replacement with a defined contribution plan.

Pooled Life Income Funds

At March 31, 1999, funds then valued at $271,000. were held by the Society to pay income for life to the donors after which principal will be paid over to the Society. The investment objectives are income and safety of principal, and these are being pursued through Vanguard's Wellesley Fund, a conservative, balanced investment vehicle.

As an adjunct to its oversight of the financial assets, the Committee monitors the Society's "spending rule" and makes periodic recommendations to the Executive Committee regarding its provisions and application. Currently, that rule provides that an amount equal to 5% of a three year moving average of endowment market value shall be made available for support of the Society's operations.

William B. Eagleson, Jr.
Chairman

REPORT OF THE LASHLEY AWARD COMMITTEE

The members of the Lashley Award Committee consisting of Sanford Palay, Floyd Bloom, Torsten Wiesel, and Eric Kandel have circulated among themselves a list of 23 candidates for the Lashley Award. After due discussion, the committee unanimously voted to recommend that the Lashley Award go to Michael Merzenich from the Departments of Otolaryngology and Physiology at the University of California, San Francisco, for his contributions to the plasticity of the cortical representation of the body surface.

Michael Merzenich has pioneered the study of cortical plasticity. The Lashley Award is given "In recognition of his original contributions to cortical plasticity."

Eric R. Kandel, M.D.
Chairman

REPORT OF THE LIBRARIAN
1998
TOWARD A NEW MILLENNIUM

On November 11, 1959 Library Hall was officially dedicated after nearly two and a half years of construction. Thus a hundred year dream of the American Philosophical Society to provide a safe and secure fire-proof facility for its invaluable books and manuscripts was finally fulfilled. This next November will mark the fortieth anniversary of the Society's second building, Philosophical Hall being the first and Benjamin Franklin Hall the third. The building was a state-of-the-art library and archival research facility when it was built, and it has served the needs of the Society and the readership admirably. The Library, the repository of over seven million manuscripts and 250,000 printed items, supported by a first-rate conservation facility, has over the years increased the size of its holdings and broadened the scope of collections in a manner unthought of in 1958. It has provided research spaces for thousands of readers during this time, and the staff of the Library has been cited over and over again for the quality of its reference service. In these forty years, the main reading room of the Library has been the site of hundreds of scholarly talks, colloquia, seminars, presentations, and of course, holiday parties and Friends of the Library events.

Eventually, however, utilization of the building simply exceeded the use anticipated for it by its architects. The manuscripts' vault, for example, once thought large enough to accommodate that entire collection, now holds less than twenty percent of it. In the 1970s new acquisitions threatened to burst the Library's seams, but the purchase and renovation of Benjamin Franklin Hall (much of which is devoted to library stack areas), has alleviated that problem for the foreseeable future. However, demand for the collections—and all the services that implies—has continued to rise. Reader days have nearly tripled in the past fifteen years alone, and on occasions staff have often found it necessary to accommodate more users than the building was designed to hold. As many as 12,000 tourists per year pour through the front doors to view the lobby exhibits created by the curators and conservators. Under these circumstances, Library Hall has stood up well indeed. Still, the building itself has been aging, and showing signs of this ever-increasing use. As it weathered forty often icy Philadelphia winters and sweltering summers, the elements began to take their toll; its magnificent hardwood floors grew dark and stained with use, the splendid oriental carpets in the reading room and offices became a bit tatty, and the furniture also began to show the years. Clearly it was time to turn our attention to the job of safekeeping and servicing the Library's collections in a pleasant, modern, and well-maintained environment. The heating and cooling system, which was antiquated and unreliable, was replaced by a modern, computer-controlled HVAC in 1995. Last year, the roof was repaired and tiles were fixed, new dormers were constructed, the balustrades replaced, exterior windows were re-painted, chimneys were re-pointed, downspouts were cleared. The exterior of the building was significantly improved. Meanwhile, staff made plans for much-anticipated interior improvements.

A priority has been the restoration of the hardwood floors throughout the building. In 1998, the hardwood floors in the administrative offices were sanded and re-finished, and electrical improvements were made. The same treatment is scheduled for the Reading Room, Manuscripts Room, and Board Room, in December 1999 (a job so large it will require the suspension of public services for a month). In addition, with the generous support of the Pew Charitable Trusts (see below for a full description), other significant improvements and renovations have also begun. These include the replacement of the Halon fire suppression equipment in the manuscripts' vault with a new, environmentally safe system; the construction of new storage spaces for oversized manuscripts; and the replacement of the exhibit cases in the main lobby with state-of-the-art, environmentally safe vitrines. Workmen have also started the repair of numerous cracks and fissures in the decorative woodwork throughout the building, and the refurbishment or replacement of many of the Library's carpets and working furniture. Numerous other smaller projects complement the major ones, and the Library staff has responded with enthusiasm and cooperation to smooth the difficulties and disruptions of contractors, noise, and construction. This renovation, rejuvenation, and modernization of the physical fabric of Library Hall has been one of the Librarian's most heartfelt, long-term priorities. He looks forward to January 2000 when the building is returned to its beautiful state of four decades ago, and, in fact, made even more attractive and useful.

As this Report will make clear, however, the renovations to the building have not slowed the pace of scholarship or service in the Library. Indeed, special projects involving technological improvements, OPAC construction, conservation of rare documents, and the dissemination of special facsimiles of American icons in the Library's collections continue apace. Library staff have been asked to cope with a tremendous three-pronged workload of simultaneous regular duties, special projects, and renovations, and have responded splendidly. More importantly, readership statistics continue to show a robust continued interest in the Library's collections, and a high level of satisfaction with service rendered by Library staff.

As we look to the future, the Library will continue to be adapted to modern standards and conventions, and we will strive to maintain our reputation as a comfortable and well-appointed place in which to pursue scholarship. At the same time, we will continue our dedication to fulfilling our environmental and professional stewardship of one of the great independent library collections in the world. The building contains the two great assets of the Society—its collections and its staff. We are pleased to think that we will start the new millennium with those assets well-protected in a safe, appropriate, and attractively enhanced milieu.

GRANTS, SPECIAL PROJECTS, AND PROGRAMS

Generous outside support continues to provide the impetus for numerous special projects and programs in the Library. In 1997, the Library received a $600,000 grant from the Andrew W. Mellon Foundation to support a nearly $900,000 installation and renovation of technology in the Library. Besides the retrospective conversion of the printed materials card catalogue and the construction of an online public access catalogue (OPAC), the ambitious plans called for a new local area network (LAN), the retro-fitting of the Library with optical and other wiring, a complete in-house internet communications infrastructure, automation of numerous collection management functions, and the installation of a sophisticated computer center powered by four separate servers. It is with great pleasure that we can now report much of the work of this program has been completed. The retrospective conversion of the card catalogue, and general public access to the OPAC, is on schedule for completion in September 2000. This project has been ably directed by Dr. Martin Levitt, with Dr. Alison Lewis and Ms. Marian Christ handling much of the responsibility for the OPAC.

In January 1999, the Pew Charitable Trusts awarded the Society a generous grant in excess of $435,000 to conserve, preserve, and exhibit notable documents of America's history from the Society's collections in the Library. The most prominent of the seven groups of documents to be conserved are: Jefferson's handwritten draft of the Declaration of Independence and the journals of the Lewis and Clark Expedition. The project includes the creation and free distribution of hundreds of high-quality facsimiles of the Jefferson's Declaration and sets of three selected Lewis and Clark journals, and the upgrade of the Library's exhibition facilities and manuscript vault.

Challengingly complex, the successful implementation of the various components of the grant has involved nearly the entire Library staff, and seven separate action committees have been established to insure the timely completion of the various grant elements. The entire project is scheduled to be concluded early in 2000.

In part due to the extraordinary Friends of the Library record-breaking 1998 contribution described below, the successful Mellon Library Resident Research Fellowship program has been augmented and strengthened by support from the Isaac Comly Martindale Fund, the Grundy Foundation, and the Phillips Fund. Now called the Library Resident Research Fellowship program, recipients of fellowships are now designated by the source of their support. In 1999, this additional support allowed for the appointment of twenty-two resident Fellows from over eighty applicants. They will pursue research on topics as far-ranging as eugenics, ethnohistory, and the social history of colonial America. Dr. Levitt continued to administer this and several other Library programs. The program continues to be among the most important outreach initiatives in the Library.

ACCESSIONS, PUBLIC SERVICE, AND CATALOGUING

The Library accessioned several notable items in Printed Materials this year. Among them was Constantine S. Rafinesque's *The World, or, Instability; a poem* (second edition: Philadelphia and London, 1836). The very rare second edition, printed the same year as the first, is an eccentric volume of poetry in support of a proto-theory of evolution. Rafinesque, the Franco-American polymath and naturalist, was ahead of his time in his belief in a system of evolutionary development of species. This year Head Cataloguer Marian Christ also catalogued 1,270 other printed items. For the first time, these new catalogue records were not added to the venerable card catalogue, but instead were integrated into the Library's OPAC.

The Manuscript Department added 88 accessions in 1998, including a few new collections along with the usual additions to existing collections. The majority of new accessions came as a result of Phillips Fund Grants, but important additions were also made to the Seymour S. Cohen Papers, the Records of the International Union of Physiological Sciences, the Smith Family Papers, the John Wheeler Papers, the Records of the Society for the Study of Evolution, the Leonard Carmichael Papers, the Carleton Gajdusek Papers, the Ruben Reina Papers, and the Philip Klass Papers. Among new materials, two collections stand out as particularly significant: The Mary R. Haas Papers and the Floyd Lounsbury Papers.

Donations of manuscripts were received from the grandson of Franz Boas,

Norman Boas, from Nathaniel Comfort, and from Herman Goldstine. Clearly the most unusual donation, however, was a clasp from one of the Lewis and Clark journals. After editing the journals in the mid-1890s, Elliott Coues presented the clasps as mementos to friends and associates with an interest in historical matters, and apparently kept no records of where the non-descript pieces of brass were disseminated. The generous donor of the clasp was Dr. Russell Bagley of Minneapolis, Minnesota.

Library staff answered a record 3,600 reference queries by telephone, fax, e-mail, and postal mail this year. Meanwhile, use of the Library continues to expand, with reader days expected to exceed 1,400 in 1999.

PERSONNEL

Since the last Report of the Librarian, a number of important changes occurred in both the composition of the staff and the administrative structure in the Library. Marian Christ's service to the Society and newly assigned responsibilities were recognized by a change in her title from Head Cataloguer and Bibliographer to Assistant Librarian, Head Cataloguer and Bibliographer. Likewise, Roy Goodman was appointed Assistant Librarian, Curator of Printed Materials. Joseph Pannella, whose service has been exemplary in implementing the many renovation projects in the Library, was appointed Physical Plant Supervisor. More recently, Lydia Marrero was named Technical Services Manager, and J.J. Ahern was appointed Library Technical Assistant, Programs Assistant.

After an extensive national search, Robert S. Cox was appointed the new Manuscripts Librarian of the Society as of September 1998. Following in the footsteps of such distinguished predecessors as Beth Carroll-Horrocks, Stephen Catlett, and Murphy Smith, Mr. Cox brings with him both an impressive record of scholarly achievement and eight years knowledge of the application of technology in libraries gained as Curator of Manuscripts and Photographs at the William L. Clements Library of the University of Michigan.

Staff members continued the Library tradition of personal scholarship and service. Librarian Edward C. Carter II is Adjunct Professor of History and the History and Sociology of Science at the University of Pennsylvania, while Associate Librarian for Administration Martin L. Levitt is Adjunct Associate Professor of History at Temple University; Conservators Hedi Kyle and Denise Carbone are adjunct faculty at the University of the Arts. In addition to the numerous university courses these educators offer in their areas of expertise, they also conduct workshops, seminars and individual lectures.

CONSERVATION AND PRESERVATION

Once again, the Conservation Department had a most productive year, creating numerous preservation boxes, enclosures, special folders, slipcases, and custom-designed enclosures. In addition to this important work, Head of Conservation Hedi Kyle and Assistant Conservator Denise Carbone continued to revise the Library's extraordinarily important disaster plan, were significantly involved in the creation, installation, and subsequent dismounting of last year's exhibit "*Insects: Our Principal Earthly Partners*," helped to create and install yet another new exhibit in the Library foyer (*How Sweet It Is: Sugar Materials from the Collections of the American Philosophical Society*), and gave numerous well-attended and highly praised workshops. The Conservation Department also was involved in the training of four summer interns.

FRIENDS OF THE LIBRARY

In 1998, the Friends of the Library contributed the largest amount of funds in its history: 440 Friends generously gave the outstanding total of $92,000. This figure is up from contributions of $52,190 from 327 gifts in 1997; $56,720 from 341 gifts in 1996; and $49,786 from 356 gifts in 1995. The largest single gift in the history of the Friends was made by a long-time supported and researcher Mme. Meredith Frapier of Paris in honor of her great-grandfather Isaac Comly Martindale, a noted nineteenth-century naturalist and officer of the Society. The generous contributions of the Friends continue to provide an important source of funds for the purchase of especially desirable manuscripts and books that would otherwise be outside of the Library's acquisitions budget. For example, the Friends provided funds for the purchase of numerous items including an original manuscript letter from William Leach to Constantine Rafinesque, September 5, 1818. As we have in years past, it with a deep sense of appreciation that we thank the Friends for their generous support.

CONCLUDING REMARKS

While we have spent a great deal of time in this report recounting improvements to the building, I would like to again state my belief that in addition to its outstanding collections, the greatest intellectual asset of the Library is its staff. This combination of bright, enthusiastic professionals, and outstanding collections, continues to keep the Library a vital center of scholarship. I would like to express my gratitude to all those who have supported our enterprise: the Committee on Library; Chairman Hatten S. Yoder, Jr.; Executive Officer Alexander G. Bearn, and many other friends and advocates.

Edward C. Carter II
Librarian
Martin L. Levitt
Associate Librarian for Administration

REPORT OF THE COMMITTEE ON LIBRARY

The Committee on Library met on 17 December 1998 in the Board Room of the Library. The Chairman welcomed the new members of the Committee and staff and expressed his appreciation of the large attendance.

The Librarian reported on the strong support of the Friends of the Library with record annual contributions. The Pew Charitable Trust Grant was being used to preserve historical documents, improve the storage vault, and exhibition space. The scholarly activities of staff included teaching, book preparation, and organizing exhibitions.

The new Manuscripts Librarian, Mr. Robert Cox, described his efforts in automating the Library work, especially in regard to the response to requests and the assembly of the shelf list. He was investigating the back-up of digitized sound recordings. Mr. Cox anticipated that the remaining 10 percent of items to be catalogued would be completed within a year.

Assistant Librarian, Ms. Marian Christ, reported on the progress of converting the card catalogue to on-line public access. Some 2,000 records per week were being processed. About 65,000 were completed. The initial error rate of 1 percent was being reduced by a factor of 100!

The Committee was most pleased with the detailed and thorough document prepared by Ms. Hedi Kyle on the Disaster Plan for Benjamin Franklin hall. The steps for recovery and preservation of the library's assets were particularly noteworthy and may well serve as a model for other organizations. Prof. Gillispie noted the unacceptable deterioration he observed in the collections of the College of Physicians' Library and the Library of the Academy of Natural Sciences, and complimented Ms. Kyle on her expertise in maintaining the APS collections.

The outreach programs of the Library were reviewed by Mr. Roy Goodman. In addition to cooperating with the Discovery Channel in regard to Benjamin Franklin's Birthday Celebration, the staff made presentations at the local schools. (Mr. Goodman edits the Friends of Franklin Newsletter.) He related the plans for a Neighborhood Consortium, the Millennium Conference, the 300th Anniversary of John Bartram (initiator of APS), and the Chemical Heritage Exhibition. It was noted that 1,100 book titles had been acquired in 1998. About 500 catalogues were searched for appropriate additions of significance to the Landmarks of Science Collection.

In the discussion of the budget, it was noted that the salaries of staff were reasonable, but not attractive. With the support of the Executive Officer, the

Librarian enjoyed some flexibility with the budget. Monies to be carried forward from 1998 were to be spent for books.

The progress on renovation of the Library building included refinishing some of the floors, installing a new telephone system, painting the iron railings, replacing the wood in the attic dormers, and stripping and painting all exterior woodwork. The items still to be carried out were installation of the surge suppressors, an emergency power line, replacement of pumps in the mechanical room, and the cleaning of the ducts and filters. The wish list includes completion of refurbishing all remaining wood floors, replacement of the rugs, refinishing the furniture, and the purchasing of new chairs.

The tremendous progress on upgrading the technology in the Library was reported by Mr. Levitt. There had been a great increase in the number of people logging on to the Society's web site. A large increase in the number of colleges using the Library was observed, and in the number of inquiries. Mr. Carter believed the Library could accommodate at least another 200 visits per year, but he was more interested in upgrading the quality of scholars. He planned to revive the Library Bulletin to focus on specific themes. For example, the Library could serve as a focal point for Philadelphia history. The Library Bulletin was strongly endorsed by the Committee.

Again, the strong commitment of the Library Staff to serving scholars was praised by the Committee.

Hatten S. Yoder, Jr.
Chairman, Committee on Library

REPORT FOR THE HENRY ALLEN MOE COMMITTEE

The Henry Allen Moe Prize in the Humanities was presented on November 13, 1998 to Gerhard Böwering, Professor of Islamic Studies at Yale University, for his paper "The Concept of Time in Islam," which was read to the Society on November 3, 1995.

The Committee consisted of Richard Herr, Professor of History, Emeritus, University of California, Berkeley, Bruce M. Metzger, George L Collard Professor of New Testament Language and Literature, Emeritus, Princeton Theological Seminary, and Helen F. North, Centennial Professor of Classics, Emerita, Swarthmore College, Chairman.

REPORT OF THE COMMITTEE ON PUBLICATIONS

Five *Memoirs* were published in 1998: *Patriot-Improvers,* Whitfield J. Bell's first volume of biographical sketches of APS members), R.A. Donkin's *Beyond Price: Pearls and Pearl-Fishing Origins to the Age of Discoveries;* Edith Balas's *Joseph Csáky, A Pioneer of Modern Sculpture;* Rick Tilman & Charles Rasmussen's *Jacques Loeb: His Science and Social Activism and their Philosophical Foundations,* and Davis Jerome's edition of Herschel's oboe concerti. In 1999 the symposium, "Surveying the Record," sponsored by the American Philosophical Library in March 1997 was published in the *Memoirs,* as was Marshall Clagett's third volume of *Ancient Egyptian Science* and Alexander Jones's *Astronomical Papyri from Oxyrhynchus.* Two other books, Whitfield Bell's second volume of *Patriot-Improvers* as well as a compilation of the papers delivered at the Millennium Meeting in April 1999 (*Useful Knowledge: The American Philosophical Millennium Program)* are also scheduled for publication.

In the first part of 1999, the Committee on Publications accepted several outstanding manuscripts. One is a biography of Humphry Davy by Professor June Fullmer of Ohio State University. This large manuscript will be published in the *Memoirs* next year. A monographic study recently accepted for the *Transactions* is "Kos Between Hellenism and Rome: Studies on the political, institutional and social history of Kos." The author is K. Buraselis of the University of Athens. For the *Proceedings,* the Committee recently accepted a manuscript entitled, "The Gita of J. Robert Oppenheimer" by James A. Hijiya of the University of Massachusetts.

For the first time, the Publications Office published some of its papers on the Internet. Papers from the symposium of last November on the "Globalization of the Economy" (moderated by Gerard Piel) are available by accessing the Publications web site, www.aps-pub.com. This procedure expedites accessability of important papers before they appear in our *Proceedings.* As of September 1999 many of the latest *Proceedings* articles will be published on-line.

Eight recent publications in the *Memoirs* and *Transactions* were exhibited at the London Book Fair in March. Several more will be exhibited at the Frankfurt Book Fair and various other smaller meetings in the United States.

A recent book in the *Memoirs* series, *Cavendish,* for which the author (Russell McCormmach) received the 1997 Lewis Award, is generating many favorable reviews. The *American Historical Review* says the volume "will long stand as the definitive study of his life and work" and the *Bulletin for the History of Chemistry* calls it "an invaluable addition to the secondary literature on Cavendish."

The sales figure for 1998 was somewhat lower than in recent years. The final figure was over $127,000. Because several *Memoirs* and *Transactions* scheduled for production last year were not completed until early 1999 (because of the Editor's illness), payments for them were not recorded in 1998.

The dearth of quality manuscripts submitted for the *Transactions* has prompted the Committee on Publications to reexamine its publications program. A short-term solution has been the initiation of a Millennium Monograph Award for the best manuscript accepted for the *Transactions* after February 1999. The award, $5,000, will be given annually at the APS Autumn Meeting for the next five years. The deadline for submissions is December 1 of each year. Manuscripts must be in English and to qualify must be in one of the following subjects: history (European, American, Asian, African, South and Central American), history of medicine, history of science, anthropology, archaeology, linguistics, classics, medieval studies, paleontology. Notices about the award have been sent to a dozen scholarly societies for announcement in their newsletters, an announcement was also sent to mailing lists (approximately 10,000 names), a notice has been placed on H-Net, and an advertisement appears in the latest issue of *Perspectives.*

Other suggestions by the Committee for enhancing the program were:

1. More advertisements in scholarly journals and newsletters
2. An announcement should be placed on H-Net
3. Representatives of the program should attend scholarly meetings where they can discuss the program with prospective authors
4. Members of the Society could take a more active role by referring young scholars with manuscripts, particularly monograph size works, to the Society
5. The program as a whole should be examined, the distinction among the three publications clearly defined, the focus of the program as a whole studied carefully. Carole Le Faivre-Rochester presented President Frank Rhodes with a brief history of the *Memoirs* and *Transactions.*

The *Transactions,* first published in 1771, recorded Society activities, meetings, deaths, elections and papers read at meetings. When the *Proceedings* was initiated in 1838, most of the Society's activities began to be recorded there. The *Transactions* started a new series in 1818 and published papers delivered by members; William Maclure's *Geology of the United States of America* was in the first volume of this second series. Volumes were published sporadically during the 19th and early 20th centuries, each containing one report. Volume 22, for example, covered 1911 through 1925 and was issued in five parts containing lengthy papers on parabolic and planetary orbits, (parts 1 and 2), tertiary vertebrate fauna (part 3), pseudomyrmine ants (part 4), and the order Doradidae (part 5). This tradition of publishing monographs such as those just listed seems to have begun with volume 12 in 1862. There was a lull between 1936 and 1947.[1] The next volume, 37, contained four monographs and the number gradually increased through the years. There were eight published per year during the 1970s. When submissions began to decrease, the number was lowered to seven per year (1984) and six per year (1996).

The differences between the *Transactions* and *Memoirs* have become less distinct, seemingly relying on size and, perhaps, on marketability. R.F. Fortune's *Manus Religion,* for example, published in the *Memoirs* in 1935 was 391 pages and a bestseller. Later a university press sought permission to reprint it. That same year in the *Transactions, Anatomy of a Rat,* 370 pages, was published, another bestseller. It was later reprinted by Hafner. An examination of the two series for the last 25 years shows the following:

1. Multi-volume works by APS members have been published in the *Memoirs.* Correspondence indicates that APS members have often specified where they want their manuscripts published (especially if they have provided subsidies).[2] Some general characteristics of the *Memoirs* are:
   A. many are oversized, $8\frac{1}{2} \times 11$ or 9×12 trim size
   B. they are case bound
   C. they are expensive to produce and have frequently been subsidized by authors' institutions.

2. Other *Memoirs* have required special, expensive designs, multiple four-color illustrations, case binding: Bartram's botanical drawings, Thompson's *Commentary on the Dresden Codex, Benjamin Franklin's Philadelphia Printing* are examples.

3. Some *Transactions* have been generated from odd-sized manuscripts: those that number from 100 to 200 pages and do not fit in the *Proceedings.* A recent example is an article that was accepted last February for the *Proceedings* but was moved to the *Transactions* because the revised version is now 114 pages with 15–20 illustrations.

4. Some *Transactions* are specialized, focusing on one aspect of a subject; for example, one author has published two monographs with the Society on Ptolemy's *Optics:* one on his theory of visual perception and a second on the foundations of ancient mathematical optics.

---

[1] *During this period, after the Penrose legacy was received, the* Memoirs *series was begun with the first volume issued in 1935,* General Analysis, Part I. The Algebra of Matrices.
[2] *If an author wanted a specially designed book, the* Memoirs *was the series of choice until 1993 when the* Transactions *were redesigned so that each has a distinctive cover.*

In marketing the two series, there is little distinction. Both are featured on our web site; review copies are sent to journals for both series; both are sent on exhibits; mailing lists are rented to advertise both. The *Transactions* has a subscriber base of about 400 libraries; the *Memoirs* has a standing-order base of about 200. For that reason, there is usually more agressive marketing of the *Memoirs*.

With the proliferation of monograph series in many scholarly disciplines and with the increased publication of many on the Internet, the Society will have to examine carefully its publications program.

Carole Le Faivre-Rochester
Editor

REPORT OF THE COMMITTEE ON RESEARCH

At its three scheduled meetings during 1998, the Committee on Research considered 256 proposals, and approved 90 awards totaling $361,020 (average $4,011). This dollar figure represents the amount of funds actually paid out. The amount budgeted to our committee for 1998 was $365,757, representing the sum of both restricted and unrestricted funds. In the course of the year, a total of $3,360 was returned to the Society by grantees who did not spend the entire amount of their award. In the last weeks of the year, $4,355.50 was returned by the institution of a grantee, from whom the Committee on Research had requested an accounting in 1997.

At year-end, $1,000 returns to principal in a restricted fund, and a small amount is unexpended from a restricted fund. Unrestricted funds not expended by year end will be used to update computer equipment in the office.

Members of the Committee on Research in 1998 were: Ludo Rocher, chair; David Bevington, Mildred Cohn, Robert Dyson, Joseph Gall, Herman Goldstine, Ward Goodenough, Stanley Katz, Peter Paret, and Russell Weigley. In the early part of the year the committee learned with regret of the death of two of its most devoted and long-term members: Arthur Link, on March 26, and Marvin Wofgang, on April 12.

Respectfully submitted,
Ludo Rocher
Chair, Committee on Research

REPORT OF THE SABBATICAL FELLOWSHIP PROGRAM IN THE HUMANITIES AND SOCIAL SCIENCES

The Sabbatical Fellowship program, open to mid-career faculty of universities and four-year colleges in the United States for whom financial support of a sabbatical/research year is available from the parent institution for only half of the year, held its first competition in the winter of 1998–1999.

Dr. Alexander Bearn began his initiative in the spring of 1998, submitted a formal proposal to the Andrew W. Mellon Foundation in June, and received notification that the appropriation was approved for approximately four years in a letter dated October 9, 1998.

The program was advertised through a mailing to 14,900 names of deans and department chairs of humanities and social sciences divisions, and in the *Chronicle of Higher Education*. The information was posted on the Society's website and sent to all the grants offices at colleges and universities on the mailing list of the research office.

Members of the humanities panel were: Bernard Bailyn (chairman), Glen Bowersock, Robert Nozick, Eugene Rice, Debora Silverman, and Helen Vendler. Of these, Professors Nozick of Harvard University, Rice of Columbia University, and Silverman of the University of California at Los Angeles were not members of the Society. After the first competition was completed, Bernard Bailyn requested that he be succeeded by Glen Bowersock, who has accepted the humanities chairmanship.

Members of the social sciences panel were: Gardner Lindzey (chairman), Patrick Kirch, Margaret Levi, Samuel Preston, Herbert Scarf, Stephen Stigler, and Patrick Suppes. Of these, Professors Levi of the University of Washington and Stigler of the University of Chicago were not members of the Society.

Three hundred and seventy applications were received. The Humanities panel reviewed 251 applications, and the Social Sciences panel reviewed 119 applications. Applicants represented 41 states. There were 156 women applicants, and 214 men applied.

Each panel selected 7 fellows, with an alternate list of 3 names. The geographic distribution of fellows in the humanities encompasses Arizona, Indiana, Iowa, Massachusetts, New Jersey, New York and Oklahoma. States represented by the social sciences fellows are California, Illinois, Massachusetts, Michigan, Minnesota and Texas. It is noteworthy that the successful fellows are drawn from

12 states and 13 institutions. The average age of fellows in the humanities is 46; in the social sciences, the average age of fellows is 45.

Although all of the fellows have accepted the award, no payments are scheduled in the first half of 1999. The list of fellows and their projects will be published in a subsequent issue of the *Year Book*.

1998 DISTRIBUTION OF RESEARCH GRANTS*
ACCORDING TO SUBJECT

Botany	4	15,900
Ecology	1	5,200
TOTAL BIOLOGICAL SCIENCES	5	$ 21,100
History: Africa	4	16,200
History: America	7	29,350
History: Asia	3	11,200
History: Europe	6	24,000
Political Science	1	2,850
Sociology	3	15,760
TOTAL SOCIAL SCIENCES	24	$ 99,360
Anthropology	8	$ 31,370
Archaeology	12	43,370
Architecture	1	6,000
Art History	12	48,970
History: Medieval	1	1,200
History: Early Modern Europe	1	4,150
History: Science and Medicine	5	23,550
Linguistics	2	9,300
Literature and Literary History: Early	11	42,100
Literature and Literary History: Modern	3	12,800
Musicology	1	3,450
Philosophy	2	8,900
Religion	2	5,400
TOTAL HUMANITIES	61	$ 240,560
TOTAL GENERAL RESEARCH GRANTS	90	$ 361,020
TOTAL DALAND FELLOWSHIPS	8	141,000
TOTAL MELLON RESIDENT RESEARCH GRANTS	9	20,600
TOTAL PHILLIPS GRANTS (Jurisprudence)	4	12,900
TOTAL PHILLIPS GRANTS (North American Indian)	24	32,310
SLATER FELLOWSHIP	1	12,000
TOTAL ALL GRANTS and FELLOWSHIPS	136	$ 579,830

*The chart indicates grants disbursed in 1998.

GENERAL RESEARCH GRANTS 1998

During 1998 the Society awarded 90 grants to help individual scholars conduct their research. Some Society grants are paid for with funds from the Penrose and Johnson bequests; Hays and Jayne bequests, and the Goldstine fund supply monies for others.

Barcham, William L., Fashion Institute of Technology, $4000, *Federico Cornaro (1579–1653): Patron of the Arts*

Beck, Lois G., Washington University, $2000, *Qashqa'i Tribespeople in Post-revolutionary Iran*

Bornstein, Daniel, Texas A & M University, $4150, *Rejection of the Sacraments in Renaissance Italy*

Brauckmann, Sabine, University of Münster, $5000, *Paul A. Weiss: from Field Theory to Molecular Ecology*

Brown, Carolyn A., Rutgers University, $5000, *Space, Leisure and Time in Enugu, Nigeria, 1914–1955*

Busing, Richard T., Oregon State University, $3000, *Dynamics of Old-growth Forests in the Smoky Mountains*

Colish, Marcia L., Oberlin College, $1400, *Edition of the Pseudo-Peter of Poitiers Gloss*

Connolly, Thomas H., University of Pennsylvania, $4000, *Jewish-Christian Communities of Late Imperial Rome*

Conte, Christopher A., Utah State University, $5200, *Biodiversity Management in Tanzania's East Usambara Mountains*

Cormack, Margaret J., College of Charleston, $3500, *Genealogy and Annals in Medieval Icelandic Literature*

Cortijo-Ocaña, Antonio, University of California, Santa Barbara, $6000, *Six Previously Unknown Manuscripts of Golden Age Dramas*

Costa, James T., Western Carolina University, $5600, *History of Social Insect Biology*

Courtenay, William J., University of Wisconsin, $1200, *Rotuli of Supplication for the University of Paris in the Fourteenth Century*

D'Antuono, Nancy L., Saint Mary's College, $1400, *Reception of Calderón's Theater in Italy, 1642–1800*

Daly, Douglas C., New York Botanical Garden, $2400, *Forgotten Expeditions and New Flora in Amazonia*

Demarest, Arthur A., Vanderbilt University, $5200, *Laboratory Study of Artifacts of Cancuen*

Desjarlais, Robert, Sarah Lawrence College, $3850, *Life-histories among the Yolmo People of Helambu, Nepal*

Diemer, John A., University of North Carolina, Charlotte, $6000, *R. Murchison's 1840 and 1841 Geological Research in Russia*

Edlund-Berry, Ingrid E., University of Texas, Austin, $3200, *The Central Sanctuary at Morgantina*

Erdman, Joan L., Columbia College Chicago, $3600, *Uday Shankar and the Oriental Dance*

Evans, James C., University of Puget Sound, $3550, *History of the Optical-mechanical Analogy*

French, John D., Duke University, $3600, *Mobilization in Brazil, 1950–1980: The Metalworkers of ABC*

Gibson, Mary S., John Jay College, $4000, *History of the Roman Prison for Women, 1860–1915*

Goldsmith, Elizabeth C., Boston University, $2400, *Letters of Maria Mancini Colonna (d. 1715)*

Gürsan-Salzmann, Ayse, Bilkent University, $4000, *Pastoral Activities at Gordion*

Helmreich, Anne L., Texas Christian University, $600, *National Identity and the Garden in England, 1870–1914*

Hood, R. Chalmers, Woodbridge, Va., $6000, *Biography of Admiral François Darlan*

Ivory, Carol S., Washington State University, $4100, *Tapa in the Marquesas Islands of French Polynesia*

Joyal, Elaine, Arizona State University, $4500, *Museum Survey of Basketry Ecology*

Kaplonski, Christopher, Rutgers University, $6000, *Political Repression in Socialist Mongolia*

Lamprakos, Michele, Venice, Italy, $6000, *Commercial Architecture in Late Medieval Venice*

LePage, Ben A., University of Pennsylvania, $6000, *Ecology of Pinaceae in the Nepalese Himalayas*

Lepore, Jill M., Boston University, $6000, *Noah Webster, Sequoyah, Gallaudet and the Language of Nations*

Letwin, Daniel, Pennsylvania State University, $5000, *Black Political Thought in the Age of Jim Crow*

Levine, Frances, Santa Fe Community College, $6000, *Maintaining Cultural Identity: Research in Australia*

Lewis, Beth I., College of Wooster, $5720, *The Public and Modern Art in Late Nineteenth-century Germany*

Lindenmeyr, Adele, Villanova University, $3500, *Philanthropy to Revolution: Countess Sofia Panina (1871–1956)*

Lindgren, James M., State University of New York, Plattsburgh, $2450, *Marine Museums in America*

Link, William A., University of North Carolina, Greensboro, $2300, *Slavery and Politics in Virginia, 1851–1861*

Lubenow, William C., Richard Stockton College, $4000, *Roman Catholic Peerage, 1815–1914*

Malamud, Margaret, New Mexico State University, $6000, *Imperial Rome in American Culture*

Mann, Janice, Bucknell University, $3000, *Romanesque Churches in Eleventh-century Spain*

Marlow, Louise, Wellesley College, $3300, *Medieval Islamic Advice Literature*

Marx-Scouras, Danielle C., Ohio State University, $4800, *Jean Sénac (1926–1973) and his Times*

Matney, Timothy, University of Akron, $4000, *Urban Planning at Ziyaret Tepe in the Diyarbakir Province*

McCollum, Melanie A., Case Western Reserve University, $4370, *Remodeling of the Early Hominid Bony Palate*

Meadows, Patrick A., Indiana University, $4000, *Vietnamese Francophone Literature*

Merelman, Richard M., University of Wisconsin, $2850, *The Yale School of Political Science*

Montias, John M., Yale University, $4850, *Art Auctions in Amsterdam, 1598–1638*

Namias, June, University of Alaska, $4000, *Alaska's Aleut Women, and Captain Cook's Third Voyage*

Parkes, Graham, University of Hawaii, $5900, *Nietzsche: a Philosophical Biography*

Paz, Denis G., University of North Texas, $4050, *Martin Tupper and Nineteenth-century British Identities*

Peters, Julie S., Columbia University, $6000, *Print and the Stage in Early Modern Europe, 1470–1870*

Phipps, Elena, Metropolitan Museum of Art, $5000, *Tapestries from Southern Peruvian and Bolivian Collections*

Pinti, Daniel J., New Mexico State University, $2500, *Chaucer and Commentaries on Dante: Research in Florence*

Powers, C. John, Australian National University, $3000, *Buddhist Oral Literature in Contemporary Himalayan Societies*

Puglisi, Catherine R., Rutgers University, $6000, *Italian Baroque Sculpture and Classical Antiquity*

Ragsdale, Hugh, University of Alabama, $1100, *Soviet Military Intentions at Munich, 1938*

Ramaswamy, Sumathi, University of Pennsylvania, $3500, *Anthropomorphic Cartography in Twentieth-century India*

Ramberg, Peter J., Johns Hopkins University, $3400, *Stereochemistry in Zurich, 1871–1913*

Ramirez, Susan E., DePaul University, $4800, *Andean Provincial Cosmology: Peru and Bolivia*

Rasico, Philip D., Vanderbilt University, $3300, *Joaquim Miret i Sans and the Catalan Language*

Reed, Cleota, Syracuse, N.Y., $3750, *A. Compton's Medieval Tiles Drawings*

Rigdon, Susan M., University of Illinois, $5760, *Rural Resistance in Sichuan Township*

Rivera, Mario A., Oak Creek, Wisc., $5650, *Prehistoric Agriculture at Ramaditas, Chile*

*Rollefson, Gary O., Ober-Ramstadt, Germany, $1670, *'Ain Soda, Jordan: Lower and Middle Paleolithic Tools*

Grant to Rollefson was returned to the Society in January 1999; personal circumstances prevent the grantee from making the projected trip.

Routledge, Bruce, University of Pennsylvania, $1500, *Investigations at Khirbat Mudaynat 'Aliya, Jordan*

Rubinson, Karen S., Key Perspectives, Inc., $3450, *Trialeti Culture Metalwork, Georgia*

Rugeley, Terry, University of Oklahoma, $6000, *Warfare and Social Reorganization in Yucatán, 1847–76*

Schaefer, Karl R., Drake University, $3600, *Catalog of Medieval Arabic Block Prints*

Scharf, Peter M., Brown University, $5800, *Vedarthadipika Manuscript Collection*

Scheck, Raffael M., Colby College, $5350, *Swiss Funding for the Early Nazi Movement*

Schenker, Alexander M., Yale University, $5000, *The Monument to Peter the Great in St. Petersburg*

Scott, R. T., Bryn Mawr College, $4000, *Regia/Vesta: Final Report*

Shepherd, Deborah J., University of Wisconsin, Stout, $1500, *Medieval Smelting Site at Low Birker, Northeast England*

Shields, Sarah D., University of North Carolina, $1700, *Assigning Nationalisms in Iraq and Syria*

Snead, James E., University of Arizona, $4750, *Archaeology and Society in the American Southwest, 1890–1915*

Sobania, Neal W., Hope College, $4000, *Contemporary Ethiopian Religious Painting*

Stewart, Pamela J., University of Pittsburgh, $2000, *Dreams and Historical Crisis in New Guinea Highlands*

Stokes, James D., University of Wisconsin, Stevens Point, $3500, *Medieval Dramatic Records in the Diocese of Lincolnshire*

Tatham, David F., Syracuse University, $3200, *European Sources for Winslow Homer*

Thomas, Christine M., University of California, Santa Barbara, $3200, *Roman-period Ossuaries of Western Asia Minor*

Waller, Richard D., Bucknell University, $4200, *Cattle in Colonial Kenya, 1900–1940*

Washburn, Dorothy K., Maryland Institute, $6000, *Puebloan Ceramic Design*

Watson, Richard L., North Carolina Wesleyan College, $3000, *Abolition of Slavery in South Africa, 1833–1841*

Weissberg, Liliane, University of Pennsylvania, $4000, *Life in Germany before and after January, 1933: The 1939 Harvard Essay Competition*

Westermann, Martine H., Rutgers University, $3750, *Dutch Interiors in Art, 1610–1700*

Wong, Deborah, University of California, Riverside, $3450, *Sacred Music in Bangkok*

Woods, Marjorie C., University of Texas, Austin, $4100, *Medieval Rhetoric in Humanist Italy*

Zuo, Jiping, St. Cloud State University, $6000, *Present-day Labor Market Status of Women and Men in China*

PUBLICATIONS SUPPORTED BY THE SOCIETY'S RESEARCH GRANTS RECEIVED IN 1998

Agenbroad, Larry D. "New Pygmy Mammoth (*Mammuthus exilis*) Localities and Radiocarbon Dates from San Miguel, Santa Rosa, and Santa Crux Islands, California." In: *Contributions to the Geology of the Northern Channel Islands, Southern California*, ed. P. Weigand. Bakersfield, Calif.: American Association of Petroleum Geologists, 1998. pp. 169–75

Attoh, Kodjopa. "High-pressure Granulite Facies Metamorphism in the Pan-African Dahomeyide Orogen, West Africa." *Journal of Geology* 106 (1998): 236–46

———. "Models for Orthopyroxene-plagioclase and other Corona Reactions in Metanorites, Dahomeyide Orogen, West Africa." *Journal of Metamorphic Geology* 16 (1998): 345–62

Becker, M[arshall] J. "Cremated Human Skeletal Remains from three Roman Glass Urns from Italy in the National Museum of Denmark." *International Journal of Anthropology* 12 (1997): 51–62

Bedford, J. M[ichael]. "The 'Hybrid' Character of the Gametes and Reproductive Tracts of the African Shrew, *Myosorex varius*, Supports its Classification in the Crocidosoricinae." *Journal of Reproduction and Fertility* 112 (1998): 165–73

Bellesiles, Michael A. "Gun Laws in Early America: the Regulation of Firearms Ownership, 1607–1794." *Law and History Review* 16 (1998): 567–89

Berezin, Mabel. *Making the Fascist Self: The Political Culture of Interwar Italy.* Ithaca, N.Y.: Cornell University Press, 1997. 296 pp.

Bernays, E[lizabeth] A. "The Value of Being a Resource Specialist: Behavioral Support for a Neural Hypothesis." *American Naturalist* 151 (1998): 451–64

Bornstein, Daniel. "Spiritual Kinship and Domestic Devotions." In: *Gender and Society in Renaissance Italy*, ed. J.C. Brown and R.C. Davis. London: Longman, 1998. pp. 173–92

Bruederle, Leo P., Diane F. Tomback, et al. "Population Genetic Structure in a Bird-dispersed Pine, *Pinus albicaulis* (Pinaceae)." *Canadian Journal of Botany* 76 (1998): 83–90

Burman, Thomas E. "Tasfs'r and Translation: Traditional Arabic Qur'an Exegesis and the Latin Qur'ans of Robert of Ketton and Mark of Toledo." *Speculum* 73 (1998): 703–32

Burnett, Stephen G. "The Regulation of Hebrew Printing in Germany, 1555–1630." In: *Infinite Boundaries: Order, Disorder, and Reorder in Early Modern German Culture*, ed. M. Reinhart and T. Robisheaux. Sixteenth Century Essays and Studies, 40. Kirksville: Sixteenth Century Journal Publishers, 1998. pp. 329–48

Cadle, John E. "New Species of Lizards, Genus Stenocercus (Iguania: tropiduridae), from Western Ecuador and Peru." *Bulletin of the Museum of Comparative Zoology* 155 (1998): 257–97

Crane, Elaine F. *Ebb Tide in New England: Women, Seaports, and Social Change, 1630–1800.* Boston: Northeastern University Press, 1998. x + 333 pp.

Crenson, Matthew A. *Building the Invisible Orphanage: A Prehistory of the American Welfare System.* Cambridge, Mass.: Harvard University Press, 1998. xii + 383 pp.

Dale, Richard. *Botswana's Search for Autonomy in South Africa.* Westport, Conn.: Greenwood Press, 1995. xxxvii + 256 pp.

Dickinson, Timothy A., et al. "North-American Black-fruited Hawthorns. I. Variation in Floral Construction, Breeding System Correlates, and their Possible Evolutionary Significance in Crataegus sect. Douglasii Loudon." *Folia Geobotanica Phytotaxica* 31 (1996): 533–71

Edinger, William. *Johnson and Detailed Representation: The Significance of the Classical Sources.* English Literary Studies, 72. Victoria, B.C.: University of Victoria, 1997. 105 pp.

Franko, Mark. "Nation, Class, and Ethnicities in Modern Dance of the 1930s." *Theatre Journal* 49 (1997): 475–91

Grassby, Richard. "Love, Property and Kinship: The Courtship of Philip Williams, Levant Merchant, 1617–50." *English Historical Review* 113 (1998): 335–50

Halliday, Paul D. *Dismembering the Body Politic: Partisan Politics in England's Towns, 1650–1730.* Cambridge: Cambridge University Press, 1998. xvii + 393 pp.

Heath, Martha E. and I.M. Coulson. "Preliminary Studies on Relocation of Cape Pangolins *Manis temminckii.*" *South African Journal of Wildlife Research* 27 (1997): 51–56

Hunt, James H., et al. "Nutrients in Social Wasp (Hymenoptera: Vespidae, Polistinae) Honey." *Annals of the Entomological Society of America* 91 (1998): 466–72

Kosmider, Alexia. "Strike a Euroamerican Pose: Ora Eddleman Reed's 'Types of Indian Girls'." *ATQ* 12 (1998): 109–31

Laursen, John C. "David Hume and the Danish Debate about Freedom of the Press in the 1770s." *Journal of the History of Ideas* (1998): 167–72

———. "Télémaque manqué: Reverdil at Court in Copenhagen." In: *Reconceptualizing Nature, Science and Aesthetics,* ed. P. Coleman. Travaux sur la Suisse des Lumières, 1. Geneva: Slatkine, 1998. pp. 147–56

Lease, Gary. "Exposed at Last: The Alan Rowe Expedition to Meidum, 1931–1932, the University Museum, Philadelphia." In: *Themelia: spätantike und koptologische Studien.* Sprachen und Kulturen des christlichen Orients, 3. Wiesbaden: Reichert, 1998. pp. 233–41 + 11 figs.

Meedel, Thomas H., S.C. Farmer and J.J. Lee. "The Single MyoD Family Gene of Ciona intestinalis Encodes Two Differentially Expressed Proteins: Implications for the Evolution of Chordate Muscle Gene Regulation." *Development* 124 (1997): 1711–21

Murphy, William M. *Prodigal Father: The Life of John Butler Yeats (1839–1922).* Ithaca: Cornell University Press, 1978. 680 pp.

———. *Family Secrets: William Butler Yeats and his Relatives.* [Dublin]: Gill & Macmillan, 1995. xxix + 534 pp.

Olson, Jeannine E. "Social Welfare and the Transformation of Polity in Geneva." In: *The Identity of Geneva: The Christian Commonwealth, 1564–1864,* ed. J.B. Roney and M.I. Klauber. Westport, Conn.: Greenwood Press, 1998. pp. 155–68

Ó Néill, Pádraig. "The Earliest Dry-point Glosses in Codex Usserianus Primus." In: 'A Miracle of Learning': Studies in Manuscripts and Irish Learning, Essays in Honour of William O'Sullivan, ed. T. Barnard, et al. Aldershot: Ashgate, 1998. pp. 1–27

Pohlsander, Hans A. "Die Anfänge des Christentums in der Stadt Trier: Bischöfe und Märtyrer." Trierer Zeitschrift 60 (1997): 255–302

Principe, Lawrence M. The Aspiring Adept: Robert Boyle and his Alchemical Quest. Princeton: Princeton University Press, 1998. xiv + 339

———. "Diversity in Alchemy: The Case of Gaston 'Claveus' DuClo, a Scholastic Mercurialist Chrysopoeian." In: Reading the Book of Nature: The Other Side of the Scientific Revolution, ed. A. Debus, M. Walton. Kirksville, Mo.: Sixteenth Century Journal Press, 1998. pp. 181–200

Reimers, David M. Unwelcome Strangers: American Identity and the Turn against Immigration. New York: Columbia University Press, 1998. xii + 199 pp.

Schurlknight, Donald E. Spanish Romanticism in Context: Of Subversion, Contradiction and Politics (Espronceda, Larra, Rivas, Zorrilla). Lanham: University Press of America, 1998. xii + 175 pp.

Sellin, Paul R. "Michel Le Blon and England, 1632–1649, with Observations on Van Dyck, Donne, and Vondel." Dutch Crossing 22 (1998): 102–24

Sharp, Lesley A. "Royal Difficulties: A Question of Succession in an Urbanized Sakalava Kingdom." Journal of Religion in Africa 27 (1997): 270–307

Sidebotham, Steven E. and W. Z. Wendrich. Berenike 1995: Preliminary Report of the 1995 Excavations at Berenike (Egyptian Red Sea Coast) and the Survey of the Eastern Desert. CNWS Publications, Special Series 2. Leiden: Research School CNWS, 1996. viii + 482 pp, 2 maps

REPORT OF THE DALAND FUND COMMITTEE

There were eighteen applications for first-year appointments to 1999–2001 Daland fellowships. The three current first-year fellows submitted requests for renewal.

The Committee voted two first-year appointments and granted three renewals. The total amount committed for 1999–2001 is $130,000. All candidates and scientific advisers received written notification of the Committee's decisions.

Beginning in 1999 there will be a change in the emphasis of the program, which has been accepting proposals for research "not necessarily associated directly with patients, but with clinical significance." The new orientation of the program will place the emphasis on patient-oriented research. Because the committee made only three awards in 1997, and two this year, and because of the strong financial position of the original Daland endowment fund, it will be possible to offer the sum of $50,000 for each of two years to the new clinical investigators.

The new Clinical Investigator Fellowships will be advertised in 1999 to the deans of all medical schools, in the *Journal of Clinical Investigation* and in the *New England Journal of Medicine*. The new information will become available at the Society's website in March, 1999.

The title of the program will be changed to Clinical Investigator Fellowships, but the announcement will contain the information that they are funded in part by the Daland endowment.

Members of the Daland Committee are: Victor A. McKusick, chairman; Robert Austrian, Alexander G. Bearn, Maclyn McCarty, and Jonathan E. Rhoads.

Victor A. McKusick
Chairman, Daland Committee

Eleanor Roach
Research administrator

DALAND FELLOWSHIPS FOR RESEARCH IN CLINICAL MEDICINE

First-year Fellows

Carhuapoma, J. Ricardo, Johns Hopkins Hospital, *MRI Techniques in Secondary Injury in Intracerebral Hemorrhage*

Gleit, Zachary L., Columbia-Presbyterian Medical Center, *Induction of Xenograft Tolerance by Thymic Transplantation*

Second-year Fellows

Avellino, Anthony M., University of Washington, *Cell Adhesion Molecules Mediating Macrophage Response after Axonal Injury*

Khakoo, Yasmin, Memorial Sloan-Kettering Cancer Center, *Transcriptional Control of Cell Growth and Differentiation in Neuroectodermal Tumors*

Qureshi, Adnan I., Johns Hopkins Hospital, *Effect of Hypertonic Saline on Intracranial Pressure*

REPORT OF THE HENRY M. PHILLIPS AWARD AND PRIZE COMMITTEE

In 1998 there were seven applications for Phillips grants. The proceeds of the Phillips bequest are used to recognize an important work in jurisprudence, and to fund research projects in the area of jurisprudence or related fields.

The Committee reviewed each applicant's submission. By adjusting the budgets, it was possible to make four grants, as follows:

Forest, Benjamin. University of Illinois at Chicago, $2400, *The Role of Geographic Information Systems and Racial Consciousness in Congressional Redistricting*

Hockett, Jeffrey D. University of Tulsa, $2500, *Brown v. Board of Education and the Politics of the Judicial System*

Netanel, Neil W. University of Texas, $4000, *Copyright Law and the Book Trade among Eastern European Jewry*

Steinberg, Allen R. University of Iowa, $4000, *The Becker Case and the Struggle for Law Enforcement in Progressive New York*

The Committee consisted of Judge Vincent McKusick, chairman; Professor Louis Henkin, and Lewis H. Van Dusen, Jr., Esq.

Vincent McKusick

REPORT OF THE COMMITTEE ON
PHILLIPS NATIVE AMERICAN FUND

In 1998, $59,000 was available from the Phillips Fund. The committee set aside approximately $19,000 for Library book purchases, subscriptions to journals and the audio tape conservation project.

There were 34 applications to the fund, but one of them was declared ineligible. The Committee approved twenty-four awards; they represent a total of $32,310 (average award: $1,346):

Alderete, John D., University of Massachusetts, $1100, *Tahltan Stress: Phonetics and Phonology*

Barthmaier, Paul T., University of California, Santa Barbara, $1000, *Lushootseed Discourse Data*

Caplow, Nancy J., University of California, Santa Barbara, $1200, *Western Abenaki Discourse*

Craver, Amy J., Alaska Native Science Commission, $1000, *Influence of Environmental Changes on Inupiaq Hunting*

Golla, Victor K., Humboldt State University, $1550, *Inventory of Sapir's Nootka Work*

Hahn, Steven C., Emory University, $1560, *The Creek Confederacy, 1633–1763*

Herndon, Ruth W., University of Toledo, $1400, *The Narragansett People and Rhode Island Officials*

Holton, Gary M., University of California, Santa Barbara, $400, *Tanacross Language Documentation Project*

Ishii, Izumi, University of Kentucky, $1500, *Cherokee Temperance Movement in the Nineteenth Century*

Keating, Neal B., State University of New York, Albany, $1500, *Historical Anthropology of Onondaga Art*

Kosmider, Alexia, University of Rhode Island, $1000, *Writings of Creek Writer Charles Gibson*

Maddra, Sam Ann, University of Glasgow, $2500, *The 1891–1892 Tour of Britain by Buffalo Bill*

Martin, Jack B., College of William & Mary, $1500, *The Creek Texts of Mary Haas, vols. 16–22*

Medicine, Beatrice, University of Alberta, $1600, *An Ethnohistory of the Wakpala Community*

Meya, Wilhelm K., University of Arizona, $1250, *Oglala Oral History and Winter Counts*

More, Anna H., University of California, Berkeley, $1150, *An Edition of Alonso de Benavides' Memorial of 1634*

Nakayama, Toshihide, Montclair State University, $2000, *Lexical Suffixes in Ahousaht Nuu-chah-nulth*

Ng, Eve C., State University of New York, Buffalo, $1500, *Fieldwork on Passama-quoddy*

Nichols, David A., University of Kentucky, $1200, *Indian Relations and American Political Culture, 1784–1800*

O'Neill, Sean P., University of California, Davis, *$1000, Hupa Texts*

Roy, Christopher A., Swanton, Vermont, $1200, *Nineteenth-century Abenaki Fusion*

Schrager, Bradley S., Northwestern University, $1200, *Spanish and English Colonialism, 1660–1715*

Shuck, Sheri M., Auburn University, $1500, *The Alabamas and Coushattas, 1500–1859*

Warren, Stephen A., Indiana University, $1500, *Emergence of the Shawnee Nation*

The committee consisted of Edward C. Carter, II, chairman, Regna Darnell, Eric P. Hamp, and Anthony F. C. Wallace.

Respectfully submitted,
Edward C. Carter II

REPORT OF THE JOHN C. SLATER
LIBRARY RESEARCH FUND COMMITTEE

In 1998 there were five applications for the Slater Fellowship, which supports doctoral dissertation work in the history of the modern physical sciences.

The committee judged Danian Hu of Yale University to be the strongest among a very strong set of candidates. He has accepted the award of the Slater Fellowship for 1998–1999. His dissertation topic is "Einstein and his Relativity Theory in China: Introduction, Assimilation and Reaction."

Information about the fellowship continues to be disseminated annually to the history of science departments and through newsletters. The information, and application form became available at the Society's website in October, 1997.

The committee consisted of John Heilbron, chairman; Edward Carter II, Marshall Clagett, Charles Gillispie, Gerald Holton, Abraham Pais, and Noel Swerdlow.

John Heilbron

HOWE, KELLER & HUNTER, P.C.
CERTIFIED PUBLIC ACCOUNTANTS
215 SOUTH BROAD STREET
PHILADELPHIA, PENNSYLVANIA 19107
(215) 893-9112
FAX (215) 893-9120

Independent Auditors' Report

American Philosophical Society
Philadelphia, Pennsylvania

We have audited the accompanying statements of financial position of the American Philosophical Society ("Society") (a non-profit organization) as of December 31, 1998 and 1997, and the related statements of activities and cash flows for the years then ended. These financial statements are the responsibility of the Society's management. Our responsibility is to express an opinion on these financial statements based on our audits.

We conducted our audits in accordance with generally accepted auditing standards. Those standards require that we plan and perform the audit to obtain reasonable assurance about whether the financial statements are free of material misstatement. An audit includes examining, on a test basis, evidence supporting the amounts and disclosures in the financial statements. An audit also includes assessing the accounting principles used and significant estimates made by management, as well as evaluating the overall financial statement presentation. We believe that our audits provide a reasonable basis for our opinion.

In our opinion, the financial statements referred to above present fairly, in all material respects, the financial position of the American Philosophical Society as of December 31, 1998 and 1997, and the changes in its net assets and its cash flows for the years then ended in conformity with generally accepted accounting principles.

Howe, Keller + Hunter, P.C.

March 23, 1999

Statements of Financial Position

December 31,	1998	1997
Assets		
Cash and cash equivalents	$ 1,552,949	$ 952,999
Accounts receivable, net of allowance for doubtful		
accounts of $3,000 in 1998 and 1997	18,166	16,355
Interest and dividends receivable	75,038	78,574
Prepaid expenses	29,667	45,585
Restricted unconditional promises to give	3,194	3,194
Deferred expenses	118,295	243,295
Land and buildings, at cost, less accumulated depreciation	10,644,636	10,156,656
Interest and dividends receivable from permanent endowments	1,284	1,321
Other receivables	-	66,000
Long-term investments, at market value	117,792,603	98,357,447
Total assets	**$130,235,832**	**$109,921,426**
Liabilities		
Accounts and other payables	$ 89,957	$ 99,972
Accrued postretirement benefit cost	389,545	374,569
Total liabilities	**479,502**	**474,541**
Net Assets		
Unrestricted	27,137,578	24,464,335
Temporarily restricted	2,127,778	1,082,088
Permanently restricted	100,490,974	83,900,462
Total net assets	**129,756,330**	**109,446,885**
Total liabilities and net assets	**$130,235,832**	**$109,921,426**

See accompanying notes to financial statements.

Statements of Activities

Year Ended December 31,	1998	1997
Unrestricted Net Assets		
Revenue, gains and other support		
Dividends and interest	$2,119,438	$ 2,084,320
Grants and gifts	1,032,701	624,523
Publications sales	123,913	146,910
Miscellaneous	27,995	16,981
Net realized gains on long-term investments, net of		
custodial fees of $54,725 in 1998 and $44,381 in 1997	1,858,587	2,675,001
Total unrestricted net assets	5,162,634	5,547,735
Unrealized gains on long-term investments	1,630,825	293,617
Net assets released from restrictions	678,321	985,707
Total revenue, gains and other support	7,471,780	6,827,059
Expenses and Losses		
Administrative	727,366	622,931
Research	682,055	648,130
Publications	510,656	462,092
Meetings	477,519	388,430
Library	1,791,903	1,828,351
Franklin Hall	427,012	475,699
Special purpose funds	182,026	231,663
Development	-	122,292
Total expenses and losses	4,798,537	4,779,588
Increase in Unrestricted Net Assets	2,673,243	2,047,471
Temporarily Restricted Net Assets		
Dividends and interest	413,167	398,603
Grants and gifts	1,191,656	945,380
Net realized gains on long-term investments	143,484	96,814
Net assets released from restrictions	(702,617)	(988,240)
Increase in Temporarily Restricted Net Assets	1,045,690	452,557

See accompanying notes to financial statements.

Statements of Activities

Year Ended December 31,		1998		1997
Permanently Restricted Net Assets				
Dividends and interest	$	43,828	$	43,170
Grants and gifts		7,150		79,057
Net realized gains on long-term investments, net of custodial				
fees of $308,422 in 1998 and $246,897 in 1997		6,314,502		12,155,712
Net assets released from restrictions		24,296		2,533
Unrealized gains on long-term investments		10,200,736		1,753,475
Increase in Permanently Restricted Net Assets		16,590,512		14,033,947
Increase in Net Assets		20,309,445		16,533,975
Net Assets, at beginning of year		109,446,885		92,912,910
Net Assets, at end of year		$129,756,330		$109,446,885

See accompanying notes to financial statements.

Statements of Cash Flows

Year Ended December 31,	1998	1997
Cash Flows from Operating Activities		
Change in net assets	**$20,309,445**	$16,533,975
Adjustments		
Depreciation	**386,444**	371,306
Realized (gains)	**(8,679,719)**	(15,218,805)
Unrealized (gains)	**(11,831,561)**	(2,047,092)
Provision for doubtful accounts	**-**	(4,253)
(Increase) decrease in		
Accounts receivable	**64,189**	(73,058)
Interest and dividends receivable	**3,536**	76,398
Deferred expenses	**125,000**	(122,785)
Prepaid expenses	**15,918**	13,209
Increase (decrease) in		
Accounts payable	**(10,015)**	99,117
Accrued postretirement benefit cost	**14,976**	21,430
Contributions restricted for long-term purposes	**(7,150)**	(79,057)
Interest and dividends restricted for long-term purposes	**(43,828)**	(43,170)
Net cash provided by (used) in operating activities	**347,235**	(472,785)
Cash Flows from Investing Activities		
Purchases of property and equipment	**(874,424)**	(299,347)
Net change in cash restricted for long-term purposes	**668,918**	27,051
Purchases of long-term investments	**(36,734,531)**	(80,564,310)
Sales or maturities of long-term investments	**37,141,737**	81,369,063
Net cash provided by investing activities	**201,700**	532,457
Cash Flows from Financing Activities		
Collection of gifts restricted for long-term purposes	**7,150**	80,625
Collection of interest and dividends for long-term purposes	**43,865**	44,430
Net cash provided by financing activities	**51,015**	125,055
Net Increase in Cash	**599,950**	184,727
Cash and Cash Equivalents, at beginning of year	**952,999**	768,272
Cash and Cash Equivalents, at end of year	**$ 1,552,949**	$ 952,999

See accompanying notes to financial statements.

Notes to Financial Statements

1. Summary of Significant Accounting Policies

History

The American Philosophical Society is a nonprofit corporation whose purpose is the promotion of useful knowledge. It was originally established in 1743, and incorporated under the laws of the Commonwealth of Pennsylvania in 1780. Its articles were amended in 1935. The Society receives revenues primarily from investment income, gifts and grants, and the sales of publications.

Basis of Accounting

The financial statements of the Society have been prepared on the accrual basis of accounting and, accordingly, reflect all significant receivables, payables, and other liabilities.

Basis of Presentation

Financial statement presentation follows the recommendations of the Financial Accounting Standards Board in its Statement of Financial Accounting Standards (SFAS) No. 117, *Financial Statements of Not-for-Profit Organizations*. Under SFAS No. 117, the Organization is required to report information regarding its financial statements according to three classes of net assets; unrestricted net assets, temporarily restricted net assets, and permanently restricted net assets.

Use of Estimates

The preparation of financial statements in conformity with generally accepted accounting principles requires management to make estimates and assumptions that affect certain reported amounts and disclosures. Accordingly, actual results could differ from those estimates.

Cash and Cash Equivalents

For purposes of the Statement of Cash Flows, the Society considers all unrestricted highly liquid investments with an initial maturity of three months or less to be cash equivalents.

Notes to Financial Statements

Contributions

The Society accounts for contributions in accordance with the recommendations of the Financial Accounting Standards Board in SFAS No. 116, *Accounting for Contributions Received and Contributions Made*. In accordance with SFAS No. 116, contributions received are recorded as unrestricted, temporarily restricted, or permanently restricted support, depending on the existence of any donor restrictions.

All donor-restricted support is reported as an increase in temporarily or permanently restricted net assets depending on the nature of the restriction. When a restriction expires (that is, when a stipulated time restriction ends or purpose restriction is accomplished), temporarily restricted net assets are reclassified to unrestricted net assets and reported in the statement of activities as net assets released from restrictions.

For the year ended December 31, 1998, one gift represents 30% of the unrestricted grants and gifts and one grant represents 81% of the temporarily restricted grants and gifts.

For the year ended December 31, 1997, grants from two entities aggregate 63% and 17% of the total temporarily restricted grants and gifts.

Contributed Facilities

The Society occupies, without charge, certain premises located on government owned land. The estimated fair rental value of $450,000 is reported as revenue and expense in the period in which the premises are used.

Donated Collection Items

In accordance with the provisions of SFAS No. 116, *Accounting for Contributions Received and Contributions Made*, the Society does not capitalize donated works of art, books, or manuscripts or recognize them as revenues or gains. That Statement provides that such donations need not be recognized if they are added to the collections that are held for public exhibition, education, or research in furtherance of public service rather than financial gain; are protected, kept unencumbered, cared for, and preserved; and are subject to a policy that requires the proceeds from sales of collection items to be used to acquire other items for the collections.

Fixed Assets and Depreciation

Fixed assets are stated at cost. Depreciation is provided over the estimated useful lives of the assets on a straight-line basis. Costs of office furnishings and equipment are charged to expense because the amounts are immaterial.

Notes to Financial Statements

Functional Allocation of Expenses

The costs of providing the various programs and activities have been summarized on a functional basis in the Statement of Activities. Accordingly, certain costs have been allocated among the programs and supporting services benefitted.

Income Tax Status

The Society is a publicly supported tax exempt organization in accordance with the provisions of Internal Revenue Code Section 501(c)(3) as amended by the Tax Reform Act of 1969. Accordingly, no provision for federal income taxes has been made.

Investments

Investments are valued at their fair market value based on quoted market prices.

Investment Pool

The Society maintains a master investment account for its endowments and quasi-endowments. Realized and unrealized gains and losses from securities in the master investment account are allocated quarterly to the individual endowments based on the relationship of the market value of each endowment or quasi-endowment to the total market value of the master investment account, as adjusted for additions to or deductions from those accounts.

Promises to Give

Unconditional promises to give are recognized as revenues or gains in the period received and as assets, decreases of liabilities, or expenses depending on the form of the benefits received. Conditional promises to give are recognized when the conditions on which they depend are substantially met.

2. Promises to Give

Unconditional promises to give are as follows:

December 31,	1998	1997
Receivable in less than one year	$3,194	$3,194
Less allowance for uncollectible promises receivable	-	-
Net unconditional promises to give	$3,194	$3,194

At December 31, 1998 and 1997, there were no conditional promises to give.

Notes to Financial Statements

3. Deferred Expenses

The following amounts have been designated by the Executive Committee for the following future uses.

December 31,	1998	1997
Philosophical Hall repairs	$ -	$ 90,000
Joint meeting with the Royal Swedish Academy of Sciences	-	35,000
Bell's sketches	58,785	58,785
Supplemental pension benefits	59,510	59,510
	$118,295	$243,295

4. Land, Buildings and Equipment

The following is a detail of the property and equipment account:

December 31,	1998	1997
Franklin Hall including restoration costs	$10,926,825	$10,860,808
Library Hall including renovation costs	3,537,845	3,261,777
Renovation costs including Philosophical Hall	1,102,928	570,623
	15,567,598	14,693,208
Less accumulated depreciation	4,922,962	4,536,552
	$10,644,636	$10,156,656

Depreciation expense on the above assets aggregated $386,444 for 1998 and $371,306 for 1997.

During 1998, the Society entered into contracts aggregating approximately $2,305,000 for the renovation of Philosophical Hall. At December 31, 1998, $366,436 was expended under the terms of these contracts and included in the Philosophical Hall renovation costs.

Notes to Financial Statements

5. Investments

Investments are comprised of the following:

December 31,			1998
	Carrying Value	Market Value	Gross Unrealized Gains (Losses)
Equity securities	$53,499,259	$ 82,665,688	$29,166,429
Mutual funds	35,029,015	34,433,929	(595,086)
Cash and cash equivalents	692,986	692,986	-
	$89,221,260	$117,792,603	$28,571,343

December 31,			1997
	Carrying Value	Market Value	Gross Unrealized Gains (Losses)
Equity securities	$46,534,757	$64,444,780	$17,910,023
Mutual funds	33,721,004	32,550,762	(1,170,242)
Cash and cash equivalents	1,361,905	1,361,905	-
	$81,617,666	$98,357,447	$16,739,781

6. Inexhaustible Collections

The Society's accounts do not include values for Philosophical Hall, built between 1785 and 1789, a national historic landmark, and its collection of books, manuscripts and works of art.

Notes to Financial Statements

7. Employee Benefit Plans

The Society sponsors a defined benefit pension plan that covers substantially all of its employees. The plan calls for benefits to be paid to eligible employees at retirement based primarily upon years of service with the Society and compensation rates near retirement. Contributions to the plan reflect benefits attributed to employees' services to date, as well as services expected to be earned in the future. Plan assets consist primarily of investments in money market, fixed income and equity mutual funds.

December 31,	1998	1997
Benefit cost	$ 15,918	$ 13,209
Employer contribution	$ -	$ -
Plan participants' contributions	$ -	$ -
Benefits paid	$139,027	$118,697

December 31,	1998	1997
Assumptions		
Discount rate for plan obligations	7.25%	7.75%
Expected long-term rate of return on plan assets	9.00%	9.00%
Annual compensation increases	5.00%	5.00%

The funded status of the pension plan, the prepaid benefit cost, and assumptions are as follows:

December 31,	1998	1997
Benefit obligation	$(2,114,386)	$(1,784,632)
Plan assets at fair value	2,223,912	2,098,360
Funded status	$ 109,526	$ 313,728
Prepaid benefit cost recognized in the statement of financial position	$ 29,667	$ 45,585

Notes to Financial Statements

December 31,	1998	1997
Assumptions		
Discount rate for plan obligations	**6.75%**	7.25%
Expected long-term rate of return		
on plan assets	**9.00%**	9.00%
Annual compensation increases	**5.00%**	5.00%

The actuarial valuation of projected benefit obligations is based on the actuarial reports of the 1998 and 1997 plan years as of January 1, 1998 and 1997, respectively.

Effective January 1, 1992, the Society implemented a contributory, defined contribution retirement plan in which all full-time and some part-time employees are eligible to participate. The plan has been funded through individually owned annuities issued by Teachers' Insurance and Annuity Association (TIAA) and College Retirement Equities Fund (CREF). There are no unfunded past Service Costs. The total contributions made by the Society were $27,954 and $27,419 in 1998 and 1997, respectively. Individuals are immediately vested in their contributions.

The Society sponsors a defined benefit postretirement health care plan covering substantially all employees. The plan is noncontributory. The Society currently sees no need, at this time, for setting a formal policy for funding this plan. The cost of employee and retiree health insurance is currently paid by the Society annually as the cost is incurred.

The following table sets forth the plan's funded status, the accrued benefits cost, and the assumptions:

December 31,	1998	1997
Benefit obligation	**$(523,238)**	$(469,031)
Plan assets at fair value	**-**	-
Funded status	**$(523,238)**	$(469,031)
Accrued postretirement benefit cost recognized		
in the statement of financial position	**$(389,545)**	$(374,569)

Notes to Financial Statements

Postretirement expense includes the following components:

December 31,	1998	1997
Benefit cost	$14,976	$21,430
Employer contribution	$ -	$ -
Plan participants' contributions	$ -	$ -
Benefits paid	$39,217	$23,068

For measurement purposes, 5.5% and 6.5% annual rate of increase in the per capita cost of covered health care benefits was assumed for 1998 and 1997, respectively. The rate was assumed to decrease gradually to 5.5% in 1998 and remain at that level thereafter.

The weighted-average discount rate used in determining the accumulated postretirement obligation was 6.75% in 1998 and 7.25% in 1997

8. Restrictions on Net Assets

Temporarily restricted net assets are available for the following purposes or periods:

December 31,	1998	1997
Administrative activities	$ (7,124)	$ 3,035
Research activities	73,509	136,000
Publications activities	3,433	337
Meetings activities	(2,092)	45
Library activities	128,686	144,574
Special purpose funds activities	1,928,171	794,902
Buildings and equipment	3,195	3,195
	$2,127,778	$1,082,088

Permanently restricted net assets are restricted to:

December 31,	1998	1997
Administrative activities	$ 1,938,032	$ 1,606,697
Research activities	8,804,841	7,336,712
Publications activities	1,770,717	1,475,479
Meetings activities	506,545	415,957
Library activities	6,562,691	5,465,322
Franklin Hall activities	154,894	125,809
Any activities of the organization	80,753,254	67,474,486
	$100,490,974	$83,900,462

Notes to Financial Statements

9. **Concentrations of Credit Risk**

The Society has cash and cash equivalents in excess of $100,000 on deposit in its bank. The Federal Deposit Insurance Corporation (FDIC) insures only the first $100,000 of funds at member banks.

10. **Beneficial Interest Trusts**

The Society is the beneficiary under a number of trusts administered by two banks. The assets of the trusts are not included in the Statement of Financial Position of the Society since the Society does not exercise any control over those funds. The income from the trusts for 1998 and 1997 was $73,294 and $115,576, respectively.

11. **Pooled Life Income Fund Plan**

The Society has established a Pooled Life Income Fund Plan exclusively for the management and investment of property transferred to the Society by donors contributing irrevocable remainder interests in the property and creating income interests for the life of the donor or donor's beneficiaries. Upon death of the last income beneficiary, the Society shall receive an amount equal to the fair market value of the donated property. The plan is operated in accordance with the Internal Revenue Code and Rulings governing Pooled Life Income Funds. Accordingly, assets that are applicable to donors with living income beneficiaries (market value of $281,723 in 1998 and $269,169 in 1997) are not reflected in the accounts of the Society as of December 31, 1998 and 1997.

12. **Year 2000 Issues**

Like other entities, the Society could be adversely affected if the computer systems our suppliers or grantors use do not properly process and calculate date - related information and data from the period surrounding and including January 1, 2000. This is commonly known as the "Year 2000" issue. Additionally, this issue could impact noncomputer systems and devices such as alarm systems, etc. At this time, because of the complexities involved in the issue, management cannot provide assurances that the Year 2000 issue will not have an impact on the Society's operations.

13. **Subsequent Event**

On March 11, 1999 the Society received a bequest of "not less than one million five hundred thousand dollars and not more than two million five hundred thousand dollars" to be used by the Society for its general purposes.

No specific amount for this bequest has been determined as of the date of this report.

Independent Auditors' Report on Additional Information

American Philosophical Society
Philadelphia, Pennsylvania

Our report on our audits of the basic financial statements of the American Philosophical Society for 1998 and 1997 appears on page 3. Those audits were conducted for the purpose of forming an opinion on the basic financial statements taken as a whole. The accompanying information on pages 18 to 31 is presented for purposes of additional analysis and is not a required part of the basic financial statements. Such information has been subjected to the auditing procedures applied in the audits of the basic financial statements and, in our opinion, is fairly stated in all material respects in relation to the basic financial statements for the years ended December 31, 1998 and 1997, taken as a whole.

Howe, Keller & Hunter, P.C.

HOWE, KELLER & HUNTER, P.C.

March 23, 1999

Schedules of Investments
Common Fund

December 31,			1998
Number of Shares	Description	Cost	Market Value

Common Stock

Number of Shares	Description	Cost	Market Value
26,400	American Home Products Corp. Com.	$1,506,830	$1,488,300
32,300	Applied Materials, Inc. Com.	1,212,862	1,378,806
16,050	American International Group, Inc. Com.	232,525	1,550,831
16,900	Archstone Communities Trust Sh. Ben. Int.	382,896	342,225
44,400	Associates First Capital Corp. CL A Com.	1,203,845	1,881,450
26,100	Avery Dennison Corp. Com.	444,731	1,176,131
30,923	BankAmerica Corp. Com.	1,286,972	1,859,245
22,800	Bell Atlantic Corp. Com.	1,159,186	1,231,200
5,800	Bowater, Inc. Com.	311,725	240,338
33,800	Carnival Corp. CL A Com.	247,204	1,622,400
6,000	Champion International Corp. Com.	298,076	243,000
8,755	Chris Craft Industries, Inc. Com.	430,607	421,882
30,300	Cisco Systems, Inc. Com.	1,013,995	2,812,219
36,250	Citigroup, Inc. Com.	548,164	1,801,172
39,200	Compaq Computer Corp. Com.	1,198,107	1,646,400
6,700	Conseco, Inc. Com.	272,740	204,350
16,400	Cooper Tire and Rubber Co. Com.	387,743	335,175
23,700	Cyprus Amax Minerals Co. Com.	472,809	237,000
19,200	Duke Realty Investments, Inc. REIT	432,541	446,400
15,133	EEX Corp. Com.	384,771	105,931
19,700	EMC Corp. Mass. Com.	882,562	1,674,500
10,100	Entergy Corp. New Com.	307,870	314,363
26,700	Exxon Corp. Com.	1,096,862	1,952,438
19,000	Firststar Corp. Wisconsin Com.	1,062,053	1,767,000
12,700	Fleetwood Enterprises, Inc. Com.	393,954	441,325
10,000	Freddie Mac Com.	327,700	644,375
30,900	General Electric Co. Com.	1,488,574	3,151,800
30,014	Gillette Co. Com.	921,529	1,435,044
9,500	Healthcare Realty Trust Com.	269,484	210,188
29,000	Hollinger International, Inc. CL A Com.	439,972	404,188
27,000	Home Depot, Inc. Com.	371,065	1,652,062
21,600	Illinois Tool Works, Inc. Com.	1,241,923	1,252,800
15,900	Intel Corp. Com.	746,043	1,885,144
18,300	Interpublic Group Cos, Inc. Com.	1,168,162	1,459,425
19,200	Estee Lauder Cos., Inc. CL A Com.	923,503	1,641,600
8,900	LTV Corp. New Com.	113,962	51,175
11,200	MBIA, Inc. Com.	656,984	734,300
37,160	MCI Worldcom, Inc. Com.	1,131,475	2,666,230
17,500	Meditrust Paired CTF	470,002	262,500
32,400	Medtronic, Inc. Com.	1,846,843	2,406,714
10,960	Merck & Co., Inc. Com.	804,045	1,616,600
19,000	Microsoft Corp. Com.	842,926	2,635,062

Schedules of Investments
Common Fund

December 31,			1998
Number of Shares	Description	Cost	Market Value

Common Stock

18,700	Mobil Corp. Com.	$ 1,041,072	$ 1,629,237
19,000	NCR Corp. New Com.	609,132	793,250
6,800	New England Electric Systems Com.	263,799	327,250
6,700	Nucor Corp. Com.	321,514	289,775
11,500	OM Group, Inc. Com.	417,611	419,750
12,700	PP&L Resources, Inc. Com.	319,104	354,013
32,800	Parker Drilling Co. Com.	422,956	104,550
11,200	Pfizer, Inc. Com.	594,367	1,400,000
12,100	Pinnacle West Capital Corp. Com.	432,294	512,738
30,005	Pioneer Hi Bred International, Inc. Com.	941,675	795,132
20,200	Proctor & Gamble Co. Com.	1,524,149	1,844,512
33,900	Ralston Purina Co. Com.	900,540	1,089,037
3,900	Readers Digest Assn., Inc. CL A Com.	97,421	98,231
5,050	Reinsurance Group America, Inc. Com.	194,641	353,500
40,300	SBC Communications, Inc. Com.	1,725,618	2,161,087
35,700	Safeway, Inc. New Com.	966,195	2,175,469
16,300	Santa Fe Energy Resources Com.	152,120	118,175
5,700	Sbarro, Inc. Com.	150,951	149,269
28,800	Schering Plough Corp. Com.	999,903	1,591,200
30,200	Schlumberger Ltd. Com.	1,053,532	1,400,525
17,600	Seagate Technology Com.	557,510	532,400
11,000	Silicon Graphics, Inc. Com.	144,818	141,625
20,745	Sprint Corp. Com. (FON Group)	981,335	1,745,173
8,222	Sprint Corp. Com. (PCS Group)	76,008	190,134
36,100	Staples, Inc. Com.	557,478	1,577,118
10,050	Sunamerica, Inc. Com.	377,846	824,100
15,700	Texas Instruments, Inc. Com.	848,697	1,344,313
8,900	Tidewater, Inc. Com.	452,965	206,369
13,300	Trigon Healthcare, Inc. Com.	305,301	496,256
15,000	Triton Energy Ltd. Com.	579,879	119,063
1,080	Triton Energy Rights	1,080	1,080
18,900	Trizec Hahn Corp. Sub. Vtg.	427,946	387,450
8,300	UNIFI, Inc. Com.	314,722	162,369
28,200	WalMart Stores, Inc. Com.	1,154,332	2,296,538
17,800	Warnaco Group, Inc. CL A Com.	556,186	449,450
11,800	Washington Real Estate Inv. Tr. SBI	189,373	219,775
15,100	Wellman, Inc. Com.	345,307	153,831
6,900	Wellpoint Health Networks, Inc. CL A Com.	350,744	600,300
58,300	Wells Fargo & Co. New Com.	1,213,316	2,328,356
	Total Common Stock	**$53,499,259**	**$82,665,688**

Schedules of Investments
Common Fund

December 31,			1998
Number of Shares	**Description**	**Cost**	**Market Value**
	Mutual Funds		
2,142,009	MAS - Fixed Income Institutional	$25,806,019	$25,082,925
438,741	Vanguard International Growth Fund	8,117,395	8,235,177
	Total Mutual Funds	**$33,923,414**	**$33,318,102**
	Cash and Cash Equivalents		
	SEI Daily Income Trust Prime Obligation Fund	$ 807,474	$ 807,474
	Total Cash and Cash Equivalents	**$ 807,474**	**$ 807,474**

Summary of Investments
Common Fund

December 31, 1998

# of Units Outstanding	Name of Fund	Cost	Market Value	Cost Per Unit	Market Value Per Unit
6,077,916	Common Fund	$88,230,147	$116,791,264	$14.52	$19.22

Schedules of Expenses

Year Ended December 31,	1998	1997
Administrative		
Society operations		
Financial and legal services		
Bank charges	$ 5,052	$ 7,266
Custodian	3,802	257
Investment advisor	55,898	42,717
Auditor	45,881	43,731
Actuary	28,766	16,909
Legal counsel	41,790	29,837
Payroll service	3,327	2,543
Curator allowance	570	10,000
Insurance	63,963	61,280
Office expenses		
Supplies	15,156	20,296
Telephone	48,109	33,856
Postage	27,625	22,577
Copier	12,257	8,272
Office machine maintenance	2,407	2,287
Computer services	39,847	43,521
Travel and public relations		
Professional services	-	5,000
Exchanges	1,805	59
Committees	16,546	21,097
Development expenses	3,326	-
Staff	11,484	5,140
Dues	4,400	3,654
Newsletter	-	-
Publications		
Yearbook and Proceedings	12,126	11,925
Total society operations	**$444,137**	**$392,224**

Schedules of Expenses

Year Ended December 31,	1998	1997
Administrative (continued)		
Building maintenance		
Janitorial supplies	$ 1,852	$ 799
Miscellaneous services		
Exterminator	720	121
Elevator	25	-
Window cleaning	625	1,338
Drinking water	632	1,142
Repairs	17,472	6,379
Air conditioning		
Machinery (includes controls and water treatment)	17,856	20,802
Utilities		
Electricity	15,689	12,845
Steam	5,214	9,858
Gas	-	468
Water and sewer	899	918
Security		
Burglary	6,548	6,536
Fire	3,956	3,417
Fire extinguishers	-	23
Jefferson Garden	673	725
Michaux	43,615	-
Total building maintenance	**$115,776**	**$ 65,371**
Prizes and honoraria		
Jacques Barzun Prize	$ 3,037	$ 3,518
Franklin Award	-	795
Franklin Medal	1,497	1,656
Jefferson Medal	1,372	552
Lashely Award	26,589	-
J.F. Lewis Prize	8,394	-
Rhoads Lecture	4,245	-
Moe Prize	2,774	2,847
Penrose Lecture	-	2,000
Phillips Prize	-	5,295
Magellanic Premium	3,314	2,904
Total prizes and honoraria	**$ 51,222**	**$ 19,567**

Schedules of Expenses

Year Ended December 31,	1998	1997
Administrative (concluded)		
Temporary help services	$ 3,831	$ 1,084
U.C. reimbursement	9,379	6,973
General contingency	43,139	82,196
President's discretionary	65	302
Hays Bequest	7,500	7,500
Periodic pension cost (FASB)	15,918	13,209
Periodic postretirement benefit cost (FASB)	14,976	21,430
Depreciation	17,923	13,075
Portraits expense	3,500	-
	116,231	145,769
Total administrative	**$727,366**	**$622,931**
Research		
Personnel	**$139,955**	**$129,662**
General		
Society appropriation	277,705	269,780
Hays Bequest	42,200	49,610
Jayne Bequest	15,000	15,000
Goldstine	3,550	2,300
Specialized		
Daland Bequest	141,000	124,000
Michaux Bequest	3,000	3,505
Phillips Library	31,666	25,698
Phillips Prize	12,900	9,500
Slater	12,000	12,000
Economic Research	-	1,730
Supplies	3,079	5,345
Total research	**$682,055**	**$648,130**

Schedules of Expenses

Year Ended December 31,	1998	1997
Publications		
Personnel	$275,374	$250,802
Newsletter	6,774	5,783
Printing, binding and advertisement	104,397	112,466
Manuscript review	3,728	6,998
Yearbook/Grantee Report	14,637	10,823
Fulfillment		
Storage	17,653	13,513
Postage and freight	10,556	10,323
Outside services	7,925	8,376
Supplies	4,258	2,710
Sales expense	856	1,050
Bad debts (recoveries)	-	(5,053)
External bequests		
J.F. Lewis	14,193	10,049
Moe	-	2,400
Moe Prize	-	800
University Extension - Jayne	8,855	12,861
Neugebauer Fund	3,000	3,081
Delmas - Publications	15,647	13,098
Miscellaneous	2,064	2,012
Bell's sketches	20,739	-
Total publications	**$510,656**	**$462,092**

Schedules of Expenses

Year Ended December 31,	1998	1997
Meetings		
Personnel	$234,241	$231,044
Accommodations	33,674	33,073
Meals		
Luncheons	49,088	42,949
Dinners	41,404	45,019
External bequests		
Jayne Bequest	15,598	7,261
Entertainment	4,528	900
Program	4,201	3,796
Audio/video	5,678	8,960
Travel	9,112	3,730
Special meeting	53,271	3,293
Miscellaneous	880	-
Nominations and ballots	6,439	865
Supplies	260	3,058
Meetings/events	262	-
Members directory	1,313	608
Wistar meetings	12,521	3,216
Professional services	-	62
Engraving/calligraphy	1,015	596
Temporary help services	130	-
Dues and subscriptions	956	-
Printing, binding and advertising	2,948	-
Total meetings	**$477,519**	**$388,430**

Schedules of Expenses

Year Ended December 31,	1998	1997
Library		
Personnel		
Personnel	$737,734	$747,241
Delmas	13,978	12,617
Greenewalt	10,389	9,377
Mellon VI	53,706	48,478
Total personnel	815,807	817,713
Books and manuscripts		
Hays Bequest	69,126	54,989
Hays Reserve	1,661	6,262
External bequests		
Balch	436	4,034
Boye	128	-
Michaux	2,996	5,227
Magellanic	275	120
Internal bequests		
Carlier	7,450	7,276
Seybert	1,679	1,597
Stephanson	1,100	-
Tilghman	(28)	616
Friends of the Library	3,814	210
Total books and manuscripts	88,637	80,331
Library operations		
Office equipment and supplies	$ 9,821	$ 9,340
Office machine maintenance	754	621
Dues and subscriptions	508	1,100
Computer services	25,666	46,944
Professional services	1,250	1,300
Photography department		
Contract services	9,499	5,482
Supplies	861	155
Copier	135	3,722
Manuscripts department		
Supplies	-	1,798
Conservation department		
Supplies	15	322
Travel and public relations		
Staff	10,693	9,443
Friends promotion	16,712	17,641
Mendel newsletter	947	1,064
Rent	450,000	450,000
Exchanges	9,726	10,924
Special funds		
Lindback Bequest	3,728	6,142
Mellon I Bequest	19,866	41,103
Osterhout Bequest	2,520	8,173
Phillips Bequest	4,138	3,447
Temporary help services	6,257	-
Total library operations	573,096	618,721

Schedules of Expenses

Year Ended December 31,	1998	1997
Library (concluded)		
Library building maintenance		
Janitorial supplies	$ 3,102	$ 4,880
Miscellaneous services		
Exterminator	638	523
Elevator	7,032	6,309
Window cleaning	3,700	3,830
Drinking water	1,158	500
Repairs	51,522	38,635
Air conditioning		
Machinery (includes water treatment)	10,772	18,614
Controls	9,260	9,740
Carnegie	17,204	17,335
Utilities		
Electricity	63,989	60,551
Steam	38,853	37,508
Gas	95	(78)
Water and sewer	4,252	4,806
Security		
Burglary	3,991	22,968
Fire	10,208	113
Fire extinguishers	152	340
Halon	2,091	5,330
Total library building maintenance	228,019	231,904
Depreciation	86,344	79,682
Total library	**$1,791,903**	**$1,828,351**

Schedules of Expenses

Year Ended December 31,	1998	1997
Franklin Hall		
Building maintenance		
Janitorial supplies	$ 3,859	$ 1,354
Miscellaneous services		
Exterminator	905	678
Elevator	7,634	6,760
Window cleaning	640	662
Lift	317	2,046
Repairs	20,956	75,766
Air conditioning		
Machinery	36,839	12,416
Utilities		
Electricity	53,385	54,880
Steam	12,309	22,432
Water and sewer	-	2,268
Security		
Fire extinguishers	214	4,158
Burglary	5,133	4,385
Halon	934	7,094
Sprinkler	1,710	2,250
Total building maintenance	144,835	197,149
Depreciation	282,177	278,550
Total Franklin Hall	**$427,012**	**$475,699**
Special purpose funds		
Curatorial	$ -	$ 11,604
Mellon Humanities	7,815	-
Mellon III Grant	17,021	21,613
Mellon IV Grant	-	790
Mellon V Grant	15,582	10,500
Mellon VII Grant	-	22,116
Mellon VIII Grant	112,372	87,740
Hewlett-Research	12,500	-
Hewlett-Library	3,536	-
Rhoads Lecture	-	27,234
Publication subsidies		
Consolidated Publication	13,200	46,566
Haney	-	3,500
Total special purpose funds	**$182,026**	**$231,663**

Schedules of Expenses

Year Ended December 31,	1998	1997
Development		
Fund raising		
Personnel	$ -	$ 104,114
Program		
Publications	-	1,082
Travel	-	1,235
Supplies	-	830
Subscriptions	-	1,546
Telecommunications	-	1,752
Postage	-	909
Computer services	-	23
Bad debts	-	800
Professional services	-	10,001
Total development	$ -	$ 122,292
Total expenses	**$4,798,537**	**$4,779,588**

THE ORIGINS OF THE AMERICAN PHILOSOPHICAL SOCIETY, like those of most institutions, antedate its founding. For some years during the second quarter of the eighteenth century Philadelphians like James Logan and Joseph Breintnall had corresponded with the Royal Society of London, to which nineteen Americans were elected before 1743. They and practical men of affairs were also acquainted with the purposes and work of the Dublin Philosophical Society, founded in 1731 "for improving Husbandry, Manufactures, and other useful Arts." In 1739 John Bartram, a Philadelphia Quaker farmer with a taste for natural history, who was a correspondent of several English and Continental botanists, proposed that a society or academy of the "most ingenious and curious men" be established in America to promote inquiries into "natural secrets, arts & syances." It should have a house of its own, sponsor lectures, and underwrite expeditions. The plan was, of course, too ambitious for the colonies, as Bartram's friends quickly told him. But four years later, in 1743, Benjamin Franklin took up Bartram's idea, revised and simplified it, and offered his fellow Americans "A Proposal for Promoting Useful Knowledge among the British Plantations in America."

The first Drudgery of Settling new Colonies, which confines the Attention of People to mere Necessaries, is now pretty well over; and there are many in every Province in Circumstances that set them at Ease, and afford Leisure to cultivate the finer Arts, and improve the common Stock of Knowledge. To such of these who are Men of Speculation, many Hints must from time to time arise, many Observations occur, which if well-examined, pursued and improved, might produce Discoveries to the Advantage of some or all of the British Plantations, or to the Benefit of Mankind in general.

But as from the Extent of the Country, such Persons are widely separated, and seldom can see and converse, or be acquainted with each other, so that many useful Particulars remain uncommunicated, die with the Discoverers, and are lost to Mankind; it is, to remedy this Inconvenience for the future, proposed. That One Society be formed of Virtuosi or ingenious Men residing in the several Colonies, to be called the American Philosophical Society; who are to maintain a constant Correspondence.

That Philadelphia being the City nearest the Centre of the Continent-Colonies, communicating with all of them northward and southward by Post, and with all the Islands by Sea, and having the Advantage of a good growing Library, be the Centre of the Society.

* * *

That the Subjects of the Correspondence be, all new-discovered Plants, Herbs, Trees, Roots, &c. Methods of Propagating them, and making such as are useful, but particular to some Plantations, more general. Improvements of vegetable Juices, as Cyders, Wines &c. New Methods of Curing or Preventing Diseases. All new-discovered Fossils in different Countries, as Mines, Minerals, Quarries, &c. New and useful Improvements in Distillation, Brewing, Assaying of Ores. &c. New mechanical Inventions for Saving Labour; as Mills, Carriages, &c. and for Raising and Conveying of Water, Draining of Meadows, &c. All new Arts, Trades, Manufactures, &c. that may be proposed or thought of. Surveys, Maps and Charts of particular Parts f the Sea-coasts, or Inland Countries; Course and Junction of Rivers and great Roads, Situation of Lakes and Mountains, Nature of the Soil and Productions, &c. New Methods of Improving the Breed of useful Animals, Introducing other Sorts from foreign Countries. New Improvements in Planting, Gardening, Clearing Land, &c. And all philosophical Experiments that let Light into the Nature of Things, tend to increase the Power of Man over Matter, and multiply the Conveniences or Pleasure of Life.

The American Philosophical Society was organized on this plan in early 1744. It held several meetings, elected to membership such men as the naturalists Dr. John Clayton and Dr. John Mitchell of Virginia, and the mathematicians James Alexander and Cadwalader Colden of New York, and received learned papers, which Franklin planned to publish in an American philosophical miscellany. But interest soon lagged—the Philadelphia members, on whom success depended, Franklin complained, "are very idle Gentlemen; they will take no Pains"—and by 1746 the Society was moribund, if not dead.

Twenty years later, in the wake of American resistance to the Stamp Act, another society was formed. Calling itself the American Society for Promoting Useful Knowledge, it was composed of younger Philadelphians, generally antiproprietary in politics, champions of American rights, who were determined to strengthen the colonies economically as well as politically. Charles Thomson, later secretary of the Continental Congress, spelled out its program: improved methods of farming, including the breeding of livestock, new medicines and cures for specific diseases, new manufactures and improvements in the old, new sources of mineral wealth. "But it is not proposed," he added, "to confine the view of the Society, wholly, to these things, so as to exclude other useful subjects, either in physics, mechanics, astronomy, mathematics, &c." The Society proved astonishingly successful. But older men, including survivors of the 1743 group, many of whom were members of the Proprietary Party, taking umbrage that they had not been invited to join, revived the American Philosophical Society, which they claimed had only been "dormant." In 1768, therefore, there were two societies of similar purpose, organization, and scope, though distinguished by the political and religious views of their Philadelphia members. Both were intercolonial and even international in membership. Good sense and good will eventually prevailed, and on 2 January 1769, the two societies were merged as "The American Philosophical Society, held at Philadelphia, for Promoting Useful Knowledge." Franklin, who was then a colonial agent in England, was chosen president. In its work the new society reflected both the spirit of the Royal Society, its prototype, and the practical concerns of the original American Society for Promoting Useful Knowledge and its model, the Society of Arts of London. It sponsored the survey of a canal to link the Chesapeake Bay to the Delaware River, and so bring the trade of Maryland into the port of Philadelphia; and it conducted observations of the transit of Venus in 1769, which, published in the Royal Society's *Philosophical Transactions*, at once established the Philadelphia society's international reputation. These observations were also reported in the Society's own *Transactions*, of which the first volume appeared in 1771. Copies were sent to the learned academies of Europe, which responded with copies of their own publications: and thus were established exchanges which continue to the present day.

Meetings of the Society were interrupted for a short time during the American Revolution, but were resumed in 1779. The next decade saw a vigorous renewal of activity. A second volume of *Transactions* was issued in 1786, a bequest of £200 was received to establish the first of the Society's prizes, a charter was obtained from the Commonwealth in 1780, a portion of the State House Yard was deeded to the Society in 1785, and there Philosophical Hall was constructed in 1785–89. The persons principally responsible for this reawakening were Francis Hopkinson, a state official and signer of the Declaration of Independence, and Samuel Vaughan, an English Whig and friend of America, now a resident of Philadelphia. Vaughan's son John remained in Philadelphia, where he became treasurer of the Society in 1791 and librarian in 1803, holding both posts until his death in 1841.

As the principal learned society in the United States, the Society in the early years of the republic often served as a national library, museum, and academy of sciences. Thomas Jefferson, who was president of the United States and of the Society simultaneously, called on it for advice: at his request, for example, the Society prepared what were in effect the scientific instructions for Lewis and Clark, and Jefferson deposited the report of their expedition in the Society's library, where it remains. Other officers and departments of government called on the Society for the loan of maps, telescopes, and other scientific apparatus; while John Quincy Adams borrowed from the Society a crate of books on weights and measures, which he consulted at Quincy during the summer he composed his great report on the subject.

Accepting the presidency of the Society in 1797, Jefferson asserted that the Society "comprehends whatever the American World has of distinction in Philosophy & Science in general." So it must have seemed. The members felt their obligation to promote American science and learning in all possible ways. They offered a premium for the plan of education best calculated to promote the welfare of a republic, and another on whether it was "the duty and interest of the Community, to provide for the Education of Youth." At the same time they continued to encourage discoveries in new and applied science—ships' pumps, stoves and fireplaces, peach blight, vegetable dyes, street lighting. And Jefferson and others placed in the library hundreds of word-lists and other materials that recorded and illustrated the life, customs, and languages of the Indian inhabitants of America.

After mid-century, however, the Society's position in the learned world was no longer unique or preeminent. Other institutions were meeting the needs of the growing scientific community. Societies like the Academy of Natural Sciences of Philadelphia appealed to specialists; Silliman's *Journal* offered speedy publication of learned papers. Furthermore, the federal government, which originally supported no agencies for science, now created several of its own—the Coast and Geodetic Survey, the Corps of Topographical Engineers, and finally the Smithsonian Institution. The Society, on the other hand, though it recognized men of distinction throughout the country and seldom failed to elect those who might be thought to deserve election, was primarily a Philadelphia institution, in the hands of local people. On top of all this, the Society suffered from an ill-advised scheme to move away from Independence Square, which left it so deeply in debt that at one point the sheriff nearly levied on its Library. The centenary of its founding, in 1843, was an occasion of thoughtful reassessment by some members, but in the end few hopeful answers were offered to changing conditions and new problems and opportunities. One of the few was the establishment of the monthly *Proceedings*. Joseph Henry's reports of his researches at Princeton were printed in them.

In the last half of the nineteenth century the Society continued in its traditional pattern, without vigor or originality. Henry Thoreau on a visit to Philadelphia was told its members were "a company of old women"; Sidney George Fisher thought meetings "insufferably dull and stupid"; while the geologist J. Peter Lesley recalled that when he was a new member in the latter 1850s, the older members raced through the formal business meeting, offering scant comment or praise to the authors of papers, then drew their chairs around the fire to exchange gossip, jokes, and even ribald stories. Though some significant proposals were made—one by Ferdinand V. Hayden, for example, for a photographic survey of the Indians of the West, another to study an international language—the Society had neither staff, financial means, nor, it seems, sustained interest, to carry them forward. The Society did not even control all of its own hall: tenants, whose rental payments were necessary to pay expenses, occupied space there until 1934.

A significant revival began early in the twentieth century, thanks to the imaginative and energetic leadership of Dr. I. Minis Hays, librarian from 1897 to

1922. Historical documents in the Society's Library were edited and published, calendars of several large collections were prepared, and in 1902 a general annual meeting was instituted. This did much to engage the interest of the members in their Society and, by making it worthwhile and attractive for non-resident members to come to Philadelphia, gave a national flavor to the meetings and signalized the national character of the Society. The annual general meeting, in the judgment of one officer, soon became "the most important and most interesting scientific event of the year."

A reassessment of the Society's achievements and possibilities in 1927–29 led to plans to make it a kind of clearinghouse of scientific information pouring in upon the public. This required the construction of enlarged quarters—an "Aristotle's House"—in a more prestigious location than the now-deteriorating Independence Hall area. A building campaign was inaugurated in 1930 but the time was unpropitious—the great depression was then spreading over the country—and though some contributions were received, the plans were laid aside. Meanwhile, however, in 1931 the Society received a magnificent bequest from Dr. Richard A.F. Penrose, Jr., for the promotion of scholarly research. Now capable of "promoting useful knowledge" in ways never before possible to it, the Society revised its structure, appointed an executive officer, and soon initiated the basic programs and activities that have distinguished it in the past forty years. A program of grants in aid of research was inaugurated. The *Transactions* was revived, the *Proceedings* revamped, and a series of *Memoirs* instituted. The Library's collections, which had once been used by working scientists like Joseph Henry and Joseph Leidy, were recognized as a principal resource for the small but growing number of students of the history of science and learning. The Society, which had once stood aloof from most of the city's civic life, soon took a leading part in planning the restoration of colonial and federal Philadelphia; instead of moving away, the Society decided to remain on Independence Square and keep its old hall. The exterior of Philosophical Hall was restored to its original appearance in 1949, and a library building, copied from the hall of the Library Company, which stood on the site from 1789 to 1884, was opened ten years later. In 1981 pressing needs for housing Library holdings and the Society's own publications, as well as an opportunity to benefit the Society's future plans, were met through the purchase of the nineteenth-century Farmers' and Mechanics' Bank Building at 427 Chestnut Street. Renovations commenced that summer.

By now the American Philosophical Society is the oldest and one of the most prestigious learned societies in the United States. During the past 256 years it has played an important role in the cultural life of the country. Philosophy in the eighteenth century meant knowledge, as it is used with a doctoral degree today, rather than the specific field of philosophy, and members now, as then, reflect a broad span of knowledge. Former members include Jefferson, Washington, Adams, John Bartram, John James Audubon, Charles Darwin, Elizabeth Cary Agassiz (founder of Radcliffe College), Thomas Edison, Mme Marie Curie, and Louis Pasteur. Today membership is limited to about 800 people, and includes about 100 Nobel laureates. The public would also recognize names of members such as J. William Fulbright, the Rev. Father Theodore Hesburgh, William R. Hewlett, Beverly Sills, Robert S. McNamara, and Walter Cronkite. The Society promotes useful knowledge through its research grants program (the first private foundation to establish such a program), an internationally renowned Library for the history of science, scholarly meetings, and publications.

Since the first grant to aid the Second Byrd Antarctic Expedition in 1933, the Society has awarded more than $14,000,000 for research to over 12,000 scholars. It has provided over $30,000,000 to promote other scholarly projects. In recent decades about $400,000 a year has been distributed. These grants enable scholars to produce a steady flow of books and articles to advance our knowledge. The Library, which houses over 158,000 volumes and bound periodicals, has important scientific publications from the eighteenth century on including first editions of Newton's *Principia* and Darwin's *Origin of Species*. There are also outstanding collections of manuscripts ranging from natural history, to Indian linguistics and ethnohistory, to nuclear physics, genetics, and computers. Among the Society's treasures are Jefferson's handwritten draft of the Declaration of Independence, a large portion of Franklin's letters and part of his library, the original Lewis and Clark journals, paintings by Charles Willson Peale, and portraits by Thomas Sully.

The Society also advances the frontiers of scholarly knowledge and practical achievement through its annual spring and fall meetings which explore many topics in a wide range of subjects; the Library sponsors numerous seminars and professional meetings as well. The Society is also an active partner in such scholarly enterprises as *The Papers of Benjamin Franklin*, the *Collected Letters of Charles Darwin, The Joseph Henry Papers, and Papers of Benjamin Henry Latrobe*. Since 1771 the Society has published scholarly works. Now each year it publishes one stout volume of *Proceedings* and another of *Transactions*, containing respectively short articles and longer monographs, as well as five to eight volumes of *Memoirs* or books. In recent years its books have won awards from the Medieval Academy and design awards at the Philadelphia Book Show.

Now well into its third century, its form and flavor remarkably little changed, the American Philosophical Society is engaged in promoting and disseminating useful knowledge, as it always has been.

A PROPOSAL for Promoting USEFUL KNOWLEDGE among the *British Plantations* in *America.*

THE *English* are poſſeſs'd of a long Tract of Continent, from *Nova Scotia* to *Georgia*, extending North and South thro' different Climates, having different Soils, producing different Plants, Mines and Minerals, and capable of different Improvements, Manufactures, &c.

The firſt Drudgery of Settling new Colonies, which confines the Attention of People to mere Neceſſaries, is now pretty well over ; and there are many in every Province in Circumſtances that ſet them at Eaſe, and afford Leiſure to cultivate the finer Arts, and improve the common Stock of Knowledge. To ſuch of theſe who are Men of Speculation, many Hints muſt from time to time ariſe, many Obſervations occur, which if well-examined, purſued and improved, might produce Diſcoveries to the Advantage of ſome or all of the *Britiſh* Plantations, or to the Benefit of Mankind in general.

But as from the Extent of the Country, ſuch Perſons are widely ſeparated, and ſeldom can ſee and converſe, or be acquainted with each other, ſo that many uſeful Particulars remain uncommunicated, die with the Diſcoverers, and are loſt to Mankind ; it is, to remedy this Inconvenience for the future, propoſed,

That One Society be formed of Virtuoſi or ingenious Men reſiding in the ſeveral Colonies, to be called *The American Philoſophical Society* who are to maintain a conſtant Correſpondence.

That *Philadelphia* being the City neareſt the Centre of the Continent-Colonies, communicating with all of them northward and ſouthward by Poſt, and with all the Iſlands by Sea, and having the Advantage of a good growing Library, be the Centre of the Society.

That at *Philadelphia* there be always at leaſt ſeven Members, *viz.* a Phyſician, a Botaniſt, a Mathematician, a Chemiſt, a Mechanician, a Geographer, and a general Natural Philoſopher, beſides a Preſident, Treaſurer and Secretary.

That theſe Members meet once a Month, or oftner, at their own Expence, to communicate to each other their Obſervations, Experiments, &c. to receive, read and conſider ſuch Letters, Communications, or Queries as ſhall be ſent from diſtant Members ; to direct the Diſperſing of Copies of ſuch Communications as are valuable, to other diſtant Members, in order to procure their Sentiments thereupon, &c.

That the Subjects of the Correſpondence be, All new-diſcovered Plants, Herbs, Trees, Roots, &c. their Virtues, Uſes, &c.; Methods of Propagating them, and making ſuch as are uſeful, but particular to ſome Plantations, more general, Improvements of vegetable Juices, as Cyders, Wines, &c. ; New Methods of Curing or Preventing Diſeaſes. All new-diſcovered Foſſils in different Countries, as Mines, Minerals, Quarries; &c. New and uſeful Improvements in any Branch of Mathematicks; New Diſcoveries in Chemiſtry, ſuch as Improvements in Diſtillation, Brewing, Aſſaying of Ores; &c. New Mechanical Inventions for ſaving Labour ; as Mills, Carriages, &c. and for Raiſing and Conveying of Water, Draining of Meadows, &c.; All new

new Arts, Trades, Manufactures, &c. that may be proposed or thought of; Surveys, Maps and Charts of particular Parts of the Sea-coasts, or Inland Countries; Course and Junction of Rivers and great Roads, Situation of Lakes and Mountains, Nature of the Soil and Productions; &c. New Methods of Improving the Breed of useful Animals, Introducing other Sorts from foreign Countries. New Improvements in Planting, Gardening, Clearing Land, &c.; And all philosophical Experiments that let Light into the Nature of Things, tend to increase the Power of Man over Matter, and multiply the Conveniencies or Pleasures of Life.

That a Correspondence already begun by some intended Members, shall be kept up by this Society with the ROYAL SOCIETY of *London*, and with the DUBLIN SOCIETY.

That every Member shall have Abstracts sent him Quarterly, of every Thing valuable communicated to the Society's Secretary at *Philadelphia*; free of all Charge except the Yearly Payment hereafter mentioned.

That, by Permission of the Postmaster-General, such Communications pass between the Secretary of the Society and the Members, Postage-free.

That, for defraying the Expence of such Experiments as the Society shall judge proper to cause to be made, and other contingent Charges for the common Good, every Member send a Piece of Eight *per Annum* to the Treasurer, at *Philadelphia*, to form a Common Stock, to be disburs'd by Order of the President with the Consent of the Majority of the Members that can conveniently be consulted thereupon, to such Persons and Places where and by whom the Experiments are to be made, and otherwise as there shall be Occasion; of which Disbursements an exact Account shall be kept, and communicated yearly to every Member.

That at the first Meetings of the Members at *Philadelphia*, such Rules be formed for Regulating their Meetings and Transactions for the General Benefit, as shall be convenient and necessary; to be afterwards changed and improv'd as there shall be Occasion, wherein due Regard is to be had to the Advice of distant Members.

That at the End of every Year, Collections be made and printed, of such Experiments, Discoveries, Improvements, &c. as may be thought of publick Advantage: And that every Member have a Copy sent him.

That the Business and Duty of the Secretary be, To receive all Letters intended for the Society, and lay them before the President and Members at their Meetings; to abstract, correct and methodize such Papers, &c. as require it, and as he shall be directed to do by the President, after they have been considered, debated, and digested in the Society; to enter Copies thereof in the Society's Books, and make out Copies for distant Members; to answer their Letters by Direction of the President, and keep Records of all material Transactions of the Society, &c.

Benjamin Franklin, the Writer of this Proposal, offers himself to serve the Society as their Secretary, 'till they shall be provided with one more capable.

Philadelphia, May 14. 1743.

STATUTES AT LARGE OF PENNSYLVANIA

CHAPTER DCCCXCIV.

AN ACT for incorporating the American Philosophical Society held at Philadelphia for promoting useful knowledge.

Whereas the cultivation of useful knowledge, and the advancement of the liberal arts and sciences in any Country, have the most direct tendency towards the improvement of agriculture, the enlargement of trade, the ease and comfort of life, the ornament of society, and the encrease and happiness of mankind; **And whereas** this country of North America, which the goodness of Providence hath given us to inherit, from the vastness of its extent, the variety of its climate, the fertility of its soil, the yet unexplored treasures of its bowels, the multitude of its rivers, lakes, bays, inlets, and other conveniences of navigation, offers to these United States one of the richest subjects of cultivation, ever presented to any people upon earth; **And whereas** the experience of ages shows that improvements of a public nature, are best carried on by societies of liberal and ingenious men, uniting their labours, without regard to nation, sect or party, in one grand pursuit, alike interesting to all, whereby mutual prejudices are worn off, a humane and philosophical spirit is cherished, and youth are stimulated to a laudable diligence and emulation in the pursuit of wisdom; **And whereas,** upon these principles, divers public-spirited gentlemen of Pennsylvania and other American States did heretofore unite themselves, under certain regulations, into one voluntary Society, by the name of "The American Philosophical Society held at Philadelphia, for promoting useful knowledge," and by their successful labours and investigations, to the great credit of America, have extended their reputation so far, that men of the first eminence in the republic of letters in the most civilized nations of Europe have done honour to their publications, and desired to be enrolled among their members; **And whereas** the said Society, after having been long interrupted in their laudable pursuits by the calamities of war, and the distresses of our Country, have found means to revive their design, in hopes of being able to prosecute the same with their former success, and being further encouraged therein by the public, for which purpose they have prayed us, "the Representatives of the Freemen of the Commonwealth of Pennsylvania," that they may be created One Body Politic and Corporate forever, with such powers, privileges, and immunities, as may be necessary for answering the valuable purposes which the said Society had originally in view.

[1] *Original Charter, Granted in 1780. Article of Amendment added 1935.*

Wherefore, in order to encourage the said Society in the prosecution and advancement of all useful branches of knowledge, for the benefit of their country and mankind.

[SECTION I.] **Be it enacted, and it is hereby enacted by the Representatives of the Freemen of the Commonwealth of Pennsylvania, in General Assembly met, and by the authority of the same,** That the Members of the said American Philosophical Society heretofore voluntarily associated for promoting useful knowledge, and such other persons as have been duly elected Members and Officers of the same, agreeably to the fundamental laws and regulations of the said Society, comprized in twelve sections, prefixed to their first volume of transactions, published in Philadelphia by William and Thomas Bradford in the year of our Lord one thousand seven hundred and seventy-one, and who shall in all respects conform themselves to the said laws and regulations, and such other laws, regulations and ordinances, as shall hereafter be duly made and enacted by the said Society, according to the tenor hereof, be and forever hereafter shall be, One Body Corporate and Politic in Deed, by the name and style of "The American Philosophical Society held at Philadelphia, for promoting useful knowledge," and by the same name they are hereby constituted and confirmed One Body Corporate and Politic, to have perpetual succession, and by the same name they and their successors are hereby declared and made able and apable in law, to have, hold, receive, and enjoy lands, tenements, rents, franchises, hereditaments, gifts, and bequests of what nature so ever, in fee simple or for term of life, lives, years or otherwise, and also to give, grant, let, sell, alien, or assign the same lands, tenements, hereditaments, goods, chattels, and premises, according to the nature of the respective gifts, grants, and bequests, made to them the said Society, and of their estate therein. **Provided,** that the amount of the clear yearly value of such real estate do not exceed the value of ten thousand bushels of good merchantable wheat.[2]

[SECTION II.] **And be it further enacted by the authority aforesaid,** That the said Society, be, and shall be for ever hereafter able and capable in law to sue, and be sued, plead and be impleaded, answer and be answered unto, defend and be defended in all or any of the courts or other places, and before any Judges, Justices, and other person or persons, in all manner of actions, suits, complaints, pleas, causes, and matters of what nature or kind so ever within this Commonwealth; and that it shall and may be lawful to and for the said Society, for ever hereafter to have and use one common seal in their affairs, and the same at their will and pleasure to break, change, alter and renew.

---

[2] *See Amendment,* ART. *I, p. 20.*

[SECTION III.] **And be it further enacted by the authority aforesaid,** That for the well governing of the said Society, and ordering their affairs, they shall have the following officers, that is to say, one Patron, who shall be his Excellency the President of the Supreme Executive Council* of this Commonwealth, for the time being, and likewise one President, three Vice Presidents, four Secretaries, three Curators, one Treasurer, together with a Council of twelve members; and that on the first Friday of January next, between the hours of two and five in the afternoon, as many of the members of the said Society as shall have paid up their arrears due to the Society, and shall declare their willingness to conform to the laws, regulations and ordinances of the Society then duly in force, according to the tenor hereof, by subscribing the same, and who shall attend in the Hall or place of meeting of the said Society, within the time aforesaid, shall chuse by ballot, agreeable to the fundamental laws and regulations herein before referred to, one President, three Vice Presidents, four Secretaries, three Curators, and one Treasurer, and at the same time and place, the members met and qualified as aforesaid shall in like manner chuse four members for the Council, to hold their offices for one year, four more members for the Council to hold their offices for two years, and four more members for the Council to hold their offices for three years. And on the first Friday in January, which shall be in the year of our Lord one thousand seven hundred and eighty-two, and so likewise on the first Friday of January yearly and every year thereafter, between the hours of two and five in the afternoon, the Members of the said Society met and qualified as aforesaid, shall chuse one President, three Vice Presidents, four Secretaries, three Curators and one Treasurer, to hold their respective offices for one year, and four Council Men to hold their offices for three years, Provided that no person residing within the United States shall be capable of being President, Vice President, Secretary, Curator, Treasurer, or member of the Council, or of electing to any of the said offices, who is not capable of electing and being elected to civil offices within the State in which he resides. *Provided also, that nothing herein contained shall be considered* as intended to exclude any of the said Officers or Councillors, whose times shall be expired, from being re-elected, according to the pleasure of the said Society; and of the day, hours and place of all such elections, due notice shall be given by the Secretaries, or some one of them, in one or more of the public newspapers of this State, agreeable to the said fundamental laws and regulations before referred to.[3]

[SECTION IV.] **And be it further enacted by the authority aforesaid,** That the Officers and Council of the said Society shall be capable of exercising such power for the well governing and ordering the affairs of the Society, and of holding such

---

* *[Now His Excellency the Governor of this Commonwealth.]*
[3] *See Amendment,* ART. II, p. 20.

occasional meetings for that purpose, as shall be described, fixed, and determined by the statutes, laws, regulations and ordinances of the said Society, hereafter to be made. Provided always, that no statute, law, regulation or ordinance shall ever be made or passed by the said Society, or be binding upon the members thereof, or any of them, unless the same hath been duly proposed, and fairly drawn up in writing, at one stated meeting of the Society, and enacted or passed at a subsequent meeting at least the space of fourteen days after the former meeting, and upon due notice in some of the public newspapers, that the enacting of statutes and laws, or the making and passing ordinances and regulations, will be part of the business of such meeting; or shall any statute, law, regulation or ordinance be then or at any time enacted or passed, unless thirteen members of the said Society, or such greater number of members as may be afterwards fixed by the rules of the Society, be present, besides such quorum of the Officers and Council, as the laws of the Society for the time being may require, and unless the same be voted by two-thirds of the whole body then present; all of which statutes, laws, ordinances and regulations, so as aforesaid duly made, enacted and passed shall be binding upon every member of the said Society, and be from time to time inviolably observed, according to the tenor and effect thereof; provided they be not repugnant or contrary to the laws of this Commonwealth, for the time being in force and effect.

And whereas nations truly civilized (however unhappily at variance on other accounts) will never wage war with the Arts and Sciences, and the common Interests of humanity:

[SECTION V.] Be it further enacted by the authority aforesaid, That it shall and may be lawful for the said Society by their proper officers, at all times, whether in peace or war, to correspond with learned Societies, as well as individual learned men, of any nation or country, upon matters merely belonging to the business of the said Society, such as the mutual communication of their discoveries and proceedings in Philosophy and Science; the procuring books, apparatus, natural curiosities, and such other articles and intelligence as are usually exchanged between learned bodies, for furthering their common pursuits; Provided always, That such correspondence of the said Society be at all times open to the inspection of the Supreme Executive Council of this Commonwealth.

[Signed]   JOHN BAYARD,   *Speaker*

Enacted into a Law at Philadelphia on Wednesday the fifteenth day of March anno Domini one thousand seven hundred and eighty.

[Signed]   THOMAS PAINE   *Clerk of the General Assembly.*

COMMISSION FOR THE COMPILATION OF THE LAWS OF PENNSYLVANIA PRIOR TO 1800.

CLERK'S OFFICE,
1211 BETZ BUILDING.

JAMES T. MITCHELL,

} Commissioners

HENRY FLANDERS,

CHAS. R. HILDEBURN, *Clerk*.
PHILADELPHIA, March 12, 1898.

Compared, revised and found to be a correct copy of the original enrollment in the archives of the Commonwealth, by me the custodian of the said original as clerk of the commissioners appointed under the act of May 19, 1887, entitled, AN ACT FOR THE COMPILATION AND PUBLICATION OF THE LAWS OF THE PROVINCE AND COMMONWEALTH OF PENNSYLVANIA PRIOR TO THE YEAR ONE THOUSAND EIGHT HUNDRED, P.L. 1887, pp. 129 and 130.

CHAS. R. HILDEBURN,
Clerk of the Commissioners.

Witness as to Chas. R. Hildeburn:
WM. NEWBOLD ELY,
JULIUS F. SACHSE.

Sworn to and subscribed before me this 19th day of May, 1898.

[SEAL]

JAMES P. STERRETT,
Chief Justice of the Supreme Court
of Pennsylvania

ARTICLES OF AMENDMENT

ARTICLE I

Notwithstanding the Proviso at the end of the first paragraph following the preamble of this Charter, or any other proviso thereof, the Society shall have the capacity and authority without limitation by this Charter to purchase, take, receive, lease as lessee, take by gift, devise or bequest, or otherwise acquire, and to own, hold, use, and otherwise deal with any and all real or personal property, or any interest therein, wherever situated.

ARTICLE II

Any provisions of this Charter which are purely administrative in their nature, including those concerning the officers, the members of the council and the date and time of meetings may be altered by a law, regulation or ordinance of the Society duly adopted and not repugnant or contrary to the laws of this Commonwealth.

CERTIFICATE OF ACCEPTANCE

1. The name of the accepting corporation is The American Philosophical Society held at Philadelphia for promoting useful knowledge.

2. The American Philosophical Society was created by the Act of Assembly approved March 15, 1780, L.B. No. 1, 363.

3. The American Philosophical Society herewith accepts the Constitution of Pennsylvania and the provisions of the Nonprofit Corporation Law.

4. The acceptance made herewith was duly authorized by a meeting of the members called for that purpose, held in Philadelphia on the 6th day of December, 1935.

ROLAND S. MORRIS
President

Filed this 12th day of December, 1935

C. F. SKINKER
Assistant Secretary

J. WARREN MICKLE, Deputy Secretary of the Commonwealth

Recorded in Miscellaneous Corporation Record Book 210, P. 125

CHAPTER I

Members both resident and foreign: their classification, nomination, and election; termination of membership.

ARTICLE 1. The resident members of the Society are elected from among citizens or residents of the United States who have achieved distinction in the sciences or humanities, in letters, in the practice of the arts or of the learned professions, or in the administration of affairs; who, in the phrase of the Society's Act of Incorporation, possess and cherish "a humane and philosophical spirit"; who manifest devotion to the public good; and who give promise of advancing the purposes and welfare of the Society.

Not more than forty persons of any age may be elected to resident membership each year to maintain a membership of those under eighty-five years of age of approximately six hundred. (Those eighty-five years of age or over are entitled to all privileges and rights of membership and will not be designated in any way to distinguish them from other members.) Should total membership rise substantially above, or fall substantially below, the desired total of six hundred, the Advisory Committee on Elections shall make appropriate recommendations to the Council.

ARTICLE 2. The foreign members of the Society shall be elected from among persons who are neither citizens nor residents of the United States, and who have attained the greatest eminence for their achievements in the sciences, in letters, in the liberal arts or in other scholarly activities of interest to the Society.

Not more than eight may be elected in any one year, of whom not more than three may be citizens or residents of any one country. Foreign members may not vote, sign instruments of election of members or officers of the Society, or be eligible to be officers of the Society.

ARTICLE 3. Upon recommendation of the Advisory Committee on Elections the Council shall from time to time establish classes, each of which shall consist of members of kindred societal, scholarly, or scientific disciplines. Any member whose field of interest has changed substantially may apply to the Council for a change of classification. The present classes are enumerated in Appendix I hereto.

ARTICLE 4. In each of the classes of members there shall be a COMMITTEE ON MEMBERSHIP consisting of a chairman and four additional members, appointed by the President. Appointments shall be made for a three-year term, once renewable, but a member may serve as chairman for only a single three-year term. Appointments shall be staggered to insure continuity on the Committee.

[1] *Wherever the words "he" "him" or "his" occur, they should be understood to apply to both sexes.*

ARTICLE 5. Nominations to membership shall be made in writing by the Committee on Membership. In addition, five or more members may nominate, in writing, a candidate for membership; however, a member may not sign more than one membership nominating petition in any one year. Such nominations shall be listed on the *class* ballot as "Member Nominees."

A nominee may be considered for election jointly by two Classes. Such a person shall be indicated on the class ballots of these Classes as an "Interclass Nominee." To be carried forward to the final ballot, he must receive at least fifty percent of the combined vote on the class ballots of the relevant Classes.

To qualify for the *class* ballot, nominations must be filed with the Executive Officer before October 1. Nominations, on forms provided by the Executive Officer for that purpose, shall include a brief "curriculum vitae" of the nominee and a statement of approximately one hundred words reciting the personal and professional characteristics of the candidate.

ARTICLE 6. At its discretion the Council may place on the *final* ballot the names of up to three persons per year whose election it deems to be in the best interests of the Society.

ARTICLE 7. The Council, after consultation with the Advisory Committee on the Election of Members, may create in any class a Temporary Nominating Group with a term of five years or less in order to strengthen existing disciplines or to introduce new disciplines into the field of learning represented by that Class. The Temporary Nominating Group shall nominate new members for election, subject to the approval of the Advisory Committee, just as if it were itself a Class. Each year Council will fix a quota for the maximum number of members to be elected by each such Temporary Nominating Group.

Members asked to serve on a Temporary Nominating Group and members elected through its auspices shall be considered members of the Class from which the Group was selected as well as the Group until its termination.

Council may create not more than three Temporary Nominating Groups at a time.

ARTICLE 8. Immediately after December 1 of each year the Executive Officer shall submit to the members of each class a ballot listing all nominations in that class. The members of each class will indicate on this *class* ballot the names of those persons they would recommend for membership. The ballot should be signed and returned to the Executive Officer before January 1.

ARTICLE 9. Before February 1 each Committee on Membership with the concurrence of the Advisory Committee shall select for inclusion on its *final* ballot not more than twelve of the names from among the nominees on its *class* ballot for resident membership and not more than three for foreign membership. These names shall be chosen giving due regard to a proper representation of the various fields within the *class* and to the votes cast in the class ballot. Moreover, the name of each Interclass Nominee who shall have received the requisite number of votes shall appear on the final ballot in whichever class the Advisory Committee shall have chosen, bearing in mind the advice of the Class Committee Chairmen.

Each committee shall then prepare, with such outside assistance as it may choose, a brief biographical sketch of each nominee, listing the nominee's profession, position, qualifications, and important publications or contributions to scholarship, science, or public affairs. The names of these nominees on the *final* ballot together with the biographical sketch of each, shall be printed in a list indicating their rankings arrived at by the Advisory Committee on Elections and the Class Membership Committees, taking into account the results of the *class* ballot, and shall be sent confidentially to all resident members of the Society not later than March 1. Members shall be asked to return to the Executive Officer not later than March 21 the *final* ballot on which they have checked names of nominees for resident and foreign membership in the numbers indicated in the letter transmitting the ballot. Members are urged to vote for candidates in all classes.

ARTICLE 10. There shall be an ADVISORY COMMITTEE ON THE ELECTION OF MEMBERS, to include the President, who shall act as chairman, the Executive Officer, and the chairmen of the Class Committees on Membership. In addition, there shall be one member from each class, nominated by the President and appointed for a term of three years by the Council, none of whom shall serve more than two consecutive terms. This Committee, acting on behalf of the Council between its meetings, shall have general responsibility for the election process, with particular reference to the following duties:

a) After completion of the *class* ballot and before the *final* ballot is submitted to the membership, the Committee and the Class Committees shall meet at their next regularly scheduled joint meeting to review all candidates proposed for the final ballot to determine that each of them meets the criteria set forth in Article 1. Where differences of opinion between the Advisory and Class Committees cannot be resolved, the Executive Committee shall resolve the difference.

b) The Advisory Committee shall also make tentative allocation of existing vacancies among the classes, for final approval by the Council, having in mind a reasonable balance among the classes and the disciplines represented within each class.

c) Where there is a question as to the class most appropriate for a nominee, the Advisory Committee shall make the allocation.

d) On completion of *final* balloting, the Advisory Committee shall meet with the Class Committees, who will present the names of the candidates recommended for election to the Society, taking into account the voting of the membership and the desirability of a reasonable balance among the several disciplines as well as the presence of such Interclass Nominees as they recommend. The Advisory Committee shall prepare for submittal to the Council during the Annual General Meeting a list of candidates supported by both Advisory and Class Committees.

Should there be disagreement between the Advisory and Class Committees with respect to a particular candidate, not resolved at this meeting, that candidate's name shall be brought before the Council at its meeting during the Annual General meeting, at which time the Council will make a final decision after hearing views from both committees.

ARTICLE 11. The Council shall make a final selection of the nominees to be recommended to the Society, taking into account the votes of the membership in the *final* ballot, the recommendations of the Advisory Committee on Elections, and the comments of the Class Membership Committees. The list of nominees so chosen, according to ranking by classes, shall be reported to the Society at the business meeting of members held during the Annual General Meeting.

ARTICLE 12. Election to membership both resident and foreign, may be by a showing of hands at the business meeting during the Annual General Meeting if requested by the President and if without objection by those present. Should there be objection, the vote shall be by written ballot. A two-thirds vote of those present and voting shall be necessary to elect. A quorum at the Annual General Meeting shall be twenty members.

ARTICLE 13. The members are mutually pledged not to mention to non-members of the Society the name of any nominee proposed, or of any withdrawn or unsuccessful nominee.

ARTICLE 14. Every person who is elected a resident or foreign member shall signify his acceptance in writing within one year after the mailing of notification of such election. In default of such acceptance the election shall be void.

ARTICLE 15. The formal admission of a member into the Society shall be at his first attendance at a meeting of the Society after his election and in the manner and form following: He shall subscribe to the Laws in the Roll Book and be introduced to the President, who, taking him by the hand, shall say:

"By the authority and in the name of the American Philosophical Society held at Philadelphia for Promoting Useful Knowledge, I do admit you a Member thereof."

ARTICLE 16. The Society may from time to time assess membership dues in accordance with its needs and policies.

ARTICLE 17. The membership of any resident or foreign member may, for good cause, and upon recommendation by the Council, be terminated by the Society at the business meeting during a General Meeting by a vote of two-thirds of the members attending, provided that a quorum of twenty is present.

ARTICLE 18. Recipients of the Benjamin Franklin Award for Distinguished Public Service shall be notified of the meetings of the Society, invited to participate in its scholarly sessions, and receive the *Proceedings* and the *Year Book*.

CHAPTER II

*Patron and Elective Officers, qualifications, nominations and elections,
terms of office, suspension or removal, vacancies.*

ARTICLE 1. The Governor of Pennsylvania shall be ex officio the Patron of the Society.

ARTICLE 2. The Officers of the Society shall be a President, three Vice-Presidents, two Secretaries, two Curators, a Treasurer, and an Executive Officer. There shall also be three Councillors elected for each class.

ARTICLE 3. Only resident members are eligible for election to the offices listed in Article 2.

ARTICLE 4. Nominations to the elective offices of the Society are made by the Committee on Nomination of Officers as hereinafter provided, and may also be made by petition signed by not less than twenty members, in such manner as prescribed in these Laws.

ARTICLE 5. The election of Officers shall be held at the Annual General Meeting at a time announced in the program. The election may be by a showing of hands, if requested by the President and if without objection by those present. Should there be objection, the vote shall be by written ballot. A majority of all votes cast is necessary for the election of an officer. A quorum at the Annual General Meeting shall be twenty members.

ARTICLE 6. The President, the three Vice-Presidents, the two Secretaries, the Treasurer, and the Councillors shall be elected for a term of three years, once renewable. They shall be ineligible for reelection to the same office after serving two consecutive terms until one year after the expiration of a second term.

The two Curators (the Curator of Fine Arts and the Curator of the Jefferson Garden) shall be appointed by the President for an indefinite term at the President's discretion.

ARTICLE 7. Three Councillors shall be representative of each class and of the interests of members. One for each class shall be elected at each Annual General Meeting.

ARTICLE 8. The Executive Officer, having been nominated by the President from the membership of the Society, with the assistance of a search committee, shall be elected by the Council for an indefinite term to serve the Society at the pleasure of the President and the Council.

ARTICLE 9. Any elective Officer or Councillor may be suspended or removed from office, for good cause, at a meeting of the Council, by a vote of two-thirds of all its members.

ARTICLE 10. A vacancy occurring in any elective office other than the Presidency may be filled for the unexpired term by the Executive Committee, such action to be ratified at the next Council meeting.

If a vacancy occurs in the office of the President because of death or other disability, the Executive Committee shall select one of the Vice-Presidents to act as President until a new President is elected at the next annual meeting of the Society.

ARTICLE 11. The two Curators (the Curator of Fine Arts and the Curator of the Thomas Jefferson Garden) shall be appointed by the President for an indefinite term at the President's discretion.

CHAPTER III

Officers and their Duties

ARTICLE 1. The President shall preside at the meetings of the Society and the Council. With such assistance as he requires, he shall formulate recommendations on policy for consideration by the Council or its Executive Committee. He shall appoint all committees except the Committee on Audit, which shall be nominated by the President and approved by the Council. (See Chapter V, Article 4 below.) The President shall designate the chairman of all committees except as otherwise provided in these Laws. He shall be a member of all committees, except the Committee on Audit. In making appointments he shall give due consideration to timely rotation of incumbents, balancing the need for experience against the need to involve a larger number of members in the affairs of the Society.

ARTICLE 2. The VICE-PRESIDENTS shall preside at scholarly sessions of the Society at the request of the President. Should the President be unable to preside at a scholarly or other type of session or occasion the President shall select a Vice-President to preside in his stead.

ARTICLE 3. The SECRETARIES, with the assistance of the Executive Officer and the Associate Secretaries, shall arrange for the custody of the Seal of the Society, record the proceedings of the Society and the Council, notify those concerned of all acts of the Society and the Council, maintain the authentic list of resident and foreign members, and have the custody of the Society's files and records. The Secretaries shall arrange among themselves each year the distribution and performance of their duties, and shall report such arrangement to the Council.

ARTICLE 4. The Curator of Fine Arts shall be responsible for all items of tangible personal property belonging to the Society excepting, as herein provided, those items which are the responsibility of the Secretaries, the Committee on Finance, the Library Committee or the Librarian. This Curator's duties shall include the care, maintenance, acquisition, loan and disposition of these.

The Curator of the Jefferson Garden shall be responsible for all matters relating to the landscape architecture, care, and design of the Jefferson Garden. This Curator's duties shall include the overall design, care, maintenance, acquisition and disposal of plants in the Garden.

ARTICLE 5. The TREASURER shall be responsible for the collection and receipt of all moneys due or payable to the Society or entrusted to its care, and all gifts and bequests made to it. He shall arrange for the payment of all bills due by the Society when properly approved, in accordance with appropriations authorized by the Society or the Council, or the Executive Committee acting for the Council, or in accordance with the terms of trust funds established for specific purposes. He shall arrange for the deposit of the funds and securities of the Society in its name with financial institutions as may be approved by the Council on recommendation of the Committee on Finance.

ARTICLE 6. The Treasurer, with the assistance of the Executive Officer and the Associate Treasurer, shall (a) keep account, in good and regular order, of all receipts and expenditures and of all moneys or other property of the Society pertaining to the financial affairs of the Society, excepting the property which is the responsibility of the Finance Committee, and (b) present such accounts for audit, as may be required by the Council or by law.

ARTICLE 7. The Treasurer may, if authorized by the Council, employ an individual or suitable corporation, selected with the advice of the Committee on Finance, for the performance of such duties as may be delegated to such agent.

ARTICLE 8. The Treasurer shall give bond, at the expense of the Society, for the faithful execution of all his duties, in such amount as may be required by the Council.

ARTICLE 9. The Treasurer shall, upon the expiration of his term of office, deliver over to the Society, for transmittal to his/her successor, the books, papers, moneys, and property remaining in his hands.

ARTICLE 10. The EXECUTIVE OFFICER shall, to the extent delegated by Council, be responsible for the day to day management of the Society's affairs, under the direction of the President. In the performance of his duties he shall be guided by general principles laid down by the Council. He shall be a member of all committees, except the Committee on Audit. He shall be compensated for his services.

ARTICLE 11. No elective officer or Councillor of the Society except the Executive Officer shall receive a salary, but they may be reimbursed for any necessary expenditures made in the performance of their duties.

ARTICLE 12. The Executive Officer shall prepare for submission to the Executive Committee and the Council for final action at the November meeting a budget for the following fiscal year including a statement of estimates of revenues and expenditures.

ARTICLE 13. The Curator of the Jefferson Garden shall be responsible for all matters relating to the landscape architecture, care, and design of the Jefferson Garden. His duties shall include the overall design, care, maintenance, acquisition and disposal of plants in the Garden.

CHAPTER IV

The Council

ARTICLE 1. The COUNCIL shall consist of the elected Officers and Councillors, and the Chairmen of the Committees on Audit, Finance, Library, Meetings, Nomination of Officers, Publications, and Research.

ARTICLE 2. The Council shall be responsible for the general management of the Society's affairs, including the authority to take action in all legal proceedings.

ARTICLE 3. The Council shall hold at least two meetings a year, and nine members shall constitute a quorum at any meeting. Minutes of the proceedings and acts of the Council shall be regularly kept. The Council shall hold its meetings during the Annual and Autumn General Meetings and at such other times as it shall deem necessary. A vote of the Council may be taken by mail, the result being promptly reported to all members of the Council.

ARTICLE 4. The Council shall require reports to be presented to it at least once a year by such officers, committees, and employees of the Society as they may designate, or as may be required by the Laws to present such reports.

ARTICLE 5. Each Council member as well as the Officers is in a fiduciary relation to the Society and shall perform his duties in a manner reasonably believed to be in the best interests of the Society, and with such care, including reasonable inquiry, skill and diligence, as a person of ordinary prudence would use under similar circumstances. In performing his duties, a Council member shall be entitled to rely on information, opinions, reports or statements, including financial material, prepared or presented by: (a) officers or employees of the Society whom the Council member reasonably believes to be reliable and competent in the matters present; (b) counsel, public accountants or other persons as to matters which the Council member reasonably believes to be within the competence of such persons; and (c) a committee of the Council upon which he does not serve, duly designated as to matters within its authority, which the member reasonably believes to merit confidence.

ARTICLE 6. In discharging their duties, the Council, committees of the Council and individual members may, in considering the best interests of the Society, take into account the effects of any action upon employees, suppliers and patrons of the Society and the community generally.

Absent a breach of fiduciary duty, lack of good faith, or self-dealing, actions or failure to take action shall be presumed to be in the best interests of the Society.

A member shall not be personally liable for monetary damages for action taken, or for failure to take any action, unless the member has breached or failed to perform the duties of his office, and the breach of failure to perform constitutes self-dealing, willful misconduct or recklessness.

The provisions of this Article shall not apply to the responsibility or liability of a Council member pursuant to any criminal statute, or for payment of taxes pursuant to local, state or federal law.

CHAPTER V

Committees of the Society

ARTICLE 1. Except as otherwise prescribed in these Laws, committee members shall be appointed or elected for terms of three years, renewable; chairmen of committees may serve at most for three consecutive terms of three years.

ARTICLE 2. There shall be an EXECUTIVE COMMITTEE consisting of the President, the Executive Officer, the chairmen of the Committees on Audit, Finance, Library, Meetings, Nomination of Officers, Publications, and Research, plus such additional Council members as may be proposed by the President and elected annually by the Council. The Executive Committee may exercise the authority of the Council over the affairs of the Society between meetings of the Council.

Minutes of its meetings shall be transmitted promptly to the Council. A majority of the Committee shall *constitute* a quorum at any meeting. The Council, or in its absence, the Executive Committee, after consulting with the Committee on Finance and the Treasurer, may authorize appropriations over and above the annual budget.

ARTICLE 3. In the absence or disqualification of a member or members of the Executive Committee, the President or his acting successor may appoint another member or members of the Council to act at the meeting in place of such absent or disqualified member or members. Actions taken at such a meeting shall be reported promptly to the full Executive Committee.

ARTICLE 4. There shall be a COMMITTEE ON AUDIT, nominated by the President and approved by the Council, consisting of not less than three members, which shall review the report of the Society's auditors and any other financial records of the Society which it deems pertinent, and report to the Council at least once a year regarding its review of the accounting procedures of the Society and any financial irregularities it may detect, making recommendations at its discretion.

ARTICLE 5. There shall be a COMMITTEE ON FINANCE, consisting of the President, Treasurer and Executive Officer, ex officio, and not fewer than five other members who shall be nominated by the President and elected by the Society at an Annual General Meeting for terms of three years, renewable. If a member is unable to perform his/her responsibilities, the President may appoint a successor to complete the term of the former member. A majority of the Committee shall constitute a quorum at any meeting. The Committee shall keep a record of all its acts and proceedings, which shall be communicated to the Council.

ARTICLE 6. The Committee on Finance shall supervise the custody and control of all securities and investments of the Society, both real and personal, with power and authority to buy and to sell, and to invest and reinvest the same, including the power to delegate investment decisions to professional advisers. The Committee shall study and make recommendations to the Council with respect to the purchase and sale of real estate, the placing of such insurance as it may deem necessary, and the financial aspects of the Society's pension plan. It shall have the power also to transfer registered securities; to subscribe to bondholders' agreements to plans of reorganization involving any securities held by the Society or in which it has an interest, and to do all such acts as are necessary in pursuance of the foregoing powers.

ARTICLE 7. There shall be a COMMITTEE ON LIBRARY, consisting of the President, Executive Officer and Librarian ex officio, and not fewer than one member from each of the classes.

ARTICLE 8. The Committee on Library shall, with the approval of Council, establish policies for the governance, administration and use of the Library collection of the Society.

It shall nominate to the President and Council a Librarian who, when appointed by the Council, shall be responsible for carrying out these policies and for directing and developing the Library as an institution in the scholarly community. Subject to these policies, the Librarian shall have charge of, and be responsible for, all books, manuscripts, maps, photographs and the like constituting the Library collection of the Society, their care, maintenance, acquisition, loan and disposition. The Librarian shall also report to the Executive Officer.

ARTICLE 9. There shall be a COMMITTEE ON MEETINGS, consisting of the President and Executive Officer, ex officio, and not fewer than one member from each of the classes.

ARTICLE 10. The Committee on Meetings shall be charged with the preparation of the scientific and scholarly programs of all meetings of the Society, and of all meetings held under the Society's auspices, and with the organization of discussions, symposia, and conferences. It shall name special subcommittees to assist it, and invite suitable persons, whether members of the Society or not, to participate in such programs, discussions, symposia, etc.

ARTICLE 11. There shall be a COMMITTEE ON MEMBERSHIP for each class, composed of five members from each class, whose appointment and duties are prescribed in Chapter I, Articles 4–8 of the Laws.

ARTICLE 12. There shall be a COMMITTEE ON NOMINATION OF OFFICERS consisting of six members proposed by the President, and elected by the Council. The President shall appoint the chairman of this Committee.

ARTICLE 13. The Committee on Nomination of Officers shall, not later than December 1, invite all members of the Society to submit to it suggestions for nominations to all offices to be filled by election at the next General Meeting.

ARTICLE 14. The Committee on Nomination of Officers shall, not later than March 1, submit to all members of the Society one or more nominations to each office to be filled by election at the next Annual General Meeting. Additional nominations may be made by petition signed by twenty or more members and submitted to the Chairman of the Committee on Nomination of Officers not later than March 25. Notice of such additional nominations must be sent to all members by April 1.

ARTICLE 15. The Committee on Nomination of Officers shall prepare for use in the elections at the General Meeting a ballot in which shall be included, under each position to be filled by election, the names of the Committee's nominees, and the names, in alphabetical order, of any nominees included in petitions duly received in accordance with the Laws.

ARTICLE 16. There shall be a COMMITTEE ON PUBLICATIONS, consisting of the President and Executive Officer, ex officio, and not fewer than one member from each of the classes.

ARTICLE 17. The Committee on Publications shall supervise the contents, editing, and printing of all publications issued by the Society or in its name. It may employ necessary editorial assistance, and shall nominate to the Council an Associate Editor who shall report to the Executive Officer. The Executive Officer as Editor shall cause the necessary contracts for the manufacture of the Society's publications to be drawn up and executed.

ARTICLE 18. The Committee on Publications shall, with the approval of the Council, prescribe regulations for receiving and considering proposals for publication, and may take such action as it shall see fit with respect to proposals so received, including the allotment of funds appropriated to the Committee by the Council. The Committee shall appoint referees or special subcommittees to assist it in the examination of material presented to it for publication and, in its discretion, may give honoraria for services so rendered. It shall report all its acts to the Council.

ARTICLE 19. There shall be a COMMITTEE ON RESEARCH, consisting of the President and Executive Officer, ex officio and not fewer than one member from each of the classes.

ARTICLE 20. The Committee on Research shall, with the approval of the Council, prescribe regulations for receiving and considering proposals for the advancement of knowledge through investigation. It may take such action as it shall see fit with respect to proposals received by it, and may, with the approval of the Council, itself initiate and cause to be executed investigations for the advancement of knowledge.

ARTICLE 21. The Committee on Research shall report all its acts to the Council, and from time to time submit reports to the Society on the progress of the investigations aided by it, and on the contributions to the advancement of knowledge made upon them.

ARTICLE 22. In addition to the committees discussed in these Laws the Council shall have the authority to create such other committees as it deems desirable.

CHAPTER VI

Meetings of the Society

ARTICLE 1. The Annual General Meeting shall be held in April, on days designated by vote of the Council adopted at least three months before the date fixed therefor, at which meeting it shall be lawful to transact all business not in contravention of the Laws.

ARTICLE 2. The Autumn General Meeting shall be held on days designated by vote of the Council, usually in the month of November, at which meeting it shall be lawful to transact all business not in contravention of the Laws.

ARTICLE 3. Special meetings may be called by order of the President, or, in his absence or in case of his disability, by order of a Vice-President, or by vote of the Council, for the consideration of matters of scientific or scholarly interest or for the transaction of such business as shall be specified in the order or vote calling the meeting.

ARTICLE 4. Where possible, scholarly and scientific sessions of the Society shall be open to the public. Business sessions shall be closed.

ARTICLE 5. At all business sessions of the Society and of its committees *Robert's Rules of Order (Revised)* shall be the rules of order.

CHAPTER VII

Publications of the Society

ARTICLE 1. The publications of the Society shall consist of PROCEEDINGS, TRANSACTIONS, MEMOIRS, YEAR BOOK and of such other serial or separate publications as may be authorized by the Council upon recommendation by the Committee on Publications.

ARTICLE 2. The PROCEEDINGS shall contain papers that are read before the Society at its meetings and obituaries of deceased members. Other papers from whatever source may also be published in the PROCEEDINGS if approved by the Committee on Publications. The PROCEEDINGS will be distributed to all members.

ARTICLE 3. The TRANSACTIONS shall consist of contributions in the form of monographs, treatises, collections of documents, and other materials, approved by the Committee on Publications. The TRANSACTIONS shall be issued in complete parts, one or more of which may constitute a volume.

ARTICLE 4. The MEMOIRS shall consist of books on major topics of scholarly importance approved by the Committee on Publications. They may each consist of one or more volumes.

ARTICLE 5. The YEAR BOOK shall contain, among other items, the Charter and Laws, list of Officers and Committees, the annual report of the President and Officers, important acts of the Society and the Council, reports of all standing Committees, a catalogue of prizes, premiums and lectureships, lists of all members including those elected and those deceased during the year. It shall be published as soon as possible after the close of each calendar year and shall be sent gratis to all members of the Society.

CHAPTER VIII

Indemnification of Elected Officers, Councillors, Employees and Agents

ARTICLE 1. The Society shall indemnify any officer or councillor, and may indemnify any other employee or agent who was, is or may be a party to or who is called as a witness in connection with any proceedings, civil, criminal, administrative or investigative, including an action by or in the right of the Society, by reason of the fact that he is or was an officer, councillor, employee or agent of the Society, or is or was serving at the request of the Society as a director, officer, employee or agent of another enterprise, against expenses, including fees, judgments, fines and amounts paid in settlement incurred in connection with such act giving rise to the claim as determined by a court to have constituted willful misconduct or recklessness.

ARTICLE 2. Indemnification and advancement of expenses granted pursuant to this Chapter shall not be deemed exclusive of any other rights to which those seeking indemnification or advancement of expenses may be entitled under any law of the Society, agreement, contract, vote of members or pursuant to the direction of any court or otherwise, both as to action in his official capacity and as to action in another capacity while holding such office. It is the Society's policy that indemnification of and advancement of expenses to officers and councillors shall be made to the fullest extent permitted by law. To this end, the provision of this Chapter shall be deemed to have been amended effective immediately upon any modification of applicable law which expands or enlarges the power or obligation of corporations to indemnify, or advance expenses to such persons.

ARTICLE 3. The Society shall pay expenses incurred by an officer or councillor, and may pay expenses incurred by any other employee or agent, in defending a civil or criminal action or proceeding in advance of the final disposition of such proceeding upon receipt of an undertaking by or on behalf of such person to repay such amount if it shall be ultimately determined that he is not entitled to be indemnified by the Society.

ARTICLE 4. Indemnification and advancement of expenses pursuant to this Chapter shall, unless otherwise provided, continue as to one who has ceased to be an officer, councillor, employee or agent and shall inure to the benefit of his heirs, executors and administrators.

ARTICLE 5. The Society shall have the authority to create a fund to secure its indemnification obligations, whether arising under these laws or otherwise.

CHAPTER IX

Laws of the Society and their Amendment

ARTICLE 1. No amendment or supplement to these laws, nor any new law shall be made or passed by the Society, unless the same has been duly proposed in writing at least thirty days prior to a General Meeting of the Society and enacted at that General Meeting. Due notice of the proposed law or amendment shall be sent by mail to the members qualified to vote thereon.

ARTICLE 2. Should Council express reservation or opposition to a proposed amendment or supplement that amendment or supplement will be deferred to the next General Meeting of the Society for consideration by the members qualified to vote thereon.

ARTICLE 3. At the General Meeting no amendment or supplement to these laws shall be made, nor shall any new law be made, unless there be present a quorum of at least thirty members, of whom not fewer than five shall be members of the Council, and the same be voted by two-thirds of the whole body present.

APPENDIX I

The classes at present are:

Class I   Mathematical and Physical Sciences
Class II   Biological Sciences
Class III   Social Sciences
Class IV   Humanities
Class V   The Arts, Learned Professions, and Public Affairs

APPENDIX II

The following fields of learning are included *inter alia* within the present classes: Class I: Mathematics, Astronomy, Physics, Chemistry and Chemical Biochemistry, Engineering, Physical Earth Sciences. Class II: Molecular Biology and Biochemistry; Cellular and Developmental Biology; Evolution and Ecology, Systematics, Population Genetics, Paleontology, and Physical Anthropology; Medicine, Surgery, Pathology, and Immunology; Microbiology, including Bacteriology, Virology, and Protozoology; Physiology, Biophysics, and Pharmacology; Genetics; Plant Sciences; Neurobiology; Behavioral Biology, Psychology, Ethology, and Animal Behavior. Class III: Economics; Statistics, Political Science and Law; Sociology; Social Anthropology; Social Psychology; Modern History. Class IV: Language and Languages: ancient, classical, modern (with some kinds of linguistics more properly assigned to Class III); Literature, Literatures, and Literary Theory (including hermeneutics and the comparative study of literature); History: ancient, classical, medieval, and early modern (by concordat, history since the Enlightenment, including most American history, is in Class III, but Archaeology is in Class IV); Philosophy: the history of philosophy as well as the philosophy of history, logic, ethics, aesthetics, metaphysics, and epistemology; History of art and of the arts (including Music and Architecture); Religion in its historical and comparative dimensions, with certain aspects assigned to Social Anthropology is in Class III. Class V: The creative and performing arts; the learned professions including physicians, theologians, lawyers, jurists, and architects; and public affairs including those persons who have distinguished themselves in the public eye and the commonwealth such as administrators, bankers and opinion leaders.

ADMINISTRATION AND STAFF

General Telephone Number .... (215)440-3400
Executive Office FAX Number .... (215)440-3436
Library FAX Number .... (215)440-3423
Librarian FAX Number .... (215)440-8579
Publications FAX Number .... (215)440-3450

Executive Office

	EXTENSION
Alexander G. Bearn, Executive Officer	3435
Susan M. Babbitt, Associate Editor	3426
Celeste M. Bivings, Part-time Publications Secretary	3451
Christine Brisson, Special Projects Officer[1]	
Margie Gaffner, Executive Assistant	3434
Nikolaj A. Goripow, Custodial Supervisor	3102
Deidre A. Greggs, Accountant	3431
Carole Le Faivre-Rochester, Editor	3425
Eileen Massi, Publications Customer Service Coordinator	3427
Carl F. Miller, Financial Officer	3433
Nora Monroe, Membership Officer	3430
Andrea B. Nicotera, Special Assistant to the Executive Officer and Program Officer	3438
Julia A. Noonan, Associate Secretary Emerita	
Eleanor Roach, Research Administrator	3429
Ann S. Westcott, Development and Special Events Officer	3441

Library

Joseph-James Ahern, Library Technical Assistant, Programs Assistant	3417
James Buchanan, Custodian	3102
Denise Carbone, Assistant Conservator	3413
Edward C. Carter II, Librarian	3404
Marian L. Christ, Assistant Librarian, Head Cataloguer and Bibliographer	3407

[1] *Resigned July 1999*

Robert S. Cox, Manuscripts Librarian	3409
Scott DeHaven, Assistant Manuscripts Librarian	3409
Sandra T. Duffy, Secretary to the Librarian	3405
Lois Fischbeck, Manuscripts and Printed Materials Assistant[2]	
Roy E. Goodman, Assistant Librarian,	
Curator of Printed Materials and Bibliographer	3408
Mark Harwell, Library Technical Assistant	3417
Hedi Kyle, Head of Conservation	3413
Martin L. Levitt, Associate Librarian for Administration	3403
Valerie-Anne Lutz, Library Technical Assistant	3416
Frank W. Margeson, Photographer	3422
Lydia E. Marrero, Technical Services Manager	3406
Karen Payano,	
Secretary to the Librarian and Secretary to the Friends[3]	
Joseph Pannella, Physical Plant Supervisor	3421
Selma Rabinowitz, Library Technical Assistant	3408

SPECIAL PROJECTS

Whitfield J. Bell, Jr., APS Biographical Dictionary Project	3420
Charles J. Fitti, Volunteer	3417
Carmen Lee, Volunteer	3409
Alison Lewis, OPAC and Retrospective Conversion Manager	3444
Carmen Lee, Volunteer	3409
Joel Loeb, Volunteer	3408
C. William Miller, Library Research Associate	3411
Alfred C. Prime, Volunteer	3418
William Severson, Volunteer	3413
Milton D. Shapiro, Volunteer	3408
Hildegard Stephans, Volunteer	3413

[2] *Resigned June 1999.*
[3] *Resigned August 1999.*

www.ingramcontent.com/pod-product-compliance
Lightning Source LLC
Chambersburg PA
CBHW061754260326
41914CB00006B/1107